PELICAN BOOKS

THE PELICAN GUIDE TO ENGLISH LITERATURE

I

THE AGE OF CHAUCER

THE EDITOR

Boris Ford read English at Cambridge before the war. He then spent six years in the Army Education Corps, being finally in command of a residential School of Artistic Studies. On leaving the Army, he joined the staff of the newly formed Bureau of Current Affairs and graduated to be its Chief Editor and in the end its Director. When the Bureau closed down at the end of 1951, he joined the Secretariat of the United Nations in New York and Geneva. On returning to England in the autumn of 1953, he was appointed Secretary of a national inquiry into the problem of providing a humane liberal education for people undergoing technical and professional training.

Boris Ford then became Editor of the *Journal of Education*, until it ceased publication in 1958, and also the first Head of School Broadcasting with Independent Television. From 1958 he was Education Secretary at the Cambridge University Press, and then in 1960 he was appointed Professor of Education and Director of the Institute of Education at Sheffield University. In 1963 he became Professor of Education and subsequently Chairman of Education at the University of Sussex. He is editor of *Universities Quarterly*. Since 1973 he has been Professor of Education at the University of Bristol.

The Age of Chaucer

VOLUME

I

OF THE PELICAN GUIDE TO ENGLISH LITERATURE

★

EDITED BY BORIS FORD

★

*With an Anthology of
Medieval Poems*

PENGUIN BOOKS

Penguin Books Ltd, Harmondsworth, Middlesex, England
Penguin Books Inc., 7110 Ambassador Road, Baltimore, Maryland 21207, U.S.A.
Penguin Books Australia Ltd, Ringwood, Victoria, Australia
Penguin Books Canada Ltd, 41 Steelcase Road West, Markham, Ontario, Canada
Penguin Books (N.Z) Ltd, 182–190 Wairau Road, Auckland 10, New Zealand

—

First published 1954
Reprinted 1955
Reprinted with revisions 1959
Reprinted 1961, 1962, 1963, 1965, 1966
Reprinted with revisions to Part V 1969
Reprinted 1971, 1972, 1974, 1975

—

Made and printed in Great Britain
by Hazell Watson & Viney Ltd, Aylesbury, Bucks
Set in Monotype Bembo

CONTENTS

CONTENTS

PART IV

An Anthology of Medieval Poems:

EDITED BY FRANCIS BERRY

PART V

COMPILED BY MARGARET TUBB

GENERAL INTRODUCTION

In introducing this *Guide to English Literature*, it is well to remember that this is the age of the Digest and the Headline, of the Comic and the Tabloid, of the Best-seller and the Month's Masterpiece, an age when a 'deep-seated spiritual vulgarity . . . lies at the heart of our civilization', in the words of the novelist L. H. Myers. Perhaps in response to this the twentieth century has also been a period of unusually lively criticism, a time when a small number of writers and critics have made a determined effort to elicit from literature what is of living value to us today; to re-establish, that is, a sense of literary tradition and to define the high standards that this tradition implies. At the same time it is also important that this feeling for a living literature and for the values it embodies should be given as wide a currency as possible, and that literature – both today's literature and yesterday's – should have a real and not merely a nominal existence among a comparatively large number of general readers.

It is to meet this second need that the *Guide* has been planned and produced; and it is the general state of letters and reading today which has determined the shape that it has taken. For this *Guide* has been expressly designed for those thousands of people who might be described as something less than advanced and specialist students of literature, but who accept with genuine respect what is known as 'our literary heritage'. For many of them this amounts, in memory, to an unattractive amalgam of set texts and school prizes, and as a result they have come to read only current books – fiction and biography and travel. Though they are probably familiar with such names as Pope, George Eliot, Langland, Marvell, Yeats, Dr Johnson, Hopkins, D. H. Lawrence, they might hesitate to describe their work intimately, or to fit them into any larger pattern of growth and achievement. If this account is a fair one, it seems probable that very many people would be glad of guidance that would help them respond to what is living and contemporary in literature, for like the other arts it has the power to enrich the imagination and to clarify thought and feeling. Not that one is offering literature as a substitute religion or as providing a philosophy for life. Its satisfactions are of their own kind, though they are satisfactions intimately bound up with the life of each individual reader, and therefore not without their bearing on his attitude to life.

At any rate, it is in this spirit that the *Guide* is offered to the general reader. For this reason it does not set out to compete with the standard Histories of Literature, which inevitably tend to have a take-it-or-leave-it attitude about them. This is not a time-table nor a *Whitaker's Almanack* of English Literature. Nor is it a digest or potted-version, nor again a portrait-gallery of the Great. Works such as these already abound and there is no need to add to the number. What this work sets out to offer is, by contrast, a guide to the history and tradi-tions of English literature, a contour-map of the literary scene. It at-tempts, that is, to draw up an ordered account of literature that is concerned, first and foremost, with value for the present, and this as a direct encouragement to people to read widely in an informed way.

The *Guide* consists of seven volumes:

1. *The Age of Chaucer*
2. *The Age of Shakespeare*
3. *From Donne to Marvell*
4. *From Dryden to Johnson*
5. *From Blake to Byron*
6. *From Dickens to Hardy*
7. *The Modern Age*

The boundaries between the separate volumes cannot be sharply drawn, and in many instances there is an overlap. Far from being a disadvantage, however, this should help to make the *Guide* a single work rather than seven distinct works. Each separate volume, with the exception of the last, has been named after those writers who dominate or stand conveniently at either end of the period, and who also indicate between them the strength of the age in literature.

Though the *Guide* has been designed as a single work, in the sense that it attempts to provide a coherent and developing account of the tradition of English literature, each separate volume exists in its own right. Thus each volume sets out to provide the reader with four kinds of related material:

(i) An account of the social context of literature in each period, at-tempting to answer such questions as 'Why did the literature of this period deal with this rather than that kind of problem?', 'What factors tended to encourage the play rather than the novel, prose rather than verse, in this period?', 'What was the relationship between writer and public?', 'What was the reading public like in its tastes and make-up?' This section of each volume provides an account of contemporary society at its points of contact with literature.

(ii) A literary survey of the period, describing the general characteristics of the period's literature in such a way as to enable the reader to trace its growth and to keep his bearings. The aim of this section is to answer such questions as 'What *kind* of literature was written in this period?', 'Which authors matter most?', 'Where does the strength of the period lie?'. In this first volume there are two such surveys, one on the poetry and the other on the prose of the period.

(iii) Detailed studies of some of the chief writers and works in the period. Coming after the general surveys, the aim of this section is to convey a sense of what it means to read closely and with perception; and also to suggest how the literature of a given period is most profitably read, i.e. with what assumptions, and with what kind of attention. This section also includes an account of whichever one of the other arts particularly flourished at the time, as perhaps throwing a helpful if indirect light on the literature itself: here it is architecture.

(iv) An appendix of essential facts for reference purposes, such as author's biographies (in miniature), bibliographies, books for further study, and so on.

(v) In this first volume, an anthology of verse is also included, since many medieval texts are virtually inaccessible to the general reader. (This anthology, which makes this a unique volume, is described at greater length in the separate Introduction on pp. 255-8.)

Thus each volume of the *Guide* has been planned as a whole, and the contributors have been chosen as people whose approach to literature is based on common assumptions; for it was essential that the *Guide* should have cohesion and should reveal some collaborative agreements (though inevitably, and quite rightly, it reveals disagreement as well). They agree on the need for rigorous standards, and they have felt it essential to take no reputations for granted, but rather to examine once again, and often in close detail, the strength and weaknesses of our literary heritage.

BORIS FORD

REVISED EDITION 1959

The opportunity was taken in the 1959 edition to enlarge quite considerably, as well as to bring up to date, the bibliographies in Part V. The revisions were proposed by Mrs Elizabeth Salter and Dr A. I. Doyle, to whom my thanks are due.

R. B. F.

NOTES

In this volume, three kinds of notes are provided. Numbered notes (1, 2, 3) provide glossaries of words and phrases and are placed either at the foot of the page or immediately beneath a passage of quotations. Notes denoted by symbols (*, †) are also placed at the foot of the page and provide clarification or guidance to the reader. Lettered notes (a, b, c) are placed at the end of each chapter and provide references for further study or of contrary opinions, etc.

PART
I

A SURVEY OF MEDIEVAL VERSE

BY JOHN SPEIRS

Reader in English, the University of Exeter

ANYONE interested to read English medieval literature, for its own sake and as a preliminary to a fuller enjoyment of modern English literature, will first ask himself a number of questions. There is the question of what to read, and in what order to read it; and then there is the question of how to read each particular work of literature. These questions turn out to be anything but simple, especially in regard to English medieval literature where the task of criticism has been very insufficiently performed.

The question of what to read, for example, is not the same as the question of what exists to be read. The answer to the latter would be merely an exhaustive bibliography of all the works that constitute English medieval literature – or the fragment of it that has chanced to be preserved. The problem involved in the first question is, on the other hand, one of judicious selection. We must wish to know what is *best* to read. Life is too short for reading much more than what Arnold once called 'the best that is known and thought in the world'. Yet English medieval literature should present no such overwhelming problem of selection as do the multitudes of more modern books. What needs to be recognized, however, is that even among the much smaller number of English medieval works still happily extant there *is* a task of selection to be performed; that there *are* works which are of more value than others; that among these there are certain works which might indeed be a serious loss for any reader of English to have missed. The task is specifically one for literary criticism. Moreover, at a time when the function of criticism is neither widely respected nor always competently performed, the individual reader himself has to be unusually critical or, in other words, an uncommonly good reader. There is, of course, no doubt about Chaucer. At least since Dryden, he has been established, for our assent or dissent, as the first great classic of English literature. But apart from the traditional agreement about the greatness of Chaucer, the situation is one in which the task of critical selection remains largely unperformed. This introductory survey must therefore be mainly an expression of an individual's taste rather than the outcome of a wide collaboration in criticism of medieval English literature. But even that is perhaps useful as a provisional guide to new readers, and as something to agree or disagree with.

The question of what there is in English medieval literature which is most worth reading narrows down to the immediate practical question of what to read *first*. Clearly, since one reads a succession of works, it is desirable that the succession should form a better rather than a worse order. Mr Eliot, in his essay, *Tradition and the Individual Talent*, has suggested how the individual works constituting a literature establish an order among themselves – an order modified by every new work.

Moreover, once the reader has made out a provisional order of reading (with such aid as he can gather from other readers), there is always finally the question of how to read each particular work. It is often forgotten, in these times of newspaper reading, that reading in the fullest sense is not easy. One should not approach the reading of medieval English literature with confidence unless one is already fairly experienced in the reading of more modern English literature. Such reading involves a kind of active and intelligent collaboration on the part of the reader in re-creating each unique work of literary art from the words on the page. It follows that generalizations about how to read are of little use and may be positively obstructive. Each work of literature requires to be individually re-made (or 'realized') by the reader for himself; but the more experience the reader has previously had in reading literature and the more experience of life the better, even if it has only taught him always to expect something different, to expect the unexpected.

There is, of course, a solid body of academic opinion which holds that we are not competent to read the poetry of Chaucer and his contemporaries until we have acquired what is often called 'background'. There is no end to the acquisition of 'background'. One might spend a lifetime reading a multitude of books that are not themselves literature in the determination to acquire the 'necessary background', and so *never* come to the poetry itself. Such of Chaucer's 'background' as is relevant to his poetry is, after all, implied and indicated in the poetry itself, and the most relevant way to that background is surely through the reading of the poetry. The best preparation for reading the poetry of Chaucer and his contemporaries is experience in reading poetry. The acquisition of background is no compensation for the kind of illiteracy that makes little of poetry or tries a circuitous approach.

It may perhaps be assumed from the start that English medieval literature is a part of a still larger whole – indeed, of several larger wholes; that it is part of English literature as a whole and, at the same time, part of European medieval literature. The idea that English readers should approach it by way of previous readings in European medieval literature rather than from experience in reading modern English literature is one of those ideas that turn out to be the less satisfactory the more they are examined. Until a reader has made himself proficient in reading literature – poetry, drama, novels – in his own language, he is unlikely to make much of literature in a language other than his own. The English reader who aspires to read European medieval literature will do well to begin by steeping himself in English medieval literature, and to approach the troubadours and trouvères through the poetry of Chaucer, rather than attempt to approach Chaucer through the poetry of the troubadours and trouvères. As he extends and deepens his reading of English medieval literature, he may, indeed, find that it will of itself lead him outward to the European literature of which it is a part – and not only to the French and Italian and medieval Latin literature, but also to the Old Norse and German and Celtic literatures. Thus with a certain inevitability he will be led to appreciate that throughout the Middle Ages there must have been the liveliest inter-connexion and interplay between these diverse written and oral literatures. In the meanwhile, he will gradually have come to recognize that in reading English medieval literature he is at the beginning of modern English literature and that his understanding and enjoyment of modern literature will have been enriched by his medieval reading. He would recognize, for example, what was new in what Chaucer did as distinct from what was medieval. As Matthew Arnold recognized in 'The Study of Poetry':

If we ask ourselves wherein consists the immense superiority of Chaucer's poetry over the romance-poetry, [we shall find that it] is given by his large, free, simple, clear yet kindly view of human life – so unlike the total want, in the romance-poets, of all intelligent command of it. Chaucer has not their helplessness; he has gained the power to survey the world from a central, a truly human point of view.

Chaucer's Art

Chaucer (c. 1340–1400) is by general concurrence the greatest English medieval author, the centre of English medieval literature, as it seems to exist for us.

Furthermore, for readers accustomed to modern literature – not only non-dramatic poetry, but dramatic poetry and novels – Chaucer is the medieval author who is likely to appear most familiar and congenial. What was new and unfamiliar in Chaucer for his contemporary audience is probably just what seems most familiar to us. It is therefore not so easy for us to recognize that Chaucer was a very remarkable innovator. He adapted certain modes, themes, and conventions of French and Italian medieval poetry to English poetry for the first time. But he was a still more remarkable innovator than that might suggest. He developed the art of literature itself beyond anything to be found in French or Italian or any other medieval literature. (This is not, of course, to deny that he necessarily lost certain qualities in the process.) In *Troilus and Criseyde* he gave the world what is virtually the first modern novel. In the *Canterbury Tales* he developed his art of poetry still further towards drama and towards the art of the novel.

It should not be surprising, therefore, that Chaucer has seemed to many readers to stand at the beginning of modern English literature – as Homer has seemed to stand at the beginning of Greek, indeed of European, literature – almost as if he had founded or invented it. But it should equally be observed that the practice of the art of poetry had been continuous and widespread throughout the Middle Ages and that Chaucer comes towards the end of that whole period. Implicit in his art are centuries of both oral and written poetic practice and development in several European languages, including English itself, though Chaucer *does* consciously borrow very much from French and Italian poetry. Any idea that, because (from our viewpoint) Chaucer is an 'early' English poet, he is 'primitive' or 'naïve' should be impossible to anyone who responds to his poetry. The civilized delicacy of Chaucer's poetic art cannot be dissociated from that of his mind and spirit. Consider the witty urbanity of the opening of the Prologue to the *Legend of Good Women*, its delicate poise between polite scepticism and modest (perhaps essentially religious) recognition of the limits of human reason and experience; the polite ease of its conversational tone and manner is itself an aspect of the art:

> A thousand tymes have I herd men telle,
> That ther is joye in heven, and peyne in helle;
> And I accorde wel that hit is so;
> But natheless, yit wot[1] I wel also,
> That ther nis noon dwelling in this contree,
> That either hath in heven or helle y-be,
> Ne may of hit non other weyes witen,
> But as he hath herd seyd, or founde hit writen;
> For by assay ther may no man hit preve.
> But god forbede but men shulde leve[2]
> Wel more thing then men han seen with ye!
> Men shal nat wenen[3] every-thing a lye
> But-if him-self hit seeth, or elles dooth;
> For, god wot, thing is never the lasse sooth,
> Thogh every wight ne may hit nat y-see.
> Bernard the monk ne saugh nat al, parde!
>
> (1–16)

Chaucer's mastery of his art – which is at the same time a mastery of life – is rooted deep in past poetic practice and in a civilization already centuries old. On the other hand, his originality marks a new beginning. It would indeed be misleading to place the emphasis finally on Chaucer's urbanity rather than on the wealth and depth of his humanity and the fertility of his inventiveness. His genius owes more perhaps to the English language of which he is a master, the English that was *spoken* around him, than to the French and Italian poets from whom he consciously borrowed and to whom he certainly owes much.

Chaucer begins as a trouvère in English. It is very likely that his earliest work has not been preserved. But, in his poetry as we have it, he begins as a translator of *Le Roman de la Rose*. Thereafter, throughout his work, we see that he has continued to borrow and adapt from French and Italian poets freely even when he is most 'English'. The art of Chaucer, therefore, implies and includes the art – the conventions and themes – of the trouvères and of his French and Italian

1. know, 2. believe, 3. consider.

contemporaries. But the language of Chaucer's poetry is English; and, if we consider the colloquial character of Chaucer's English, even in such of his poetry as is not dialogue or monologue, it is unmistakably the English spoken by the community to which he belonged. English was, of course, the language of a people who were largely country folk, though there was already a middle class becoming wealthy, independent and important. Chaucer's poetry gained immensely in the vividness and variety of its imagery and its idioms from being in the spoken language of the medieval English people. But the language of Chaucer's poetry is unmistakably that English further shaped, refined, and pointed in the conversation of cultivated and witty courtly folk. If Chaucer's audience – though a portion of it may have been bilingual – was not English-speaking as well as courtly, why are his poems English and courtly? 'All art is a collaboration.' Chaucer's English poetry cannot be felt to be over-sophisticated, over-refined, or artificial. It is anything but superficial in that sense. There is nothing exclusive about it. It implies a whole varied community and a single civilization. There are implied in Chaucer's English not only the courtly folk, but the country folk and the new bourgeoisie, who figure also as characters in his human comedy; and for all its diversity, the community implied in Chaucer's English – in Chaucer's poetry – strikes us as a remarkably harmonious whole.

The modern reader should not assume that, as a reader of poetry, he is more accomplished than the audience for whom the poems of Chaucer were originally composed. None the less, however knowledgeable he is about poetry, he is necessarily a different kind of person with a very different viewpoint from a member of Chaucer's original audience. As such he may surely be allowed to have his own judgement and be required to exercise it, in reading the poetry of Chaucer, without dutiful reference to the way the original audience might be supposed to have exercised *its* judgement. The poetry of Chaucer today is an object detached from Chaucer the man and his original fourteenth-century audience; it is an object with which the modern reader in his turn must now come to terms. It belongs to that impersonal realm (as Mr Leavis calls it) in which works of art may take effect and minds of different ages may meet.

Certainly, no amount of background knowledge is likely by itself to assist a reader in apprehending more sensitively and intelligently such essential aspects of a poem as its rhythm and imagery or, indeed, its whole structure, effect, and import. On the other hand, many of the subtleties and delicacies of Chaucer's poetry – the finer shades and subtler points of his irony and wit, for example – must at first be uncertain to a modern reader, before he has read his way into a certain inwardness with Chaucer's idiom and mode of speaking. But the best way to attain this inwardness is, I suggest, by frequent and alert reading of his poetry itself. We may agree that the poetry itself shows that it was composed in the first instance not only for an intelligent, lively, and cultivated audience, but also for a circle of people who had common standards and who very well understood each other. We may agree that we modern readers of Chaucer are, in that respect, comparatively outsiders. Nevertheless, we must also ask why modern readers should want to read Chaucer at all; and why we are justified in saying that Chaucer, like Shakespeare, is for all time. One partial answer is perhaps that the greatness of his poetry – particularly as a presentation of the human comedy – depends on an inexhaustible 'source' in the life and speech of a whole varied community.

Reading Chaucer

Before proposing an order of reading Chaucer, I may here presume to interpose some preliminary advice for the reader who takes from the shelf his Chaucer for the first time – at least, since he read some of Chaucer as a set task at school.

Many readers seem to make unnecessarily heavy going of Chaucer's poetry from the beginning. They make it out to be more difficult in certain initial respects than it really is, and as a consequence are slow to recognize the subtle and delicate delightful thing it turns out to be when one has finally come to read it, as we say, 'easily'. Yet, paradoxically, it is rather at this later stage – as the subtleties and delicacies become apparent – that the real difficulties, such as arise in the exact appreciation of any complex work of art, begin to engage most fully the intelligence and sensibility of the reader. Many of the pioneer teachers of English in schools appear to have found no better way of treating Chaucer than as if he were a Latin (or an Anglo-Saxon) text. The habit has been formed of approaching Chaucer's English almost as if it were a foreign language. New readers set themselves – as they may have been set at school – to 'translate' passages of Chaucer's poetry. A process of reading what is after all English poetry begins laboriously as one of looking up words and substituting the modern equivalents, often crudely approximate, which are listed in the glossary. My own observation has convinced me that one's first reading in Chaucer had much better be a reading of all the *Canterbury Tales* straight through at an easy pace but without allowing oneself to be interrupted by looking up every unfamiliar word. It will generally be found that enough of the interest comes through even in such a superficial first reading to carry the reader enjoyably on. As he reads, the unfamiliarity of many of the words begins gradually to wear off. It is only by coming across particular words (such as 'curteisye', 'gentilesse', 'vileinye', 'fantasye', 'semblaunce', 'maistrye', 'kinde', 'vertu', 'corage', 'usage') again and again in the various living and changing contexts of Chaucer's poetry that the reader begins to acquire a feeling for their specifically Chaucerian shades of meaning and implications, a feeling more delicate and exact than he would get by providing himself with modern equivalents from a glossary or notes. Words acquire their *exact* meaning in Chaucer's, as in any other, poetry from the way in which they are used, from their interplay in particular arrangements or structures of words. There is no shorter cut to learning to be a Chaucerian reader than by constant and extensive reading of Chaucer.

The reader's initial interest in the *Canterbury Tales* may well be of the kind that is found in reading a novel or volume of *nouvelles*. But from the beginning, even if he is as yet only imperfectly understanding it, he should try to *listen* to the poetry; it appears to have been intended to be read aloud, as for centuries previous to Chaucer poems had been recited to companies of listeners. Though Chaucer was in some ways a new kind of poet in English, the art of poetry was to Chaucer still a social art, intended for the entertainment or instruction of a company. All poetry should be listened to, at least with the inner ear, and in the case of Chaucer that means listening to a kind of talking, even when it is the poet himself who seems to be talking familiarly to the company he is entertaining. But, above all in the *Canterbury Tales*, we are listening much of the time to the talking of *characters*, listening not merely to 'vowel music' but to full-bodied conversation implying in its movement and rhythm the accents, inflections, and even the bodily gestures of live speakers.

Chaucer's verse was not only spoken, but spoken differently from our own; it is therefore probably best to try to accustom ourselves to pronouncing it as nearly as possible in the way it is supposed to have been pronounced, yet to do this only in so far as it can be done easily and without becoming a distracting preoccupation. The key to the pronunciation which most modern editions provide is probably sufficient for this practical purpose. The spelling, which must surely have been intended by the scribes to be phonetic, is, after all, the principal guide. It is the vowels which have chiefly to be attended to, until with some little practice the reader falls into the habit of pronouncing the poetry in an approximately Chaucerian way without any longer being conscious that he does so. (This question of pronunciation is discussed in greater detail in the Introduction to the Anthology: see page 255.)

It need scarcely be added that it is essential to read Chaucer's verse metrically if we are not to fall into the error of supposing it to have merely what Dryden called 'the rude sweetness of a Scotch tune'. For this purpose it has to be recognized that the -e ending of so many of the words was generally pronounced (except when the succeeding word begins with a vowel). The surest guide as to when or when not to pronounce the -e is the metre itself, once the reader has instinctively fallen into it. Gradually his feeling for the variety and flexibility, the subtle and dramatic changes in conversational movement within the strict metrical formality, will grow from reading the poetry itself.

Chaucer's Poems and Medieval Genres

I have already suggested that Chaucer's greatest achievement, the *Canterbury Tales* (c. 1386–1400*), is what the modern reader will probably read first. It will also be what he is most likely to return to again and again. For depth of interest, for the wealth of its impressions of the human comedy, and for its mature wisdom, it is unrivalled among Chaucer's works. *Troilus and Criseyde* (c. 1380–85) is its greatest predecessor among these. In this poem the modern reader will discover, emerging out of a medieval romance, what is virtually a great novel – the first modern novel. Once again, the more conventional elements in the poem, which were probably the most

* The chronological order of the poems is fairly well established, but their dates can only be conjectured.

familiar to the original fourteenth-century audience, will be the least familiar to the modern reader. But he will make their acquaintance in this poem in the way that should be the most intelligible to a modern mind; even the medieval convention of courtly love, for instance, is handled critically in the poem. This criticism of conventions is, of course, part of the poem's 'criticism of life' in the Arnoldian sense of the endeavour to see life as it is; it is not abstract, but is presented, as by a great novelist, in terms of contrasts between flesh-and-blood persons – Pandarus, Criseyde, Troilus – and of live and developing human relationships. Thus Pandarus, the first great comic creation in English, contrasts with Troilus, the courtly lover of trouvère poetry; Criseyde, so various, so alive, seems to fluctuate between the two, though she is always a vivid and complex individual, the first complete character of a woman in English literature. The poem is both comedy and tragedy. It is comedy in its searching, though infinitely charitable, contemplation of human frailties, in the setting of the social scene; and it is tragedy in its recognition of the impermanence of human relationships and, finally, in the disastrous conclusion of the loves of Troilus and Criseyde and the defeat of the wordly wisdom of Pandarus.

The reader who eventually reads Chaucer's poems in chronological order, will begin with the Chaucerian *Romaunt of the Rose* (before 1373). In doing so he will make his acquaintance with a delightful new English poem and at the same time with the nearest thing in English to the original *Roman de la Rose*. The English reader could have no more intimate introduction to the medieval French romances and allegories of courtly love, to the poetry of the trouvères, and, ultimately, of the troubadours. At the same time the poem may well come to seem to him the embryo out of which all Chaucer's poetry grows, although it is clear that the 'sources' which at different stages nourish the varied growth of Chaucer's poetry are many and diverse and are not all 'literary'. Chaucer's principal 'source' may surely be said to be the English that was spoken around him and out of which he made his poetry, drawing on it abundantly in his later poetry to express his direct observation and knowledge of the life around him. But the *Roman de la Rose*, his original *literary* source or model (in his poetry as we have it), may be observed to underlie not only the succession of dream-vision poems, but even, in some measure, the

Canterbury Tales. Thus, right through Chaucer's poetry, the personifications of the *Romaunt of the Rose* may be observed in process of growing into the persons of the *Canterbury Tales*; and thus, out of the allegory of courtly love, comes *Troilus and Criseyde.*

The two parts of the *Roman de la Rose* are in effect two quite different poems. The original courtly love allegory of Guillaume de Lorris (thirteenth century) is continued in a very different key by the sceptical Jean de Meung (c. 1250–1305). Both poets were of considerable importance for Chaucer. A reading of the first part of the Chaucerian *Romaunt of the Rose* will introduce the modern English reader in the most direct way possible for him to medieval courtliness and courtly love. It will introduce him to a poetry that was intimately associated with the spring festivals when both peasant and courtly folk danced and celebrated the annual triumph of summer over winter. This spring note continues right through Chaucer's poetry. Not least, the first part of the poem will introduce the reader to medieval allegory and its setting within a dream-vision. Although Chaucer's poetry not only grows out of but away from allegory towards a larger, freer realism, allegory still underlies even the *Canterbury Tales.*

Allegory was the way the medieval mind characteristically worked; it was a mode of seeing; by its means what was dimly thought or felt was made visible, the abstract made concrete, the barely intelligible made imaginable and so more clearly intelligible. The power of visualization is controlled, concentrated in allegory until it attains the order and lucidity of vision. The medieval allegorical habit modified the language itself. The English of our medieval literature is full of personifications or of words and phrases that are on the point of becoming so; and personifications are a feature of allegory. As in Dante, so in Chaucer frequent similes promote the distinct visualization which is an essential aspect of allegory and is still an aspect of the 'realism' of the *Canterbury Tales.*

In his part of *Le Roman de la Rose* Jean de Meung contributes a sceptical tone and attitude which, as we can observe in Chaucer's poetry, had a share in promoting the growth and maturity of Chaucer's much larger, more humane wisdom. The mocking spirit of Jean de Meung is by no means discordant with that of the *fabliaux*, those ribald and anti-clerical tales which appear to have been particularly popular among the new, increasingly independent bourgeoisie of both France and England. The *fabliaux* provide Chaucer with a contrast of attitude to the poetry of courtly love, as well as a disrespect for clerics, which he made the basis of a more profound comic criticism. Certainly it cannot be accidental that in the *Canterbury Tales* Chaucer has turned to the *fabliaux* as a source of several of his best tales. Chaucer's *fabliau* tales must, of course, be distinguished from the rudimentary tales that the *fabliaux*, as they existed orally, must in general have been. In Chaucer's hands they have been shaped with masterly comic art.

The poem which the reader will come to next after the *Romaunt of the Rose* – because it appears to be the nearest to it both in composition and in its form and nature – will be the *Boke of the Duchesse* (c. 1369). Though the poem is an elegy, the lady who is dead is seen in recollection as when alive, the lady of the poetry of courtly love and something more, the first Chaucerian impression of a lady. From this still somewhat immature poem, the reader might well pass next to the *Parlement of Foules* (c. 1380). In this delightful poem in celebration of St Valentine's Day, the garden has borrowed – or Chaucer has borrowed from the poetry of Boccaccio – something of the quality of early Renaissance Italy. But the liveliest passages of the poem are the very dramatic dialogues between the assembled birds.

Apart from the unique value of this poem as a poem, the reader will find that with it he has been introduced to one of the most popular *genres* of medieval literature, the Bird and Beast Fable. These tales of talking birds and beasts were certainly not invented in the Middle Ages, though they were then added to and elaborated upon – when folks in the villages and small towns still lived familiarly with animals. (There is a theory that this species of tales may have originated in the impersonating of animals and birds by humans dressed in skins or feathers in the dramatic rituals of the ancient communities. In the same way there might well have originated the innumerable tales of metamorphoses, humans changed into animals or animals changed back again into humans; and thus might also have originated the tales of talking animals.) The possibility of a rich human comedy, playing upon the absurd resemblances between humans and animals, was realized from these tales by various medieval poets and above all by Chaucer himself in his masterpiece, *The Nonne Preestes Tale* of Chauntecleer and Pertelote.

In the clash between the 'gentils' and the 'cherles' in the bird-debate of the *Parlement of Foules* we can also see emerging one of the *social* comedy themes of Chaucer's later poetry. The modern reader will find, in addition, that in their *flyting* – exchange of satiric abuse – he has been introduced to yet another of the recurrent features of medieval poetry. (It is again a feature which has a long ancestry, for it has been traced back to the flyting-match that was a regular pre-liminary to, or substitute for, the combat between the two antagon-ists – Summer and Winter, the Old Year and the New, the Old Divine King or God and the New – in ancient dramatic rituals. It is said to have been the origin of the boastings and abuse exchanged by heroes in Epic poems and, indeed, in tragedies. In its humorous or satiric as-pect it is more evidently a feature of comedies, and it has been con-vincingly claimed as the origin of satiric poetry itself.)

From the *Parlement of Foules* the reader will pass on to *The House of Fame* (c. 1380), which – at least in the second and third books – is a masterpiece of comic fantasy, with a graver undertone of contempla-tion of the vanity of human wishes. Out of his reading of Dante, and also of Ovid, Chaucer has made something entirely his own – in-formal, easy, familiar, conversational in tone. Thus, by way of these delightful poems, the reader will find himself back with *Troilus and Criseyde* and will better appreciate its magnitude and significance. Between *Troilus and Criseyde* and the *Canterbury Tales* he will then come upon the *Legend of Good Women* (c. 1385). The Prologue to the *Legend* is, perhaps, the loveliest of Chaucer's May vision poems. The God of Love and the Lady clothed in green, whom he conducts as his Queen at the head of a long procession of women across a meadow, are surely a happy reminiscence of the King and Queen of the May festivals, and this is not incompatible with their particular significance in the poem. The tales – the Legends themselves – appear to have come mostly or ultimately from Ovid. But they show already that poetic-dramatic genius in presenting scenes and persons which is one of the characteristics of the far greater *Canterbury Tales*, the great human comedy of the literature of the Middle Ages.

The *Canterbury Tales* should be read as a whole poem and not simply as a collection of tales from among which one may pick self-contained masterpieces. The unity of the *Canterbury Tales* as it stands is not altered by the fact that the whole poem as planned remained incomplete and that several of the individual tales appear not yet to have been arranged in any final order when the poet died. In what we do have, there are indeed more than the beginnings of a formal arrangement: certain groupings of the tales have been made, sequences have been established, deliberate contrasts between tales are apparent. Nevertheless, there had been no final arrangement, and it seems superfluous for modern editors to attempt to do more in that way than Chaucer himself had already done. It is superfluous principally because the tales themselves seem to have the power to combine, in more or less any order in which one reads them, into a unity that builds up out of contrasts, an orderly impression of the rich disorder of life. The reader, therefore, should not allow what he happens to know of the uncompleted scheme to interfere with his feeling for the organic completeness of the poem as it stands and for its inclusiveness as an impression of the diversity of human life.

It follows from this that while each tale has its own individuality and can be enjoyed in and for itself, in relation to the other tales it has a far richer significance. The *Clerkes Tale* of Patient Griselda, for example, so often studied out of its context, is a deliberate contrast with the Wife of Bath's Monologue and with the tale of the disillusioned Merchant, whose own wife has proved no Patient Griselda at all. A tale unusually solemn in itself – and too good to be true, so to speak – thus becomes part of the comedy.

But each tale has still further significance not only in relation to other tales but also in relation to the great *Prologue*, to the interludes between the tales, to the character of its own teller, and to the characters of the other Canterbury pilgrims who tell the other tales and who are imagined to make up the audience – indeed, in relation to the whole movement and animation of the larger dramatic poem which the *Canterbury Tales* virtually is. In its total impression, the Canterbury Pilgrimage of the poem is the procession of the human comedy itself. The diversity of the tales fulfils the promise of that initial diversity of pilgrims presented in the *Prologue*, 'characters' who are individuals and at the same time are morally and socially representative. In the interludes between the tales these 'characters' are set in action, talking, disputing, and the tales themselves are a livelier extension of their talk. These tales are the entertainment the pilgrims provide for each other and at the same time they are a fuller revela-

tion of themselves, their interests, attitudes, and antagonisms. For example, the *Freres Tale* is directed against the Somnour: he tells how
a rascal somnour falls in with a fellow-traveller, a forester clad in green
who turns out to be a fiend and carries the somnour off to hell; the
Somnours Tale is at the expense of a friar and is his reply to the *Freres
Tale*. Thus the two rascals mutually expose one another in their tales.

Most of the tales appear, with regard to their sources, to be old
traditional tales that were told in this age of story-telling when there
were rich oral as well as written traditions to draw on. In making his
Canterbury Tales Chaucer appears to have drawn much more freely
than in his earlier poems on less narrowly 'literary' sources. Some
of the tales are based on old romances or 'Breton lays', others on
fabliaux or 'merry tales'. But of almost every one he makes a work of
the maturest and wisest art. Yet where the art seems most mature,
the traditional roots are also the deepest. The Wife of Bath's great
dramatic monologue is a brilliant new invention of sophisticated art.
But it grows out of ancient roots, partly the traditional flytings between man and wife, contentions for the 'maistrye' such as that between Noah and his wife in the Miracle Plays. The Wife of Bath herself is a new type - the bourgeois woman, one might call her - yet in
essentials she is as old as humanity.

In reading and re-reading, one will necessarily exercise one's judgement as to which are the outstanding masterpieces among the tales.
Apart from the *Nonne Preestes Tale* and the *Pardoneres Prologue and
Tale* (which are discussed in some detail later in this volume), I would
myself mention the *Wyf of Bathes Monologue and Tale*, the *Mar-
chauntes Tale* of January and May, the *Chanouns Yemannes Prologue
and Tale*, the *Frankeleyns Tale*, and the tales of the Miller and Reve
and of that other quarrelling pair, the Friar and the Somnour. If it
seems surprising that I have not mentioned the *Knightes Tale* or the
Clerkes Tale or the *Prioresses Tale*, that may be due to the prejudice that
finds it hard to accept the comic as potentially a work of art - the
prejudice that, in the nineteenth century (in spite of the example of
Byron's *Don Juan*) prevented *The Dunciad* from being recognized as
a great imaginative poem. But the *Milleres Tale* is not only Chaucer's
comic art at its maturest but - and this is only another way of saying
the same thing - it is his poetry at its richest. Consider the fertility of
the imagery out of which Alisoun, the rich old carpenter's young

wife, is created. The tales are poetry – the *fabliaux* tales no less than the others – poetry that in its creation of characters, scenes, episodes and dialogues is of the nature of dramatic poetry.

The *Canterbury Tales* is one of the two greatest achievements in English medieval literature, the other being a poem of a very different kind, the alliterative *Sir Gawayne and the Grene Knight*. The contrast between some of Chaucer's tales is sufficiently striking. But the contrast which these two masterpieces make with each other is even more striking, and their creative diversity is a remarkable testimony to the flourishing condition of English poetry in the fourteenth century.

The Alliterative Poems

When he has reached the stage of reading Chaucer with a certain accomplishment and appreciation, the reader has also qualified himself in the best possible way to read such other English medieval poetry as has been preserved, and to appreciate it specifically in relation to Chaucer. This is not to say that he will find all the rest of English medieval poetry closely resembling Chaucer. On the contrary, he will discover that much of it – particularly the alliterative poems of the West Midlands and the North-west – is very unlike Chaucer's poetry in important respects and, indeed, makes a most stimulating and interesting contrast with it.

These alliterative poems show by comparison in what respects Chaucer was an innovator in English – the extent to which he brought English poetry into accord with the poetry of France and Italy, and also what he did that was new not only in English but in European literature. At the same time, the comparison with the alliterative poems is not all to Chaucer's advantage. While he has gained in witty urbanity and courtly ease and smoothness of versification, he has sacrificed certain extra-rational and pre-Christian elements and a certain massive native strength, all of which are found in the alliterative poems. Moreover, the latter are just as much works of art, in their different traditional kind, as are Chaucer's poems, and they imply as noble and as cultivated audiences – though these were evidently located in the provinces and were naturally conservative in their tastes.

The masterpiece among the alliterative poems which have survived from the fourteenth century is undoubtedly *Sir Gawayne and the*

Grene Knight.* But there are others which in their nature may properly be grouped with that poem, and which are scarcely less masterly; these include *Wynnere and Wastoure,** *The Parlement of the Thre Ages,** *The Awntyrs of Arthure at the Tarn Wadling,* the alliterative *Morte Arthur,* and *The Destruction of Troy* (this and Lydgate's *Troy Book* are the two principal English medieval Troy books). It is a remarkable fact that *Sir Gawayne and the Grene Knight* itself and most of the other alliterative poems which we may associate with it are virtually accidental survivors from the Middle Ages. Had it not been for the chance preservation of a single MS. – the only MS. in which the poem is preserved to us – we should have known nothing of this masterpiece. The same is true of most of the poems which constitute the so-called alliterative 'revival' of the fourteenth century. (*Piers Plowman,* which has been preserved on forty-seven MSS., is a very special case.) Now, since these poems have been preserved virtually by accident, we may surely conclude that there must have been others; that, magnificent poems as several of them are, they are the accidental survivors of what – judging from these poems alone – must still have been a widespread and flourishing tradition of alliterative poetry in the West Midlands and the North-west of England. Not one of these poems reads like a self-conscious attempt by an isolated poet to 'revive' what was felt to be a disused and archaic mode. The reason why the predecessors of these poems in the same living tradition have not been preserved to us must either be that these predecessors were never written down or, if they were, the MSS. have been lost. Whichever explanation is the right one (and I am inclined to the former), these poems seem to me unmistakably the final poems we have in English of the great oral tradition of Northern European alliterative poetry, oral in the sense that they could have been originally composed and remembered and recited without the intermediary of writing and reading. In such a tradition, their art, much more even than Chaucer's, must have been the product of a collaboration between the poet and his audiences as well as between the poet and his predecessors. For although Chaucer's art is still largely social, he is much more the new kind of individual artist than his contemporaries of the West Midlands and North-west.

It would be a pity indeed if the modern reader felt he was excluded

* These three poems are included in the anthology in this volume.

from such a great poem as *Sir Gawayne and the Grene Knight* because of
the very wealth of the vocabulary on which the strength and vividness of the poetry depends. It is well worth taking the necessary pains
to overcome that difficulty. Once again it is essential to read the poem
aloud to enable the masterly rhythm to come into play. The reader
will then realize for himself how little this alliterative verse is awkward and uncouth. The varied and profound significances of this
great poem, symbolical as well as realistic, are considered in detail in
a later essay and are beyond the scope of this preliminary survey.

From *Sir Gawayne and the Grene Knight* the reader might well pass
to the other associated poems of the Gawain Cycle, such as *The
Awntyrs of Arthure* and *The Avowing of Arthure*. Alternatively, he might
turn to *Wynnere and Wastoure* or *The Parlement of the Thre Ages*. These
latter vivid, satiric, and weighty poems are, in structure, flyting-
matches and the nearest thing to a kind of ritualistic dramatic poem.
The fact that the dramatis personae (the Three Ages, incidentally, are
Youth, Middle Age, and Old Age) appear in a vision in alliterative
poems of this nature should make us hesitate to derive the dream-
vision convention in English medieval poetry solely from *Le Roman
de la Rose*. The vision had also been a feature of the poetry of the
North of Europe, where the poet was, perhaps, longer regarded as
having the sacred character of a prophet than in the South.

Piers Plowman is generally approached from Chaucer's *Canterbury
Tales*, and, indeed, it provides a usefully sharp and decisive contrast.
But if we approach it from the reading of the other fourteenth-century alliterative poems – particularly *Wynnere and Wastoure*, its immediate predecessor in the tradition in which it belongs – we shall perhaps be in a better position to estimate its individual value as one
among a number of alliterative poems. It is difficult to judge the
poem as a whole because of the vastness of its bulk. The poetry has
not, throughout the whole work, the density and richness of texture
and significance of *Sir Gawayne and the Grene Knight* and *Wynnere and
Wastoure* and *The Parlement of the Thre Ages*; nor has it, at a first impression, the organic completeness of these masterpieces of art.
Passages stand out from it very strikingly, and it may be that the new
reader would be well advised to begin by appreciating them first, before attempting to grasp the work as a whole. These individual passages usually turn out to be those in which the poet is most 'traditional'

– as in the presentations of the Seven Deadly Sins and the episode of the Harrowing of Hell.* The Seven Deadly Sins appear to have been creations (or re-creations from some older mythological or ritual figures) of the folk imagination as it took possession of the vernacular preachers. Through the vernacular sermons the Seven Sins evidently passed into the poetry and drama of the Middle Ages. These monstrous caricature figures – radically simplified or selected aspects of human nature, magnified and distorted, yet not less real than ordinary human life, though imbued with a fearful intensity – are early expressions of a large and important element in what became the English comic tradition, notably in Ben Jonson, and still present as an element in the kindlier comedy of Dickens. The Harrowing of Hell was an episode in the annually performed Miracle Cycle, and the moving rendering of it in *Piers Plowman* may well have been inspired by actual performances witnessed by the poet. Indeed, it is remarkable how much of the imagery in *Piers Plowman* could have come from the seeing of Miracle Plays.

The poem has been much investigated as a social document rather than as poetry. It contains – even as an allegorical vision poem – a large element of realistic social and moral satire. But the innermost core of its significance is certainly a mystical one. Its central symbol is that of Piers the Plowman as Christ.

Another poem which should be distinguished, for very different reasons, from the main group of fourteenth-century alliterative poems is *Pearl*. This poem has been preserved on the same manuscript as *Sir Gawayne and the Grene Knight* and is in the same dialect: it has thus come to be associated with it. But *Pearl* is a very different kind of poem. It is much more personal and private, less social in that it could not be described as being of the nature of 'oral' poetry or intended for the entertainment, or even enlightenment, of the convivial company in the great hall. It is made up of 101 elaborately rhymed and alliterated stanzas arranged into twenty sequences, the stanzas of each of these sequences being knit together by a final line refrain rather as in a ballade. The landscape of the dream-vision, the Earthly Paradise, is opulently decorative and brilliantly coloured in effect like a MS. illumination or stained glass.

* Passus xviii from the B Text, which contains the Harrowing, is included in the anthology in this volume.

Nevertheless it would be grievously unjust to the poem to suggest that its interest and value are purely 'aesthetic' in the narrower sense. It has, of course, a mystical and theological significance, and is related to a public occasion – a high feast of the Church:

> In Auguste in a high sesoun
> When corne is corven with crokes kene.

Harvest is here associated not only with fruition but with cruel death. The poet has lost a 'pearl of price' which has slipped through the grass (the usual interpretation is that the loss was that of the poet's infant daughter). In a dream-vision he finds himself wandering in what seems to be the Earthly Paradise. It is distinguished from the garden of the Rose by its 'chrystal cliffs' and generally from all mundane gardens by the suggestion of its eternal, unfading, jewel-like quality, and by its quality of light. On the opposite bank of a river which he cannot at present cross (the water of life is crossed only at death), he sees his Pearl transformed and transfigured now to a 'Heavenly Pearl', a maid decked in pearls as a Queen of Heaven, his daughter lost and restored, but still separated from him. The grain sown in the earth has flowered in heaven; the Rose that fades in nature has been eternalized as an unfading jewel – 'gathered into the artifice of eternity'. The child (cf. Beatrice) now instructs the man in heavenly wisdom and sacred theology and shows him finally a vision of Heaven. The poem appears to be in the nature of a religious exercise, the elaborate craftsmanship being itself a part of the disciplining perhaps of a rebellious personal grief. A detailed analysis of this poem would I think, bring out the essential differences, rather than resemblances, between it and the other alliterative poems.

The Metrical Romances

There are about sixty English medieval metrical romances extant. These, though they should all be studied in relation to each other, are of varying quality and require to be sorted out judiciously. But a few of them have some distinction and deserve to be known and valued by the general reader. Workers in the field of the origins of literature[a]* have shown in great and convincing detail that the medieval romances are at the end of a process of evolution from myth or ritual to romance. The reader ignores their findings at some risk of an impoverished reading of the romance. Once the Arthurian romances – and other romances that may be associated with them – are recognized as being rooted in mythology, they at once begin to show themselves full of meaning and the more interesting as poetry.

The extant English metrical romances appear to belong to stages in the transition – during the thirteenth, fourteenth, and fifteenth centuries – from oral poetry to written composition. *King Horn* (c. 1225), which is perhaps the earliest, and *Havelok the Dane* (c. 1275) are explicitly minstrels' lays; and even those that come at the very end of this phase of minstrelsy (which was virtually over by the fifteenth century) cannot be dissociated from the recital, though some of them may have been written compositions and not merely written down. Many, in the form in which we have them, are evidently English redactions of earlier French romances. The tales which form the substance of these poems, and of the French romances on which many of them seem to be based, must have existed earlier and been transmitted and continually reshaped orally. Many of these tales, particularly those which form the substance of the Arthurian romances and of the Breton lays, have been regarded as Celtic, and their principal channel of development into French and English and German as the Breton story-tellers who were bilingual.[b] (As Bretons these *conteurs* would have had access to the rich storehouse of Celtic tales that had their origin in ancient Celtic myth and ritual. The richest original source may have been Irish; but Brittany and Wales, Cornwall and the West of Scotland shared much the same ancient culture. As professional story-tellers at the courts of kings and nobles in early medieval France and England, the Bretons told their tales in French.) Thus what may have been originally Celtic tales were made into French romances, influenced in greater or less degree by the spirit of courtliness and chivalry, the spirit of the troubadours and the trouvères. From French they passed into German and English. So the gods of ancient mythology became, on the one hand, medieval knights

* This note, and all subsequent *lettered* notes, appear at the end of their respective essays. Notes indicated by *numbers* and *symbols* appear as footnotes.

and, on the other, their monstrous or other-world antagonists; the spring or earth goddesses became courtly ladies or queens or, retaining their other-world character, fays.

If we compare the extant romances we should quickly recognize that a number of themes or *motifs* keep recurring in them, though always as variations. The impression grows that these themes are – or were at one time – related. There is, for example, the theme of the union of a mortal with an other-world being. Sometimes a mortal queen meets a splendid other-world stranger, or she is abducted by the King of the Other World. Or a mortal man – a knight – may meet in a forest a lady, surpassingly lovely, who is clearly a fay and who woos him. The knight may dwell in the other world with his faery mistress for, perhaps, seven years until he breaks some taboo which deprives him of her, to his inconsolable grief. Sometimes a knight may pursue through the forest a hart which turns out to be a faery messenger or guide. Often, indeed, the faery cavalcade are seen by a solitary mortal as they ride, in splendid attire, hunting through a forest or hawking by a river.

In one or two romances which have evidently come under ecclesiastical influence, such unions with an other-worldly being are regarded as unions with the devil, and the offspring may show demonic tendencies or be possessed of the devil (*Sir Gowther*, *Richard Coeur de Lion*). But in most of the romances there is no such sinister interpretation. Instead, we have the theme of the marvellous child, born of a union between a mortal and an other-world being, who is exposed or lost, and then found. This is the theme of the boy born to be king, exposed or exiled, who grows up in a poor man's hut perhaps or in some menial station in some other king's court, and in the end returns to claim his kingdom and be recognized as the true king. In several of the romances a similar cycle of separation and restoration is undergone by a wife or queen. Indeed, the theme of the child or wife lost and eventually found again is one of the most recurrent in the romances.

In many romances the theme is of a succession of tests – a kind of initiation – which a knight must undergo to prove his manhood; of a contest between a knight and some other than human or other-world character. This contest may be prolonged and may take many forms other than that of a direct combat. But a combat – often of an unusual kind – is frequently the climax, perhaps with the owner of what may be an other-world castle.

There can be no doubt that these themes are fragments of what was originally a mythology or several. R. S. Loomis and J. L. Weston in particular have gone far in an endeavour to reconstruct that mythology; and they regard it as (in relation to the Arthurian and associated romances) specifically Celtic. Thus the antagonists – the knight and the keeper of the other-world castle – were originally different phases of one and the same god, perhaps the old and the young sky-god, or the old and the new year, winter and summer. They are opposites and yet one and the same. The young god slays and supplants the old; yet he *is* the old renewed, become young again. In the original ritual – for a myth is the story of a ritual, the story the ritual enacts – the old divine king and the young king who supplanted him evidently impersonated one and the same god.

After the ritual combat follows the ritual marriage. The victor marries the goddess or queen. This goddess, the spring or earth goddess, has become in the medieval romances the faery lady or queen. She may correspond, in the Celtic mythology, to Proserpine. The loathly lady and the lovely lady of the romances are also essentially one and the same, as can be seen in those tales in which the former, disenchanted by the embrace of a courteous knight, changes back again into her original lovely and youthful self (e.g. Chaucer's *Wyf of Bathes Tale*).

Least influenced by French romances and perhaps nearest to the Old Irish tales (perhaps combined with Norse), are the poems of the Gawain cycle which comes from the North-west of England – these include, besides *Sir Gawayne and the Grene Knight* itself, *The Avowing of Arthure* and *The Awntyrs of Arthure*, already mentioned. One of the most interesting of the northern English romances that may be associated with these is *Sir Perceval of Galles* (fourteenth-century MS.). Perceval is brought up in the woods by his mother – evidently a water-sprite – as a 'wild man' and has the task of revenging his slain father, like Orestes or Hamlet. Among the first of the romances to be read might well be the charming group that are based on the Breton lays – *Sir Launfal*, *Sir Degare*, *Le Freine*, and perhaps *Sir Orfeo*★ (all in MSS. of the fourteenth century). These are not specifically Arthurian,

★ This poem is included in the anthology in this volume.

but they unmistakably belong with the Breton lays. In the lay of *Sir Orfeo* we meet the legend of Orpheus and Eurydice taken (at some time) possibly from the *Metamorphoses* of Ovid, but, having become associated with medieval traditional tales in the stream of oral tradition, it has been itself completely transformed into the nature of a Breton lay. The first of the other romances to be read should, perhaps, be those that have been regarded as peculiarly English or Scandinavian – *King Horn*, *Havelok the Dane*. But even those tales, from quite other sources and places, which form the substance of romances other than the Arthurian romances and the Breton lays, appear to have been modified by the influence of the latter and shaped according to the familiar traditional pattern. Even the latest of the 'new' compositions are combinations of the old.

Some of the English medieval romances appear to have passed through a process of remaking – or at least of rehandling – for successive recitals, until each was given the shape it had when written down on the MS. on which it has been preserved. We must not assume that this process was always, or even usually in later tradition, one of improvement. On the contrary, many of the romances (such as those interesting ones preserved in the Percy Folio MS. c. 1650) look like poems which have deteriorated in the process. It may be that some of them were originally works of individual genius, comparable even to *Sir Gawayne and the Grene Knight*, and have fallen into their present confusion in later tradition.

The process was, we know, complicated for medieval English poetry by the fact that there was undoubtedly in early medieval England a phase of bilingualism – a phase when many people were both French- and English-speaking. During this phase, we may guess, the redactions from French into English were made. We have no right to assume, however, that such redactions were necessarily what we think of as translations, involving the intervention of reading and writing. As poems were made and shaped orally by minstrels, the redactions could be (and possibly often were, up to the fourteenth century) made orally. Poems were made to be heard, not read; and by the makers themselves, we may assume, the poems were heard as they were composed, rather than composed in writing. There was, of course, a long phase of both oral and written traditions, existing side by side. These traditions were certainly not isolated from one another;

on the contrary, they drew freely from each other's repertory. Thus tales that were told were made into written tradition and later taken back again into the stream of oral recital and re-shaping.

It seems certain that many of the ballads that were collected in the seventeenth, eighteenth, and nineteenth centuries originated from the medieval minstrels' lays, though many were modified also (judging from their formal structures) by the medieval dance-songs. The ballads must have been flourishing among the unlettered people earlier than the centuries in which they were collected. The balladists (like the Elizabethan dramatists, in their different way) must have been successors of the minstrels of the early Middle Ages and of still earlier communities – no longer honoured and listened to by kings and nobles, but now occupying a humbler station among the people. Ballad recital and composition were still, to some extent, a collaborative activity. It is possible to see in the ballads – the ballads as they were sung or recited dramatically – a social and popular dramatic art that still flourished among the people, particularly in Scotland, up to the eighteenth century. Moreover, the themes of many of them are recognizably those of medieval romances. Thus, the minstrel's lay of *King Horn* is of the thirteenth century: the ballad of *Hind Horn* was there to be collected 600 years later (c 1825).[c]

Malory's 'Morte D'Arthur'

Though this chapter is primarily a survey of poetry (prose being left to the next chapter by Mr Doyle), there are some advantages in including at this point Malory's prose *Morte D'Arthur* (printed by Caxton 1485). For it is best approached after a reading of the English Arthurian verse romances which preceded it, rather than from the poetry of Tennyson and other poets who have since used it as a source. As Professor Vinaver has shown in his edition of the works of Malory, what is really a succession of separate prose romances has been given an appearance of unity, of being one 'book', by the way they were edited and printed by Caxton (under the misleading title of *Morte D'Arthur*). There could be no greater contrast than that between Malory's exceedingly 'literary' fifteenth-century prose romances and the English verse romances or lays of the thirteenth and fourteenth centuries. Malory's prose, with all its seeming simplicity – it is a stylization of earlier medieval prose – is in some respects the nearest thing in medieval English to the prose of Walter Pater. There is a tone of *fin de siècle* about Malory's book.

At the end of the Middle Ages and the end of the long efflorescence of medieval romance in many languages, Malory endeavoured to digest the Arthurian romances into English prose, using as his source chiefly an assortment of French Arthurian prose romances. But this traditional material has not been organized so as to convey any coherent significance either as a whole or, for the most part, even locally. Malory persistently misses the meaning of his wonderful material. (This may have been partly because apparently he had no access to the earlier and better sources – if we except the fourteenth-century English alliterative *Morte Arthure* – and was dependent, or chose to be dependent, on his French prose romances.) The comparison with *Sir Gawayne and the Grene Knight* is in this respect – as, indeed, in nearly all respects – fatally damaging to Malory's *Morte D'Arthur*. The modern reader does best to accept the book as essentially episodic, a book to be dipped into rather than read through. Once we have fallen under the spell of such an episode as that of the Maid of Astalot, it is to it that we shall return.

What is it, then, that constitutes the charm of the book, that draws readers back to parts of it again? Partly it is the 'magic' of its style – those lovely elegiac cadences of the prose, that diffused tone of wistful regret for a past age of chivalry, that vague sense of the vanity of earthly things. Yet the charm of the prose is a remote charm; the imagery is without immediacy; there is a lifelessness, listlessness, and fadedness about this prose for all its (in a limited sense) loveliness. There is also the fascination of the traditional Arthurian material itself, even though we feel it is not profoundly understood. The material fascinates the reader in spite of Malory's 'magical' style, which seems to shadow and obscure rather than illuminate it. Malory's Grail books, for example, include some of the most fascinating of his traditional material. We find here once again the Waste Land, the Grail Castle, the Chapel Perilous, the Wounded King, and so on, but reduced to little more than a succession of sensations and thrills. The recurrent appearance of the corpse or corpse-like figure on a barge and the weeping women – fragments of an ancient mythology though they are – become in Malory merely tedious after a number of repetitions, and the final effect is one of a somewhat morbid sensationalism.

Some qualifications of these strictures should be made on behalf of the last four books of Caxton's Malory, which may be felt to have an impressive kind of unity of their own. The lawless loves of Lancelot and Guinevere, the break-up of the fellowship of the Round Table through treachery and disloyalty, the self-destruction of Arthur's knights and kingdom in a great civil war, the last battle and death of Arthur, and the deaths of Lancelot and Guinevere have, as they are described, a gloomy power, and are all felt as in some degree related events. This set of events appears to have been deeply felt by Malory, partly as a reflection of the anarchy and confusion of the contemporary England of the Wars of the Roses.

Medieval Lyrics and Carols

About the English poetry of the end of the fourteenth century it is still possible to make two broad distinctions. There is what may by then be called the old-fashioned kind of poetry; this is represented by the alliterative poems of the West and North Midlands which appear to come at the end of the oral tradition of Northern European poetry. On the other hand, there is the new-fashioned kind of poetry that is captivating the Court, London, and the South; this poetry, though English, is recognizably related to the traditions of the troubadours and the trouvères. Chaucer is the great poet of this new kind of poetry in English, though he went on to do things that were newer still. This newer kind of English poetry shows itself already in the century before Chaucer, in some of the features of the English songs and lyrics that have chanced to survive in about half-a-dozen MSS., and of an early thirteenth-century debate-poem or flyting called *The Owl and the Nightingale*.

The character of many of the thirteenth-century lyrics itself suggests clearly enough that they are words intended to be sung. Furthermore, the earliest of the English lyrics that have survived are anything but simple in the sense of being rudimentary or primitive, first awkward attempts. On the contrary, their genuine simplicity and spontaneity of effect are those of a complex and subtle art or craft of song-making. The word-structures of the songs were probably evolved in association with the music-structures which they were intended to fit. Moreover, the basic or original structure both of the music and of the words was evidently often determined by the dance – particularly by the ring dances. Thus several of the medieval songs, for example four short pieces preserved together on a fourteenth-century MS., 'The Irish Dancer', 'The Hawthorn Tree', 'All Night by the Rose', 'Maiden of the Moor', appear to belong with the rites and ceremonies and sacred dances of the old Nature religion, and may have been evolved for special festival occasions, such as the May Day rites.

The division between secular and religious (Christian) lyrics appears to be somewhat artificial, or at least superficial. If one considers their imagery, versification, and indeed total textures, no radical division is observable. Moreover, the Christian lyrics are just as much rooted in pre-Christian myth and ritual, in the rites and ceremonies of the old Nature festivals, as are the so-called secular lyrics. Many of the Christmas songs were evidently associated with the ceremonies, games, and plays of the Christmas feast, and are explicitly songs for the boar-feast or ale-feast as the Christmas feast still largely was. With the more convivial of the Christmas carols we may associate the body of songs and lyrics which express the jollity of the medieval English folk on festive occasions.

As distinguished from the more boisterous jollity there is a note of 'mirth' (a word used then with a fuller and richer meaning than to-day) in many of the lovely hymns to Mary. Some of these are lyrics of courtly love transformed or transmuted. But also, in several of the most beautiful of them, Mary has something of the significance still of the tree goddess, the flower goddess, or the spring goddess. In such carols as 'There is a floure sprung of a tree', 'Of a rose, a lovely rose', 'There is no rose of swich vertu', she is either herself the Rose or she is the tree out of which the Rose, who is Christ, springs. In other lyrics Mary is the tragic mother whose child is slain. The unusual, original beauty of the Corpus Christi Carol depends largely on the medieval association of the Crucifixion with the Grail myth.

While very many of the best lyrics are either spring songs or songs for Christmas, it would be giving a one-sided impression not to refer also to the lyrics on the decline of the year, the onset of winter, melancholy utterances or meditations on the uncertainty of the human lot, such as 'Wynter wakeneth al my care'.

In the fifteenth century many more of the lyrics seem 'literary', though there are still nearly as many of the 'traditional' kind. Towards the end of the fourteenth century already, Chaucer and Charles d'Orleans (in his English lyrics) are composing ballades and roundels modelled on the French with deliberate literary craftsmanship. But the old close association between words and music was never quite broken and continues and leads up to the songs of the glorious Elizabethan song-books.

'The Owl and the Nightingale'

There is one English poem of about 1200 (the earlier of the two MSS. is c. 1220), *The Owl and the Nightingale*, which, though not a song but a debate-poem of considerable length, may properly be associated with the thirteenth-century English lyrics and read along with them. Moreover, it provides a contrast with a contemporary alliterative work, Layamon's *Brut* (also c. 1200) which is much more the kind of thing one might have expected. If one were attempting to plot a history of early medieval English literature on the evidence of the scanty number of stray texts that have been preserved, *The Owl and the Nightingale* would have a place out of all proportion to its intrinsic merits, though these are not inconsiderable. There seems to have been nothing like it in English before, though it is improbable that so accomplished an English poem of its particular kind could in fact have been an isolated work. As it now stands among what has survived, a poem earlier perhaps than the earliest surviving group of medieval English lyrics, it seems to represent all by itself an immense modification of the English sensibility, indeed to be almost the first evidence of an English sensibility as we have come to recognize it in English medieval poetry as distinct from Anglo-Saxon poetry. The English language, accustomed to move in the traditional alliterative kind of verse, is here discovered moving easily in rhymed verse (octosyllabic couplets) as to the manner born, as if this kind of verse had long been natural to English. This new kind of verse has certainly been adapted from French and medieval Latin. Yet the English of the poem still instinctively, as it seems, forms itself into frequent alliterative phrases. This poem also may well have been the work of a poet who was bilingual or trilingual, familiar with the contemporary French and Latin poetry, including debate-poems, and perhaps capable himself of composing in these languages. But, if so, he has in this English poem let the genius of his English language have full scope.

The greater part of *The Owl and the Nightingale* is a dialogue between the two birds, and it is thus very near to being a dramatic poem. The rest of the poem sets the scene and provides a spectator's impressions of the quarrelling birds. The opposition is not merely one of ideas but of persons; it is no impersonal academic debate on a set subject. It is essentially a flyting match in which the two birds are the antagonists. As such, it has an ancient ancestry, for the ceremonial flyting match is a phenomenon much older than the Middle Ages and seems to have been almost universal.

The nightingale starts the flyting match by abusing the owl. Her vivid description of the owl, head bigger than all the rest of him, accurate in relation to the bird, is of course a caricature if he is thought of as human. The effect on the owl is vividly seen; he is all swollen and bulged with inarticulate rage as though he had swallowed a frog. The debate thus begins dramatically as an exchange of abuse. Instead of fighting, however, the hostile birds agree to argue. The arguments are full of sense as well as being lively and satiric, and thus the poem is substantial and yet never dull. Nor, at the end, is either bird felt to have decisively the upper hand; the two are well matched, judiciously balanced against each other by the poet. The satiric flyting match and the seriously thoughtful debate – for the poem delightfully combines both these aspects – are sustained to a well-managed dramatic climax. For a critical moment there is a threat of actual battle. But the tiny wren intervenes as peace-maker, and the birds agree to fly off to seek judgement from a certain Master Nicholas of Guildford (perhaps the poet's friend or even, it has been suggested, the poet himself). We are not told what the judgement is. The balance is held, judgement suspended to the end.

The poet's greatest asset is his English vernacular. In listening to his disputing birds, we are listening to English as it must then have been talked in the poet's particular locality. With the conversational language, the contemporary life of the people has entered the poem – and the wild life of the countryside as it was familiar to the people. The satiric humour of the disputants is often of a savage kind, but one becomes aware that the violence of the disputing birds is comprehended within an understanding humour and humanity on the part of the poet as comic observer of life. The final impression of this familiar-talking poem is paradoxically not one of quarrelsomeness, but rather of friendliness, intimacy, and sociability. The colloquial English of the poem is saturated with the traditional wisdom of the people as it has been stored up in proverbial phrases. The wisdom of the poem as a whole is not so much a clerkly wisdom (though the poet may have been a clerk), as of a broad human experience.

The Miracle Cycles

Four versions of the complete English Mystery (or Miracle) Cycle have been preserved – the York, Chester, 'Towneley MS.' (probably Wakefield), and 'N-towne' (probably East Anglian) Cycles. These have evidently been fashioned and shaped for the annual performances by the work of many hands. Though they have been preserved in MSS. of the fifteenth century and later, it is probable that they had assumed or been given much the form in which we find them in the MSS. by the end of the fourteenth century or the beginning of the fifteenth. Certain of these plays will seem to stand out from the rest of the Cycle as being more what we think of as plays – Comedy or Tragedy – presented to an audience. But even these should be viewed in their places in the Cycle – the larger play – in which they are episodes.

The Cycle as a whole appears to be still essentially at the stage of ritual drama. Probably those present at the annual performances should be regarded as worshippers and therefore, to a greater or less extent, participants. The actors or more active participants were probably, for most of the Cycle, not yet actors performing for the entertainment or edification of an audience, but rather impersonators in a ritual. We should probably not think of there being a marked division into spectators and actors as yet, although a few of the plays are beginning to imply an audience and therefore the beginnings of such a division. From our viewpoint, of course, we see the Mystery Cycle as in process of becoming what we may call, for the sake of suggesting the distinction, *art* drama. The few outstanding plays have, indeed, already become so. But even these are dramatic poems, the fullness of whose meaning depends on their still being rooted in ritual and ritual drama. The annual performance was, it would seem, nothing less than the great occasion of the year in the town-community life of the Middle Ages. The townspeople, as organized and incorporated in their Craft Gilds, performed it as an intrinsic part of the Corpus Christi procession at the height of the year (June). It was clearly what gave significance to the life of each year for both the individual and the community in which he belonged. Indeed, this Cycle of events and participation in it each year was probably felt to be more important to the townspeople than what we now look back to as the historical events of that year.

The Mystery Cycle represents or reproduces what might perhaps be called a history of the world – of mankind in relation to God – from the Creation to the Last Judgement. But, if so, it is a history different in kind from what we recognize as history today. The frequent anachronisms are not blunders. Past and future co-exist in the immediate present of each performance. Thus the whole Cycle itself concludes with what we should think of as a future event, the Last Judgement. The purpose or effect of the annual performance was evidently that of a ritual, namely to give significance or meaning to life for that year. The significant past had to be, and therefore was, annually recreated in order to make, and make fortunate, the future for that year, fortunate for the community as a whole and for each individual member of it. Between the Creation and the Judgement the central mystical events – central for everyone concerned – are the birth, death, and resurrection of Christ. The Old Testament episodes between the Creation and the birth of Christ are no more than a preparation for this great central sequence. The whole corresponds, of course, to the cycle of the Christian year.

The historical origins of the plays that have come to form the Mystery Cycle can, we know, be traced back to the embryo Latin plays which appeared first as intrinsic parts of the Church services at Easter and at Christmas. The first of these formal liturgical plays seems to have been the representation of the Resurrection. But corresponding to this little play – almost exactly parallel to it even in the phrasing – there appeared at almost the same time also a Nativity Play. Thus, the Sepulchre approached by priests impersonating the three Marys was the central object in the Easter Play: the cradle approached by priests impersonating the Three Shepherds was the central object in the Christmas Play. Yet the size and nature of what by the end of the fourteenth century had become the English Mystery Cycle cannot be entirely accounted for as a straight development or expansion from these priestly performances. The Mystery Cycle is a truly communal or national drama. There are things in the plays of which the Church became more than doubtful and, indeed, the whole Cycle became, from the Church's point of view, something which had got entirely out of hand. Was it merely the tendency in unregenerate human nature to turn sacred things to buffoonery and farce which was responsible for the transformation? There is surely a profounder explanation. It is clear that for the people the Mystery Cycle was profoundly important and not merely an opportunity for releases of rowdiness.

The explanation almost certainly is that there always had been – among the Scandinavian, Teutonic, and Celtic peoples as still earlier among the Greeks – a ritual drama since before Christianity. Everywhere among the people in the Middle Ages there were fragments of this older, pre-Christian dramatic ritual – ceremonies, dances, games – still being practised. They were being practised in some cases almost desperately, in defiance of the prohibitions of the Church, because they were still obscurely felt to be sacred and fundamental to life. Certain of these survived almost to our own day among the folk, as the Mummers' Play, the Wooing (or Plough) Play, the Morris Dance, and the Sword Dance. It is now generally agreed that these are not the blundering efforts of the folk at spontaneous dramatic creation, but are the degenerate and confused remnants of the dramatic ritual of an ancient Nature religion that had survived among the folk. We have come to think of the Miracle Plays as standing alone, as virtually the only thing in the nature of drama in the Middle Ages (apart from the Morality Plays which the ecclesiastical authorities tried to offer as a substitute in the fifteenth century and which by the early sixteenth century had begun to be secularized). But that is because we too easily assume that only what has been recorded existed. There was, on the contrary, a great deal in the nature of dramatic ritual outside the Church with which the new Christian drama could become at least partially associated; and what we do in fact find in the Mystery Cycle itself is a profound union of the new and the old – such as the priestly class could not by itself have accomplished, even supposing it had wanted to do so.

The classical Greek drama was developed, we know, out of earlier dramatic rituals. The evolution of the English drama – the drama, above all, of Shakespeare – is perhaps more complex. It is necessary in its case to take account of the influence of Classical models at the Renaissance. Nevertheless, the only truly national or English drama before the Shakespearean is the Mystery Cycle – and that is certainly already the outcome of a union, a unique combination, of the dramatic rituals of the old religion and the new. Thus the Herod and the Pilate of the Mystery Cycle bear an unmistakable resemblance to the Turkish Knight of the Mummers' Play. But do we not also see them again on the Elizabethan stage itself as the prototypes of some of the villains and of the clowns (or at least farcical characters)? The Elizabethan dramatists did not need to borrow the stage type of the ranter or the boaster from Latin comedy or the Senecan tragedy – though the more scholarly were quick to find a classical sanction for their own creations. These types were vividly there already in the English dramatic tradition itself as Herod and Pilate, and generally as the antagonists in the flyting matches that so frequently enliven the Mystery Cycle. The association of buffoonery with death, which is another feature of the plays of the Mystery Cycle, has again its counterpart later in the mixture of comedy and tragedy which is so characteristic of Elizabethan drama and which so distressed neo-classic critics. Furthermore, certain of the themes and symbolisms which are to be found in Shakespearean drama – such as some of the symbolical significance of storms and disorders, both social and natural, the themes of winter and spring, of youth and age, of death and birth, of the lost one and the found one, and of disguises and metamorphoses, recognitions and restorations – are already present in the English Mystery Cycle and, more universally, in the dramatic rituals with which the Cycle had undoubtedly become associated and upon which it drew.

The modern reader will wish to know which of the extant plays he is likely to find most interesting to read. These yield their full meaning only when they are recognized as poetic drama rooted in ritual drama. They should be responded to fully as poems. The formula that drama is 'character in action' will only tend to inhibit this complete response, just as it does in regard to Shakespeare. In these plays it is of no use always to be looking for something in one of the characters to account for what happens. The dramatis personae can be vivid persons or presences, created in the poetry of the dialogues and monologues; but what happens can never be explained simply in terms of character or motive. Impersonal forces, forces outside and often greater than personality, have as much or more to do with the shaping of events; and these impersonal elements and conditions are what the poetry makes us apprehend as much, at least, as it makes us apprehend the persons involved.

Many of the best individual small plays are to be found in the Towneley Cycle. The fact that several of these are so similar in texture has produced the hypothesis of a single dramatic poet of genius – the so-called Wakefield Master – as having been their maker. They include the *Noah Plays*, the two *Shepherds' Plays*,* and the dialogues between devils (or demons) which form the bulk of the *Play of the Last Judgement*. The devils are grimly humorous characters who have every appearance of being descendants of the earth demons or demons of darkness of some earlier mythology. The *Abraham and Isaac Play*, both in the Towneley version and in the versions in the other Cycles, will also be found especially interesting as having the elements, to some extent realized, of a tragic situation, a family tragedy (not unlike some of those to be found in the Sagas), the tragedy of a father under an overriding obligation or doom to slay his son. Nearness of kinship between the slayer and the slain (though in this case, after prolonged suspense, the slaying is prevented just in time) is, as the Greeks knew, peculiarly tragic. In the Crucifixion sequence the slain god of ancient ritual and myth is Christ; but the new Christian significance is developed, in the dramatic presentation of it, largely in terms of the older symbolism. Two of the most impressive of the York plays, in addition to the York *Crucifixion*,† are the *Fall of Lucifer* and the *Harrowing of Hell* (the Towneley *Harrowing of Hell* appears to have been borrowed from the York Play). The *Harrowing* is conceived largely in terms of the triumph of light over darkness, and it seems to bear a relation to the first breaking of light on Easter Morning. It is immediately succeeded in the Mystery Cycle by the *Play of the Resurrection*.

Gower and Manning

After the wide sweep of reading through the poems of the thirteenth

---

* The Towneley *First Shepherds' Play* is included in the anthology in this volume.

† This play is included in the anthology in this volume.

and fourteenth centuries – the alliterative poems, the minstrels' lays or verse romances, the songs, the plays – we shall perhaps be in a better position to see the new, fashionable, more purely 'literary' poetry in true perspective. After Chaucer, the 'literary' poetry – at least the English (as distinct from the Scottish) poetry of the fifteenth century – is very derivative from his work, and from his earlier poems in the French dream-vision mode rather than from the *Canterbury Tales*. But the freshness has quite faded.

The poet who is perhaps nearest to Chaucer – in so far as it is possible to be near to Chaucer without having anything of the Chaucerian genius – is Gower. Gower's verse (he was Chaucer's contemporary and friend) certainly implies the same social and cultural *milieu* as Chaucer's. In Gower's English book, *Confessio Amantis* (1390-3) – it is notable that of the three books he composed, one is in Latin, one in French, one in English – we recognize again the well-bred, easy conversational tone and manner that we are familiar with in Chaucer, and the smooth-flowing – perhaps in Gower's work, too smooth-flowing – verse. Yet *Confessio Amantis*, for all its great length and considerable achievement in workmanship, is a pale shadow compared not only with the *Canterbury Tales* but also with the other poems of Chaucer.

Here, more than 300 years before the eighteenth century, is a kind of poetry which has the prose virtues, which is, in fact, more prosaic than a great deal of prose. What we are given by Gower is seldom more than simply the adequate statement. His modesty or sobriety of style must be allowed its due; his is the middle way of style. But it is hard to be sure whether, in Gower's case, the middle way is not simply the way of mediocrity. Gower's very lack of emphasis, whether studied or not, becomes in time monotonous.

If we compare *Confessio Amantis* with a somewhat earlier collection of plainly told tales in verse, Robert Manning of Brunne's *Handlyng Synne* (early fourteenth century), the comparison is not in every way to the advantage of Gower. The octosyllabic couplets of *Handlyng Synne* may lack Gower's smoothness, but several of the tales, if cruder, are more vigorous and vivid than most of Gower's. *Handlyng Synne* has a plain practical moral intention, though this does not interfere with the traditional tales themselves; and the tales are retold as *exempla*, as it was the custom to introduce tales into sermons as *ex-*

empla. 'The Dancers of Colbek'* is an interesting case of such a rehandling of a traditional tale. As it stands in *Handlyng Synne*, it purports to be a warning to people of what might happen to them if they
dance in church. But it appears to have been originally a tale warning
of the dangers of interfering with sacred or magical dancers. The
Christian priest who curses the dancers gets the worst of it in the end;
he and his daughter both die. The dancers who cannot stop dancing
appear, on the other hand, in an ecstasy or trance, to be dancing in
paradise or fairyland, because at one point it is said of them that they
feel neither snow nor hail.

In *Confessio Amantis* – otherwise a typical medieval collection of
tales within a framework – Gower is less single-minded than Manning
and manages, indeed, to combine the roles of a courtly-love poet and
a Christian moralist; the courtly lover must learn to be a good and
virtuous man. Following Gower – in the dream-vision of the fifteenth century – moralizing heavily invades the poetry of courtly
love; whereas in the literature preceding Gower, the allegory of
courtly love and moral allegory – the allegory of the Seven Deadly
Sins – had been fairly distinct, though the Sins do appear marginally
even in Guillaume's part of *Le Roman de la Rose*. The tales in each
book of *Confessio Amantis* purport to exemplify one of the Seven Sins.

But the principal interest of *Confessio Amantis* is as a collection of
tales. Many of them appear to have come originally from Ovid, and
all appear to be among the innumerable tales which were in circulation in this great age of tale-telling and had become part of medieval
tradition, both oral and written. A few are found also in Chaucer, in
the *Legend of Good Women* and in the *Canterbury Tales*; the tale of
Constance is rendered both by Gower and by Chaucer (the *Man of
Lawes Tale*), and Gower's tale of the Knight Florent is Chaucer's *Wyf
of Bathes Tale*. Even the tales from Ovid have been modified by their
association in medieval tradition with those numerous other tales that
had been made into romances. Among the best of the renderings in
Confessio Amantis is that of the tale of Ceix and Alceone from the
Metamorphoses. The impression of the distraught Alceone rushing into the waves to take her drowned husband in her arms has, indeed,
some power and is one of the very few moments in which Gower
merits comparison with Chaucer himself. Another of Gower's best

* This poem is included in the anthology in this volume.

tales is that of Rosiphele, and particularly the passage in which the faery company is seen riding by, as in so many medieval romances. The impression of Medea as a witch (in Gower's tale of Medea*) gathering herbs by moonlight to renew old Aeson, is become characteristically medieval in quality; it is another passage of unusual interest as compared with *Confessio Amantis* as a whole.

The Scots Poets

The most living poetry in the fifteenth century and early sixteenth century until we come to Wyatt was composed in Scotland, for it is unlikely that even the Skelton enthusiasts would claim that he is the equal of the Scots poet, Dunbar.

The poet of *The Kingis Quair* (attributed to James I of Scotland, 1394–1437, though the attribution has been disputed and the poem certainly seems to belong with a group of poems of the *latter* half of the fifteenth century) may properly be called a Chaucerian, though in a very limited sense. The poem purports to be autobiographical, and this may account for its fresher quality as compared with other poems derived from Chaucer. This kind of poetry may also have been still something of a novelty in the North, something fairly recently transplanted; Chaucer's poems were perhaps being read more freshly by Northerners. *The Kingis Quair* is full of Chaucerian echoes and reminiscences – often closely verbal. The poet is evidently thoroughly familiar with the Chaucer of the earlier poems and of *The Knightes Tale*, rather than of the *Tales* as a whole.

The poem begins and ends with the medieval conception of human life as within a fixed frame, our fortunes determined by the stars. Throughout the poem there is an interplay on the Boethian themes of necessity and free will, fortune and freedom. The man (unlike the birds whose spontaneous joy he wonders at) has not yet experienced love – whose service is freedom – until he looks down from the tower in which he is imprisoned and sees for the first time his lady in the garden below. This lady is very unlike the flower-like and springlike Emily of *The Knightes Tale*, her prototype, in that she is a heavily ornamented princess dressed rather as if she were going to a fashionable ball, though again it is a May morning. Suddenly the lady is no longer there; her departure is felt as a desolating loss, and the prisoner's

* This tale is included in the anthology in this volume.

day is turned to night. He lays his head on a stone and has a vision. He ascends to the palace of Venus, who refers him to Minerva for good advice. Minerva, indeed, fills the poem with too much 'sentence'. But the poetry recovers freshness when the poet finds himself in a meadow by a river – surely not only the garden of *Le Roman de la Rose* but the meadow of numerous medieval romances. When the dreamer awakes, a turtle-dove comes to his prison window (like the dove to Noah's Ark), bearing a message of hope from his lady, a bunch of flowers.

The most stimulating transition from Chaucer to the great Scots poets would be by a reading of the *Testament of Cresseid* by Henryson (before 1450–before 1508). We at once draw breath in a harsher air. *The Testament of Cresseid* is a Lent poem, a poem for the season of repentance, a wintry season in the North; it is a winter night's tale. The poem opens with a huge impression of a cold wintry night and the ageing clerk among his books in a very human domestic scene. Himself past love, the book he takes to shorten the night is Chaucer's *Troilus and Criseyde*. He wonders what could have happened to Cresseid in the end, and the *Testament* describes what he imagines to have been her end. He sees her as the cast-off mistress of a great lord, Diomede. There is little of the 'courtesye' of Chaucer here; the *Testament* is altogether grimmer, though this poet, too, has 'pitie' for Cresseid. She returns to her old father, who takes her back compassionately. Praying in the temple of Venus, Cresseid bitterly accuses Cupid and Venus for her unhappy fate. She is rebellious, not yet recognizing her fault in deserting Troilus. Then a tremendous event seems to happen (in a dream-vision). As if the universe is moved, the divinities of the Seven Planets descend to judge Cresseid for her rebellion against the nature of things.

As Cresseid awakes, there comes the moment of recognition when she looks in a glass and sees her face disfigured with leprosy. There is no such grim moment in Chaucer. Though the primitive notion of pollution seems to have something to do with it, the leprosy seems, partly at least, to represent (in a grim form) the transformation or metamorphosis from youth to age, the withering of the flesh; it is the work of the moon and of Saturn, who is Elde and Winter. The suddenness comes partly from the recognition that this subtle, silent, gradual change has, in her own case, occurred. It is the common fate of humankind, man or woman, sinful or innocent. The leprosy – in the Middle Ages an ever-present threat to the reader himself – enormously intensifies the horror.

Cresseid can never again belong to the human community, the normal social round, represented by the boy who comes in cheerfully to call her to supper. Her aged father delivers her in at the 'spital-house' at the town's end, and we pity both father and daughter. From melancholy recollection of her vanished youth, gay and beautiful, she is recalled by a leper woman to the actuality of her present condition, recalled to the bleak, dreary round, the mechanical monotony of a leper's begging existence – 'Go leir to clap thy clapper to and fro'.

One of the great moments in literature – once read, unforgettable – is towards the end of the poem when Troilus himself rides past the group of lepers, among whom is Cresseid. The episode recalls to the reader of Chaucer the other and so different occasion when Troilus rode in triumph down the street past Criseyde's house. Though neither knows the other, there is a half-conscious recognition on Troilus's part; it seems to him that he has seen that face somewhere before and he flings to Cresseid his purse. When she learns who it was who has passed by, then at last she recognizes and acknowledges her fault. She dies, and a leper man takes from her dead finger the ring that Troilus had once given her. The poem ends with an epitaph which sums up her life and death in brief contrasts.

Henryson is no moralist, in the narrower sense of the word. His background is not simply the Abbey School of Dunfermline (where he is reputed to have been a schoolmaster), but the surrounding Scottish countryside and community to which he belonged. His wisdom – and his poems are very wise about life – evidently came from his having lived long and profoundly as a member of that whole Scottish community. We may come into direct touch with this wisdom by reading his *Fables*, where it is dramatically and humorously presented through the talk and adventures of his beasts and birds. They are essentially Scottish peasant folk talking and acting, the country folk Henryson knows and whose shrewd and humorous knowledge of life, particularly of human weaknesses, he shares. The wisdom of each tale is not in the added *moralitas*, but is conveyed concretely and dramatically in the tale itself. Several of the best are tales of the fox; others are of mice, diminutive creatures whose troubles and perplexities are sympathetically imagined. The fable of the Swallow and the Other Birds is one of the wisest. The poet's interest and pleasure in the work going on in the fields as he takes his walks in spring, and at a later stage in summer, can be felt in the descriptions. Through his intimate connexion with the local life, with the life and labour going on around him and changing with the seasons, the poet seems to establish a sense of the whole life of the earth.

In Henryson's *Orpheus and Eurydice*, particularly Orpheus's journey through Hell in quest of his lost Eurydice, the myth from Ovid has again come to have a perceptible affinity with the medieval traditional tales. The landscape of Hell, through which Orpheus makes his way, is so real because it is Henryson's own. Among Henryson's shorter pieces, *The Garment of Gude Ladies* – a poem with a very taking metrical movement – describes the dress the poet would have his lady wear; she should be dressed in virtues and heavenly graces. A charming portrait of a lady is revealed, and here Henryson is a very tender moralist.

It will not do to describe Dunbar (c. 1460–c. 1515) as a Chaucerian. He certainly inherits the Chaucerian modes and themes, as he inherits others which, though medieval, are not specifically Chaucerian. Thus in several of his poems he seems rather one of the last of the goliards, the *clerici vagantes* of the earlier Middle Ages, in this respect more like his near contemporary Villon. But even when Dunbar borrows from Chaucer, it is always the difference from Chaucer that is most striking. He is, among other things, a 'court man', as Henryson is not, perhaps even something of a 'malcontent'.

Dunbar comes very late, at the culmination of medieval poetic practice. Perhaps because he is more of a fashionable poet than Henryson, this 'lateness' is more apparent in his work. He has at his command – and is well aware that he has – a variety of alternative modes in which he can choose to work. His technical skill and versatility are what may first strike the reader. It may be that Dunbar's poetry appears to be more various than it really is. There is a great variety of modes and forms, but perhaps not a corresponding variety of experience. It may be said, further, that he is technically brilliant without being really very new. He made new formal combinations, but he is not essentially an innovator. He does not invent anything really new as Chaucer, for example, virtually invents the English novel in *Troilus and Criseyde*. By Dunbar's time among the poets there was, it seems, a dying or decaying of the finer inventive spirit of the Middle Ages.

There are several fairly distinct varieties of language in Dunbar. Thus he draws upon the medieval Latin and French vocabularies to aggrandize his Scots in forming the poetic diction – the 'aureate diction' – in which a number of his show-pieces are composed; and he frequently interpolates Latin lines or phrases effectively On the other hand, the largest proportion of his poems is colloquial Scots in character, evidently based on the language that was actually spoken by the people in Dunbar's part of Scotland. Dunbar, then, draws for his different kinds of poems on different vocabularies. His show-pieces and ceremonial poems – corresponding, we may imagine, to the pageants and processions of public or royal occasions – are those in which he uses lavishly the 'aureate diction'. These heavily ornate poems, with their bejewelled and formal landscapes, dazzle one, but except here and there life has largely escaped from them. It seems that poems at a remove from spoken language must necessarily lose touch with life. There is little that is spontaneous about Dunbar's two principal show-pieces, *The Goldyn Targe* and *The Thrissil and the Rose*. *The Thrissil and the Rose* celebrates, with its assembly of heraldic beasts and emblematic flowers, the marriage of James IV of Scotland with Margaret Tudor, daughter of Henry VII. The shorter poem, *To Aberdeen*, also seems to correspond to what it describes, the formal processions, pageants, plays, and dances on the occasion of a royal visit to the Scottish town.

Though, among such a bewildering variety of modes, it may be difficult at first to find the living core of Dunbar's poetry, it is undoubtedly to be found among the poems in colloquial Scots. It is here that the sap flows vigorously. These familiar, realistic poems are mostly comic or satiric, though a number are gloomy or morose; indeed, many of the comic or satiric poems also have something of a sardonic or morose tinge, and even Dunbar's mirth is often of a violent or desperate character. The wealth and vitality of Dunbar's colloquial Scots is indeed remarkable, and his vocabulary of scurrility and abuse is particularly rich; the old flytings renew themselves in many of his poems.

It is once again the differences between Dunbar's alliterative poem,

Tua Mariit Wemen and the Wedo, and Chaucer's *Wyf of Bathes Prologue*, rather than the resemblances, that are most striking. Dunbar's wives are much less complete human beings than the Wife of Bath. In them, human nature is reduced to its animal elements, and they contrast with the profound and rich humanity of Chaucer's Wife. Though outwardly they are noblewomen, splendidly arrayed, gay courtly ladies, they expose themselves in their private gossip as merciless, primitive creatures, at the level of instinct and appetite. They tear at their men 'with murderous paws'. The poem is very strong meat, and presents the brutal obverse side to the poetry of courtly love. The descriptions of the midsummer night, which draw upon the 'aureate diction' and contrast effectively with the colloquial Scots of the monologues, produce an effect of midsummer opulence, rococo June with its festoons of flowers and leaves and its singing birds, and contrast sharply with the horrors exposed.

Another of Dunbar's most striking poems is his *Dance of the Seven Deadly Sins*. It is to be remarked that it is a *dance* of the Sins. The characters of the satanic pageant are imagined as caught up in a dance frenzy, communicated in the rhythm of the poem. (The relation of this episode to the witch cult might be worth investigating. Similarly, the scene in Alloway Kirk in Burns' *Tam o' Shanter* is probably not purely the invention of the poet.) For all their weirdness, Dunbar's Seven Deadly Sins are local characters, rooted in a particular locality. The poem ends with a wild dance of Highlanders whom the Devil smothers – Dunbar being a Lowlander. Indeed, the whole poem seems to go to the pipes or the fiddle.

Among Dunbar's many flyting poems there is one on a considerable scale, *The Flyting of Dunbar and Kennedy*. In this poem the two poets abuse each other like two fish-wives. But, of course, it is a game – a game which (most readers would agree) Dunbar wins. In Dunbar's comic-satiric poem, *To the Merchants of Edinburgh*, the reader gets to know the character of the town, what it was like to live in, its noises and its smells. The impression is of a lively place, the habitat of a boisterous and vigorous community living among high houses which shut out the sun from each other and from the streets.

Two of the most individual of Dunbar's gloomier poems are *Meditatioun in Wynter* and the famous *Lament for the Makars*. In the former, it is not only winter that oppresses his spirits, but his own morbid moods. He turns with anxiety to summer, as he has turned to song, dances, plays, wine, and some 'lady's beautie', turning away from his oppressive fears of old age and death. In the *Lament for the Makars*, the procession of life is dominated by Death. The Latin phrase, *timor mortis conturbat me*, is impressively used, lending a liturgical solemnity to the contrasting familiar Scots, like a funeral bell tolling. But what makes Dunbar's poem speak directly to us is its homely, personal note – the makar's concern about his friends and about himself.

Spiritually as well as technically, Dunbar's poetry is late: it has a disenchanted and distrustful sardonic air. The poet's temperament appears to have been peculiarly sensitive to the gloomy, indeed often morbid, spirit of the end of the Middle Ages. There could be no greater contrast than between this tone of Dunbar's poetry and Chaucer's spring-like gaiety. It is with certain of the Jacobeans – notably Ben Jonson – not with the earlier Elizabethans, that Dunbar may be felt to have some affinities of mood, though his forms and modes are still those of medieval poetry.

Lastly, the reader should not miss Gavin Douglas's (1475?–1522) Scots translation of the *Aeneid*. It is the first version of the complete poem in any branch of English, and in the opinion of some critics, the greatest. Ezra Pound said (I think rightly) that Douglas gets more poetry out of the *Aeneid* than any other translator. But it is a different poetry from that of the *Aeneid*. As a poem in its own right it is the culmination of the medieval Scots poetry and in the succession from Henryson and Dunbar. Its characteristics are those of medieval Scots poetry; the differences between Douglas's Scots *Aeneid* and the original *Aeneid* are the differences between the Scots and Latin sensibilities.

In Douglas's Prologues to different books of his *Aeneid*, his indebtedness to his Scots predecessors is even more evident than in the translation itself. He renders again, but with a new particularity of observation, the seasonal theme of so much medieval poetry. His winter, as might be expected from the nature both of his Scots language and his experience, is the most real of his seasons and may be compared with the winter in *Sir Gawayne and the Grene Knight*.

The Morality Plays

The Morality Plays are a species of allegorical plays or dramatic allegories, presenting a somewhat drastic simplification of life. There is no use assuming that the few specimens we have (from the fifteenth and early sixteenth centuries) are intrinsically very remarkable or interesting. But the *kind* of thing they are may be interesting to us for special reasons. They may be interesting to us not only because Morality art is one of the elements in the more complex Elizabethan dramatic art, but also because they are a species of drama that is different both from the modern naturalistic drama and also, on the whole, from Elizabethan poetic drama.

The kind of allegory which, as a Morality Play, is set upon the stage is *moral* allegory. The germ of it may, perhaps, be traced back to the medieval sermons and to the kind of thing that is found in *Piers Plowman*. Such a play is a theatrical projection of the moral consciousness, the knowledge of good and evil. A man – any or each or every man – is imagined as faced with two alternative sets of choices, sharply distinguished as good and evil, right and wrong. These are visualized as two sets of persons and, indeed (when the moral allegory is made into a Morality Play), impersonated by actors together with Everyman himself. The idea of two sets of alternatives gives rise to the idea of a conflict between them for possession of the soul of each man. Where there is conflict there is certainly the potentiality of drama.

The difficulty is that the moral conflict in general is not – or is not primarily – a conflict between persons. It has its centre in the mind of a man. To attempt to project the moral conflict on to a stage is to attempt to externalize an inner drama. Allegory was the established medieval method of visualizing or imagining the inner workings of the mind; it had been very much developed in the earlier literature of the Middle Ages. The new problem was how to set it upon a stage.

The characters proper to allegory are personifications; they are impulses, moods, attitudes and states of mind, qualities, virtues and vices, physical (and mental) conditions such as old age and youth personified. In a typical Morality Play these personifications, as separate figures impersonated by separate actors, are grouped round a central figure who is a man. This man is not a particular but a representative man. Everyman or *Humanum Genus*. It is for possession of his soul that these personified impulses and forces contend. Though the contention is for a human soul, and is focused in that human soul, the characters in a Morality Play are mostly not themselves human. I say *mostly* because we do have, for instance, Everyman's Friend and his Relations among the *dramatis personae*. But even they are generalized (as Everyman himself is); they are the Friend and any Relations of anybody.

Further, in a typical Morality Play there are, in addition to the straight personifications, other important *dramatis personae* who are not human. They are the metaphysical or supranatural beings or powers of medieval theology or mythology – Angels and Devils. These Good and Bad Angels (or Devils) imply a metaphysical or supranatural universe, Heaven and Hell – what E. M. Forster calls 'the huge scenic background' which in the ages of faith lent dignity and significance to human life. The moral conflict is thus conceived as not merely of concern to the man in whose mind it takes place. Powers from the outside – supranatural powers – meet in his mind and contend for his soul. (Indeed, it is very unlikely that the majority of the audience at a Morality Play, or even the authors of these plays, conceived these supranatural or magical powers as non-material. Certainly, if we take into account the contemporary witch cult, they were popularly believed capable of assuming material shapes and liable to intrude physically upon human life as they were seen to do in the plays. This popular belief would undoubtedly be of assistance to a dramatist.) But the presence of the Angels and the Devils – in so far as they could be freed from popular beliefs or superstition – implies that the moral law is not merely man-made, that the necessity or obligation of moral choices is not merely a human idiosyncrasy, but that it has a universal or absolute validity. Behind the forces of evil, as they concentrate in the mind of a man for possession of his soul, is Hell; behind the forces of good, as they concentrate for his protection, is Heaven.

The conventions of Morality art – the art of dramatic moral allegory – should be of special interest to us who have experienced for so long a narrow and rigid naturalistic drama which seeks to confine the dramatist to the superficies, to what people *say* to each other, whereas what they do *not* say may be much more significant. Here, in the Morality Plays, is almost the opposite extreme from our naturalistic drama, a drastically non-naturalistic mode. Of course, there is a certain amount of realism in the Moralities as there is in *Piers Plowman*, and these realistic passages are often the more lively passages; but the whole conception and framework of a Morality Play is non-naturalistic. There could be no easy confusion between Morality art and everyday life or surface appearances.

We have to admit that this non-naturalistic drama, as represented by the Morality Plays still extant, was on the whole a failure. But it did not, I think, fail because of the nature of the form itself, as has been generally argued. The causes of the failure were, no doubt, sociological rather than purely literary. The conditions of civilization in England in the fifteenth century, when the Morality Play should have developed, appear to have been unfavourable to the development of poetry as a whole. If the 'types' in the Moralities had been as vividly re-created as those in Bunyan's *Pilgrim's Progress* (e.g. Mr Worldly Wiseman), or if the Seven Deadly Sins as they appear in the Moralities had even been as real as they are in *Piers Plowman*, they would have been effective dramatic characters. That they have not this degree of reality is not the fault of the form itself. But there is no Chaucer among the authors of the Morality Plays, no dramatist capable of writing dialogue as dramatic as that of the *Canterbury Tales*.

The earliest extant Morality Play is *The Castell of Perseverance* (c. 1405). One of the latest, and probably the best, is *Everyman*, extant in a printed edition of the beginning of the sixteenth century, a play which is still very moving. The note of unexpected parting – a parting that has the aspect of a desertion – is peculiarly poignant in this play. To the careless Everyman comes a messenger – the moment of recognition that he must die. The world, everything, and everyone, that Everyman has loved forsake him. He is deserted by Fellowship, his Kindred, his Goods, and, at the very end, also by Strength, Beauty, even Knowledge. Only his Good Deed is entirely faithful. Though the play is the play of the Salvation of Everyman, it has the late medieval awareness of mortality; shadowing it, as shadowing the Moralities in general, is the *Danse Macabre*. The play has a simple elegiac style and dignity and is certainly impressive in its grave ecclesiastical way.

Among the more interesting of the Early Tudor or early sixteenth-century Moralities are Skelton's *Magnificence* and Sir David Lindsay's *Satyre of the Three Estaitis*. Whether these are, strictly speaking,

Morality Plays, might, however, be disputed. They are more concerned perhaps with social and political satire than with the salvation of the soul. They are, however, in themselves none the less interesting; they may even be found more interesting. The later Moralities in general have lost the wholeness or single-mindedness of the medieval Catholic moral vision; they attempt less to deal with the human moral situation as a whole. They are more fragmentary in that sense, but they contain a farcical element which becomes interesting for its own sake. Indeed, we find in the Tudor Moralities the morality and the farce falling apart. Several of the best survivors of the Early Tudor dramatic pieces appear to be the work of members of Sir Thomas More's household, and of these the farcical Interludes attributed to the John Heywood who married More's niece are still entertaining reading. These are essentially farces and, as such, should be dissociated in one's mind from the Morality proper. They are not just broken-down Moralities, but a distinct *genre*. They go to a jigging, dancing movement, and their themes are similar to those of the old *fabliaux*. The Interlude has sometimes been explained as an entertainment devised to fill a gap in an evening, but it may be that the word carries the idea of a play (*ludus*) performed by or between (*inter*) two or more players to entertain the company after dinner in the hall. There is a fragment of an English Interlude preserved from as early as the thirteenth century, *The Clerk and the Maiden*. There may have been many such, having nothing to do with the Morality Plays.

From Medieval to Elizabethan

One of the benefits the reader may expect to obtain from an acquaintance with medieval English literature is a sharpened appreciation both of the ways in which Elizabethan literature still has deep-rooted affinities with that earlier literature out of which it has grown, and also of the ways in which it is different and new and sometimes more complex. The resemblances are implicit in the fact that the Elizabethans are using the same English language at a not so very much later stage of development, and often in much the same ways as their not so distant predecessors. The age of Shakespeare is much closer, not only in time but in other respects, to the age both of Chaucer and of the minstrels than it is to ours. The traditional order which Elizabethan and Jacobean England inherited from the Middle Ages appears, throughout the country as a whole, not to have been radically changed from what it had been. As ever, the Court circle appears to have been the most susceptible to the new fashions from the Continent – now principally the new fashions from Renaissance Italy. But if the court of Elizabeth was, at least to some extent, a Renaissance court, England as a whole appears to have been still to a great extent medieval.

This survey cannot attempt to retrace the history of the emergence of the 'new' drama in the sixteenth century in relation to the 'old'. The traditional art which shows itself at intervals throughout the Miracle Plays has had, perhaps, less acknowledgement as an element in the Elizabethan drama than has (at any rate recently) Morality art. Yet, when taken together with the dramatic games, ceremonies, and dances widespread among the people, it may be even more deep-rooted, subtler in its shaping influence, and certainly not less important. The Morality element is now beginning to be recognized as at least as important as the more famous Senecan or Classical influence, important though the latter was stylistically and in other ways. Together with the traditional morality itself, the Elizabethans did not fail to inherit and make use of some of the forms in which it had been expressed.

Broadly speaking, Shakespeare and his fellow dramatic poets may be regarded as the Elizabethan successors of the minstrels of the former age. The plays performed in the London theatres by companies of actors have taken the place of the near-dramatic recitals by single minstrels in the great halls. The audience in the great hall must have been comparable in its diversity to the audience in an Elizabethan theatre: all ranks and stations from the nobles downward were assembled in the former, and from the courtly and scholarly folk downward in the latter. Thus in both places one finds the conditions for an intimate relationship and critical collaboration between entertainer and audience. What must have altered unfavourably the conditions of minstrel art – apart from the increase in the habit of private reading, resulting from the accumulation of MSS. and, later, printed books – was the withdrawal of lord and lady to private apartments in the manor-houses in and about the fifteenth century. Though in Tudor times Interludes appear to have been performed in great households for (and by) the assembled family, these performances had become something in the nature of private family entertainments. But the Elizabethan drama was a truly national drama. As has been well said, the Elizabethan theatre held a cross-section of the English nation. Consequently the Elizabethan drama appealed at various levels, and is both popular and sophisticated art. It grew out of the traditional civilization of England as a whole and was at the same time in touch with the new Renaissance culture of the scholarly and courtly poets, sensitive to Classical and Italian influences and models, but not subservient to them.

The advantages which the dramatic poets enjoyed are apparent if we compare them with Spenser (1552–99), the greatest genius among the non-dramatic poets before Donne – and Donne is peculiarly close to the dramatic poets.[d] The comparative rootlessness of Spenser is implied in his curiously rootless language, so far removed from the current speech of his own or any time. Spenser became, of course, an exile from the Court and from the courtly and scholarly circle with whom he felt he belonged and to whom he aspired to return. But his exile from the courtly circle did not plant him any more deeply in the English people. It merely removed him still farther away from them (into Ireland). The *Faerie Queene* (c. 1590), brilliant as it is with a remote moon-like brilliance, is indeed a poem of exile. The landscapes of the poem through which the knights wander are wildernesses which surely bear some relation to the wild country of Ireland, inhabited by 'savages', as Spenser must have viewed it from his castle window. The *Faerie Queene* is the work of a poet of genius who has the grave disadvantage of really belonging to no particular country. Medieval romance and allegory float in the poem together with elements of Renaissance Italy and Classical mythology, mingle vaguely as in a dream-pageant, and this they can do because, despite the glowing colours and the music, all are insubstantial and remote. Spenser is, of course, as different as can possibly be from Chaucer, though he drew upon some of the decorative aspects of Chaucer's poetry and also upon Chaucer's vocabulary for some of his archaisms: but they were not archaisms in Chaucer. Spenser is also essentially different from his own contemporary Elizabethan dramatic poets (though Marlowe learned what Mr Eliot has called 'melody' from him). The dramatic poets are rooted in a past traditional England that was still immediately present around them, and yet they are at the same time alive and alert to all that was new.

Of all the English – as distinct from Scottish – poets of the fifteenth and sixteenth centuries, the one who occupies a central and connecting position between Chaucer and the Elizabethans is Sir Thomas Wyatt (1503–42). His verse (composed in the reign of Henry VIII) both relates back to medieval English verse, including the alliterative verse, and points forward to Elizabethan and Jacobean verse. He is as much a precursor of Donne in some of his poems as, in others, of the Elizabethan lyric poets; for while certain of his smoother musician's poems (under the influence of Italian and French models) come somewhere between the medieval lyrics and the conventional Elizabethan songs and lyrics, others, notably the Satires, because of their more dramatic, colloquial, or introspective character, point forward to Donne as well as backward to Chaucer.[e]

NOTES

a. See particularly R. S. Loomis, *Celtic Myth and Arthurian Romance*, and J. L. Weston, *From Ritual to Romance*. But see also C. B. Lewis, *Classical Mythology and Arthurian Romance*.

b. On the other hand, C. B. Lewis in his *Classical Mythology and Arthurian Romance* argues with considerable weight of reason and evidence that the Arthurian romances are only superficially Celtic and that the tales out of which they were made were a residue of Classical myths and accounts of ritual performances circulating as tales, oral and written, throughout the West in the early Middle Ages. May we not perhaps conclude, very tentatively, that in this age of tale-telling there was a great flowing-together of tales from many and diverse sources, combining and coalescing, to form the rich repertory of the medieval *conteurs*?

c. The ballad-romance of *Thomas of Ercildoune and the Quene of Elf-Land* (fifteenth-century MSS.) is one of the finest of the medieval romances and deserves to be at least as well known as its folk-ballad successor, *Thomas the Rhymer*.

d. The best essay on Spenser's poetry is Yeat's essay 'The Cutting of an Agate'. See Yeats's collected *Essays*.

e. See H. A. Mason's distinguished book *Humanism and Poetry in the Early Tudor Period*.

A SURVEY OF
ENGLISH PROSE IN THE MIDDLE AGES

BY A. I. DOYLE

Keeper of Rare Books, Durham University Library

THE fact that this chapter alone is concerned with prose compositions is due mainly to the inherent limitations of prose during the Middle Ages. Not that the general quantity and interest of surviving Middle English prose are less than those of poetry, but medieval circumstances did not promote many prose works of the same degree of artistic self-sufficiency as those in verse sometimes attained. Since popular poetry, in competition with other entertainments, had to be primarily diverting and yet was deeply valued for its serious content, its lessons and sentiments were best supported by, or presented through, mythical or fictitious stories and in a plainly attractive and persuasive manner. This gave many poems and plays a rudimentary, and some a unique, shape and style, whose exact success can be well elucidated by the critical method of later chapters of this *Guide*: that is, by estimating the significance of the individual piece predominantly in its own terms, as well as in relation to literature and life at large. Prose, on the contrary, being ordinarily the instrument of direct and simple information, instruction, and exhortation for supposedly undistracted audiences, had less excuse for elaboration, and its narrative and rhetorical features tended to be subsidiary and unsustained. It offers, therefore, little scope for the minute interpretation of particular items and its success is less readily appreciable apart from its contemporary context. The most that can be done here is to indicate some of its more distinctive qualities and where they are to be found, within the outlines of the whole production of Middle English prose. In the words of W. P. Ker, 'English literature contains and preserves, in a better and completer form than elsewhere, the common ideas, the intellectual and educational groundwork of the Middle Ages'; and this is especially true of the prose. It can, therefore, afford to the modern reader an explanation and enlargement of the implications of other medieval activities, in many ways better than he can get from secondary descriptions by recent scholars. One may also trace in it characteristics to some extent approaching modern uses of prose for what may be called imaginative effects, and consider how and why they so occur.

It may be useful to start with a summary of the main lines of development of medieval English prose, in order to show the necessity for confining detailed investigation and discussion to a selected range and number of books, and to define their place amidst the general body of work.

Some of the chief written uses of Old English, which persisted for some time after the Conquest, were the maintenance of the Anglo-Saxon annals, the copying of sermon-collections, and the study of glosses on scriptural books, and though they all finally ceased, nevertheless each affected (in conjunction with Latin) later vernacular compositions of the same sort. Didactic lives of the saints were repeatedly rendered from Latin into both Old and Middle English, without any decisive change between the two periods, and were constantly associated with sermons and other homilies containing similar legendary illustration. Popular preaching itself went on continuously and increasingly, formed on native models as well as on learned and foreign sources. With it was naturally connected the growing body of treatises of diverse scope and length, meant for communication to readers just as much as to listeners, and especially for those of enough leisure and education to want more provision of this sort in English.[a] That, true of one class (the religious, notably nuns) throughout the Middle Ages, became almost universal in the last century and a half. With the middle and latter part of the fourteenth century came the great extension of the use of English, particularly for prose writing, and largely by the translation and adaptation of Latin and French originals. The earliest were complete renderings of Biblical texts, with commentaries and exhaustive treatments of vices and virtues, with examples; both allied to previous applications of prose. Then, from the last quarter of the century onwards, followed versions of standard historical and scientific expositions, certain dialogues and allegories containing philosophical and theological argument and speculation, and straightforward religious and political controversy not entirely echoing thought in other languages. Only relatively late in the fifteenth century did prose romances appear in any number; while there was virtually no true invention of anything of importance in this or the other *genres* of English prose just named, before the very end of the period in view. A work by Thomas More (1478–1535) may be judged the first wholly successful specimen of native prose history, biography, and, paradoxically, fiction too: his *History of Richard III*, made about 1513 out of report and imagination. And his other writings are among the best, as well as the last, representatives of medieval ideas in English.

For an adequate knowledge of Middle English prose, one would have to study items from each of the categories mentioned above. But simply to obtain a grasp of the points of most interest to a modern outlook it should be enough to read and to consider here a limited number of the more significant works (not taken equally from every branch of literature), and to examine one kind of composition more closely.

The main continuity of English theological prose from Anglo-Saxon times up to the sixteenth century and later has been discussed by Professor R. W. Chambers,[b] and there would be no advantage in repeating or modifying his observations here. There is also little value in considering externals of alliteration, rhythm, syntax, and so on, divorced from the objects to which they were attached and from which they arise. Instead, we can note some special concerns and virtues of early and later Middle English prose, in a few of the chief works of moral instruction and spiritual counsel for people whose life was devoted to prayer and contemplation, and who therefore needed appropriate reading-matter in the vernacular and could develop an exceptional responsiveness by habituation to those ideas.

The first masterpiece of such religious guidance, unrivalled for almost two centuries afterwards, scarcely ever surpassed, and certainly never displaced, during the Middle Ages, was the anonymous *Ancrene Riwle* (the Anchoresses' Rule; 1175–1200?), which had probably a greater influence on subsequent writing than anything else of English origin.[c] It is not easy to give sufficient samples of the staple of its and its successors' plain style of advice, concerning the right observance of both the 'outer rule' – physical duties and discipline – and the 'inner rule' – devout conduct and conscience – necessary for regular religious life. The authors, men of learning, had to render in common idiom the fundamentals of an ancient tradition of ascetical doctrine and its up-to-date developments, and to apply universal principles of ethics and psychology to the experience and capacities of their known or likely readers and hearers. This they did with such common sense and tact, that to isolate striking instances of their approach is inevitably somewhat misrepresenting, and the persistent quality can only be appreciated properly by consecutive reading of the whole, or the greater portion, of the books themselves. But to show how the authors' broad learning and calm wisdom were admirably combined with nonetheless strong sympathies and shrewd opinions, some short passages may be extracted for inspection and comment, which should also assist the reading of others.

We may take first a piece of methodical distinction and exemplification from the *Riwle*, typical of the medieval manner of persuading and demonstrating by means of parallels drawn from life and literature jointly; as the author says here, 'vor hit is almest Seint Beornardes sentence', yet it is truly his own perception, too:

Threo manere of Godes icorene[1] beoth on eorthe. The one [2]muwe beon iefned to gode pilegrimes; the other to deade; the thridde to ihongede[3], mid hore gode wille[4], o Jesu Cristes rode[5]. [6]The vorme beoth gode; the other betere; the thridde beoth best of alle. To the vorme gredeth[7] Seinte Peter inwardliche[8] and seith 'Obsecro vos tanquam advenas & peregrinos ut abstineatis vos a carnalibus desideriis que militant adversus animam'. [9]'Ich halsie ou', he seith, Seinte Peter, [10]'alse unkuthe & pilegrimes, thet ye withholden ou from vlesliche lustes, thet weorreth ayean the soule'. The gode pilegrim halt[11] ever his rihte wei vorthward; [12]thauh he iseo othere ihere idele gomenes & wundres bi the weie, he ne etstont[13] nout ase foles doth, auh[14] halt forth his rute & hieth toward his giste[15]; ne he ne bereth no garsum[16] bute[17] gnedliche his spense, ne clothes nouther, bute one theo thet he haveth neod to. This beoth holie men, thet [18]thauh heo beon ithe worlde heo beoth

1. chosen (people), 2. 'may be likened', 3. (men) hanged, 4. willingly, 5. cross, 6. 'The former are good', 7. cries, 8. heartily, 9. 'I beseech you', 10. 'like strangers', 11. holds, 12. 'though he see or hear idle games', 13. does not stop, 14. but, 15. lodging, 16. possessions, 17. 'barely his expenses', 18. 'though they be in the world'.

therinne ase pilegrimes, & goth [1]mid gode liflode touward
the riche[2] of heovene, & siggeth[3] mid the apostle, 'Non
habemus hic manentem civitatem, sed futuram inquirimus':
thet is, [4]'Nabbe we none wununge her, auh we secheth other
wununge', and [5]beoth bi the leste that heo ever muwen; ne
heo nabbeth, [6]ne ne holdeth none tale of none worldliche
vroure, thauh heo beon ine worldliche weie, ase ich seide er[7],
of pilegrimes, auh habbeth hore heorte ever touward heovene.
[8]Heo ivindeth, iwis, Sein Julianes in[9], thet weiverende[10] men
yeorne[11] secheth.

1. 'with good lifeleading', 2. realm, 3. sayeth, 4. 'We have not any
dwelling place here', 5. 'make do with the least that they possibly can'(?),
6. 'and do not pay any attention to any worldly pleasure', 7. before,
8. 'They find, indeed', 9. St Julian's inn (the model of hospitality; cf.
Chaucer's Franklin), 10. wayfaring, 11. eagerly.

This amply reveals the intellectual and imaginative powers by
which a whole situation and its emotions can be re-created, and a
categorical assertion and a conventional metaphor both be elaborated
and enlivened. It is basically the same expanded commonplace as in
a passage of Walter Hilton's *Scale of Perfection* (c. 1390–5?), or the
whole of John Bunyan's *Pilgrim's Progress* (1678), to compare only
well-known works, yet hardly inferior to either, for its length.
Another passage of the *Riwle*, likening God and the human soul to a
mother and child, equally sensitive and profound, though no more
original or peculiar to the author, was so closely echoed by writers
of later centuries that it is one of the keys to the influence of the *Riwle*,
historically considered.

A further didactic method, allied, of course, to pulpit practice like
that just specified, is the partial dramatization of vices:

The thridde cumeth efter, & is wurst fikelare[1], ase ich er
seide: vor he preiseth [2]thene uvele & his uvele deden, [3]ase
the the seith to the knihte thet robbeth his poure men, 'A sire!
[4]Hwat tu dest wel! [5]Vor evere me schal thene cheorl pilken
& peolien: vor he is [6]ase the withi thet spruteth ut the betere
[7]thet me hine ofte croppeth.'

1. flatterer, 2. 'the evil (person) and his evil deeds, 3. 'like he that says',
4. 'How well you act', 5. 'One should always pluck and peel (i.e. pillage) the
peasant', 6. 'like the willow', 7. 'when one frequently crops it'.

This gains in force from being topical social satire, employing the very phrase and tone of contemporary speech, hardly exaggerating but simply leaving the over-robust expression to reveal its real nature. The blunt human cost of that glib prudence (note the ambiguity of 'wel') is suddenly felt in 'pilken & peolien', and the final stroke ('croppeth') comes to destroy the treacherous parallelism of the proverb. Fellow-feeling with men reduced to the plight of animal and vegetable stock awakens moral indignation and judgement against the offenders, and deepened distrust of all such professions and motives for the future.

The sympathetic disposition on which the last passage turns was one which may be thought distinctively (though not, of course, solely) medieval, since in the Middle Ages it was inculcated more widely and fruitfully than ever before or since, so far as can be seen from the evidence of art and history. A direct exhortation from the *Riwle*, moving in itself, may serve to represent and explain more clearly this habit of mind, so crucial for both the composition and the comprehension of medieval literature:

> Bi deie summe time other bi nihte, [1]thencheth & gedereth in owere heorte alle sike & alle sorie, thet wo & poverte tholieth[2], the pine thet prisuns tholieth, [3]thet heo liggeth mid iren hevie iveotered; nomeliche[4] of the Cristene thet beoth in hethinesse[5], summe ine prisune, summe ine [6]alse muchele theudome alse oxe is other asse; [7]habbeth reouthe of theo thet beoth ine stronge temptaciuns; [8]alle monne sores setteth in ower thouhte, & siketh[9] to ure Louerd thet he [10]nime yeme & habbe reouthe of ham, & [11]biholde touward ham mid the eie of his ore ...

1. 'consider and imagine', 2. undergo, 3. 'that they lie heavily fettered with irons', 4. especially, 5. heathen regions, 6. 'as much bondage', 7. 'Have pity', 8. 'everyone's sorrows', 9. sigh, 10. 'take care', 11. 'look at them with the eye of his mercy'.

Acute awareness of the physical endurance of all sentient things may be attributed partly to the inescapably primitive sides of medieval life, but this controlled compassion was, besides, an achievement of conscious religious and artistic cultivation. The sufferings and longings of every member of mankind (and animal-kind, too, by a natural 'pathetic fallacy' – the 'overflow of powerful feelings') are concentrated in the sense of one pitying personal omniscience. It would be hard, and mistaken, for anyone accustomed to the Christian gospels and legends to exclude from his mind here suggestions of the inhabitants of the stable of Bethlehem, the incarceration of John the Baptist and Peter the Apostle, perhaps even adding some historical knowledge, the later subjection of the Holy Land itself, other parts of Christendom, and many individual Christians, to loss of freedom, persecution, and martyrdom for their beliefs. More immediately may be discerned a basic allusion to the Beatitudes and their specification of the temporal trials of patience and charity, and the ultimate consolations; and all such recollections are gathered up in the explicit final appeal, in homely, affectionate language, to the supreme participant of the experiences of each of his creatures. Thus, by a deliberate exercise of imaginative meditation, suitable for the simplest or the subtlest mind, may be evoked an appropriate attitude and mood for contemplative prayer, which the *Riwle* and its kind were principally meant to foster.

This habit, incumbent chiefly on the cloistered religious, was besides recognized and adopted commonly by pious people whatever their social rank or condition. In the words of Professor E. F. Jacob (speaking of fifteenth-century foreign piety): 'In such an atmosphere *compunctio cordis*, the most characteristic virtue praised in the *Imitatio*,[d] can be practised. The words imply a mixture of sensitiveness and intelligence. It is this quality that keeps the believer open to good impressions and "ready to take and bear all well that is enjoined upon him".' Formalization and repetition could not deaden this ingrained sensibility, and its benefits may be traced throughout medieval literature and life. Such reflections as those encouraged by the piece last quoted were not only potentially affecting but even practically effective, as is proved by such events as the Crusades or the Franciscan movement (despite the rapid disappointment and degeneration of their ideals). The same emotions are at the core of the mystery plays of Abraham and Isaac, or the Shepherds, the most striking passages of *Sir Gawayne* and *Piers Plowman*, the opening of Chaucer's *Canterbury Tales*, or his Clerk's Tale of Griselda, to mention only obvious places, and there are innumerable examples in medieval painting and sculpture.

The counterpart or obverse of the capacity just discussed is the sharp perception of what is spiritually contemptible or abhorrent, through its external manifestations, real and imaginary: in the latter respect, for instance, the monsters and fiends of saga and legend, the dragon of *S. Marherete* (c. 1175–1200?), the deadly sins in the *Ancrene Riwle* and *Piers Plowman*, the devils of medieval drama, or the tempter of Lady Julian (c. 1373–93) – all seriously (whether solemnly or comically) conceived. Antipathy is rarely called into play alone, and unqualified disgust is uncommon, like undisguised evil itself, even in medieval ideology and imagery. The *Riwle* and its heirs and allies more often engage and excel in exposing the insidious and confusing forms ordinarily assumed by malice and concupiscence. One specimen was given earlier in this chapter; many other degrees of satire appear, going so far as purely humorous (because consciously unfair) caricature of what is to be seen as harmless in itself, yet definitely discouraging from things of greater importance. This may be noticed in certain passages of the *Riwle* relating to the recluses' domestic affairs, and in much of the rhetoric against marriage of the contemporary homily on *Hali Meidenhad*, both written for similar audiences. To quote the latter:

> [1]And hwat yif ich easki yet, thah hit thunche egede, hu that wif stonde, that ihereth, hwen ha cumeth in, hire bearn screamen, seoth the cat at te flicke[2], & te hunde at te huide[3]. Hire cake bearneth o the stan, & hire calf suketh; [4]the croh eorheth i the fur, [5]& te cheorl chideth. Thah hit be egede sah[6], hit ah, maiden, [7]to eggi the swithre therframward, [8]for nawt ne thunche hit hire egede that hit fondeth.

1. 'What if I ask besides, though it may seem absurd, in what circumstances the housewife is placed', 2. the flitch (of bacon, etc.), 3. the hide (of a beast), 4. 'the pot runs over into the fire', 5. 'and the man (servant?) grumbles', 6. tale, 7. 'to egg you on more sharply from it', 8. 'for it does not seem trivial to her who feels it'.

The author of this, like that of the *Riwle*, had a nice appreciation of actual domestic life, and an artist's ability to evoke an amusingly exaggerated scene and apt reactions almost visually. It is a typically medieval parody of an oft-applied story, that of Martha and Mary – one of the chief authorities for the accepted distinction between the active and contemplative manners of life. The humour serves to support, not to subvert, the conviction of the incompatibility and superiority of the one in relation to the other, by proving the point in un-ideal contemporary conditions; yet without slighting seriously, even by implication, anything of value in normal life. The author as good as admits that this is not the whole case or argument – either for the housewife's or the maiden's vocation.

The foregoing quotations are surely as effective and impressive as much of the popular poetry of the Middle Ages, or any comparable writing of a later date. Despite, or perhaps because of, the need to embrace many intervening changes, social and intellectual, the religious treatises of the fourteenth and fifteenth centuries maintained and perhaps improved this quality, certainly above all other species of prose at that time. The enthusiastic piety encouraged, if not introduced, by Richard Rolle (d. 1349) may at first seem to contradict the sober devotion and constant self-scrutiny taught by the *Riwle*. His proficiency in straightforward narrative and emotive prose – for instance, in the autobiographical 'tale that Rycherde hermet made', too long for quotation here – is so great that, though one may see no inferiority and, indeed, a certain kinship in these qualities to parts of the *Riwle*, it is possible to mistrust the implications and results. In their context, however, such maxims as this:

> Better it es to say seven psalmes wyth desyre of Crystes lufe, havand[1] thi hert on thi praying, than seven hundreth thowsand suffrand thi thoght passe in vanitees of bodyli thynges. What gude, hopes thou, may come tharof, if thou lat thi tonge blaber on the boke, and thi hert ren abowte in [2]sere stedes in the worlde? Forthi[3] sett thi thoght in Criste, [4]and he sal rewle it til hym. (*Ego Dormio*)

    1. having, 2. 'many places', 3. therefore, 4. 'and he shall guide it to him'.

or this:

> [1]The thare noght covayte gretely many bokes; halde lufe in hert and in werke and [2]thou hase al that we may say or wryte. For fulness of the law es charite; in that hynges all. (*Form*)

    1. 'You ought not to covet', 2. 'you have (the essentials of) all'.

– such thoughts are elements of balance, Rolle being correspondingly and correctively insistent on 'discrecion', 'mesure'[1] and 'fastness'[2], on

---

    1. measure, modesty, etc. – a fundamental principle of the *Riwle*, and, of course, of Classical-Christian ethics, 2. stability, fixity, permanence, perseverance, etc. – physically and psychologically indispensable to a religious vocation.

the one hand, as he is, on the other, anxious for authentic and abiding inspiration. A further extract from the *Form of Living*, the fullest of his three English epistles to women disciples, may show this real, highly personal, and influential breadth of mind:

> And namely al that lufes contemplatyfe lyf, thai seke rest in body and saule. For a grete doctor[1] says that thai er Goddes trone, that dwelles still in a stede, and [2]er noght abowte rennand, bot in swetnes of Cristes lufe er stabyld[3]. And I have lufed for to sytte, for na penance, [4]ne for na fantasy that I wild men spak of me, [5]ne for na swylk thyng, bot anly for I knew that I loved God mare, and langar lasted within the comforth of lufe, than gangand[6] or standard or kneeland. For sittand am I in maste rest, and my hert maste upwarde. Bot tharfore peraventure es it noght the best til another at sitte, als I did, and wil do [7]til my dede, bot if he war disposed als I was in his sawle.

1. doctor (of the Church, teacher, theologian), 2. 'are not restless', 3. stable, 4. 'nor for any imaginary reputation I wanted', 5. 'nor for any such thing' (in fact), 6. moving, 7. 'till my death'.

Rolle's successors in English literature, Walter Hilton and the anonymous author of the *Cloud of Unknowing* and other pieces, are indebted to him for much of the sanity and wit of their diagnosis of errors which have sometimes been thought to spring from a careless or selective pursuit of his doctrine and example, but in fact are more likely owing to alien influences or spontaneous temptations and excesses of piety. In the relevant parts of the *Cloud* we find a careful differentiation of tone of portrayal and judgement, according to the degree or stage of dangerous self-delusion shown. For example:

> Somme of thees men the devil wil desceyve wonderfuly. For he wil seende a maner of dewe – aungelles foode thei wene[1] it be – as it were comyng oute of the eire, and softely & sweetly fallyng in theire mowthes; and therfore thei[2] have it in costume to sitte gapyng as thei wolde kacche flies. Now trewly alle this is bot disceyte, seme it never so holy; for thei have in this tyme ful emty soules of any trewe devocion. Moche vanitee & falsheed is in theire hertes, causid of theire corious worchyng, in so moche, that ofte-tymes the devil feyneth queinte sounes in theire eres, queynte lightes and schinyng in

1. imagine, 2. 'are accustomed'.

theire iyen, and wonderful smelles in theire nosen; and al is bot falsheed.

With this may be compared and contrasted the depiction of merely pitiful mannerisms:

> For som men aren so [1]kumbred in nice corious contenaunces in bodily beryng, that when thei schal ought here, thei writhen here hedes onside queyntely, and up with the chin; thei gape with theire mouthes as thei schuld here with hem, and not with here eres. Som, when thei [2]schulen speke, poynten with here fyngres, or on theire fyngres, or on theire owne brestes, or on theires that thei speke to. Som kan nouther sit stille, stonde styll, ne ligge stille, bot yif[3] thei be outher waggyng with theire fete, or elles sumwhat doyng with theire handes. Som rowyn with theire armes in tyme of here spekyng, as hem nedid for to swymme over a grete water. Some ben evermore smyling and leighing at iche other worde that thei speke, as thei were [4]gigelotes and nice japyng jogelers lackyng conte-naunce. [5]Semeli cher were with sobre & [6]demure beryng of body and [7]mirthe in maner. I say not that alle thees unsemely contenaunces ben grete synnes in hem-self, ne yit alle thoo that done hem ben grete synners hem-self. Bot I sey if that thees unsemely & unordeinde[8] contenaunces ben governers of that man that doth hem, in so mochel that he may not leve hem whan he wile: than I sey that thei ben tokenes of pride and [9]coriouste of witte, and of unordeinde schweyng and covetise of knowyng. And specyaly thei ben verrei tokenes of unstabelnes of herte & unrestfulnes of mynde, and namely of the lackyng of the werk[10] of this book.

1. 'encumbered with extremely studied manners', 2. 'mean to speak', 3. unless, 4. 'recklessly behaved (people) and foolish jesting buffoons, lacking restraint (in manners)', 5. 'a fitting appearance', 6. 'modest conduct', 7. cheerfulness, 8. uncontrolled, 9. 'intellectual conceit, unnecessary display, and anxiety to be known' (?), 10. business, concern.

Such satirical writing resembles a great deal of the *Ancrene Riwle*, at one extreme of date, and some of William Law's (1686–1761) at another, being in the same tradition and art of vernacular spiritual and moral teaching, not far inferior to the finest contemporaneous poetry (Chaucer's or Pope's, respectively), grounded equally in the standards and ideals of an essentially religious civilization. The power of discerning the depraved depends, indeed, not only on rational discrimination but also on positive affections, of which just as forceful expression may be found in the *Cloud* as in Rolle:

> A man or a womman, affraied with any sodeyn chaunce[1] of fiier, or of mans deeth, or what elles that it be, sodeynly in the height of his speryt he is [2]drevyn upon hast & upon nede for to crie or for to prey after help. Ye, how? Sekirly[3] not in many woordes, ne yit in o woorde of two silables. And whi is that? [4]For hym thinketh to longe tariing, for to declare the nede and the werk of his spirit. And therfore he [5]brestith up hidously with a gret spirit, & cryeth bot a litil worde of o silable, as if this worde FIIR or this worde OUTE[6]. And right as this lityl worde FIIR sterith[7] rather and peerseth more hastely the eeren of the herers, so doth a lityl worde of o sylable, whan it is not only spoken or thought, bot prively ment in the depness of spirit, the whiche is the height (for in goostlyness[8] alle is one, height and depnes, length and brede). And rather it peersith the eres of Almyghty God than doth any [9]longe sauter unmindfully mumlyd in the teeth. And herfore it is wretyn[10] that schort preier peersith heven.

1. happening, 2. 'forced by haste and necessity', 3. surely, 4. 'it seems to him to take too long', 5. 'bursts out violently in the stress of emotion', 6. common Middle English ejaculation of distress, dislike, etc., 7. excites, 8. spiritual terms, 9. 'lengthy recitation of the psalter', 10. i.e. in holy scripture or otherwise in an authority of some sort.

It should be obvious how this is developed from the earlier author, and as complete a composure of fervour and restraint as his, at the best, may be found elsewhere in the *Cloud*: in, for instance, this passage which may be compared not only to the passage just quoted, but also to the one on compassion from the *Riwle*, as well as the last adduced from Rolle:

> And this abilnes[1] is not elles bot a stronge and a deep goostly sorow. But in this sorow nedeth thee to have discrecion[2] on this maner: Thou schalt be ware in the tyme of this sorow that thou neither to rudely streyne thi body ne thi spirit, bot sit ful stylle, as it were in a [3]slepyng sleight, al for-sobbid and for-sonken in sorow. This is trewe sorow; this is parfite[4] sorow; and wel were hym that might wynne to this sorow.

1. capacity, 2. judgement, prudence, 3. 'a somnolent, pondering mood' (?), 4. perfect.

77

These are not common modern attitudes or sentiments; their meaning, however, may be well learned by a modern reader from what is, by virtue of them, the best of medieval prose, and in this regard superior to any later English prose.

The scope and style of the *Cloud* is conspicuously more complex, if not necessarily more mature, than its predecessors. It is at the same time more metaphysical and more metaphorical, while the obsolescence of inflections and vocabulary since the *Riwle* has been amply recompensed by growth in syntax and terminology, which may indeed be due as much to work in this field of literature and thought as to any single other cause, for nowhere else were they so fully utilized. In the exceptionally long and practical activity of English prose of this kind (continuing to excel in later centuries), it seems to have been the natural tension between ardent devotion and sober reflection, along with the necessity for careful expression in popular language of abstruse ideas, which helped to improve the instruments to a pitch of potency and precision beyond anything outside the finer poetry. Other kinds of Middle English prose had the disadvantages of a comparatively late start and a continual inferiority of function, and until More, hardly any first rate mind consistently tried to do its best in the medium, apart from this one domain of spiritual counsel.

Such qualifications as may be made to that generalization only tend to confirm its broad truth. In particular, two remarkable works of peculiar psychological, historical, and literary interest, the *Shewings* of Dame Julian of Norwich (b. c. 1343, d. after 1413) and the *Book* of Margery Kempe of Lynn (b. c. 1373, d. after 1438), ought to be examined specifically in relation to the tradition just treaded[e]. For despite a disparity and difference of qualities, both of them come from devout though unlearned women and are scrupulous reports of the effects of the doctrine and example received by them and their fellows under clerical guidance, and presented in prose which thus shares its virtues, though cast more or less in the form of autobiography.

Ordinary informal English writing had plain strength and occasional subtlety, as is to be found in the *Paston Letters* (1422–1509), a casual collection, though possessing something more than documentary significance, from the same region as the two books just mentioned. Deliberate prose composition, in contrast, whether of sophisticated literature or official correspondence, laboured under its mainly derivative content, and auxiliary purposes. Pedestrian translation, at the best straightforward but often halting, and adaptation admittedly deputizing for superior originals, were most usual; the fewer attempts boldly to imitate or emulate Latin models in the vernacular were almost entirely failures.

Only in prefaces, epilogues, or topical interjections, where the authors felt the need and freedom to present both personal and popular opinions on questions such as that of the legitimacy of prose translation itself, and where they consequently followed current English conversational practice and not ancient or alien literary precedent, did they achieve ease and force simultaneously. Some of their mere rendering had the one quality, and some original controversy the other, but rarely were the two well combined, for the former was directed simply to general utility while the latter was governed by partisan hostility. Conventional sermons and expositions of right and wrong belief and behaviour, no doubt because of the initial abundance and order of their materials (affiliated, as we have seen, to ascetical works, and often incorporated in them), and also because of the publicity and frequency of their performance, maintained a complexity and vivacity surpassing more thoroughly original compositions. Likewise, popular versions and revisions of learned and foreign sources in the tradition and style of contemplative piety were far more successful than literal translations and scholarly commentaries meant for academic study and teaching.

As there is nothing in Middle English prose seriously comparable (in the same *genre*) with the romances of *Sir Gawayne and the Grene Knight* or *Troilus and Criseyde*, so there are nothing but poor specimens of the other great forms of fiction in which the masterpieces of the Middle Ages were made, the story-cycle and the allegorical vision. There are pieces made according to these, or other, or even mixed prescriptions, which may be granted negative merits, but in detail and in sum they are very nearly devoid of new interest. Thomas More's *History of Richard III* (1513?) is all the more noteworthy, considering its brevity, for being not only the first attempt at English biography and history on what may be called philosophical principles, but also the first English prose in which the methods of the modern novel, and, indeed, of poetical drama, appear at large. An appreciation of the antecedents of this and More's other writings, reinforcing our impressions of what was possible and what lacking in Middle English prose generally, would provide an interesting conclusion to a study of medieval literature and a good introduction to what followed.

NOTES

a. See more detailed treatment of this in Part II.

b. See R. W. Chambers, *On the Continuity of English Prose from Alfred to More*.

c. Except perhaps the *Mirror of the Church*, by St Edmund Rich (d. 1240), originally in French and then put into Latin and later English.

d. *The Imitation of Christ*, by Gerhard Groote (d. 1384) or Thomas à Kempis (d. 1471), of which there are very many versions and editions in English (e.g. R. Whitford's, 1530, ed. G. Raynal, 1872, R. Huddleston, Orchard Books, 1929, E. J. Klein, 1941, and L. Shirley-Price, Penguin Classics, 1952).

e. Some suggestions are made in Miss Allen's introduction to the *Book*.

PART
II

THE SOCIAL CONTEXT
OF MEDIEVAL ENGLISH LITERATURE

BY A. I. DOYLE

THE Middle Ages in England are well defined by the Norman Conquest, A.D. 1066–87, and the Reformation of the Church, A.D. 1533–59. For English literature these events were decisive, the first in reducing for some time the importance and the functions of the native language, the second by greatly changing the ideals and customs of the nation, on both of which verbal compositions depend for general and permanent significance.

To realize the context of medieval English literature in the age and society in which it was composed and originally appreciated, it is necessary to understand, firstly, the part of the English language itself in the English people's life at that time, and how different its conditions were from those we assume today; secondly, the predominantly *communal* and *oral* character of literary instruction and entertainment, in contrast with our present mainly *individual* and *visual* habits; and last, but by no means least, the pervasive moral and spiritual concern of all authors, readers, and listeners.

Old English and the Conquest

Before the Conquest, English was used in almost all the ways to which we are accustomed, except that divine worship was largely conducted in Latin, which all educated Europeans spoke, wrote, and read for certain matters of professional business and learning besides; and there was for a while an additional vernacular in that part of the country under Danish domination, though this part was gradually assimilated again to the rest. With the Conquest another language, Norman French, was introduced, and therewith changes in the application of each. In the century after 1066 Latin primarily and French secondarily, in different ways, took the place of Old English in public and private written business. Latin, too, came to be used even more than it had been previously in all religious affairs, and French chiefly for the amusement and edification of the new aristocracy. English became more simply the language of unrecorded common speech, except for some copying and reading of certain theological, scientific, and historical works, which continued in a few places with the requisite libraries and traditions.

The disuse of English in some main realms of employment naturally deprived the language of its adaptability to the expression of those kinds of ideas. The growing incapacity was aggravated by the evolution and innovations that took place in the twelfth and thirteenth centuries in theology, philosophy, psychology, politics, law, and other forms of knowledge and speculation, as well as by the inevitable changes in any spoken tongue: so that it became less and less an all-effective instrument. Before the Conquest and for a time afterwards, Old English had been, like any fully developed language, both idiomatic and elaborate, with the latter (the formal and literary) side acting as a standard and check to the former, and vice versa. New needs, human inventiveness, and internal complication were constantly affecting both aspects of the language; but the advent of the Normans and the cultural revolution drastically restricted such natural processes in the native tongue.

Old and Early Middle English

With the passing of the generations and the predominance of the other languages, the old literary modes (maintained chiefly by monastic preservation and study of Anglo-Saxon compositions) reflected less and less the actual English of the day; especially as, with the loss of inflections on the one hand, and modifications in vocabulary and spelling on the other, it was being substantially transformed during the same period. When, a century or so after the Norman Conquest, authors not trained in the old literary conventions, or at any rate writing for others who were not, composed new works in English, they followed more closely contemporary manners of speech and thought, incorporating the new linguistic, intellectual, and social influences, in so far as they were relevant to their purposes. This is, roughly, the change from residual Old English to what is called early Middle English.

Middle English Prose and Verse

Beyond everyday speech, English had always been used for popular oral instruction and exhortation, until recent times principally religious. In the largely illiterate society of medieval England, addresses from the pulpit and other public places were the commonest employment of the vernacular which can be called artistic, however rarely recorded in proportion to the vast quantity delivered. Preachers must have been influenced directly or indirectly by native as well as foreign models, for they were working in a continuous tradition from Anglo-Saxon days and much of the Old English literature still known after the Conquest was made up of sermons and similar pieces. Preaching itself had throughout the Middle Ages a great influence on other literature of all sorts, and first and foremost on those homilies and treatises which, as an extension of the same pastoral activity, were written down and circulated for subsequent reading, not only in private but also aloud. In this way, at least, was perpetuated the fruitful relationship of the two sides of language mentioned earlier; in prose, for it was naturally nearest both informal speech and intimate thought; and also in Anglo-Saxon alliterative verse which had been relegated from its written status in the metropolis to provincial oral currency after the importation of French verse. It took considerable time to combine successfully the new manner and matter with the older ones, and there was an interruption or transition in the history of English verse, overcome gradually in different parts of the country and for different subjects at varying dates from the middle of the twelfth century to the middle of the fourteenth, until the foreign and native elements were amalgamated. The evolution of religious prose, by contrast, was very much more straightforward.

Anglo-Norman and English

During the twelfth, thirteenth, and first half of the fourteenth century, Anglo-Norman French (not merely imitating or inspired by the Continental variety) played a major part in the occupations of the educated classes, in other ways already united with the rest of the nation. Even in the highest, most cultivated, and cosmopolitan English circles, however, it became less and less a native possession and more and more a special accomplishment, however useful, until about the third quarter of the fourteenth century most Englishmen seem to have ceased to think freely in it, though many continued to read and understand and quite a number to speak and write it, for one reason or another. A parallel change can be traced in regard to Latin, which nevertheless remained much longer indispensable to the clergy, and in any complicated theory and business. About the same time, legal dealings and elementary schooling began to be transacted more frequently in English, though most of the text-books and documents remained in Latin and French long after the close of the Middle Ages, partly because of professional prejudice and inertia, but also because of the real deficiency of adequate vernacular terminology. An alteration came only gradually as men felt they could put and grasp certain sets of notions in English as well as or better than in any other language, and this accompanied the growth of a literate public having a thorough knowledge of English only, found to some extent in every class and circle of society from the end of the fourteenth century onwards.

Literature to be read aloud

The most distinctive feature, however, of the literary scene, both before and after the developments just described and whatever the precise degree of literacy in any group, was the natural predisposition in favour of audible, social reading of literature. There was little which was read merely in solitude, and so normal was recitation in company (silent perusal in such circumstances being an unusual ability, and suitable privacy uncommon) that the word 'read' almost invariably meant and should be taken to mean, in a medieval context, read *aloud*, implying the participation of all other persons present. Not only was written matter in English or French ordinarily communicated in this way to many more than could read it, but there is also evidence that there was a great abundance of stories, plays, songs, and other pieces rarely or never committed to a page, which were commonly known and transmitted by word of mouth by migrant professional entertainers or resident amateurs, such as there have always been in semi-literate and illiterate communities. There is reason for supposing that this now lost oral literature was not very different from much actually written down in the Middle Ages or later (before the traditions had wholly died) and still remaining to us; and it is unlikely that the more extensive and complicated compositions were ever current for long independently of some text, despite the remarkable feats of memorization performed by medieval reciters.

The physical circumstances determined that the form and content of most vernacular literature were popular, that is, potentially intelligible and interesting to members of all classes and capacities (not merely the lower ones, as the word 'popular' tends to mean today). It had to be read and heard in public and so was best when of clear metrical shape, repeatedly punctuated with appeals to the audience and summaries of the narrative and didactic burden. Since distractions must have been common, it is all the more notable that long poems, which can only have been heard interruptedly, seem to have been highly successful. The functions of any literary piece were inevitably broad and the occasions for it various, in the domestic conditions then prevailing; for large and mixed assemblies of people customarily ate and conversed together under one roof and about one hearth, and had very limited possibilities of other kinds of recreation indoors at meal-times, in the evenings, and on the frequent holidays. Within these general circumstances, of course, the scale and character of the entertainment could vary considerably, from bold enunciation or performances by several people attempting to hold the attention of casual assemblies of diverse tastes, to modest readings by individuals to small and sympathetic groups of friends.

All literature of the public type, and especially anything in the rhyming couplet and stanzaic forms, might at that time be called 'romance'. The word referred primarily to the language, French, in which the models of such poems originated; stories of courtly love were only one species, though perhaps the most distinctive and influential, but from this fact the main modern meanings of the term are descended. In the Middle Ages such compositions were usually pious in their sentiments and often religious in their purport, even though the actions and emotions they displayed did not always accord with the orthodox Christian ethical code. In fact, there was frequently no great difference between many medieval romances (in the sense of amorous adventures) and the equally numerous tales of saints or sinners, containing a similar mixture of imaginative history and psychology. Much literature, besides, was plainly instructive and hortatory, interspersed with examples and digressions. The practicality of verse in the presentation and illumination of the contemporary notions of astronomy and geography, as much as of theology and morality, is difficult for us to appreciate, but there is no doubt that for most of the thirteenth and fourteenth centuries, at any rate, it was superior to prose for these purposes, at least in the vernacular.

In either a secular household or a religious community, whatever was read had to attract, excite, and engross the minds of various members and visitors, however coherent the gathering or however general the appeal of the subject. A sharp distinction or opposition between improving and entertaining literature is a relatively modern phenomenon, and almost all medieval literature is overtly or ultimately didactic and yet, if of any competence, nonetheless lively in feeling, expression, and illustration. All actions and emotions represented in literature have to be considered in a context of contemporary convictions and conduct, and any appeal or persuasion exercised by a literary composition must accord or conflict more or less clearly with what the readers and hearers are supposed to believe, feel, and do: thus the more religious the civilization, the more religious, explicitly or implicitly, the literature, even when it depicts irreligion. Since religion itself is always open to some variety of theoretical and practical interpretation, even when as universally and on the whole as unitedly understood as in the Middle Ages, and since occasional scepticism and parody are not incompatible with it but are rather symptoms of its potency, so literature is still of religious significance when it expresses or portrays such reactions. The religious character of medieval literature was not simply due to the fact that most of its authors and interpreters were clerks in holy orders; the ability to read and write has always, until the last century, been restricted to a minority of the total population, but that has not prevented literature being truly representative, as well as formative, of general taste, for it has been written by the individuals who had the best means and reasons for making it so; and the medieval clergy had special obligations (spiritual and secular) to write, read, and preach regularly, not primarily for their own sakes, but for their subordinates, neighbours, and friends of all classes, while the literary work of laymen tended to conform with that of clerks.

The Modes of Publication

The modes of publication were such that authorship itself was in any case a good deal less important than in modern times, for a composition became very rapidly the property of its users and beneficiaries.

An idiosyncratic style was of doubtful advantage, the author's name might not even be transmitted with the work, and before the era of printing he could not hope to derive from it any personal profit, other than reputation and patronage within a limited area and time, once it had passed from his hands. Much of the matter which was communicated solely by word of mouth from region to region and generation to generation was thus not only anonymous but also, being subject to inventive or accidental alteration, virtually impersonal. But the longer and more laboured compositions and many shorter ones were from the first committed to writing, by the authors themselves or by copyists. The author (or translator, as the case might be), with the hope of reward or as a work of duty or charity, then read or gave it to one, or sometimes more than one, patron and audience. If welcomed, the text would then be transcribed for other members of the first audience and their acquaintances, and in due course it might be further gradually multiplied and disseminated, this mainly by means of personal connexions and movements. Apart from what further employment, encouragement, and esteem he might gain from the success of his efforts, the benefit to the readers and hearers and their grateful prayers for him in return were the best things the author could promote by his work and words. To put it extremely, these conditions helped to make the bulk of medieval literature devout and didactic rather than mercenary and meretricious.

In this process of circulation, texts in private ownership were the sole source of knowledge and reproduction of the work. Simultaneous duplication of copies, in anticipation of further sales, was undertaken by stationers only when a book became well-known and frequently wanted. It was not until printing that large-scale speculative book production and marketing became possible, from which arose the system of directly commissioning or accepting works from authors and translators, who are remunerated according to the number of copies sold or likely to be sold, instead of the old method of request, presentation, and reward between amateurs (neither authors nor patrons regarding literature as their main vocation or source of profit).

Since the prosperous community or household was the centre of literary occupations, its permanent members were, in emulation of the clergy and under their instruction, the first to learn and to find opportunity to read for themselves, in seclusion as well as in company. The tendency of the heads of religious community and lay household to withdraw from the common table, hearth, and hall, was one of the complaints of social critics of the fourteenth and fifteenth centuries, emphasizing both what was then taken as normal and at the same time how the balance was moving between communal and individual life. As more and more people learned to read for themselves, and as standards of social and literary refinement came to have a broader influence than hitherto, private reading became a habit with those, especially gentlewomen, who had the requisite literacy, leisure, and solitude, but it could not be predominant before the full results of printing and the decline of communal entertainment, well after the end of the Middle Ages.

Households and Communities

It is now necessary to describe more specifically the kinds of people who made, wrote, read, and heard Middle English literature, and the places where it was appreciated: that is, something of the social history and human geography of England in the medieval centuries. The reasons for the crucial importance of the secular household and religious community, and their effects on the matter and form of literature, have been sketched above. Such households and communities were dispersed widely, though not evenly, throughout the country. The household might be great or small, on a manor or in a town; that of any head of a family maintaining some servants and entertaining occasional guests along with his actual kinsfolk. The king, peers, prelates, knights, and gentry were thus not the only dispensers of hospitality (in the broad medieval and renaissance sense) and their halls not the only centres of amusements that may be called literary. The prosperous smaller owners and cultivators of land, franklins, yeomen, and husbandmen, to use the contemporary terms, had their modest yet, by modern standards, inclusive households, sometimes because of the material restrictions more truly united in character than the larger establishments, where there was more room for private and individual pursuits. The sophistication of the entertainment that was possible in each naturally differed in relation to size, wealth, rank, and education. The greater lord could maintain a number of performers of songs, ballads, romances, mummings, shows, interludes, moralities, and so on, as well as having in his service (for other purposes) persons with some proficiency in these things or simply in reading aloud; also he would attract visitors of the highest eminence, amateur and professional, in poetry, music, and drama, as well as those to whom any such authors or performers would be anxious to display their talents. His taste and that of his immediate family, friends, and followers would tend to conform and compete with that of the chief household of the land, the king's court, in what was thought most modern and refined – however, this hardly impaired, though it did gradually modify, the permanent interests they shared with their less fashionable fellows and inferiors in their neighbourhood and in the nation at large.

The noble and gentle classes and their places of residence were by no means isolated from the rest of the nation. They arose from and depended on the general economic and political structure, the mainly agricultural and feudal form of medieval English life. The manors of England were not only divisions of the land, but also groups of the inhabitants, like parishes and villages, which, having grown to a certain size, density and prosperity, and therewith self-consciousness achieved independence as towns and cities. It was within or near these centres that the households and communities of most literary significance existed.

Town Life

The core of the townsfolk was composed of tradesmen and craftsmen, organized in professional and religious gilds, many of them having some direct personal concern with agriculture apart from its indirect importance to all occupations and livelihoods. In any case, even in London very many of the inhabitants or their parents had come in from the surrounding and distant counties. The more prosperous citizens spent much of the wealth they had established by successful industry and finance, in making themselves and their children gentlefolk, acquiring lands and maintaining houses, with all that properly pertained thereto. Their education and taste were thus inevitably formed like those of their neighbours and connexions in town and country, and supplied similarly by literature. It was in the towns, besides, that most vernacular books were actually made, purchased, and read.

The Mystery Plays

As members of the gilds and associations for professional and pious objects of mutual benefit, and of a municipal corporation regulating the various activities of civic life, one of the townspeople's chief communal responsibilities was the production of a religious drama on an annual holy-day, usually the feast of Corpus Christi in May or June. The form this took was a series of scenes, each performed by the members of one gild (or more in collaboration) on a stage on wheels. The procession of 'pageants' moved round the streets of the town, repeating every episode at a number of places, a couple of dozen or more in all, taking a day or two to do so and involving one way or another the attentions of most of the inhabitants. The subject-matter was the history of mankind from the Creation and Fall, through the principal events and prophecies of the Old Testament, the Incarnation, life, death, and Resurrection of Our Saviour in the New, the foundation of the Church, the coming of Anti-Christ, the end of the world and the Last Judgement. It was fittingly called a mystery cycle, both because it concerned the essential facts or *mysteries* (incomprehensible certainties) of the Christian faith, and also because it was so produced by the gilds or *mysteries* (professional and religious confraternities).

The plays were in rhyming stanzaic verse resembling much contemporary narrative and lyrical poetry on the same themes, and structurally and verbally to a considerable extent developed from Latin semi-liturgical representations of the same events which had been acted in and near churches all over Europe for many centuries. The cycles were probably composed in the first place by clerks of the neighbourhoods where they were to be performed; the surviving texts, of relatively late in the Middle Ages, show specific inter-relationships that must be the result of imitation and borrowing amongst them, while the general likenesses indicate the similarity of the conditions in which they all originated and were carried on. The part and influence of the clergy of the town in the mystery cycles was mainly that of its individual members' contributions to the texts and performances, and occasionally as a body in putting on a particular scene (selected, like the others, to be more or less appropriate in character). The cycles as a whole were not in clerical control; they were truly popular institutions and activities, and their pious and sentimental, yet often farcical and even parodistic qualities were more the result of that inclusive proprietorship, than symptoms of their initial inspiration having become adulterated and inverted, as scholars have suggested. They were unquestionably the chief public participation of lay-people in the expression of their religious faith and of all that was related to it.

Each constituent play being the peculiar responsibility of a gild, it became one of its principal privileges and a demonstration of its solidarity and prosperity: and the whole cycle the great annual manifestation of the town. It would be difficult to overestimate the significance of the mystery cycles in the social and imaginative life of medieval townsfolk, and their attachment to them was naturally intimate and intense. The custom once established was keenly maintained, both by the smaller unit (the gild) and the larger (the corporation), with a system of rewards and fines expressing the common acceptance of the broadly distributed responsibility and a competitive confidence in their ability to sustain it. The share of the municipality itself, while the plays flourished, was confined to the supervision of the gilds and the keeping of such essential properties as the complete play-book. It was only the confiscation of this by the agents of the central government under Henry VIII, Edward VI, and Elizabeth that ended the cycles, not any general inanition of the gilds and their members, from whom, on the contrary, came for some time protests and resistance. Though a consequence of the ecclesiastical reformation, destruction was delayed in those towns farthest from the capital, and the subordinate rôle of the clergy in the cycles meant that changes in its allegiance, practices, and personnel did not immediately affect this form of medieval drama. Yet if the mystery was not wholly dependent on the externals of the medieval Church, it was so permeated by medieval beliefs that adaptations could not save it from final abolition, and little survived of its tradition and function after the last quarter of the sixteenth century, apart from some recollections and vain hopes of revival lingering in a few places in the early part of the next century.

The Secular Clergy

The ordinary clergy of town and country was made up mainly of priests serving the lay-people in churches and parishes, within dioceses whose episcopal sees were situated in the principal cities of their respective regions. The cathedrals and some other large churches (chiefly in the centres of the towns) were specially endowed with lands and revenues supporting colleges of priests: of whom some only, including their head, the dean, would at any one time be resident there, salaried deputies being employed to take their part in the regular daily services. The prebendaries or secular canons were usually clerks of good education, holding key positions in the administration of Church and State, which often required their presence elsewhere. The better parochial rectories were treated by their patrons (the king, the bishops, and wealthy laymen) and the beneficiaries in a similar way, so that they were also in fact served by permanent vicars or temporary curates paid a fixed stipend out of the revenues. There were, besides, in the later Middle Ages, in both collegiate and parochial churches, many other priests who were hired by individual lay-people and clerics to celebrate mass and other offices for a time or on a permanent basis. These helped to form large or small resident clerical communities, according to the rank and size of the church. In the cathedrals the vicars-choral and the chantry-chaplains were numerous enough to form their own associations, have their own living-quarters, and obtain recognition of their duties and rights from the authorities, thus becoming virtual colleges in addition to the chapter of canons. There were also clerks in some numbers in the greater laymen's and prelates' households, engaged as private chaplains, tutors, and assistants in both spiritual and temporal duties, as well as those who held the highest posts. When the quantity of parish and collegiate churches, still apparent in some of our older cities, the multiplication of chantries, and the general usefulness of clerks are taken together, it may be appreciated that the size and significance of the clerical segment of the nation was very much greater in England in the later Middle Ages than at any time since; even before taking account of the other half of that segment, the 'regular' as distinguished from the 'secular' clergy, which was wholly removed at the Reformation.

Academic Education

The education of the secular clergy, and of many laymen of the middle classes (from whom it was largely recruited) was obtained first in small local schools and afterwards in urban grammar schools. Since

the teaching was primarily by and for clerks, the principal subject besides the elements of religion, courtesy, calculation, singing, and other
practical necessities, was the reading and writing of Latin, in which,
after the earliest stages, almost all instruction and conversation were
supposed to be carried on. From the grammar schools some went,
with the assistance of private means, friendly gifts, or scholarship
benefactions, to the two English universities of Oxford and Cambridge (and some, usually at the more advanced stages, to foreign
ones). A large number of those who did not take or did not complete
the full arts course, did sufficient to claim and perform subordinate
ecclesiastical and educational functions. Of those who persevered to
take higher degrees after lengthy courses of study, only a few remained as masters and doctors teaching in the universities. The rest
filled the ranks of the higher clergy and civil service (under the spiritual
and temporal peers as well as the king) and were supported and re-
warded from the various benefices, pensions, and other revenues at
the disposal of their employers and friends.

The upbringing and occupations of these university graduates
were predominantly in Latin, and in the later Middle Ages they must
have been the class most at ease with that language. The libraries they
gathered for themselves and for the institutions of which they were
members and benefactors reflected this fact in the low proportion of
vernacular literature they usually contained. But since so much of
these clerics' time was spent in the company of the principal patrons
and audiences of medieval English and French literature, they could
not but be influenced thereby to some extent, and their tastes in these
ways were similar if more severe. As authors and readers in English
or Latin, their books included, besides the theology, philosophy,
science, and poetry of their academic studies, much of the staple of
interest to their fellows who were engaged mainly or solely in pastoral
work – compendia of dogma and ethics, series of model sermons, improving stories, saints' lives, and paraphrases and explanations of the
books of the Bible.

Since the chief concern of any priest, beyond the performance of his
liturgical duties and the administration of the sacraments, was the instruction of the lay-people in his care, for their better understanding and
observance of the religious beliefs and practices and the standards of
conduct they were supposed to hold, those who had, for one reason

or another, deputed most of the labour to others were by no means acquitted of responsibility for ensuring that it was properly done. The compilation of suitable literature was one of the ways in which, with their training and facilities, they could best assist. Since the knowledge of Latin of many of the lower clergy (secular and regular) and of nuns was limited to the essential and frequently repeated formulas, books intended primarily for their aid, as well as ones meant to be communciated to others, were often in English. Many English books were contrived more or less for both manners of use, and the most successful seem to have been on the whole most adaptable.

Laymen's Education

Nobles and gentlemen, brought up more often than not in their fathers' households or those of persons (sometimes ecclesiastics) of equal or higher rank, learned their reading and writing from the domestic clerks and some, subsequently, at the greater grammar schools. Some went to the universities and more to the Inns of Court in London, getting a general as well as a practical education there. Whether they later followed the law as advocates and judges, served as officers of the king or a magnate, or managed their own property, they were in constant association with clerks of the academic class treated above, and were influenced by their intellectual outlook.

Noble and Gentlewomen

The extent and variety of feminine education and vocation were much more restricted. Above the lowest ranks, where they can hardly be said to have had much chance or choice of either, formally, women were instructed in religion, courtesy and letters in secular households or convents of nuns – in the latter case often as boarders as well as prospective members. The educated lay-woman, in consequence, followed the literary and devotional habits of her enclosed relatives and friends as best she could amidst the distractions of the bourgeois or courtly world. There is little doubt that for many the amusements of secular life, especially stories of amorous intrigue (according to the strictest doctrine incompatible with true piety), were equally engrossing. But, as said earlier, few specimens of this literature contraverted, and most maintained conventional medieval morality more or less strongly, the worldly condition of the audience being reflected rather in elaborateness of imagery and sophistication of sentiment. Feminine taste probably more often than not compromised between the inclinations to triviality and to sobriety, a fact on which a masterpiece like *Troilus and Criseyde* could be built.

When, however, the noble or gentle widow happened to survive her husband and children who had died through violence and disease and lived herself to an advanced age, she had exceptional opportunities and motives to pursue a more consistent life of seclusion, reading, reflection, and prayer, approximating to that of a nun or a solitary, sharing their circumstances and even taking their vows. It was for the private and domestic reading of such women, lay and religious, who would know little Latin beyond a few of the church services, that the most impressive works of English prose were translated or composed by their clerical counsellors; and it was by exchange of copies amongst them and their sympathizers and friends that this literature obtained wider circulation and influence.

Monasteries and Nunneries

Monastic houses for men and for women had existed in England from long before the Norman Conquest, but they were greatly increased in the two centuries afterwards, by foundations and endowments from the king, noblemen and women, and ecclesiastics. Many of the members of the richer abbeys and priories were themselves drawn from the wealthier classes – much more so in the nunneries, whereas the convents of men always contained a substantial proportion of humbler origin. The rulers of the important houses maintained something like a noble household, with lay officers, servants, and visitors of their own. Proper hospitality was also an obligation of the community as a whole, performed by special officers and in appointed buildings for the rank and file of guests. In either case the entertainment must have resembled what has already been described, except no doubt for appropriate differences of matter and tone.

The main regular occupations of monks and nuns were common worship and private prayer, diversified by some form of practical labour or business and a certain amount of conversation and exercise, together with study and meditation. In church their task was the singing and saying of the Latin liturgy, chiefly the Psalms (which had a profound effect on medieval literature, since all the clergy and many of the laity were so habituated to them), and hearing some of their number deliver sermons and lessons, for the most part in Latin, as the monastic business meetings in the chapter-house were also supposed to be. At meals, Latin reading of extracts from the rule of the order, Holy Scripture, and the Fathers of the Church was customary. Vernacular writings were, it seems, rarely thus read and then only as a concession to the poorly educated, particularly lay-brethren and servants or nuns. They played, however, a larger part in the private reading of both male and female religious during the periods assigned for the purpose between their other duties. The monastic libraries reflected this situation, for they contained only a small number of English books, though the proportion increased towards the end of the Middle Ages in certain places. But some individual members of communities had, by custom or consent, their own collections of books for their own use (if not for free disposal), and here writings in the native tongue were quite common.

Not all monks, let alone nuns, were deeply educated, and only a minority had a thorough scholastic training, starting in the monastic school and ending at one of the universities; but the majority were literate in at least one language, and acquired some knowledge of the Bible and of standard expositions of the chief scriptural texts, of the lives of the saints, and of traditional teaching concerning Christian belief and conduct; and in particular about the ideals and rules of the kind of formal religious life they were supposed to be leading (of which the intention was to give, through alternating worship, prayer, work, and meditation, as undistracted attention to God as possible). The degree to which these things were realized varied in each house in accordance with its general prosperity, the competence and diligence of its governors, and the severity of the vocation and enclosure enforced. It was in the wealthiest which were also the strictest houses that the pursuit of the contemplative life was most notable and the relevant English literature best cultivated, until the abrogation of both by Henry VIII.

The Mendicant Religious

Besides the monks of various rules and varying zeal, and the regular canons of very similar life, there was another great body of clergy in religious orders, namely the friars, called mendicant because they maintained themselves by begging and gifts, and who (by the principles of their establishment in accordance with the hardest precepts of the Gospel) had no material property or assured revenue beyond the bounds of their actual convents and the essentials of clothing and food. The four principal orders – the Franciscans, Dominicans, Carmelites, and Augustinians – started in the early part and arrived in this country in the middle of the thirteenth century. Their object of spreading the Gospel by word as well as by example, and the encouragement and recruitment they received from eminent secular clerks, led them soon to enter the universities, where they established houses of study and took degrees, especially in theology, in which some of their members became the outstanding scholastic thinkers and popular teachers of the later thirteenth and early fourteenth centuries. Practically, as preachers and confessors, and as compilers of handbooks for these purposes, they greatly stimulated pastoral work, though across the ordinary diocesan and parochial structure; for their practice was periodical migration from convent to convent and 'limitation' or making rounds in the neighbourhood of each; while they were only permitted to perform certain functions not infringing too severely the rights and rewards of the secular clergy. In the later thirteenth and early fourteenth centuries (the period of their academic pre-eminence), the friars seem to have been outstanding as authors and popularizers of devotional lyrics and didactic poems, as well as ordinary sermons, in English; the surviving compositions of these kinds are notable not only for their spiritual fervour but also for their social criticism which caused resentment in those clerks and laymen exposed to it. Accusations were made by the enemies of the friars that they showed no scruples in the means by which they acquired popularity and remuneration, but it would be unwise to accept such charges as objective, and not to appreciate that the mendicants were normally regarded from soon after their arrival as neither a dissident nor a despised sect but as a regular element of Church and nation.

Lollardry and Wycliffitism

By the end of the fourteenth century, however, criticism of the religious orders and ecclesiastical system in general were not uncommon in some circles of the clergy and laity, expressed not merely in the incidental satire of Langland or Chaucer, but also in direct attacks on the principles of their foundation and maintenance, or on their divagations from their original ideals, as by Wyclif and his academic and political predecessors and followers. The opposition of the friars to this movement, which from being merely one of reform rapidly became one for revolution in the Church (and potentially in the State, too), was strong and soon strongly supported by other classes and groups. The Lollard movement at first embraced many ordinary priests and laymen with a simple enthusiasm for the improvement of themselves and their neighbours by the greater use of the English language, and without any intention of subverting orthodox belief and the established Church order, only deploring what were thought to be abuses in them. A few, however, of the most energetic clergy and gentry involved were from an early stage of radically different theological and social views, and their bitterness and intransigence, confronted with the restraints and censures of the ecclesiastical and civil authorities, served to separate them from the body of their fellow Christians and citizens. Many of those who were initially prominent in the movement later disclaimed or retracted whatever was objectionable in their conduct. The basis of Lollardry in its two strongholds, at Oxford and in Parliament, was destroyed in the last decade of the fourteenth and first of the fifteenth century, along with its influence on the secular clergy and the country gentry of the West Midlands, and the clergy and bourgeoisie of London and the Home Counties; thereafter it was confined chiefly to the lower middle classes of the larger towns of Eastern England, where it continued to enlist some support, despite persecution, yet without any apparent force in intellectual or social changes, until the sixteenth-century Protestant reforms fulfilled many of its tenets and prescriptions. The apologetic and polemical writings in English of the Wycliffite clerks (vitiated as literary models by their ill-controlled feeling) continued to be copied and read somewhat and to be rebutted by orthodox authors during the fifteenth century; whilst their scriptural and instructive translations and compilations, of overwhelmingly orthodox content and function, were more freely multiplied.

The types of English prose literature just mentioned were suitable for reading in small circles or in solitude, habits which were growing in popularity in the last century and a half of the Middle Ages in England, not merely among Lollards and the religious. In the course of the period there was a great increase in the quantity of English books of all sorts, and the advent of printing in the last quarter of the fifteenth century not only vastly multiplied the numbers, but also helped to make them cheaper and more readily obtainable. The national commercial system to which we are accustomed was not realized at once; but for this survey the middle of the sixteenth century may be regarded perhaps as an approximate and convenient term, for by that time the old processes of manuscript production were of little effect, there were many printers in the capital and in the provinces bringing out an ample stream of publications, and the book-selling business was being reorganized to suit the new growth and conditions; while the bulk of medieval literature of all kinds, religious and secular, which remained the staple of printing until about 1540, came in the course of the next twenty years (with some intermission in Mary's reign) to be prohibited or despised as erroneous and mis-chievous, being contrary to the reformed belief, ethics, and worship introduced under Henry VIII and Edward VI and established by Elizabeth.

The End of the Middle Ages

It is outside the scope of this chapter to assess at all adequately the methods and effects of the religious and social revolution of the six-teenth century, but it may be useful to add some more reasons why it may be taken as the conclusion of the Middle Ages in England from the point of view of this survey of the context of literature.

The assertion of royal supremacy in matters of faith, morals, organization, and conscience struck at the tradition of the subordina-tion of arbitrary local and temporal power to constant universal and supernatural authority; the objective efficacy of sacramental and sacerdotal functions was denied or slighted in favour of private ex-perience and judgement; and the dissolution of the religious orders uprooted the medieval expression of the value of a dedicated spiritual life. Since dogmatic, moral, and ascetical theology were thus trans-formed, many medieval conventions lost their authentic inspiration and original sanctions, though some received fresh justification, so that preaching and casuistry, on lines differing somewhat but not per-haps as greatly as might be expected from the medieval ones, flour-ished for the rest of the sixteenth and most of the seventeenth century.

The putting of the Scriptures and liturgy into English for general use familiarized the mass of the population with what was before known rather indirectly or incompletely – the restrictive effects of Latin on the use of English during the Middle Ages have been so prominent in this survey that it would require another to appraise the less obvious but equally important advantages English literature derived from the traditions and international currency of the now 'dead' language. It was only in the realm of religion that the Reformation caused its immediate diminution, but since that was the key of its medieval life, what survived of the old applications for more than another century was of altered and declining influence on national civilization.

The destruction of hundreds of communities of clergy, regular and secular, throughout England, and the dissipation of their possessions, premises, and customs, led to the decline of whole towns and villages economically and culturally, removing from the countryside so many centres of hospitality and entertainment, as well as of education and edification: features which were esteemed all the more as they tended to disappear from the national scene during the next century or two. Some of the former ecclesiastical revenues, buildings, and books helped to enlarge lay fortunes, households, and libraries in the provinces, but most of the spoils went in less fruitful royal expenditure in the metropolis and abroad. In certain ways (as the contemporary portraits, music, and poetry indicate) the court of Henry VIII and the families of his peers and gentlemen were as cultivated as any which had preceded them, but for the last fifteen years or so of his reign (1533–49) there is no doubt that they were dominated by a spirit of fear and flattery. The sense of moral expediency in promotion of material comfort, characteristic of most of the nobility and gentry during the next three reigns, was a corollary of this. It was not so much the heirs and survivors of the ancient and illustrious lines (decimated and dispirited by the Wars of the Roses and Tudor attainders) who most energetically encouraged and aided the policies of Henry, Edward, and Elizabeth, but rather members of rising families of middle station, who benefited greatly from their sovereigns' depredations and from the accompanying economic changes. It is doubtful how far these men can be said to have fostered literary composition of more than ephemeral and partisan character. A generation or two elapsed before their heirs seem to have welcomed and sponsored more amiable artistic conditions and creations.

Social developments are always reflected more obviously in architecture and drama than in the other arts. The first of these activities is dealt with in another chapter (pp. 229–251); a few more remarks concerning the second are perhaps in place here. The companies of professional players who had earlier in the sixteenth century been actual servants and entertainers of particular noblemen, performing moralities and interludes in their houses and elsewhere to various assemblies, were but nominally so by the end of the century, when they stationed themselves more or less permanently in the suburbs of London. After the suppression of the mystery cycles the civic authorities became indifferent or hostile to acting of any sort, except occasional topical pageants and processions. The Elizabethan-Jacobean-Caroline drama was a much less truly communal and national thing than either the mysteries to which it owed only a few incidental features, or the morality and interlude from which many of its essentials were derived. Not only was it wholly professional in performance, but it drew its audiences from a relatively small section of the English people. Its matter and manner were frequently exotic and sensational, not mythical and pious like the ancient English (or Greek) drama; and although, at the best, playwrights such as Marlowe, Shakespeare, Jonson, and Tourneur overcame these disadvantages by the discerning incorporation of older materials along with the newly fashionable, at the worst they were incoherent and purposeless, if not demoralized and demoralizing. However mediocre the treatment of a theme of medieval drama or literature in general, the conventions there of belief, morality, and imagery were such as to save it more often than not from mere futility. Where the medieval drama may be seen to be an integral part, the later species may rather be called symptomatic, in relation to its society. Such a conclusion (admittedly relative and questionable) may at least give a measure of the necessity of knowing something of medieval life in the study of English literature.

PART
III

THE *PARDONERES PROLOGUE* AND *TALE*

(from Chaucer's *Canterbury Tales*)

BY JOHN SPEIRS

THE *Phisicien's Tale* and the *Pardoneres Prologue* and *Tale*, wherever they would finally have stood in relation to the other tales, are expressly intended to stand together. The *Pardoneres Prologue* and *Tale* are organically one, a dramatization of the Pardoner, and unmistakably one of Chaucer's maturest achievements.

The Chaucerian dramatic interest is less in the *Phisicien's Tale* itself than in the Host's reaction to it. The good-natured fellow is powerfully affected, his Englishman's sense of justice outraged:

> 'Harrow!' quod he, 'by nayles and by blood!
> This was a fals cherl and a fals justyse! …'

He declares he is in need of a drink to restore his spirits, or else of a merry tale; so he calls upon the Pardoner. At that the 'gentils' are fearful of hearing some 'ribaudye' and insist 'Tel us som moral thing'. The Pardoner has, as he says, to 'thinke up-on som honest thing' while he drinks. The irony is that he does indeed tell a moral tale with a vengeance.

But first, after this interlude, comes the *Pardoneres Prologue* to his *Tale*. This consists, as he drinks, of his 'confession' – a 'confession' of the same order as that of the Wife of Bath. The 'confession' should simply be accepted as a convention like those soliloquies in Elizabethan plays in which the villain comes to the front of the stage and, taking the audience entirely into his confidence, unmasks himself ('I am determined to prove a villain'). The consideration that the rogue is here apparently giving away to his fellow-pilgrims the secrets he lives by will intervene only when we refuse (incapacitated, perhaps, by modern 'naturalistic' conventions) to accept the convention – and that would be just as unreasonable as if we were to refuse to accept the other convention by which he speaks in verse. Even by 'naturalistic' expectations the phenomenon is not outrageously improbable. In an excess of exhibitionism, glorying and confident in his invincible

roguery, his tongue loosened by drink, the Pardoner is conceivable
as sufficiently carried away to boast incautiously as well as impudently.
But such considerations are hardly the relevant ones here. A conven-
tionalized dramatic figure – such as could not be met with off a stage
– is not necessarily less living or less of a reality than one that has not
been treated conventionally. It partly depends on the vitality of the
convention itself, which may concentrate instead of dissipate, elimin-
ate all but essentials, sharply define, focus, and intensify. Within the
frame of the present convention – the 'confession' – a dramatization
of spectacular boldness, remarkable intensity and even subtlety is presented. By its means the Pardoner exhibits himself (like the Wife of
Bath) without reserve.

The themes of the Pardoner's initial characterization in the great
Prologue are developed and illustrated dramatically in both the *Pardoner's Prologue* and his *Tale*, which together may be regarded as all the
Pardoner's monologue. He combines several rôles. His chief rôle, in
which he most prides himself, is that of the fraudulent preacher who
preaches against the sin which he himself typifies – Avarice. The object of his emotional and vivid sermons against Avarice is to loosen
his hearers' heart-strings and purse-strings for his own profit. To this
immoral end he is consciously the declamatory preacher, the spell-
binder, in the guise of holiness. He presents, for admiration, the image
of himself in the pulpit, incidentally revealing his contempt for the
'lewed peple' whom he deceives:

> I stonde lyk a clerk in my pulpet,
> And whan the lewed peple is doun y-set,
> I preche, so as ye han herd bifore,
> And telle an hundred false japes more.
> Than peyne I me to strecche forth the nekke,
> And est and west up-on the peple I bekke,
> As doth a dowve sitting on a berne.
> Myn hondes and my tonge goon so yerne[1],
> That it is joye to see my bisinesse.
> Of avaryce and of swich cursednesse
> Is al my preching, for to make hem free
> To yeve her pens[2], and namely un-to me.
>
> (63–74)

1. briskly. 2. money.

He will do no honest work (such as weave baskets). His other profitable rôles are those of a pedlar of parsons and sham relics, and a
medicine-man selling false remedies and formulas to induce people
to feel and believe what they would like to – against the evidence of
their own senses – and to multiply the crops and cure sick animals:

> For, though a man be falle in jalous rage,
> Let maken with this water his potage,
> And never shal he more his wyf mistriste,
> Though he the sooth of hir defaute wiste;
> Al had she taken preestes two or three.
> Heer is a miteyn eek, that ye may see,
> He that his hond wol putte in this miteyn,
> He shal have multiplying of his greyn. ...
>
> (39–46)

Part of the power he exerts is unmistakably as a survival of the traditional medicine-man. As the eternal charlatan, showman, or quack,
his rôles are still being played not only in market-places and at street
corners.

The *Pardoneres Tale* has the dual character of a popular sermon and
a moral tale. The tale itself is such as might have been grafted on to a
popular sermon on Gluttony and Avarice as an *exemplum*, to show
Death as the wages of sin. It belongs (though in its origins clearly an
old traditional tale) with the Pardoner's own preaching as he has been
describing and enacting it in his *Prologue*. But the order by which the
tale is subsidiary to the sermon is in this case reversed. Instead of the
tale growing out of the sermon, the sermon here grows out of the
tale; instead of incorporating the tale, the sermon is here incorporated
in the tale; and the tale concludes, not only with a final condemnation
of the sins of Gluttony and Avarice, but a confident attempt by the
Pardoner to make the most of its terrifying effect by yet another production of the scandalous bulls and relics. The Pardoner's preaching
and entertaining are entangled, perhaps confused in his own mind,
share an identical lurid life, and are calculated by him to promote his
private business ends.

The lurid opening of the tale startles us sensationally into attention
with its images of ferocious riot, and with the tone of moral indignation which accompanies these images, a moral indignation that on examination turns out (as frequently with moral indignation) not to be

so moral after all, but to be itself an accompanying emotional orgy
on the part of the Pardoner:

> ... yonge folk, that haunteden folye,
> As ryot, hasard, stewes, and tavernes,
> Wher-as, with harpes, lutes, and giternes,
> They daunce and pleye at dees[1] both day and night,
> And ete also and drinken over hir might,
> Thurgh which they doon the devel sacrifyse
> With-in that develes temple, in cursed wyse,
> By superfluitee abhominable;
> Hir othes been so grete and so dampnable,
> That it is grisly for to here hem swere;
> Our blissed lordes body they to-tere;
> Hem thoughte Jewes rente him noght y-nough;
> And ech of hem at otheres sinne lough,
> And right anon than comen tombesteres[2]
> Fetys[3] and smale, and yonge fruytesteres[4],
> Singers with harpes, baudes, wafereres,
> Whiche been the verray develes officeres
> To kindle and blowe the fyr of lecherye,
> That is annexed un-to glotonye;
> The holy writ take I to my witnesse,
> That luxurie is in wyn and dronkenesse.
>
> (136–156)

The images are presented along with a thunderous overcharge of
shocked and outraged half-superstitious, half-religious feeling:

> ... they doon the devel sacrifyse
> With-in that develes temple, in cursed wyse.

Blasphemy is visualized as an act monstrously unnatural and ghastly,
the mutilation of the body of Christ.

Our imagination having been seized by these sensational means, we
find ourselves launched first not into a tale but into a sermon. This
'digression' – a sermon on gluttony and drunkenness, gambling and
swearing – again serves an integrating and dramatic purpose. Not
only are the themes of the sermon themes which the suspended tale
will illustrate, but the sermon is a further exhibition by the Pardoner
of his powers, and also a further exhibition of himself. He consciously

1. dice, 2. female tumblers, dancing-girls, 3. neat, 4. fruit-sellers.

dramatizes certain aspects of himself – he is a play-actor by nature and profitable practice – but equally is unconscious of other aspects. He is half-horrified and half-fascinated by the subject-matter of his sermons. He unconsciously gloats over the sins he zestfully condemns. There is in his sermon (as, according to T. S. Eliot, may lurk even in some of Donne's sermons on corruption) a sly yielding to what for him is the grotesque fascination of the flesh. The dramatization here is more inclusive than the Pardoner's own conscious self-dramatization as a popular preacher, and it completely detaches and objectifies even the sermon as comic dramatic art.

After a succession of popular *ensamples* from the Bible, the Pardoner in his sermon dwells on the original instance of 'glotonye' – the eating of the forbidden fruit by Adam and his wife – and this produces a succession of indignant (or mock-indignant) apostrophes and exclamations – 'O glotonye … O glotonye …':

> Allas! the shorte throte, the tendre mouth,
> Maketh that, Est and West, and North and South,
> In erthe, in eir, in water men to-swinke
> To gete a glotoun deyntee mete and drinke!
>
> (189–192)

The idea corresponds to the Jacobean feeling that the fine clothes on a courtier's or lady's back may have cost an estate – evidence again that the Jacobean social conscience was inherited from the medieval religious attitude. The poetry here depends particularly on the contrasts arising from the conjunction of vigorous popular speech with scholastic phraseology:

> O wombe! O bely! O stinking cod,
> Fulfild of donge and of corrupcioun!
> At either ende of thee foul is the soun.
> How greet labour and cost is thee to finde!
> Thise cokes[1], how they stampe, and streyne, and grinde,
> And turnen substaunce in-to accident,
> To fulfille al thy likerous talent!
> Out of the harde bones knokke they
> The mary[2], for they caste noght a-wey,
> That may go thurgh the golet softe and swote[3].

1. cook, 2. marrow, 3. sweet.

> (206–215)

A fantastic-comic effect is produced by the virtual dissociation of the belly and gullet – as, just before, of the throat and mouth – from the rest of the body, their virtual personification and consequent magnification; and by the impression of the wasted labour and sweat of the cooks in the contrasting metaphysical phrase – 'turnen substaunce into accident'. The vigorous coarseness and the metaphysics come together, momentarily, in the term 'corrupcioun'. How close Chaucer can sometimes come, in some of the elements of his art, to the vernacular sermons and *Piers Plowman*, is once again shown in the Pardoner's farcical impression of Drunkenness:

> O dronke man, disfigured is thy face,
> Sour is thy breeth, foul artow to embrace,
> And thurgh thy dronke nose semeth the soun
> As though thou seydest ay 'Sampsoun, Sampsoun';
> And yet, god wot, Sampsoun drank never no wyn.
> Thou fallest, as it were a stiked swyn. ...
>
> (223–8)

Gluttony has been visualized in the sermon as parts of the body that have taken on a kind of independent life of their own as in the fable of the rebellious members; drunkenness is impersonated realistically as a drunk man.

The tavern scene is before us again – on the resumption of the suspended tale – and has as its sombre and sinister background one of those periodic visitations of the pestilence (the Death) which made such a profound impact on medieval religious feeling as retribution for sin. The 'ryotoures' seated in the tavern are suddenly confronted in the midst of their ferocious lusts by an image of death:

> And as they satte, they herde a belle clinke
> Biforn a cors, was caried to his grave.
>
> (336–7)

Death was a person to the medieval mind, with its deep-rooted personifying impulse, and Death's victim is correspondingly seen as a sharp visual image:

> He was, pardee, an old felawe of youres;
> And sodeynly he was y-slayn to-night,
> For-dronke, as he sat on his bench up-right;
> Ther cam a privee theef, men clepeth Deeth,
> That in this contree al the people sleeth.
>
> (344–8)

In their dunken rage the rioters therefore rush forth to seek and to slay Death:

> And we wol sleen this false traytour Deeth;
> He shal be slayn, which that so many sleeth.
>
> (371–2)

As they are about to cross a stile they do, indeed, meet someone who is equally anxious for death, an old man:

> Right as they wolde han troden over a style,
> An old man and a poure with hem mette.
> This olde man ful mekely hem grette,
> And seyde thus, 'now, lordes, god yow see!'
> The proudest of thise ryotoures three
> Anserde agayn, 'what? carl, with sory grace,
> Why artow al forwrapped save thy face?
> Why livestow so longe in so greet age?'
> This olde man gan loke in his visage,
> And seyde thus, 'for I ne can nat finde
> A man, though that I walked in-to Inde,
> Neither in citee nor in no village,
> That wolde chaunge his youthe for myn age;
> And therefore moot I han myn age stille,
> As longe time as it is goddes wille.
> Ne deeth, allas! ne wol nat han my lyf;
> Thus walke, I lyk a resteless caityf,
> And on the ground, which is my modres gate,
> I knokke with my staf, bothe erly and late,
> And seys, 'leve moder, leet me in!
> Lo, how I vanish, flesh, and blood, and skin!
> Allas! when shul my bones been at reste? ...'
>
> (384–405)

The huge power of the impression of that old man seems to proceed from the sense that he is more – or at least other – than a personal old man; that he possesses a non-human as well as a human force; that he seems, in Yeats' phrase, 'to recede from us into some more powerful life'. Though it is not said who he is, he has the original force of the allegorical Age (Elde). As Age he is connected with Death, comes as a warning of Death, knows about Death, and where he is to be found:

> To finde Deeth, turne up this croked wey,
> For in that grove I lafte him. ...
>
> (433–4)

('Croked wey' belongs to the traditional religious allegorical land-scape.) The old man therefore knows more, is more powerful, for all his apparent meekness and frailty, than the proudest of the rioters who foolishly addresses him as an inferior and who may be supposed to shrink from the suggested exchange of his youth for the old man's age. The bare fact that we are impelled to wonder who or what the old man is – he is 'al forwrapped' – produces the sense that he may be more than what he seems. He has been guessed (too easily) to be Death himself in disguise. Since that idea evidently occurs, it may be ac-cepted as an element of the meaning; but there is no confirmation, though he says that he wants to but cannot die and has business to go about. He has the terrible primitive simplicity – and therefore force – of an old peasant man whose conception of death is elementary and elemental.

> And on the ground, which is my modres gate,
> I knokke with my staf, bothe erly and late,
> And seye, 'leve moder, leet me in! ...'

(401–3)

When the rioters come to the tree to which the old man directs them, they find not Death, a person, but a heap of bright new florins. We are thus brought round again to the theme of Avarice. The florins are the cause of their discord and several mutually inflicted deaths. The heap of florins turns out to have been indeed Death in one of his diverse shapes. The recognition that Death is not after all a person, as we have been led to expect, and as the rioters as medieval folk had imagined, but that Death is more subtle, elusive, and insidious – in this instance, the deadly consequences of Avarice – comes as the last shock in the tale's succession of disturbing surprises.

Presuming his tale to have awakened in the company the full terrors of death and damnation, the Pardoner loses no time in producing his bulls and relics and offering them as a kind of insurance policy against accidents on the journey:

> Peraventure ther may falle oon or two
> Doun of his hors, and breke his nekke atwo.

(607–8)

He has the effrontery to call first upon the Host – 'for he is most en-voluped in sinne' – to kiss, for a small fee, his assoiling relics; but he quite loses his good humour when at last he gets the answer from the Host he has richly deserved:

> Thou woldest make me kisse thyn old breech,
> And swere it were a relik of a seint.
>
> (620–1)

Yet even the Pardoner had deepened to a momentary sincerity (we cannot mistake it) when he said:

> And Jesu Crist, that is our soules leche,
> So graunte yow his pardon to receyve;
> For that is best; I wol yow nat deceyve.
>
> (588–590)

Thus the conclusion provides a final view of the queer teller of the tale and by so doing sets the tale in a completed frame. With much the same skill, the opening description of the peasant widow's poverty frames the tale of the brilliant Chauntecleer and provides a contrast between the widow's life of sensible sobriety and the pretensions that so nearly cause Chauntecleer's downfall.

NOTE

This essay is taken from *Chaucer the Maker*, by John Speirs (Faber & Faber 1951), and is reproduced, slightly revised, by kind permission of the pub lishers

THE NONNE PREESTES TALE

(from Chaucer's *Canterbury Tales*)

BY DAVID HOLBROOK

THE *Nonne Preestes Tale* can be read, with very little explanation of words and phrases, to an audience of people who have never come across Chaucer before, and they will enjoy it immensely. The witty and vivid story of the cock and the fox, and the other subsidiary stories in it of medieval life, make an immediate impact. What need is there, then, to say any more about it? Can the *Tale* not stand for itself? In theory it can: but at a time when one feels that Chaucer's poetry can give us an understanding of civilization so different from our own, most things said about Chaucer today tend to have a limiting effect, getting between us and the full life of the poetry.

The kinds of limiting attitudes to Chaucer I mean are perhaps fairly summarized by saying that he is held either to be 'having his little joke' or, if he is allowed to be serious, to be offering a slight improving moral, after the fashion of an Aesop's *Fable*. So even when we are told that the *Nonne Preestes Tale* is concerned with 'central truths about human nature' and about 'moral disorder'[a], we remain unconvinced, asking, What central truths? What moral disorder? The answer – and this is a significant point – is there in the poetry: the moral concern of the *Tale* cannot be simply summarized. The life of the *Tale* is there in the living language, and it comes to our senses and mind, our feeling and thought, though the poetry: in reading it, we experience the medieval community, its values, and something of the way human life was carried on in it.

The judgements which most limit Chaucer, and which prevent his achievement from being seen as standing behind Shakespeare, spring from a failure to treat his poetry as poetry. There is evidence enough of this in the amount of translation and modernization of Chaucer which appears without any apparent recognition of what is lost in the process. Compare, for instance, the first lines of the *Prologue* of the *Canterbury Tales* with two 'translated' versions[b]:

Whan that Aprille with his shoures sote
The droghte of Marche hath perced to the rote. ...

When the sweet showers of April fall and shoot
Down through the drought of March to pierce the root ...

When April with sweet showers has ended the drought of March. ...

Look at the soft fall of Chaucer's first line – the voice falls assuredly on 'shoures sote' after the light stresses of 'with his', but is softened by the consonance of the long vowels and by the gliding transition from 'sh' to 's'. And then note how this liquidness of sound ('Aprille ... shoures sote') is followed by the arid contrast of 'droghte ... Marche' and by the strong movement and feel of 'perced' – for it is the 'shoures sote', the light fall of rain, that is piercing to the root with such force. What is lost by the 'translations' isn't simply 'rhythm' as part of the 'style', but a rhythm and movement which are an integral part of the very meaning of the poetry itself. The reader feels the spring coming, feels the light fall of water stirring the parched ground: and the better he feels it, the more he is aware of the sense of harmony between man and Nature as the medieval poet experienced it. If one pays the same attention to the first translation, one can only be disturbed by that 'shoot down' – 'shoot', coming on the line-break with such emphasis, brings with it a degree of activity that quite inappropriately suggests storm and pandemonium. In the Chaucer it is the drought which is pierced, not the root, so that all this activity of 'fall', 'shoot', and 'pierced' destroys the image completely, and with it the poetry by which we can respond to the experience offered.

The *Nonne Preestes Tale*, then, needs to be read with a higher degree of seriousness and with greater expectations than the general account of Chaucer would suggest. In fact, the *Tale* could only have been written for a medieval audience which looked at life seriously, and which had a sensitive popular tradition of its own; and written by a mind which could add to that tradition complexities of its own. If we turn to the poetry, we can see that it is of a kind which could only proceed from a fine moral concern. Take, for instance, the masterly opening. On the one hand there is the old widow:

> Thre large sowes hadde she, and namo,
> Thre kyn[1], and eek a sheep that highte[2] Malle

(10–11)

1. cows, 2. was called.

On the other hand there is the cock:

> This gentil cok hadde in his governaunce
> Sevene hennes, for to doon al his pleasaunce,
> Whiche were his sustres and his paramours,
> And wonder lyk to him, as of colours.
> Of whiche the fairest hewed on hir throte
> Was cleped faire damoysele Pertelote.
>
> (45–50)

The difference in rhythm, imagery, and words chosen does not simply show an ability to use English to its full range in order to establish a comic, mock-heroic prince-of-a-cock in a dirty farmyard. The Cock is, of course, inflated as a character in the same way as Dryden's characters in his satire are inflated, and the French words, the long words, and the glorious trappings of Chauntecleer contribute to this effect. But to call it mere 'comic effect' is to limit the poetry, and to miss the way it brings to life for us different ways of living, different attitudes to life, so that we can judge what we see and feel 'in the round', alongside the considerations of good and evil which are raised.

The widow represents, as do the parson and the plowman in the *Canterbury Tales*, a simplicity and a goodness which were a standard in the medieval community:

> Hir bord was served most with whyt and blak,
> Milk and broun breed, in which she fond no lak.
>
> (23–4)

She represents also the plain human life which exists underneath the graces and trappings of cultivated life, and beside which man's theories of life must be set. The physical simplicity of her life is realized in poetry in which the plain rural idiom predominates: the sound and movement here are not elegant:

> A povre widwe, ¹somdel stape in age,
> Was whylom² dwelling in a narwe cotage. ...
>
> (1–2)

Notice the words that Chaucer associates with the widow – 'Stape', 'hogges', 'hyn', 'sowes', 'narwe cotage', 'fully sooty', 'sklendre' –

1. somewhat advanced, 2. once.

those harsh consonants reproduce audibly the rough simplicity of her life, and 'stape' (lit.: 'stepped') and 'narwe' give a sense of movement as of years of tramping in and out of a cramped hovel. She is not free of drudgery or weariness of the flesh: indeed, the contrary is suggested by 'narwe', 'stape', 'by housbondrye, of such as God hir sente, She fond', 'sooty'. The repetition of 'fond' and the negative phrase 'fond no lak' imply a livelihood *won* from life. She is a member of the medieval community, whom the community could recognize as good and who has 'hertes suffisaunce' in the very arduousness of her husbandry.

Chauntecleer and his wives are set in the midst of this, not only by way of visual and comic contrast, but morally, and in such a way as to give the poem more depth than is allowed by saying it has 'a moral'. For all the wit and comedy, the interest in Chauntecleer is serious, and it is of the same kind which later was to produce Shakespeare's consideration of 'man, proud man ... most ignorant of what he's most assured: his glassy essence ...' In the lines quoted above, 'gouvernaunce', 'pleasaunce', 'paramours', 'damoysele' bring forward for examination, against the recognizably real background of the yard, the graces and trimmings of the cultivated life. The 'glassy essence' of Pertclote is this:

> Curteys she was, discreet, and debonaire,
> And compaignable[1], and bar hir self so faire ...
>
> (51-2)

Yet the plain facts are that she is a hen in a hen-run, a wife ('fy on yow, hertelees!'), and her gracious social life, when we see it for what it is, amounts to this: 'He feathered Pertelote twenty tyme, And trad her eke as ofte, er it was pryme'. The 'glassy essence' of Chauntecleer is portrayed, against the widow's 'white and black', in heraldic words and phrases, he is a painted image: 'jet', 'azure', 'lyle flour', 'burned gold'. Against the widow's 'narwe cotage', his comb is 'batailled as it were a castel wal'. Contrasted with her 'hertes suffisaunce', his achievements are of voice, appearance, 'knowledge', and social grace. And just as, in the first page or so, the 'courtesy' of the yard is revealed as a surface deception, so the rest of the story concerns the consequences of Chauntecleer's self-deception, in being 'ravished' with these, his

1. companionable.

own achievements. In those opening lines Chauntecleer is established
as being compounded of 'the lust of the eyes, the lust of the flesh, the
pride of life' – and later we find that it is by a tabulated appeal to these
that the fox has him 'hente by the gargat' [*seized by the throat*].

The *Nonne Preestes Tale* is, in effect, an expansion of an *exemplum*
common in the popular medieval sermon: there were thousands of
such homiletic stories taken from the Classics, the Bible, from local
history and folk-lore, and used by popular preachers to illustrate religious precepts[c]. These stories presented the abstract moral consideration in terms of everyday life: the figure of a broken mirror would
serve to explain the doctrine of Transubstantiation, and the story
would be offered as Chaucer offers his *Tale*:

> But ye that holden this tale a folye,
> As of a fox, or of a cok and hen,
> Taketh the moralitee, goode men.
>
> (617–19)

Yet the strength of this *Tale* lies in Chaucer's individual development
from the tradition: the *exemplum* here takes on a life of its own, and
enacts in complex living terms something far more subtle than the
plain moral. As Chaucer remarks elsewhere in the *Tale*, he is not deal-
ing with the abstract but with a piece of life felt and seen; referring
to a scholastic argument, he says:

> I wol nat han to do of swich mateere;
> My tale is of a cok, as ye may heere.
>
> (430–1)

This sermon-tradition explains how the comic *Tale* can have, at
so many points, most serious religious references. Chauntecleer is
Adam:

> Wommanes conseil broghte us first to wo,
> And made Adam fro paradys to go,
> Ther as he was ful mury, and wel at ese.
>
> (437–9)

> When that the month in which the world began,
> That highte March, whan god first maked man ...
> Bifel that Chauntecleer, in al his pryde ...
>
> (367–71)

and the col-fox, black-tipped, is the Devil – Pertelote speaks of 'black
devels', referring to Chauntecleer's dream, and the fox, ironically

enough, says he 'were worse than a feend' if he should harm Chauntecleer. The farm-yard chase at the end is, in its own way, the moral
confusion following the Fall of Man:

> They yelleden as feendes doon in helle ...
> It seemed as that hevene sholde falle.
>
> (568–80)

As L. A. Cormican has written, in an article on *The Medieval Idiom
in Shakespeare*[d]:

The medieval ethic saw all human actions as replicas either of Adam
sinning or of Christ redeeming ... the principle that 'no man liveth to
himself or dieth to himself' meant not only the practice of brotherly
love towards neighbours; it implied the vast reverberations of actions,
both good and evil ... the medieval doctrine of the power of concupiscence over man (the lust of the eyes, the lust of the flesh, the
pride of life) comes from Adam's rejection of the objective divine
law. ... Lechery was the perverted, frustrated abuse of the body (or
rather the abuse of the free control of the body by the will); pride was
the abuse of the highest power, the intellect.

In a world pervaded by such a religious reality it would be apparent
that Chauntecleer's dream did mean there was something wrong with
him, something which was not simply the 'superfluytee' of his 'rede
colera': it was a supernatural warning of his evil state of soul. Neither
the dream, nor his seeing the fox by daylight, brings him to that conclusion, and much of the poem deals with recognizably human ways
of failing to see what is wrong, with self-deception. When troubled
by the dream, Chauntecleer turns in the end to the lust of the eyes,
the lust of the flesh:

> For when I see the beautee of your face,
> Ye ben so scarlet-reed about your yen,
> It maketh al my drede for tor dyen; ...
> For whan I fele a-night your softe syde,
> Al-be-it that I may nat on you ryde,
> For that our perche is maad so narwe, alas!
> I am so ful of joye and of solas,
> That I defye bothe sweven and dreem!
>
> (340–51)

But he also turns in his pride to 'abuse of the intellect', sheltering behind theories, odd scraps of knowledge, old examples. In the lines missed out above, for instance:

> For also siker as *In principio,*
> [1]*Mulier est hominis confusio*;
> Madame, the sentence of this Latin is –
> Womman is mannes joye and al his blis.

(342–5)

The irony of Chauntecleer's 'recchlessnesse' is pointed to: his self-deceit shelters behind mistranslation, misuse of his knowledge.

Indeed, much of the force of the *Tale* derives from the intention summed up by the two lines at the end of this passage:

> But what that god forwoot mot nedes he,
> After the opinioun of certeyn clerkis.
> Witnesse on him, that any perfit clerk is,
> That in scole is gret altercacioun
> In this matere, and greet disputisoun,
> And hath ben of an hundred thousand men.
> But I ne can not [2]bulte it to the bren,
> As can the holy doctour Augustyn,
> Or Boece, or the Bishop Bradwardyn,
> Whether that goddes worthy forwiting[3]
> Streyneth[4] me nedely for to doon a thing,
> (Nedely clepe I simple necessitee);
> Or elles, if free choys be graunted me
> To do that same thing, or do it noght,
> Though God forwoot it en that it was wroght;
> Or if his witing streyneth nevere a del
> But by necessitee condicionel.
> I wol not han to do of swich matere;
> My tale is of a cok, as ye may here. ...

(414–32)

Presenting a piece of life, Chaucer seems to say, produces a more useful consideration of the philosophical problem than could be dealt with in such terms as these. Chaucer does not treat lightly of scholastic debates, for instance, simply because he was so well grounded in them. It is rather part of his whole intention to set theories, attitudes, and assumptions against experience. The self-assured intellect (ours or

1. 'Woman is man's downfall', 2. 'sift it down to the bran', 3. fore-knowledge, 4. constrains.

Chauntecleer's) can be blind to something which happens in front of it:

> O destinee, that mayst nat be eschewed!
> Allas, that Chauntecleer fleigh fro the bemes!
> Allas, his wyf ne roghte[1] nat of dremes!
>
> (518–20)

– we know that whether Chauntecleer stayed on the beams or not has very little to do with his characteristic vulnerability to temptation: destiny is not something which can excuse his free choice. Again, in the debate between cock and hen on the significance of dreams, both fail, in their retreat into bogus knowledge to recognize the evidence before them. Pertelote, in recommending laxatives, errs on the side of common sense and gives the practical answer to fear of temptation. But her 'lauriol, centaure and fumetere' seem less alien than Chauntecleer's retreat into 'old ensamples' (while in the end refusing the laxatives because he doesn't like them).

That this criticism of misused intellect, allied with pride, is part of the underlying intention of the *Tale* is indicated by the following passage:

> And on a Friday fil al this meschaunce.
> O Venus, that art goddesse of plesaunce,
> Sin that thy servant was this Chauntecleer,
> And in thy service dide al his poweer,
> More for delyt, than world to multiplye,
> Why woldestow suffre him on thy day to dye?
> O Gaufred, dere mayster soverayn,
> That, whan thy worthy king Richard was slayn
> With shot, compleynedest his deth so sore,
> Why ne hadde I now thy sentence and thy lore,
> The Friday for to chyde, as diden ye?
>
> (521–31)

There are references elsewhere in the *Tale* to significant dates ('the month in which the world bigan') and the medieval mind would associate Friday, with the death of Christ. It is appropriate that the poem should draw no parallel between Chauntecleer and Christ (though the fox is the 'newe Scariot'), and appropriate too that Chauntecleer should *not* die on a Friday. But the reference amounts to a damning

---

1. take account.

comment on the invocation to Venus, Chauntecleer's goddess because of his sensuality, and to Gaufred, the author of *Nova Poetria*, whose kind of rhetoric Chaucer parodies in those passages when the world of the hen-run is taken at its face-value: ('O destinee ...' etc.) Venus and Gaufred are invoked because of Chauntecleer's associated 'abuse of body and mind'.

Such references do not come to our minds at first reading as they would have done to the medieval audience. But when explored they reveal the strength of the moral interest that Chaucer could draw on, and they show how, in turning to examine life as it is lived, he could achieve such range in his poetry, a range which gives the *Tale* its satisfying structure. The flexibility of the poetry, its varying notes from satirical inflation to lively dialogue (as in the debate between cock and hen), from 'rhetoric' to speeches 'in character' (often like the speeches of Polonius):

> Macrobeus, that writ th'avisioun
> In Affrike of the worthy Cipioun,
> Affermath dremes and seith that they been
> Warning of things that men after seen ...
> Read eek of Joseph, and there shul ye see
> Wher dremes ben somtyme (I sey nat alle)
> Warning of things that shul after falle.
>
> (301–7)

– this flexibility is controlled by the poetry in which Chaucer establishes his main reference: the medieval community on the ground. The description of the widow, for instance, seems to have a symbolic weight, and in the way it makes use of popular idiom for such a purpose, is in a tradition on which Shakespeare was to draw to explore profounder complexities in his later plays. This symbolic use of language, as in the Liturgy, is there too, in Chaucer's reference to Saint Paul: 'Taketh the fruyt and let the chaf be stille'.

It is in this kind of poetry that the medieval community itself is brought to us in the *Tale*. It is the poetry of the two vivid stories Chauntecleer tells about murder and shipwreck. These are too good to be 'in character' – they are part of the total effect of the dramatic poem: they take us out into the streets and harbours, to the daily life where the moral considerations dealt with in the tale of cock and hen will count. They bring into the *Tale* its only murder, robbery, and

THE NONNE PREESTES TALE

sudden death, without making it anything other than a comedy,
though adding to the serious bearing of it.

The kind of poetry I mean is represented at its best by this:

> 'Ha! Ha! the fox!' and after him they ran,
> And eek with staves many another man;
> Ran Colle our dogge, and Talbot, and Gerland,
> And Malkyn, with a distaf in hir hand;
> Ran cow and calf, and eek the verray hogges
> So were they fered for berking of the dogges
> And shouting of the men and wimmen eke,
> They ronne so hem thoughte hir herte breke,
> They yelleden as feendes doon in helle;
> The dokes cryden as men wolde hem quelle;
> The gees for fere flowen over the trees;
> Out of the hyve cam the swarm of bees;
>
> (561–72)

Some of the most important characteristics of medieval civilization
are evident in this poetry:

In medieval England social organization was marked by three general
characteristics; the close connexion of the whole population with the
soil; the large corporate or co-operative element in the life of the people; and the extent to which the whole structure rested upon custom,
and not upon either established law or written contract, (E. P. Cheyney,
Social Changes in England in the Sixteenth Century.[e]

The first fundamental assumption which is taken over by the sixteenth century from the Middle Ages is that the ultimate standard of
human institutions and activities is religion. (R. H. Tawney, *Religion
and the Rise of Capitalism*.)[e]

Through the excitement of the rhythm, that community reaction
('many another man', 'they ronne so, hem thoughte hir herte breke'),
and those 'hogges', 'bees', 'Malkyn with a distaf in hir hande' give
solidity to the traditions of husbandry and 'God's plenty'. And the
religious reality, as we have seen, is there too.

The range and flexibility of this poetry, and the dramatic qualities
of the *Tale* derive from a moral concern which grew out of the religious, and traditional community, and they represent a great individual achievement at the same time. Both the community and the

achievement are behind Shakespeare and much else in English literature: Chauntecleer is conceived out of the same kind of moral purpose, and performs in some ways a similar function in the poem, as
Shakespeare's Falstaff in the chronicle plays.

NOTES

a. By John Speirs, in his essay on this *Tale* in his book *Chaucer the Maker*, to
which I am indebted both for its positive suggestions and as providing a point
of departure.

b. By Nevill Coghill and by Eleanor Farjeon.

c. See G. R. Owst, *Literature and Pulpit in Medieval England*.

d. In *Scrutiny*, Vol. XVII, iv (1951).

e. Quoted by L. C. Knights, in *Drama and Society in the Age of Jonson*.

LANGLAND'S *PIERS PLOWMAN*

BY DEREK TRAVERSI

The British Council, Madrid

IT is hard to feel, reading the current histories of English literature, that justice has yet been done to the strength and variety of the achievement of the fourteenth century. Chaucer, of course, has had his due, and through him the distinctively cultured attitude to English poetry; but the alliterative tradition which has, in a sense, roots even deeper in the national consciousness, and which produced in the North-west that highly individual development of medieval romance, *Sir Gawayne and the Grene Knight*, and in the Midlands, *Piers Plowman*, has tended to receive the almost exclusive attention of the philologist and the student of social conditions. If this were rectified – and the existence of admitted linguistic obstacles should not be insuperable – we would possess a more balanced picture of what is, beyond doubt, the first great flowering period in English literary history.

Of the author of *Piers Plowman*, a work in its own kind comparable in greatness to the best of Chaucer, almost nothing is known except what the poem itself has to tell us. He seems to have been born, perhaps in 1331, in the region of the Malvern Hills. He was educated, according to his own account, at the Benedictine school at Malvern and probably took minor orders, passing at some fairly early date to London and devoting most of the rest of his life to the writing and expansion, by successive stages, of his poem. We may assume that he died somewhere near the turn of the century. Perhaps the lack of significant biographical information is not altogether a misfortune. *Piers Plowman*, although it bears the mark of an unmistakable and powerful personality, is not, in the same sense as the *Canterbury Tales*, a purely personal creation. It represents the coming together of two firmly established lines of tradition, the popular and the theological, reflected respectively in the supple, direct vigour of the alliterative line and the all-embracing scope of the allegorical design. These two aspects, strictly complementary, are alike in that they cannot be described as mere reflections of one man's experiences or opinions; and the poem that emerges from their union, proceeding though it does from the personal reactions of William Langland, is in the first place, and above all, the reflection of society and a civilization.

The first step in defining the place of *Piers Plowman* in the tradition of English poetry involves, naturally, a study of the distinctive linguistic qualities of the poem. The chief quality of Langland's language, as it appears from even a cursory reading, is the remarkable immediacy of its best passages, the power of conveying a clear picture and of suggesting without adornment the presence of direct personal emotion. In this respect, at least, not even Chaucer, whose expression is more complicated by purely literary considerations, can excel him. This quality, however, is not merely a personal creation of the poet. It is the product of a long and mainly anonymous process, associated in great part with developments particularly evident in the medieval sermon. In this eminently popular form of expression, the preacher's natural tendency to deal with abstract qualities, virtues and vices carefully differentiated by the processes of orthodox theology, was wedded to the popular instinct for realistic description to produce a remarkable development of the possibilities of common speech. The preacher came to the pulpit armed with the Church's abstract survey of human failings, accurately analysed in the shape of the Seven Deadly Sins, but he had still to put them vividly before an audience who were accustomed to translate everything into terms of their own experience. The sermons thus conceived, in fact, were what we might call proverbial, for the proverb is nothing more than the translation of general law into terms of particular knowledge.[a] They are full of such evident proverbial expressions as 'Pore be hanged bi the necke; a rich man bi the purs' or 'Trendle the appel nevere so far, he conyes (*knows*) from what tree he cam'. From these it was only a natural step to bring the well-worn virtues and vices to life, giving each of them an easily recognizable and vivid embodiment. As time passed, these in turn assumed more or less conventional shapes, and were handed from preacher to preacher until they became part of the common stock from which a writer like Langland could easily draw.

That he did draw upon them is clear from the evidence of his poem. I need not quote the famous incident (in Passus vii, C. Text) in which Glutton set out for church and ended in the tavern with 'Thomme the tynker', 'Clement the cobelere', and others; ending in tardy and half-hearted repentance, it has a long and clearly established ancestry in medieval preaching. Here is an anonymous speaker enlarging on the same theme of drunkenness:

> Thow a now se thre candels, ye, thre mones ther a nother man seth but on, yit I seye he is blynd. How truliche a may nat se what is good and what is evel! ... I pray the, is nat this a grete blindnes, thynkis te, whan a man hath sate ate nale hows or ate taverne alday, ye, nat onliche alday, but also muche of the nith therto – and ate laste cumth hom as drunke as a dosil, and chit his wyf, reprevith his children, bet his meyne, ye, unnethe a kan go to bedde but as a his browth therto with his servauntes hondis![b]

Glutton, too, returned home without the use of his faculties and was carried to bed by 'hus wif and hus wenche' with 'al the wo of the worlde'; and such a phrase as 'drunke as a dosil' (if Owst is right in suggesting that this means 'the spigot of a barrel') has about it a vivid unlikeliness that can easily be paralleled in *Piers Plowman*. All the elements of Langland's description are present in the prose passage, used by the preacher to gain a lifelike effect, to evoke states of mind likely to be uncomfortably familiar to the hearers he had particularly in mind, and even to rouse a certain amount of laughter in order to bring his point home.

The poetic qualities which this tradition made possible to Langland are present everywhere in his poem. His picture of Covetyse may be taken as typical:

> Thenne cam Covetyse · ich can nat hym discryve,
> So hongerliche and so holwe · Hervey[1] hym-selfc lokede.
> He was bytelbrowed and babberlupped · with two blery eyen,
> [2]And as a letherene pors · lollid hus chekus,
> Wel sydder then hys chyn · ychriveled for elde:
> As bondemenne bacon · hus berd was yshave,
> [3]With hus hod on his heved · and hus hatte bothe;
> In a toren tabarde · of twelve wynter age.

(C Text, 196–203)

The qualities of this passage are clearly visual qualities, and their ancestry will by now be obvious. They derive from centuries of effort

---

1. Skelton also gives the name Harvey to a covetous man, 2. 'And like a leather purse, lolled his cheeks Much lower than his chin – shrivelled for age', 3. 'With his hood on his head'.

on the part of the preacher to bring home to his audience the true nature of the great and common vices of his time. Even the alliteration, with its long literary ancestry, is as much a device of the speaker as an accepted poetic technique; note how it falls again and again upon the descriptive epithets which are the key to the whole effect. The words chosen, moreover, are precisely those which a preacher could be certain of sharing with his audience, intense, but in no way 'poetic' if by this we mean mere elaborations of feeling or a refined decoration of not too pressing emotions. These merits, once we admit them, are seen to be more than personal, more even than the qualities of Langland's own particular tradition; they are a general characteristic of the best English poetry. They are the product of an extraordinary ability to describe personal experience in terms of a common idiom, founded in this case, as so often, upon the simple but fundamental activities of a society closely connected with the land. It is unnecessary to prove Langland's close contact with rural life, for it is clear on every page of his poem. It opens with the wanderings of a shepherd on the Malvern hills, and never moves far from them in spirit. Piers Plowman, its hero, is merely a universalizing of the English rural way of living, the life which all readers of the poem would understand and in terms of which they could establish a common idiom with its author. To realize how such a symbol could be given a universal significance, we have only to see how Piers appears successively as an ideal type of the English countryman, as the expounder of Charity and the Holy Trinity, as the Good Samaritan, and finally, by a splendid and daring transformation, as Jesus himself.

Langland, in fact, was a great poet, and the quality of his greatness throws some light upon the nature of the English contribution to poetry. The greatest English poets have been those who have followed the genius of the language in resisting false convention. Shakespeare and Donne, in their day, were great poets because they freed English from the bondage of a dead scholarship and restored to it expressiveness and idiomatic strength; and Gerard Hopkins, in his, when he praised Dryden for stressing 'the naked thew and sinew of the English language' was only giving critical formulation to their practice. Their idiom was similar to that of Langland, whose language was living English and the alliterative metre into which it naturally fell the vital vehicle for it. Driven underground after the Norman Conquest

PIERS PLOWMAN

by versifiers who, for a long period, could neither make a foreign
medium live nor retain the life of the old, it revived in the fourteenth
century as a natural framework for the English language. To say this
is not to deny either the importance of Chaucer or the fruitfulness of
the foreign influences, French and Italian, upon his work. Over two
centuries of reversals and foreign domination had adversely affected
what we may call the original English tradition. More especially, they
had divorced that tradition from healthy contact with important
sources of self-consciousness and intelligence; there are places where
the allegory of *Piers Plowman* drops into heaviness and unwieldy
personification, and these are precisely the faults that Chaucer, himself certainly no less English than Langland, succeeded in avoiding.
To admit this, however, is not to minimize the importance of Langland's own contribution. The full alliterative verse represents values
more important, not, indeed, than those of *Troilus and Criseyde* and
The Canterbury Tales, but of the Chaucerian version of *The Romaunt
of the Rose*, and by virtue of these values its influence deserves to survive in later English literature. In particular, Langland's verse achieves
a peculiarly fruitful relation of rhythm to feeling, the same relation
which allowed Shakespeare to play sense and stress in infinite variety
against the restraining influence of the traditional blank verse line.

An application of these principles to the opening lines of *Piers Plowman* should make this clear:

> In a somere seyson · whan softe was the sonne,
> I shop me in-to shrobbis[1] · as I a shepherd were,
> In abit as an ermite · unholy of werkes,
> Ich went forth in the worlde · wonders to hure,
> And sawe many cellis · and selcouthe thynges.
> Ac on a may morwening · on Malverne hulles
> Me byfel for to slepe · for weyrynesse of wandryng;
> And in a launde as ich lay · lenede ich and slepte,
> And merveylously me mette[2] · as ich may yowe telle;
> Al the welthe of this worlde · and the woo bothe,
> Wynkynge as it were · wyterly ich saw hyt,
> Of tryuthe and of tricherye · of tresoun and of gyle,
> Al ich saw slepynge · as ich shal yowe telle.

(C Text)

1. shrubs, but A Text has 'schroud' and B 'schroudes' – garment(s),
2. dreamed.

131

The advantages of scansion by stress rather than by mechanical counting of syllables are obvious here. Langland may not have been fully aware of the metrical subtleties of Anglo-Saxon verse, but he realized that the break at the centre of each alliterative line was the key to the whole effect; his lines rise up to the pause, and fall as definitely away from it, and are so preserved from the dangers of a mere invertebrate flow. The exigencies of the language, in turn, dictate the position of the stresses within the individual line, and these are determined by what D. H. Lawrence described as 'the ebbing and lifting emotion'. The break in the middle of the line may serve to give point to a balanced contrast, or to emphasize a significant parenthesis in the flow of the narrative. Langland's metre, in fact, was the natural setting of a living language. One very important indication of this was the fact that he showed, in the psasage just quoted, that he could do what very few modern poets have been able to accomplish – that is, handle a plain unadorned narrative in verse, bringing out its full implications, without interrupting its natural flow. He has succeeded in telling us that his poem is to be a complete survey of human life under the aspect of good and evil (for he saw 'Al the welthe of this worlde · and the woo bothe') without in any way distracting from the preliminary statement of the circumstances of his dream. In its way, this is an achievement not less remarkable than that which enabled Chaucer to turn the highly organized stanza of *Troilus and Criseyde* to the ends of conveying the movement of natural dialogue and a keen analysis of character.

If *Piers Plowman* draws part of its individual quality, as I have been arguing, from contact with a long and still living tradition of linguistic usage, it also owes much to its foundations in medieval allegory. The allegorical habit of mind (for it was this as much as any consciously formulated philosophy that influenced Langland) has been so long dead, is so remote from modern ways of thinking, that it is hard for us to imagine that it could once have served as the basis for a satisfying and inclusive view of life. Allegory for us means much what it meant for Spenser in *The Faerie Queene*: the projection, more or less convincing according to the skill of the allegorist, of abstract qualities – virtues, vices, spiritual states – into a tangible representation. This, however, even when the process of embodiment is carried out by a writer as firmly rooted in tradition as Bunyan, is barely the husk of the complete thing. The allegorical outlook, in its full medieval form, implied the capacity to see a situation simultaneously under different aspects, each independent and existing, on its own level, in its own right, but at the same time forming part of a transcendent order in relation to which alone its complete meaning is to be ascertained.

The figure of Piers Plowman himself is a perfect example of the way in which this convergence of simultaneous attributes upon a single point provides added depth and perspective, enriches our understanding by conferring upon it moral significance without in any way detracting from the concreteness of the original experience. Piers is in the first place the English countryman of his own particular time and place, and none of his subsequent transformations will make this primary aspect of his nature irrelevant; rather they will complete it, by setting it in what the poet believes to be its natural spiritual context. This context, in turn, is indicated through the gradual transformation of Piers, which springs so naturally from his normal being that we are hardly aware of it; for Piers, simply by living in accordance with the simple set of values he has inherited in his calling, is able to pass judgement upon the world around him, to denounce its numerous failings and to indicate the way which leads to spiritual health. So far, factually and morally, the figure is still a projection of contemporary realities. It is only in the later and more daring stages of his allegorical transformation that Piers becomes something more than a fourteenth-century farmer concerned with the evils of contemporary society and with the simple, severe code by which these evils can be mastered. First as the Good Samaritan, the bodily representation of the supreme Christian virtue of Charity, and then – by the most far-reaching and inclusive transformation of all – as symbol of the humanity assumed by Jesus Christ in his Incarnation, dying on the Cross, harrowing hell, and rising again in triumph from the dead, he becomes the key, not merely to the time and place in which he originally appeared, but to the destiny of the whole human race. The successive phases of his transformation have by the end of the poem been gathered together, assumed into the unity of the complete conception.

This allegorical structure, properly conceived, may even throw some light upon the long process of growth by which *Piers Plowman* appears to have assumed its final and complete form. The facts themselves are under dispute,[c] and there is even some question as to whether the poem, in its longer versions, is the work of a single hand. Perhaps, indeed, in literature of this kind, where the continuity of tradition is clearly an important shaping factor, this is a secondary problem. A reading of the successive forms of the poem indicates, in any case, the existence of a single continuous development, in the course of which the complete allegory came into being. The three texts distinguished by the first editors – A, B, and C – undoubtedly appear to grow one from another, as though reflecting, together with the passage of time and the influence of changing external conditions, a process by which social realities are related to moral judgements and both in turn to a universal spiritual interpretation. In the working-out of this process, of course, the earlier stages are neither forgotten nor rendered irrelevant by concentration on what follows. On the contrary, the fuller, more developed versions bear embedded within them the simpler passages of the A Text, using them – so to speak – as points of departure, foundations on which to build the pattern of universal significances, which is the true aim of the poem. In this way, again, *Piers Plowman* suggests less the finality of an individual creation than the cumulative expression of a traditional conscience.

A summary consideration of the general plan will make this clear. The so-called A Text, which covers twelve Passus, represents only one-third of the completed poem. It begins with the vision of Lady Meed, in a very true sense the starting-point of the whole conception, follows this with the contrasted vision of Piers Plowman, and ends with a brief development of the vision of Do-Well, Do-Bet, and Do-Best, in which a distinctive didactic position (so to call it) begins to take shape. All three stages survive in the later, expanded versions of the poem. The poet's opening dream of a 'faire felde ful of folke' combines universality of reference with a limited, even familiar environment. The field itself might easily be a part of the poet's local experience, expressly related from the first to Malvern and its surroundings, but in it he finds –

> Alle manere of men · the mene and the ryche,
> Worchynge and waundrynge · as the worlde asketh,
>
> (C Text, 19–20)*

* Since my concern, at this point of the essay, is with the developing *structure* of the poem and not primarily with *poetic* differences between the three texts, I have taken my quotations here, as throughout the essay, from the C Text.

and it is bounded, on the east, by the Towere of Truth, and, on the west, by the Dale of Death. From the first, therefore, the setting of the poem is at once local and universal, descriptive and allegorical. Its allegorical content, however, though present from the first, deals at this stage with relatively simple ideas, themselves pictorially expressed. When Lady Meed herself, the occasion of all social disorder, makes her appearance, it is as a woman 'wonderlich riche clothed', clad in the luxury which was, for Langland, an infallible sign of degeneration:

> [1]Hure was purfild with peloure · non purere in erthe,
> And coroned with a corone · the kynge hath no betere;
> On all her fyve fyngres · rycheliche yrynged,
> And ther-on rede rubies · and other riche stones.
> (C Text, Passus iii, 10–13)

The contemplation of this figure provokes in the poet a conflict between fascination and moral condemnation which he expresses with direct simplicity when he says: 'Hure araye with hure rychesse · ravesshede myn herte'. The temptation, however, though acknowledged, does not prevail. From the superficial splendour of Lady Meed, we pass to a remorseless picture of the clerical and courtly corruption which she spreads in a world where rank and responsibility are divorced from one another. This, in turn, prompts the poet to resume the search for truth, which is found at last accompanying, in the contrasted figure of Piers, simple dedication to honest toil, 'Ich knowe hym', says Piers of Truth, 'as kyndeliche · as clerkes don hure bokes':

> Ich have yben his folwer · al this fourty wynter,
> And served Treuthe sothlyche · somdel to paye;
> In alle kynne craftes · that he couthe devyse
> Profitable to the plough · he putte me to lerne.
> (C Text, Passus viii, 188–91)

This contrast between Lady Meed and Piers is the point of departure for the whole allegorical development which follows. The later, and fuller, versions naturally expand the A Text's first direct enunciation of the main themes of the poem in the light of a more ample vision of the universal spiritual context of the immediate problems; but their foundation, as laid down in these early Passus and handed down from

1. Her robe 'was edged with fur'.

the birth of the entire conception, is the poet's concern with the gap that separated contemporary society, as he saw it, from true simplicity of life. The vision of Do-Well, Do-Bet, and Do-Best with which the first text closes is in reality a first effort to relate this description to a fuller statement of Christian doctrine.

In the later texts, B and C, this effort is both developed and surpassed. Whatever their authorship may be, these are the texts to which we have to turn for a complete picture of the poem. The result – according to Skeat – of Langland twice resuming work on *Piers Plowman*, first in 1377 and again towards 1393, they expand the original text to nearly three times its original length. The B Text, in fact, adds a considerable number of lines to the first eleven Passus of A, with the general effect of assimilating the primary vision to the more developed state of the allegory; in addition, it replaces Passus xii by no less than nine new sections. C, whilst adding little really new, redistributes further the matter of the poem, and increases the number of the Passus to twenty-three. These developments represent, in effect, an expanded treatment of the concluding vision of the original text. This concentrates first upon setting the sombre facts originally described against a system developed from moral theology and, secondly, relates this new allegorical construction, through the figure of Piers, himself finally transformed into a symbolic representation of Christ's humanity, to the doctrine of the Incarnation. The various stages of the poem, therefore, however it may have come to be written (J. M. Manly, for example, ascribes the final Passus of the A Text to a hand different from that which imagined the earlier episodes, and B itself to yet another author), follow a logic of their own in moving from the particular to the universal, from a statement of facts to a consideration, which is at the same time an interpretation, of their spiritual background. This logic seems to be an essential part of the finished conception.

The expansion of the original vision in the later texts, therefore, implies incorporation into a greater allegorical pattern. This pattern is built up primarily on a triple conception of Christian obligation, summed up in the three successive states Do-Well, Do-Bet, and Do-Best. These states, however, are not allowed to remain mere abstractions. Each of them is successively related to the facts of human behaviour, as observed by the poet in the society which surrounds

him; and the fact that the contrast assumes, as the allegorical progression advances, an air of increasing tragedy prepares the way finally
for the direct introduction of the central Christian symbols. The first
stage in this construction turns on the life of Do-Well. Do-Well
represents the acceptance of the conditions of daily life, lived truly in
the sight of God and in accordance with the precepts of the Church.
The philosophy of

> Who-so is trewe of hys tonge · and of hus two handes,
> And thorw leel[1] labour lyveth · and loveth his em-cristine[2]
> > (C Text, Passus xi, 78–9)

is sufficient, when truly followed, for salvation. By contrast with
this, the lowest form of the Christian ideal, Langland continues to set
his sombre picture of the state of the world, and more especially his
denunciation of the incapacity of the privileged and those to whom
spiritual power has been entrusted to follow even the elementary precepts of their own moral code:

> Clerkus and knygtes · carpen of god ofte,
> And laveth hym muche in hure mouthe · ac mene men in herte ...
> > so is pryde en-hansed
> In religion and al the reame · among ryche and poure,
> That preyeses han no powere · these pestilences to lette.
> For god is def now a dayes · and dayneth nought ous to huyre,
> And good men for our gultes · be al to-grunt to dethe.
> > (C Text, Passus xii, 52–3; 58–62)

It is this contrast between precept and reality, presented with a wealth
of observed detail, that gives life to the abstract structure of the poem.

Do-Well is, in any case, no more than a first step on the road to
perfection. Beyond it, including and transcending its qualities, is the
life of positive dedication to spiritual realities and to the practice of
the supreme virtue of Charity. This, the state of Do-Bet, normally
though not necessarily should find its consummation in the religious
life. Do-Bet, in other words, retains all the qualities of Do-Well,
but – as the poet puts it – 'he doth more':

> He is lowe as a lombe · and loveliche of speche,
> And helpeth herteliche alle men · of that he may aspare.

1. faithful, 2. fellow-Christian.

The bagges and the by-gurdeles · he hath to broke hem alle ...
And is ronne into religion · and rendreth hus byble,
And precheth to the people · seynt Poules wordes.

(C Text, Passus xi, 83–5; 88–9)

On this new level, the contrast between precept and behaviour looms
larger than ever. Langland does not hesitate to underline it with all
the peculiar pungency of phrase at his command:

He is worse than Iudas · that giveth a Iaper silver,
And biddeth the beggar go · for his broke clothes.

(C Text, Passus xi)

Only now, more clearly than before, man's lack of Charity stands
out against the direct evocation of God's providence:

For our ioye and oure hele · Iesu Cryst of hevene,
In a pore mannes appareille · pursueth us evere.

(B Text, Passus xi, 179–80)

With God thus incarnate in the garb of the poor, the identification of
Christ, in his human nature, with Piers is clearly foreshadowed.

The allegorical pattern, however, is still far from complete. Do-
Bet itself, in spite of the greater spiritual discernment which it implies, is not the last step in the ladder of perfection. Beyond it and
Do-Well, combining both in a higher perfection, is the state of *active*
spiritual dedication in which a human being, having grasped true
spiritual values and responded to them with a total offering of the
self in poverty, is entrusted with the task of remoulding the world to
their pattern: the state, in other words, of Do-Best. This is, in its
most complete form, the life of spiritual authority, supremely con-
fided for its selfless exercise to the rulers of the Church by Jesus Christ
himself, and implying the obligations – the most neglected of all –
described in the poet's own words:

Do-best bere sholde · the bisshope's croce,
And halye[1] with the hoked ende · ille men to goode,
And with the pyk putte downe · *prevaricatores legis*,
Lordes that lyven as hem lust · and no lawe a-counten;
[2]For here mok and her meeble · suche men thynken

1. haul back. 2. 'On account of their muck (trashy wealth) and their
movable property'.

That no bisshop sholde · here byddynge with-sitte,
Ac Do-best sholde not dreden hem · but do as god hihte.
                                        (C Text, Passus xi, 92–8)

As a combination of the active and contemplative virtues, the life of
Do-Best is the highest destiny open to man on earth; but precisely
because this is so, as Langland repeatedly asserts, it bears the greatest
responsibilities and is the most open to corruption. In his statement of
its privileges, therefore, and in the accompanying denunciations of
failure and neglect, spiritual ideal and social reality finally come together in the most universal contrast of the whole poem.

In the various stages of *Piers Plowman*, to put it more simply, the
manifold richness and continuity of the allegorical pattern is balanced
by a profoundly tragic view of the state of the world. Set against the
balanced statement of hierarchical values which constitutes the framework of his poem, Langland's repeated evocations of the lot of common humanity gain in intensity and moral urgency. As the distance
between ideal and reality grows with the unfolding of the full conception, the contrast is stated with increasing power. The happiness
which should be the poor man's inheritance, but which the social
structure so signally fails, for all its Christian pretensions, to guarantee,
is eventually sought for elsewhere in direct appeal to the justice of
God:

                    ... by law he cleymeth Joye,
        That nevere Joye hadde · of rightful Juge he asketh;
        And seith, 'lo, briddes and bestes · that no blisse knoweth,
        And wilde wormes in wodes · throw wynter hem grevest,
        And makest hem wel ney meek · and mylde for defaute;
        After then thou sendest hem somere · that is her sovereyn Joye,
        And blisse to alle that been · both wilde and tame.
        Then may beggers, as bestes · after blysse asken,
        That al her lif haven lyved · in langour and defaute.
                                        (C Text, Passus xvi, 290–8)

No lesser justice, indeed, seems at this stage conceivable. To the lot
of the poor, hard and barely changeable, corresponds – as described
in these Passus in contrast to the ideal of Do-Best – the corrupt state
of the rich and the neglect of those whose professional concern should
be with the spiritual guidance of humanity. If the sign of true Christian

living be the practice of Charity, the prospects of attaining social order in the world of Langland's poem are far from bright. The virtue was found 'once' in a friar's habit, but 'it is far and fele yeares · in Fraunceys tyme'; it appears seldom among the commons 'for brawlynge and back-bytynge' and 'bearynge of false wittnesse', and still less among the bishops, where indeed 'it wolde be' were it not that 'avaryce other-whiles halt hym with-oute the gate'. As the allegorical structure grows in completeness and coherence, the human situation, failing to correspond to its majestic inclusiveness, is revealed in pitiful inadequacy.

The conflict between good and evil, in other words, far from being settled in accordance with the dictates of reason, needs to be resolved by other means. At the end of the poem, therefore, we are brought to the last vision of all, that which transforms Piers into the human semblance of God incarnate and crucified. Freewill, we are told –

for love hath undertake,
That this Jesus of his gentrise · shal jouste in Peers armes,
In hus halme and in hus haberion · *humana natura*;
That Christ be nat knowe · for *consummatus deus*,
In Peers plates the Plouhman · this prykiere shal ryde.

(C Text, Passus xxi, 20–4)

By this supreme transformation, the scope of the whole vision is finally and decisively extended. New elements, scarcely touched on before, are added to the conception. The duel between good and evil is described in terms of a 'joust', a courtly tournament. Jesus has become a 'prykiere', a knight riding out to meet his challenger, and his armour, the humanity he has assumed for the purposes of battle, is that of Piers, who has borne his active representation of the Christian virtues through the successive stages of his allegorical pilgrimage and is now ready to play his part in the decisive encounter. As *humana natura*, the human element in the Word made flesh, he is united to the Divinity of Christ and so participates in the great Christian victory over the enemies of God and mankind; but, by a last superb and characteristic touch, the poet, having witnessed this consummation in his dream, wakes to the world to realize that the endless struggle continues. Here, too, *Piers Plowman* is faithful to the Saxon origins of its inspiration. Like the pagan Beowulf many centuries earlier, the Christian hero, if not defeated, is given no rest in this life from the conflict with evil.

The allegorical conception thus sketched, however, is not properly to be appreciated except in the light of the literary virtues that went with it. The foundation of these is a capacity to see the highest spiritual conceptions in terms of a firm grasp of the particular. When Langland desires to express his deepest feelings, and when these break through the sometimes cumbrous garb of his allegorical inventions (for the allegorical habit, as he used it, was at times clumsy and un-realized in detail), he finds it natural to rely on the simplest imagery. He writes of the Incarnation in terms of the most universal physical processes:

> Love is the [1]plonte of pees · and most preciouse of vertues;
> For hevene holde hit ne myghte · so hevy hit semede,
> Til hit hadde on erthe · goten hymselve.
> Was never lef up-on lynde · lyghter ther-after,
> As whanne hit hadde of the folde · flesch and blod ytake;
> Tho was it portatyf[2] and pershaunt[3] · as the poynt of a nedle,
> May non armure hit lette · nother hye walles;
> For thy is love leder · of our lorde's folke in hevene.
>
> (C Text, Passus ii, 149–56)

Langland's language here is the vehicle of a finely integrated experi-ence, alive and sensitive to every point of contact, and crystallizing suavely into poetry. The effect of 'pershaunt', preceded by 'portatyf' and followed by 'as the poynt of a nedle' is not so inferior to Ham-let's 'bare bodkin'; it is certainly of the same kind, and depends upon a similar keen intensity of perception. The simple alliteration of the second and third lines, charged with the sense of ripeness, reflects the 'heavinesse' of the spiritual burden which leads finally, after the pro-cess of begetting which follows so naturally from it, to the sense of joyous relief beautifully conveyed in the evocation of the leaf flutter-ing in the breeze. In writing of this kind, words become transparent vehicles for the emotion that underlies them and demands the simplest, most vital expression. Their value is, so to speak, sacramental (the word has a special relevance in view of the nature of Langland's

1. 'plant of peace', 2. easily carried, 3. piercing.

allegory) and the presence of universal physical experiences illumin-
ates even the most spiritual reality.

What is true of the language is equally true of the symbolic figures
of the poem. Langland's allegory, like his language, grew out of his
experience before sublimating it. The symbol of Piers has a content
that almost all later allegorical creations, whatever their other merits,
lack; he is fully natural both before and after he touches the supernatural. Langland's moral judgements are always founded on particular instances, and his portraits remind us of the dramatic practice
implied in Ben Jonson's conception of humours. The theory of
humours was long regarded as purely scholarly in origin, but this is
not entirely so. The essence of it consists in taking a real human type
and in stressing one aspect of it until the stress gives a peculiar life to
the whole figure. The quality of that life lies in its intensity. It domin-
ates the character even to the point of distortion, though the distortion, being to scale within the limits of the complete work, always
gives increased and not diminished reality. In Jonson, as in Langland,
moreover, the moral intention behind this conception of character
stands unconcealed. *Piers Plowman* is full of examples of it. The tavern
incident in Passus vii, already mentioned, is typical. It belongs to the
same world as *Bartholomew Fair*, similar in its fidelity to detail and in
the firmness of its moral purpose.

A single example will serve to illustrate this generality. The words
of Lechery, a typical Langlandian personification, will serve:

> To eche maide that ich mette · ich made hure a sygne
> Semynge to synne-warde · and somme gan ich taste
> A-boute the mouthe, and by-nythe · by-gan ich to grope,
> [1]Til our bothers wil was on; · to werke we yeden
> As wel fastyngdaies as Frydaies · and heye-feste evenes,
> As luf in lent as oute of lente · alle tymes liche –
> Such werkus with ous · were nevere oute of season –
> Til me myghte no more ; ·thanne hadde we murye tales
> Of puterie[2] and of paramours · and proveden thorw speches,
> Handlynge and halsynge[3] · and al-so thorw cussynge
> Excitinge oure aither other · til oure old synne;
> Sotilede[4] songes · and sende out olde baudes

1. 'Till both our appetites were aroused', 2. lechery, 3. embracing,
4. invented.

For to wynne to my wil · wommen with gyle;
By sorcerye somtyme · and soun tyme by maistrie.
Ich lay by the lovelokeste · and loved hem nevere after.
Whenne ich was old and hor · and hadde lore[1] that kynde,
Ich had lykynge to lauhe · of lecherous tales.
Now, lord, for thy leaute · of lechours have mercy!

(C Text, Passus vii, 178–95)

No passage could illustrate better the origin and development of that concreteness and vitality in delineation which is the common basis of the English comedy of humours and of Langland's allegorical method. The characteristics of Lechery are not presented in an abstract form, but through the mouth of a human being; they are, above all, visualized, given their tragic context in the light of observed experience. The feeling is human, and not only human, but dramatic; that is the essence of the practice of humours. The symbolic figure is simplified by that 'distortion' to scale of which we have spoken, but so simplified that its significance is not less but greater. Real human nature is given us, but under one aspect, seen in the light of one dominating quality. Such a simplification is essential to the dramatist, and Langland foreshadows the development of the Elizabethan theatre, not only here, but repeatedly in his work.

But this is not all. The human figure thus revealed under a dominating aspect is firmly subordinated to a moral aim which, far from tending to abstraction or unreality, is its true justification. Lechery is allowed, towards the end of the description, a certain tragic quality, expressed in the bitterness of –

Ich lay by the lovelokeste · and loved hem nevere after,

and, above all, in the vanity of –

Whenne ich was old and hor · and hadde lore that kynde.

The feeling, common in medieval work, occurs elsewhere in *Piers Plowman*:

At churche in the charnel · churles aren evel[2] to knowe,
Other a knyght fro a knave · other a queyne fro a queene.

(C Text, Passus ix, 45–6)

1. lost, 2. difficult.

143

Such sentiments are not to be confused with that haunting presence of the inevitable worm which, after the spiritual crisis of the following century, became an important part of religious experience. It is more to the point, in reading Langland's sombre passages to remember that no community can be called balanced or complete which lacks a considered attitude to the two central themes of European literature – death, and what Langland called 'the flesh'; without such an attitude, poetry, though capable of isolated achievements, degenerates inevitably into triviality or romantic pose. Langland possessed an attitude of this kind; we may find it unsatisfactory or incredible, but it gave his work a point of universal reference. He did not share the metaphysical preoccupation of the Renaissance with the idea of impersonal Time, as expressed in Shakespeare's line –

Devouring Time, blunt thou the lion's paw. (Sonnet xix)

The feeling of the sonnets is something new and complex. It is obtained here by transforming the epithet 'devouring', which belongs naturally to the lion, to Time, subjecting the classical commonplace *tempus edax rerum* to a new and highly complex emotional situation. The lion naturally raises associations of splendid life and boundless activity; but the transfer of 'devouring' suggests that all this energy is in reality self-consuming, that it involves the ultimate wearing-down of life into pure annihilation. Shakespeare's tendency, in fact, as far as this sonnet is concerned (for it is only one of his many tendencies), is to subdue the nervous activity of life to the idea of Time, 'metaphysically' apprehended. In Langland, similar poetic resources are used to a different end. Time is regarded as merely the condition under which living moral action takes place. Full value is given to the human and spiritual tragedy represented by the figure of Lechery. The tragedy is – to quote Shakespeare again – that of 'the expense of spirit in a waste of shame', and Langland's moral judgement fully recognizes, not only the 'waste' and the 'expense', but the fact that it is 'of spirit' and therefore redeemable. As always, the allegory of *Piers Plowman* follows the principle of its author's central doctrine – the Christian Incarnation. Far from imposing itself upon reality as an abstraction, it works from the body to the soul, from natural life to the consummation of grace in which its author believed. And, in so doing, it bears witness to the real strength of English literature.

NOTES

a. On this subject, G. R. Owst's *Literature and Pulpit in Medieval England* should be consulted.

b. Quoted by Owst.

c. The theory of divided authorship is most authoritatively stated by J. M. Manley in *The Authorship of Piers Plowman* (Early English Text Society, 1910). See also A. H. Bright, *New Light on Piers Plowman* (Oxford, 1928).

The substance of this essay first appeared in *Scrutiny*, Vol. v, 1936, and it has been recast for this *Guide* by kind permission of the Editors.

SIR GAWAYNE AND THE GRENE KNIGHT

*Professor of English Literature, Royal Holloway College,
University of London*

Sir Gawayne and the Grene Knight is written in an English dialect that
was fed by the experience of the communities of the North-west
Midlands, an experience, and therefore a language, that was different
from the experience and the English of Chaucer's community, and to
a lesser extent from those of Langland. Chaucer's English was also a
regional form, even though it was on the point of becoming the
standard form of the country. The *Gawayne* poet's form of English or
dialect is that of a community in a rough, mountainous country with
a scattering of castles. The landscape was sterner, the weather more
vehement, and the courts more parochial than those known to
Chaucer. The *Gawayne* poet's dialect reflects the uniqueness of his
place and generation. To illustrate: the following are a selection of
words – many of Scandinavian origin – from our poem which do *not*
appear anywhere in Chaucer:

aghlich *hideous*, a-wharf *turned aside*, cragge *crag*, dreped *knocked down,
slain*, glam and glaum *din*, jovial *uproar*, glyfte *glanced sidelong*, grymme
fierce, grindel *menacing*, yarrande *snarling*, harled *tangled*, nirt *nicke or cut*,
ratheled *entwined*, rof *gash*, ruche *turn oneself*, runisch *violent*, rusched
rushed, schaterande *shattering*, schynder *sunder*, schrank *shrank*, schunt
sudden jerk, skayned *grazed*, snart *bitter (of weather)*, snayped *nipped uncomfortably (of the snow)*, snitered *descended*, swap *make a bargain*, thwarle
intricate, wappe *rush*, wap *blow*, wharre *whirr*, wruxled *wrapped up,
clad*, wysty *desolate*.

Of these words it can be said that they accord with Paget's gesture
theory. They are onomatopoeic, or they reproduce in sound the
shape or feel of rough or intractable objects, or they re-create in sound
sensations of smart or pain, or they are mimetic of violent or laborious
body-movement and action. The words communicate the experience
of the poet's environment, but would be outside the personal experience of Chaucer as they were, in fact, outside his poetic experience.

But here is this language activated and organized into a passage of poetry:

> Sumwhile with wormes[1] he werres, · and with wolves als,
> Sumwhile with wodwos[2], · that woned[3] in the knarres[4],
> Bothe with bulles and beres, · and bores otherwhile,
> And etaines[5], that him anelede[6] · of the heghe felle;
> Nade he ben [7]dughty and drighe, · and Drighten[8] had served,
> Douteless he hade ben ded · and dreped ful ofte.
> For werre wrathed him not so much, · that winter was wors,
> When the colde cler water · fro the cloudes shadde,
> And fres er hit falle might · to the fale[9] erthe;
> Ner slain with the slete · he sleped in his yrnes[10]
> Mo nightes then innoghe · in nakedrokkes,
> Ther as claterande fro the crest · the colde borne rennes,
> And henged heghe over his hede · in hard iise-ikkles.
>
> (720–32)

A knight is undergoing a rough journey in winter, and the experience is actualized in the muscular images and rhythms, in the firm grasp of concrete particulars. Moreover, the alliterative metre of *Sir Gawayne and the Grene Knight* (as of *Piers Plowman*) was flexible, and had vast rhythmic resources and possibilities, no less so, though of a different order, than the rhymed syllabic lines of Chaucer. The order of resources and possibilities of the alliterative line was of its own order, and the triumph of *Sir Gawayne* is largely rhythmic. Here, for instance, the movement of Gawain on his journey is conveyed by rhythms which emphasize the images:

> Thay boghen[11] bi bonkkes · ther[12] boghes ar bare,
> Thay clomben bi clyffes · ther clenges the colde.
> The heven was up halt[13], · bot ugly ther-under;
> Mist muged[14] on the mor, · malt[15] on the mountes,
> Ech hille had a hatte, · a mist-hakel[16] huge.
> Brokes[17] byled and breke · bi bonkkes aboute,
> Shyre[18] shaterande on shores, · ther thay doun shoved.
>
> (2077–83)

1. serpents, 2. wild men of the woods, satyrs, 3. dwelt, 4. rocks, 5. giants, 6. pursued, 7. doughty and strong, 8. God, 9. pale, faded, 10. irons, i.e. armour, 11. turn, 12. where, 13. up-drawn, 14. drizzled, 15. melted, 16. mist-cloak, 17. brooks, 18. bright.

Contrast with this rhythmic 'enactment of sense' the much quicker rhythm that conveys the sense of delighted expenditure of energy in the hunt:

> Hunteres with highe horne · hasted hem[1] after
> With such a crakkande cry · as kliffes hade brusten[2];
> [3]What wilde so atwaped · wighes that shotten
> Was al toraced and rent · at the resayt.
> Bi thay were tened at the highe · and taysed to the wattres.
> The ledes were so lerned · at the lowe tristeres,
> And the grehoundes so grete, · that geten hem bilive[4],
> And hem to-filched, as fast · as frekes might loke,
>   ther right.
> The lorde for blis abloy
> Ful oft con launce and light,
> And drof that day with joy
> Thus to the derk night.

(1165–77)

In the narrower sense of the word 'technique', the explanation of this plasticity of the fourteenth-century alliterative measure is that the four heavily stressed syllables (three of them alliterating) in the line, two on each side of the pause, can be very freely moved about in relation to each other inside the line on account of the large freedom of choice as to the number of unstressed syllables intervening between them. This allows a line with four 'blows' of variable, often very heavy, weight (occasionally two of them immediately succeed each other to make a centre of force), and this offered the writer a variety of rhythmic contour, as well as a varied length of line. But this is not all. Each stanza of *Sir Gawayne* consists of a 'stock' of from anything between twelve and thirty-eight lines followed by a 'bob' – a very short line, or 'hinge', of two syllables leading to a 'wheel' – four short lines. This 'bob' and 'wheel' make a periodic contraction after each 'stock' of long lines, and serve as a rhythmic punctuation; and although it has not the verbal repetition of refrain, it serves as a kind of refrain, especially as these five lines carry rhyme in addition to alliteration.

Hand in hand with its exploitation of a traditional native rhythm

1. them, i.e. the hounds, 2. burst, 3. 'Whatever wild beast escaped the hunters who were out shooting was yet slaughtered at the receiving station, After they had been chivvied at the high ground and driven to the waters', 4. quickly.

goes a high degree of sophistication in the outward form of the poem. For instance, the poem begins and practically ends with almost the same line:

> Sithen the sege and the assaut · was cesed at Troye,

and

> After the segge and the asaute · was sesed at Troye,

Then there is a verbal and stanzaic pointing of the poem's cyclic theme. This is emphasized by a stylizing of episodes: there are *three* hunting expeditions and these alternate with *three* visits from the Lady to Gawain; the Green Man makes *three* blows or attempts at blows with the axe, and so on. This 'formalism' of numbers and episodes accords with, and is interwoven with, the poem's sophisticated theme of Courtly Love. Now much of the poem's success is precisely due to the tension between the 'sophisticated' and formal on the one hand and the 'primitive' rhythmic impulse on the other, and their resolution. The poem achieves an extraordinary resolution of literary and 'popular' elements.

*   *   *

The story of *Sir Gawayne and the Grene Knight* is very ancient and there are analogies in both early Celtic and French documents. But all we can say for certain is that the story was widely dispersed and may have been of remote Celtic origin.

At the start of the poem Arthur is beginning his Christmas revels at Camelot on New Year's Day when a huge figure, dressed all in green and on a green mount, intrudes into this ambit of human joy. He lays down a challenge, and as a result Gawain strikes off his green head with an axe. The Green Knight 'runischly' leaps up, catches up his 'lufly' head and remounts his horse. The severed head tells Gawain that he must repair to the Green Chapel a year hence for a return blow. The cycle of the year passes. On the morrow of All Saints' Day Gawain gears himself and sets off for the Green Chapel. He travels over rough country in wintry weather until Christmas Eve, when he comes to a castle and breaks his journey for rest. He is welcomed by the Lord of the Castle, who has a fair young wife companioned by an old and hideous lady of high status. Christmas rejoicings are celebrated in this lord's castle. On three successive days after Christmas the lord goes hunting with his retainers while Gawain spends this period in his chamber, recuperating his energies for the promised meeting with the Green Knight on New Year's Day. The lord and his guest have agreed to exchange each other's daily earnings. On each of these three days, while her husband is out hunting, the lady comes to Gawain's chamber and temps his constancy, courtesy, and chastity. Gawain survives the test well and receives no more than a kiss on the first day, which he gives to the lord in return for the buck he has killed. The next evening Gawain receives a slain boar and faithfully returns two kisses. After the third day he receives 'nobbut an old fox' for the three kisses he had received; but he breaks the bargain since he fails to surrender the green girdle which the lady had given him under a pledge of secrecy, and which she says will protect him in his encounter with the Green Knight. To fulfil his appointment Gawain resumes his journey. He has the help of a guide for part of the way. The Green Chapel turns out to be nothing but a barrow or mound with a bubbling spring or stream nearby. The Green Knight appears with his axe. After two feints the Green Knight's third blow inflicts a slight graze which draws blood. The Green Knight then discloses himself as identical with the lord who had entertained Gawain. Gawain would have got away scot-free but for his deception over the matter of the girdle. The old woman at the castle was Morgan the Fey who had urged the original apparition in Camelot a year ago to spite Guinevere. Huffily Gawain refuses further invitations from the Green Knight and betakes himself back to Arthur's court. He gives a faithful account of his adventures to Arthur, and gets some delighted laughter for his pains. From that date all of Arthur's court wear green girdles as a commemoration of Gawain's adventure with the Green Knight.

This story has ritualistic elements. *Sir Gawayne* is a poet's treatment of a myth.[a] What is the meaning of the myth, thus treated and transformed?

In the poem the main contrast is between the social joys of the court, its games and feasting at Christmastide –

> With alle the mete and the mirthe · that men couthe avyse;
> Such glaum and gle · glorious to here,
> Dere din upon day, · daunsing on nyghtes,

(45–7)

and the savagery of Nature's winter, careless of human needs –

> Highe hilles on eche a halve, · and holtwodes under
> Of hore oakes ful hoge · a hundreth togeder;
> The hasel and the hawthorne · were harled[1] al samen,
> With roghe raged mosse · railed anywhere,
> With mony briddes unblithe · upon bare twiges,
> That pitosly ther piped · for pyne of the colde.
>
> (742–7)

The contrast is dramatic. It first implies and then promotes a conflict, and the conflict is then resolved, and the highly formal mechanics of plot and stanza noted above are essential features of this resolving pattern. For the form and narrative cannot be separated. The poem in its cyclic form corresponds to that cycle of the year which forms the essence of the narrative. This poetic realization of the seasonal rhythm, while occupying the whole poem, also takes place on a smaller scale in these two stanzas:

> A yere yernes[2] ful yerne, · and yeldes never like,
> The forme[3] to the finisment · foldes ful selden.
> Forthi this [4]Yol overyede, · and the yere after,
> And eche sesoun serlepes[5] · sued after other:
> After Cristenmasse · com the crabbed lentoun,
> That fraistes flesh with the fishe · and fode more simple;
> Bot thenne the weder of the worlde · with winter hit threpes[6],
> Colde clenges adoun, · cloudes upliften,
> Sheer shedes the rain · in showers ful warme,
> Falles upon faire flat, · flowres there schewen,
> Bothe groundes and the greves[7] · grene ar her[8] wedes,
> Briddes busken to bilde, · and bremlich singen
> For solace of the softe somer · that sues therafter bi bonk;
> > And blossumes bolne to blowe
> > Bi rawes[9] rich and ronk,
> > Then notes noble innoghe
> > Ar herde in wod so wlonk[10].

> After, the sesoun of somer · with the soft windes,
> When Zeferus sifles[11] himself · on sedes and erbes;

1. tangled, 2. passes, 3. beginning, 4. 'Yule passed by', 5. in turn,
6. contends, 7. groves, 8. their, 9. rows, 10. proud, 11. whistles softly.

Wela winne is the wort · that waxes theroute,
When the donkande[1] dewe · dropes of the leves,
To bide a blisful blusch · of the bright sunne.
Bot then highes[2] hervest, · and hardenes him sone,
Warnes him for the winter · to wax ful ripe;
He drives with droght · the dust for to rise,
Fro the face of the folde · to flye ful highe;
Wrothe winde of the welkin · wrasteles with the sunne,
The leves lancen fro the linde · and lighten on the grounde,
And al grayes the gres · that grene was ere;
Thenne al ripes and rotes · that ros upon first,
And thus yirnes the yere · in yisterdayes mony,
And winter windes again, · as the worlde askes ...

(498–530)

Such an imaginative appreciation of the rhythm of the seasons involves a recognition of the indivisible process of getting and spending
(compare the poem *Wynnere and Wastour*, pp. 315, for a study of
this in a more exclusively human application), of fluorescence and
deliquescence, begetting and dying; of enjoyment of harvest and of
the deliberate letting of blood or sacrifice that is a premium for the
enjoyment of harvest. Some such principle of sacrifice, or expenditure, is implied in the beheading incident. In the poem, the striking-
off of the head of the Green Knight is like the pollarding of a tree,
and, indeed, the Green Knight in his boisterousness of confident
humour after delivering his challenge resembles a tree swayed by
gusts of wind:

> [3]The renk on his rounce · him ruched in his sadel,
> And runischly his rede eyen · he reled aboute,
> Bende his bresed[4] browes, · blicande[5] grene,
> Wayved his berde for to waite · who-so wolde rise.
>
> (306–6)

But there are other examples of spending in return for getting. The
hard journeys over inhospitable country are measures of payment
for the court festivities they follow; Gawain, in return for his getting
of the green girdle, has to pay for it by the spending of a token of

---

1. moistening, 2. hastens, 3. 'The fellow on his horse swayed himself
about in his saddle And violently his red eyes ...', 4. bristling, 5. shim-
mering.

blood. And so on. But this principle of adjustment between getting and spending is chiefly embodied in the figure of the Green Knight himself. He is huge in the richness of his personal resources and capacities of enjoyment, and in the bounty of his entertainment. But in Fitt iii, while Gawain is recuperating his energies in bed, he hunts wild beasts; we see him curb the excesses of Nature, redressing its economy. This dramatic contrast between humanity (especially in its finest aspect of the court) and harsh Nature is solved by imposing a pattern, and this pattern of narrative is itself the poet's transmutation into artistic terms of his perception of the balance and adjustment between winning and wasting, between growth and deliquescence.

* * *

It is because of, and not despite, the anthropological and the theological background that the poem has such an ample power of realized and natural human observation. The persons live in a context where their mere presences signify, and where their actions follow from choice and greatly count. And the objects in Nature, also by their mere presence, signify and can serve a purpose by their obstruction to human effort. Gawain is a type or representative, but he is also convincingly observed in his uniqueness as a person. This realism of character creation is partly due to the subtlety of the poet's psychology. This is well shown in Fitt iii where Gawain eventually 'falls' not so much through amorousness, but because of a reflection on his reputation for courtesy. A gift for observation is also apparent in this image of Arthur:

> Bot Arthure wolde not ete · til al were served,
> He was so joly of his joyfnes, · and sumwhat childgered[1]:
> His lif liked hym light, · he lovied the lasse
> Auther to longe lye · or to longe sitte,
> So busied him his yonge blod · and his brain wylde.
>
> (85–9)

or in the image of the two ladies, the young and attractive one and the old repulsive one, with its lively humour (lines 947–69). This Chaucerian sympathy extends to minor persons in the poem, such

---

1. boyish.

as to the guide in Fitt iv. Or notice the keen life in the image of people playing Christmas games in Fitt i:

> Loude crye was ther kest · of clerkes and other,
> Noël nayted[1] onewe, · nevened ful ofte;
> And sithen riche[2] forth runnen · to reche hondeselle[3],
> Yeayed[4] year's-giftes on high, · yelde hem bi hond,
> Debated busily · aboute tho giftes;
> Ladies laghed ful loude, · thogh thay lost haden,
> And he that wan was not wrothe, · that may ye wel trawe.
>
> (64–70)

But while all these are successful, even in their most restricted guises as mere characters in the plot – though this vitality in the images of persons is but an aspect of one vitality of the whole poem – the image of the Green Knight himself is more complex. He is seen by the poet from a variety of aspects and at various levels.

On one level – in Fitts i and iii, where he appears as the Lord of the Castle – the Green Knight has the kind of life of a human rather than supernatural figure. Here the poet's creation is a lord, Bercilak de Hautdesert who, whether he is entertaining his guest or hunting wild beasts, is a vigorous and ample embodiment of an amoral joy and energy. He has the profuseness and reckless vigour and the amorality of life on its purely natural level. He is jovial, and laughs at crabbed and conscientious human effort. Indeed, the main event of the whole poem, which is his contrivance, turns out to be a huge joke.

In Fitt iii, while Gawain nurses his energies indoors, this lord of the castle, whose own energies are boundless, goes hunting. The fluctuation of movement over rocky country is communicated with astonishing exactitude by the poet. And as previously noted, the variations of muscular effort of men and animals in this pursuit of game are rhythmically expressed (see lines 1428–34). What does this image of the burly, jovial host with hounds and retainers in his prodigal and joyous expenditure of energy suggest? While the chase was a prime pastime of the medieval and renaissance courtly class (cf. Uccello's picture) and the kill also provided subsistence (cf. the opening of the *Parlement of the Thre Ages*, p. 304), the hunt in *Sir Gawayne* has a further significance. For we are becoming aware

1. celebrated, 2. courtiers, 3. gifts of the season, 4. proclaimed.

that the Green Knight is prosecuting one of his necessary rôles – the purger of excess without which Nature

> Would be quite surcharged with her own weight,
> And strangl'd with her waste fertility;

as Milton puts it. For Life corrects its own over-profusion. Thus in his aspect as 'the jolly lord out hunting', the Green Knight is also functional in relation to the larger meaning of the poem.

But this bland host has other phases of being. He is elsewhere the grim and sardonically intimidating executioner stalking with his axe on the ledge overhanging the desolate Green Chapel:

> Whyrlande out of a wro[1] · wyth a felle weppen ...
> Sette the stele[2] to the stone, · and stalked bisyde,
> When he wan to the watter · wer he wade nolde,
> He hipped[3] over on his ax, · and orpedly[4] strydes,
> Bremly brothe[5] on a bent[6] · that brode was aboute,
> on snawe.
>
> (2222–4)

And this is different again from the impressive apparition in Fitt i with his rollicking and heartless laughter, his resemblance to a great tree shaken by the wind, his amazing beheading trick. But in all his different rôles, aspects and appearances, there is a common amplitude and an amoral enjoyment of life that transcend limited human capacities.

With these observations in mind, the usual title of editors* misleads as to the complexity of the Green Knight's nature. Gawain indeed is eminently a 'knight', but in the poem he encounters something other than, and larger than, himself. And it is this richness of the Green Knight's resources, his ambiguity, and multiplicity of his aspects, that may account for the very large number of designations he receives in the poem. He is called (to make a selection) *tulk, hathel, burn, mayster, freke, gome, schalke, renk,* as well as *mon.* All of these words except *mon* and *mayster* were used only in verse: while no modern synonyms exist for them all, their common meaning seems nearest to our word 'warrior', and this, or even the neutral word

1. nook, 2. handle, 3. hopped, 4. actively, 5. fiercely eager, 6. field.

* Since there is no title in the MS. this must be an editorial choice, anyway.

'man', might be a better translation, since they are more capable of distension to cover the particular and diverse shades of the image.

This impressive scale of designations for the Green Knight is indicative of the general linguistic richness of the whole poem. But what is the Green Knight? The poem is not an allegory, and we can not advise the mental substitution of a concept such as 'the Life Force' whenever the Green Knight appears in the poem. The Green Knight is himself (in fact, Bercilak de Hautdesert), but he has also the unlimited energy of a symbol. All we can say is that the poet's awareness of the generic forces of life and growth and richness and energy – all seemingly independent of men's choice or desire, and able to mock these – realizes itself in the image of the Green Knight. He testifies to an assumption that moral behaviour, though of vast importance, is subservient to and dependent on something even more primary – creative energy. In the poem, Gawain and his 'society' humbly come to terms with the Green Knight. They had been in danger of forgetting their own *sine qua non*.

The poem involves the divine and the human, the natural and the magical, and presents a pattern of these categories in which potential antagonisms between them are conciliated, and this in a partly comic temper. The very perfection of 'form' is evidence of the mastery exerted by the poet over his material, and that material was co-extensive with the writer's world. To say so much for a poem is to imply a very high value. *Sir Gawayne and the Grene Knight* is one of the great poems of the Middle Ages in English, which is to suggest that it is greater than nearly all poems except a few by Shakespeare. This is also a hint that its enjoyment is a necessary preparation for an enjoyment of Shakespeare, because Shakespeare's poetry is the culmination of those tendencies that are active in *Sir Gawayne and the Grene Knight*.

NOTE

a. For a detailed study of the poem from this point of view, see the essay by John Speirs in *Scrutiny* (Vol. XVI, iv, 1949), an essay to which I am much indebted.

MEDIEVAL LYRICS AND THE BALLADS

BY M. J. C. HODGART

Professor of English, the University of Sussex

Medieval Lyrics

The English medieval lyric, religious and secular, is a poor relation of the splendid Continental art-form, through which many of the finest writers of the Middle Ages said what they felt most deeply. We have nothing to compare with the *Dies Irae* or the *Stabat Mater* or with the great songs written in their mother-tongues by Bernart de Ventadorn, Walter von der Vogelweide, or Dante. The comparison is inevitable, since the English lyrics written during the thirteenth and fourteenth centuries are for the most part but imitations of an established European tradition; only with the carol of the fifteenth century does a native tradition of any originality begin to appear.

A lyric is a poem set to music; and so the history and criticism of the English medieval lyric should be bound up with the study of medieval music, an art which is impossible to illustrate in a short essay. It must be said in passing that lyrics during their early history were intended to be sung; that the peculiarities of their construction and style arise largely from the attempt to fit words and music together; and that 'words for music' possess a different aesthetic from 'words for speech'. You cannot judge Campion's lyrics as if they were an unsuccessful attempt to compete with Donne's; and a song like Chaucer's roundel in the *Parlement of Fowles* should not be compared even with Chaucer's own 'spoken' verse in *The Canterbury Tales*: the latter is based on the cadences of the speaking voice, while the beautifully phrased roundel has the movement of a particular melody:

> Now welcom somer, with thy sonne softe,
> That hast this wintres weders over-shake,
> And driven away the longe nightes blake.

There are many religious lyrics of the thirteenth and fourteenth centuries, but few of great literary merit. Most are conventional exercises on well-worn themes: the 'Ubi sunt?' theme ('Where are the

snows of yester-year?', 'Where are the great ones of the past?', later to
be linked with the Danse Macabre, the procession of all classes of men
to death), the five joys of the Virgin Mary, the lullaby sung over the
infant Christ, the lament on the Passion. Behind their composition
lay the movement to popularize religious concepts by translating
them into the mother-tongue and by adapting worldly literary forms
to godly ends, a movement in which the Franciscans took a leading
part. St Francis in the early thirteenth century had wished to make
religion gayer and closer to the common people: his missionary friars
were to be God's minstrels. Of the few religious lyrics which escape
from conventionality, one is the *Luve Ron* (love-song) of a Franciscan,
Friar Thomas of Hales, who treats the 'Ubi sunt' theme with the
naïve pathos and clarity of medieval pictorial art; it was written to
admonish an audience who knew the courtly romances:

> Hwer is Paris and Heleyne
>   That weren so bryht and feyre on bleo[1]?
> Amadas and Ideyne,
>   Tristram, Yseude and alle theo?
> Ector with his [2]scharpe meyne,
>   And Cesar, riche of worldes feo[3]?
> [4]He beoth iglyden ut of the reyne
>   So the schef is of the cleo.

The same theme appears in a more moral and less nostalgic poem
of the thirteenth century:

> Where beth they that biforen us weren,
> Houndes ladden and havekes[5] beren
>   And hadden feld and wode?
>   ... And, in a twincling of an eye,
> Hoere[6] soules weren forloren[7].

The most moving adaptation of a secular song to the theme of the
Passion, is the fifteenth-century *Quia Amore Langueo*. The best songs
are those which are closest to folk tradition: 'Adam lay ibounden' and
'I syng of a mayden', both of the fifteenth century; the latter shows
the threefold repetition typical of folk-song:

1. countenance, 2. powerful company, 3. goods, 4. "They have all
glided out of the realm, As the corn-sheaf has vanished from the hill-side,'
5. hawks, 6. their, 7. lost.

He cam also[1] stylle · there[2] his moder was
As dew in Aprylle · that fallyt on the gras;
He cam also stylle · to his modered bowr
As dew in Aprylle · that fallyt on the flour;
He cam also stylle · there his moder lay
As dew in Aprylle · that fallyt on the spray.

The lyrics of the fourteenth-century mystic Richard Rolle lie outside the scope of this chapter.

The Secular Lyric

The French lyric may be divided into *chanson courtois* and *chanson populaire*. The former is the sophisticated poetry invented by the troubadours as vehicles for the doctrine of courtly love. The earliest troubadour is William IX, Count of Poitiers, with whom the art is born almost fully developed: in a few of his songs, written about 1100, there appear both the elaborate rhyming stanza and the language of courtesy, with analysis of the lover's emotions, emphasis on refinement and on humility, exaltation of the lady, etc., which have now become commonplaces of romantic love poetry. Courtly love was probably a literary convention from the beginning, and had little to do with social life: William IX did not have to be humble to anyone in France, and we know from other poems of his how little refined he could be in action. Either there was an earlier development of the courtly lyric in France which left no trace, or, as some scholars now think, the early troubadours took over both technique and doctrine from the more advanced civilization of the Arabs. At its worst, Provençal poetry is full of sterile jargon; at its best, as in a few dozen poems by Bernart de Ventadorn, it is capable of expressing precise and delicate shades of feeling, especially of joy and despair. From the troubadours this art spread to Northern France and then to Germany (the Minnesingers) and to Italy (Dante and the *dolce stil nuovo*). In England we have only a few examples of courtly lyric, nearly all of them to be found in the Leominster Manuscript collection of the early fourteenth century. Even these are not purely courtly; some seem to have been written by clerics, as do the religious lyrics in the same collection; and some are closer to folk-song than to Provençal

1. as, 2. where.

rhetoric. They often show the native English habit of alliterating ('Lenten is come with love to town').

Yet the stanza-forms, phrases, and ideas of the troubadours re-appear: there are the same openings which invoke the spring, the same analyses of unrequited love; the poem in which the lover wishes he were a bird ('Between her curtel and her smock I would been hid') has a counterpart in Provençal. Sometimes the figures of speech escape from cliché into direct observation of Nature: the lady is whiter than the morning milk, the lover lies awake like water in a troubled pool, or, when rejected, falls like mud from a lifted foot.

Chanson populaire is objective where *chanson courtois* is subjective; as is usual in folk-song, the situation is described rather than the poet's feelings. In the thirteenth century the northern French produced literary imitations of various kinds of folk-song: the song of the lovers' separation at dawn; the 'pastourelle', originally a shepherd's song; the 'reverdie', which celebrates the return of spring; the com-plaint of the ill-wed wife (Gaston Paris derives this from the licentious songs of women at the rites of spring); the lament of the nun, and so on. Their forms are based on the simple dance-song with refrain, rather than on the elaborate rhyme-schemes of the troubadours. In a common pattern, the poet rides out one morning and meets a shepherdess or overhears a pair of country lovers or a woman com-plaining of her husband (*chanson d'aventure*). This poetry was also imitated in England: the famous 'Sumer is icumen in' is a 'reverdie', probably based on a dance-song, though its music is rather sophisti-cated. A pleasant lyric of the early fourteenth century has the spring setting in its refrain ('Now springs the spray; All for love I am so sick That sleepen I ne may') and begins like a *chanson d'aventure*.

> Als I me rode this endre dai
> O my pleyinge
> Seih I hwar a litel mai
> Began to singge[1]

This form in turn was imitated for religious lyrics, which often began 'As I rode out ...'

Many lyrics of this kind are fragmentary, often jotted down in the

1. 'As I rode out a day or two ago, In sport, I saw where a little maid Began to sing.'

margin of a manuscript. The purest examples of some types of *chanson populaire* can found in Scotland: the 'pastourelle' in Henryson's *Robene and Makyne* and the ill-wed wife in Dunbar's riotous *Tua Mariit Wemen and the Wedo*; the more primitive forms survive in the periphery of a cultural area. The secular lyric, courtly and popular, flourished only sporadically in England in the thirteenth and early fourteenth centuries, from the lack of an audience interested in the refinements of *amour courtois*. Chaucer was the first poet to have such an audience: and he broke away from the troubadour conventions, taking as a model instead the later and very different French lyric, and introducing a new version of the courtly doctrine into English poetry.

The Carol

The most original and fruitful development of the English lyric came about in the fifteenth century with the carol. The word had at first no connexion with Christmas or even with religion; it is derived from *carole*, or dancing-song. Dancing in the Middle Ages had a connexion with popular fertility rites, and as such was denounced as pagan superstition. In the *carole*, probably, the leader sang the stanza while the chorus danced round in a circle and all marked time in place while they sang the refrain. There seems to have been two kinds of dancing: from one developed the ballad with its alternating refrain, and from the other the carol with its separate refrain or 'burden', often of three or more lines, rhyme-linked with the stanza. Many of the Early English lyrics, both courtly and popular, possess this burden; for example, 'Now springs the spray', and 'Icham of Irlonde'.

Secular and amorous carols were written throughout the fifteenth century and even by Henry VIII and Wyatt; but the most striking growth was in the Christmas carol. Again, the Franciscans are closely associated with this spiritualization of a worldly form, and there was a special reason for their efforts. At Christmas the challenge of paganism was at its strongest, and before the Reformation there were large numbers of survivals of ancient Yule customs, such as the wassail, the eating of the boar, the hunting of the wren, hobbyhorses, mock kings, holly and ivy, ritual gifts, and, above all, the singing of improper songs, each with its ritual significance. There is a rich cluster of carols around the holly and ivy theme, some introducing primitive motifs.

There are others about the boar's head, like the one still sung at the Queen's College, Oxford. Many of the fifteenth-century carols have little beyond folkloric interest, but there are a few of great beauty, such as the macaronic Christmas song, 'There is no rose of such virtue As is the rose that bare Jesu'; the *Corpus Christi* carol on the Grail theme, with its obscure but moving group of images; some of the lullaby carols, and the shepherd songs ('The shepherd upon a hill he sat'). These have a grave sincerity, and are successful in presenting doctrine in dramatic and pictorial terms. Two of the best lyrics, 'The Coventry Carol' and the shepherd's song 'Hayle, comely and clene', come from dramas; and in many others there is some dramatic quality, such as the translation of abstractions into living symbols. The carols, like the satirical lyrics (for which there is no space here), are not strictly of the people; they were probably written by the minor clergy.[a] In this half-clerical, half-folkloric vein, England was particularly rich.

The Ballads

A ballad is a narrative song which bears the stamp of folklore. There are many kinds of poetry which have been called ballads – the broadside ballads of the Elizabethans, literary imitations like Coleridge's *Rime of the Ancient Mariner* – but the only ones to be discussed here are the *Traditional English and Scottish Ballads*, as collected in F. J. Child's work of that title. These ballads are short narratives, in stanzas of two or four lines, which tell their stories in a highly characteristic way; they are dramatic, using a high proportion of dialogue to stage direction, usually beginning in the fifth act and presenting the story in a series of rapid flashes which may be compared with the technique of the cinema. They are impersonal in their attitude, and there is little comment or moralizing. They are free from the rhetorical devices of most 'learned' poetry but possess a rhetoric of their own, using repetition, in threes ('He hadna gone a mile, a mile, A mile but barely three'), or in sevens ('For in will come my seventh bauld brither'), stock phrases ('the gold so red', 'the wan water'), and a stylized description of heroes and heroines – all this in common with folk-literature of other kinds and of other peoples. Their special narrative technique carries a folk-view of life, an ironic acceptance of tragedy, and a rich background of popular myth, of ghosts and fairies.

The result is often poetry of a high order, well known to many from the great anthology pieces like *Clerk Saunders*, *Edward*, and *Sir Patrick Spens*.

The ballads, like the lyrics, were sung, and they too must be taken with their musical settings. Not only does their full poetic effect come over when they are sung, but their history is only explicable by reference to the history of folk-song. Their metrical forms are essentially musical forms and their special narrative technique arises naturally from the dividing up of the story into clearly defined stanzas.

How did ballads begin? A great deal of discussion of this point has taken place, much of it to no purpose. But it has become clear that there are really two questions. The first, about the origin of the ballad *form*, and the second about the origin of the various stories found in our ballads. As for the form, the most probable explanation lies in the medieval dance-song, the *carole*. Whereas one form of *carole* with alternating solo and chorus led to the carol with its external burden, another led to the typical ballad stanza with its internal refrain.

> She laid her back against a thorn
> *Fine flowers in the valley,*
> And there she has her sweet babe born
> *And the green leaves they grow rarely.*

A number of ballads have these irrelevant refrains, which accidentally produce a striking poetic effect: the violence and cruelty of the story is ironically contrasted with the peaceful continuity of Nature. These refrains go to show that the original pattern of the ballad stanza was the non-narrative *carole*, to which at a later stage narrative words were attached. At a still later stage, when the dance-song went out of fashion, the refrain was often dropped, and the second and fourth lines were filled up with the narrative; hence the normal four-line ballad stanza.

The stories of the ballads, on the other hand, have originated in a variety of ways. Some ballads are part of the international treasury of folklore (especially the supernatural and romantic ballads); some were drawn from Arthurian and other romances by minstrels of the late Middle Ages, while minstrels must also have had a hand in the Robin Hood cycle; the Border and Aberdeenshire ballads were composed by local poets about local incidents of the sixteenth and seventeenth centuries; the more properly historical ballads are based rather on chronicles. The theory of communal composition can account for certain kinds of primitive folk-song, but not for any ballad as we know it. Ballads are comparatively late in date. *Judas* is a ballad-like religious poem of the thirteenth century and there is reason to believe that the Robin Hood cycle existed in the fourteenth century, but nothing else like a ballad is found until the fifteenth century; most are of the sixteenth century or later.

Nor are the ballads pure examples of folk-art. On the one hand they contain a great deal of folk-belief and primitive survivals (a rich body of lore about fairies and ghosts, tabu, enchantment and marvels). On the other hand, their texts have been greatly altered by printing as popular broadsides and by remaking by educated poets, mainly of the eighteenth century. The great anthology pieces like *Edward*, *Sir Patrick Spens*, *The Twa Corbies*, *Tam Lin*, *Thomas Rymer*, etc., as known to everyone in the finest versions, betray the hand of Percy's Scottish correspondents, and later of Burns and of Sir Walter Scott. When the images, narrative technique, and outlook of folk-tradition have been combined with a poet's skill, the ballads have become great poetry.

NOTE

a. The medieval religious lyric and carol can be fully appreciated only if they are seen in their relation to the liturgy and to theological instruction. Like the medieval drama and like the plastic arts, they are part of an attempt to diffuse doctrine in a popular medium, using the traditional symbolism of the Church. See Helen Waddell, *Medieval Latin Lyrics*, D. M. Anderson, *Misericords*.

THE TOWNELEY *SHEPHERDS' PLAYS*

BY JOHN SPEIRS

THE two *Shepherds' Plays* have their places in the version of the Mystery Cycle preserved in the Towneley MS. This version of the Cycle is thought to have been the one performed at Wakefield in Yorkshire. There is evidence from the three Northern texts preserved that towns borrowed and worked on one another's texts in producing their local versions of the Cycle. Several of the plays in the Wakefield Cycle appear to have been borrowed from the York Cycle, unless (as has been suggested) both York and Wakefield derived them from some parent-cycle. Though the Towneley MS. has been dated about the third quarter of the fifteenth century, it is generally thought that the version of the Cycle which it preserves had already assumed more or less the form in which we have it by the end of the first quarter of the century. Many different hands at different times appear to have worked on the making of the Wakefield Cycle, as in the making of a cathedral, adding to it and altering it; it appears to be more heterogeneous in this respect than the Chester and York Cycles.

*   *   *

The two Towneley versions of the *Shepherds' Play* are among those attributed to a single Wakefield Master; and if we are to have a Wakefield Master they are indeed sufficiently similar in texture to each other and to different plays of the group to justify their both being assigned to him. Though the second is the better known, the first seems to me quite as interesting; both are richly significant dramatic poems.

The first play begins with a monologue spoken by a First Shepherd (Gyb) on the theme of winter downfall and poverty – the theme of 'Wynter wakneth al my care'. He envies the dead; they are free from vicissitudes. All his sheep are gone, and his 'purs is bot wake'. The monologue is, however, not quite all a complaint; there is a more hopeful note in its ending. Gyb is on his way to the fair to buy more sheep. There is promise of a new abundance – at the next spring.

To the fare will I me,
To by shepe, perde,
And yit may I multyple,
    for all this hard case.

On his way to the fair he meets the Second Shepherd (John Horne)
who enters, speaking directly to the crowd at the play in a second
monologue, John Horne hails Gyb, who is apparently straying over
the corn, and the two Shepherds greet each other. They agree that
'poore men ar in the dyke'.

The strange buffoonery of the dialogue that follows is surely no
more accidental than is that of the mock-nativity – the dead sheep in
the cradle – in the second *Shepherds' Play*. It is in the unbroken tradition in which, all over the world almost, joking and buffoonery have
been associated with death; ceremonial joking (as Hocart explains[a])
often indicates 'the presence of death, real or mystical'. What gives
rise to this buffoonery appears to be the association of death and rebirth, the one presupposing the other and setting up an endless cycle.

In our present play, Gyb tells John Horne he is going to the fair to
buy sheep (his sheep, as he supposes, having all died in the winter).
Thereupon the two Shepherds quarrel about where he shall feed them,
since there is evidently not grass enough to go round. Suddenly Gyb
starts shouting like a madman at imaginary sheep, the sheep he has
not yet bought at the fair. Thus we have a farcical fantasy. In the
midst of the winter dearth, when the Shepherds have no real sheep
left – or only a few – there is suddenly all round them an illusion of
abundance, a multiplicity of phantasmal sheep. This make-believe
abundance – their own make-believe, it seems – is not there as a mockery of them in the season of deprivation. The tone is rather one of
jollity as if what is seen is a promise of the spring abundance that is
indeed certain. The buffoonery of the Shepherds is, apparently, a
significant Christmas game in this Christmas play – a game intended
perhaps magically to help to induce the abundance it pre-figures. Gyb
and John Horne shout contradictory orders at the (as yet) purely
imaginary sheep and involve themselves in a wildly farcical medley.

In the midst of the confusion the Third Shepherd, appropriately
named Slaw-pace, arrives – as the New Year itself seems to do in
winter – late. Like a chorus, he comments that here are two *old* knaves
fighting about nothing, and he compares them proverbially with

166

Moll. This Slaw-pace carries a bag on his back; but it is empty. He shakes it out in front of everyone – so that it can be seen to be quite empty – as a conjurer might do, because later out of the same empty sack will come food and drink in never-ending abundance.

A boy appears (Jack Garcio) and the contrast of Youth and Age must have been visible. He reveals that Gyb's sheep are not, apparently, lost after all. On the contrary, they are in grass to the knee. The wonder is whence comes this abundance of grass, this miracle of fertility, on a midwinter night. We may associate it with such legends as that of the cherry tree that bore fruit on Christmas Eve (for in this play it is also Christmas Eve).

Immediately following the good news that the sheep are found there is yet another apparent miracle. Although the Shepherds have complained of winter and starvation, they unexpectedly produce between them – and even out of Slaw-pace's empty bag – a sudden abundance of food and drink, a more than substantial Yule feast.

Having first asked Christ's blessing, the Shepherds sleep after the feast and are wakened by the angel – 'he spake of a barne'.

The dramatic poem ends with the Adoration of the Shepherds. Each of the three Shepherds, as he recites or sings (probably sings) his part in what is in effect a dramatic Christmas carol, presents a gift – a spruce coffer, a ball, and a bottle – to the new-born divine child. It is perhaps not too fanciful to suppose that the bottle is the very same as that out of which earlier in the play the 'holy ale' – 'boyte of oure bayll' – was drunk by the Shepherds. The gifts of the three Shepherds (as of the Three Kings) have surely some relation to the magical or otherwise rich gifts which are bestowed on a new-born child or found beside an exposed child in so many folk-tales and which often have to do with the ultimate recognition of his supernatural or royal origin and status.

* * *

Because the second Towneley *Shepherds' Play* includes the episode of the sheep-stealing, involving the characters Mak and his wife Gyll, it has been acclaimed the first English comedy; we should have to add 'the first that has chanced to be preserved'. Less than justice has been done to it as significant art, even by those who have praised it; they have praised it too simply as farce, light comic relief intruded into the old solemn Nativity Play. Instead, it needs to be insisted that the play *is* a poem.

The progression or whole movement of the play is again, as in the first *Shepherds' Play*, from winter sorrow and death to the joyful birth. The opening monologue spoken by the First Shepherd is a vigorous protest – no mere sorrowful musical complaint – against the winter distresses and oppressions suffered by the poor. The poor are oppressed not only by winter – that is bad enough – but in winter by the rich. Social grievances and vexations increase, once again not only because the social order seemed to be breaking up in the England contemporary with the play, but because it is winter, the season when the life-energies that hold all things together begin to fail; the winter world (it was traditionally believed) pre-figures the final end of all things when the world will fall into rack and ruin. This note of vigorous and robust protest against the oppression of powerful, rich, and evil men is the more readily absorbed – because it *is* vigorous and robust – in the jollity that strangely develops in the play; it seems, indeed, to reinforce the jollity into which it is finally absorbed.

The Third Shepherd (Daw) enters, and he appears to be the servant of the other two Shepherds; if they are poor, he, it seems, is still poorer. Yet the inhumanity of which they have just complained, they themselves in some measure enact; for when he begs for food and drink – he, too, is hungry in the winter – they upbraid him, as his masters, for being late. When the first two Shepherds ask him where their sheep are, Daw answers that he has left them in the corn. Because their sheep appear to be well provided for after all, the three Shepherds sing together a mirthful part-song – and to the accompaniment of the Shepherds' singing, Mak enters, and the Mak farce commences.

The central episode of the farce, the discovery of the stolen sheep in the cradle by the three Shepherds, is clearly a kind of parody of the serious subject of the whole Nativity Play, a mock-nativity. In the final episode of the whole play the new-born Christ in the cradle – probably, in the performance, the same cradle – is adored by the same Shepherds. In the farcical episode (the spirit of which is similar to that of the popular beast fables) a beast is found in the cradle:

> What the dewill is this? · he has a long snowte ...
> I never Sagh in a credyll
> A hornyd lad or now.

Finally, the infant God is found in the cradle between two beasts:

> In a cryb full poorely,
> Betwyx two bestys.

The phrase 'little day starne' is first used by one of the Shepherds of what he supposes to be Mak's child and the audience knows to be the sheep; the same phrase is later in the play used of the Christ child (as, indeed, it is commonly used in the carols of the Christ child).

The 'hornyd lad' in the cradle has certainly a still more particular significance. He can be none other than the 'horned god' – the God incarnated as goat or sheep, bull or stag – whose worship continued throughout medieval Britain[b]. The buffoonery in this play – the buffoonery of the dead sheep in the cradle – once again (as in the first Towneley *Shepherds' Play*) indicates the presence of death and birth in their age-old association. There is probably no irreverence to the Christian religion intended. The mock-nativity does not appear to be introduced in the mocking spirit of scepticism. The boisterousness of the Mak farce as a whole, culminating in the tossing of Mak in a blanket, may rather be interpreted as an expression of the jollity of the folk as the rebirth significance of the midwinter festival overcomes the death significance. As the consciousness of the distress of winter is absorbed into the boisterousness of the farce, so the latter in its turn is finally absorbed into the joyous wonder of the Adoration of the Shepherds. The movement of the dramatic poem is from the winter sorrow of the opening monologue, through the boisterous jollity of the Mak farce, into this final reverent joy and wonder. The Mak farce – including the mock-nativity – is thus not finally incongruous with the whole play as a Nativity Play, but indeed contributes to a total complex harmony. The boisterous jollity is resolved or transmuted into this more complete joy as the *Gloria in excelsis* is sung. We who read are apt not to appreciate what would have been the effect of this singing.

Though Mak first enters to the accompaniment of the mirthful singing of the Shepherds, the farce commences, on the part of Mak himself, on a note of distress that corresponds with that of the opening of the play. He breaks into a fit of boasting and *flyting*, like the antagonists in the Mummers' Play or like Herod or Pilate elsewhere

in the Mystery Cycle; he declares that he is a yeoman of the king and
'sond from a greatt lordyng'; but the Shepherds recognize him and
suspect him of being a thief. He is the wild man of the moor – 'a man
that walkys on the moore' – and also (in relation to the Christian part
of the significance) perhaps the unregenerate Adam whom Christ is
born to redeem. He would cheat his neighbours for the sake of a dinner for himself, his wife, and his too-numerous progeny. But he also
suffers the common lot of poor men in winter, he also is hungry; he
is as much the oppressed as he is the oppressor. Though he is a rogue,
he is (like Autolycus in *A Winter's Tale*) a merry rogue. He risks
hanging; yet, perhaps because he provides merriment, the worst that
actually happens in the end, when he is exposed, is that he is tossed in
a blanket, as if it were a Christmas game – as indeed it *is*. Thus there
is no tragedy to mar the good-humoured mirth of Christmas, and the
element of jollity achieves a boisterous victory in the play.

There follows the episode in which Mak, who is something of a
magician, pronounces a spell over the Shepherds and puts them into a
deep sleep. Meanwhile Mak and his wife Gyll devise the ruse of
swaddling the stolen sheep and putting it in the cradle. The sleepers
now wake severally ('*Resurrix a mortuis!*' exclaims the First Shepherd
awaking). Almost their first concern is as to the whereabouts of Mak,
whom, it is clear, they do not trust, and they set about counting their
sheep. In the subsequent developments of the farce there are two
'discoveries' made by the Shepherds, the first of the loss of a sheep,
the second of the sheep in the cradle. The buffoonery of the sheep lost
and found – found in a cradle – corresponds, at the farcical level, to
the death-and-birth theme of the play as a whole. (At the highest and
most serious level, the daughter lost and found in *A Winter's Tale*,
Pericles, and *Lear*, has a corresponding symbolical meaning.)

To the accompaniment of Mak singing a lullaby and Gyll groaning
as in childbirth, the three Shepherds arrive to seek their lost sheep. All
that the Shepherds can find in Mak's cottage are 'bot two tome platers'
that have plainly the significance in this play that, in the first *Shepherds' Play*, Slaw-pace's empty bag has.

Just when, at the departure of the Shepherds, the suspense has re-
laxed and the audience has begun to draw breath again, the Shepherds
return – a well-managed dramatic surprise – and make the discovery
of the sheep in the cradle:

FIRST SHEPHERD. Gaf ye the chyld any thyng?
SECOND SHEPHERD. I trow not oone farthyng.
THIRD SHEPHERD. Fast agane will I flyng,
      Abyde ye me there.
  Mak, take it to no grefe · if I com to thi barne.
MAK. Nay, thou dos me greatt represe · and fowll has thou farne.
THIRD SHEPHERD. The child will it not grefe · that lytyll day starne.
  Mak, with youre leyfe · let me gyf youre barne,
      Bot sex pence.
MAK. Nay, do way: · he slepys.
THIRD SHEPHERD. Me thynk he pepys.
MAK. When he wakyns he wepys.
     I pray you go hence.
THIRD SHEPHERD. Gyf me lefe hym to kys · and lyft up the clowtt.
  What the dewill is this? · He has a long snowte.

Yet Gyll persists in maintaining that the sheep is not a sheep but her child – 'A pratty child is he as syttys on a woman's kne'. In this mock nativity in which Gyll comically corresponds to, or pre-figures, Mary, there is the suggestion, if not of a miraculous birth, at least of a supernatural occurrence; her child (Gyll claims) has been metamorphosed by an elf:

> He was takyn with an elfe,
> I saw it myself.
> When the clok stroke twelf
> Was he forshapyn.

The farce attains its climax with the tossing of Mak in the air – a death in terms of buffoonery. The change or transformation in the play thereupon comes about with the Angel's singing of the *Gloria in excelsis* and the Shepherds' wondering recognition that 'He spake of a barne'. They marvel that the new-born Saviour is 'poorly arayd' and comes 'to so poore as we ar'. He is the Saviour of all mankind – of the poor above all. Thus the note of the distresses of the poor in the opening of the play finds its response towards the close. The play concludes, as does the first Play, with the Adoration of the Shepherds. The natural human tenderness towards a child is expressed and is at the same time hallowed by the recognition that this child is God. The three Shepherds approach each with a gift – a 'bob of cherys', a bird, and a ball:

Lo, he merys;
Lo, he laghys, my swetyng,
A welfare metyng,
I have holden my hetyng;
    Have a bob of cherys. ...
Hayll! I kneyll and I cowre, A byrd have I broght
    To my barne.
Hayll, lytyll tyne mop!
Of oure crede thou art crop:
I wold drynk on thy cop,
    Lytyll day starne. ...
Hayll! put furth thy dall!
I bryng the bot a ball:
Have and play the with all,
    And go to the tenys.

We should not jump to the conclusion that 'go to the tenys' is naïvety on the part of the Shepherd, that he is unconscious of such a remark being incongruous to a new-born infant. On the contrary, it is surely intended as this Shepherd's conscious humour. It has been far too easily assumed that everything in these plays is naïve.

NOTES

a. A. M. Hocart, *Kingship*.
b. See the evidence assembled by Miss Margaret Murray in *The God of the Witches*.

TWO SCOTS POETS:
DUNBAR AND HENRYSON

BY PATRICK CRUTTWELL

Professor of English, the University of the West Indies, Jamaica

OF Dunbar's life we know almost nothing. He was born about 1460 and had died by 1513. He lived in and wrote for the court of James IV; his life was that of a court-poet at a court, which it would seem, had little use for poetry. His verse shows all the uneasiness, the spiritual discomfort and self-disgust, the financial anxieties, the bitter brew of envy and contempt for those more favoured, which seem the inevitable lot of the artist who must be also a courtier. Sometimes he is familiar and jaunty; sometimes envious, disgruntled, and melancholy; sometimes obsequious and mendicant; sometimes 'polished' and artificial. His work, though its compass is comparatively small, is as varied, as his personality.

Within it, there are immediately apparent two styles, two dictions; one could almost say, so great is the difference, two poets. The one is ornate, artificial, and English; the other colloquial, natural, and Scottish. Of the former, the two allegorical poems *The Goldyn Targe* and *The Thrissill and the Rois*, are the most complete examples. In one thing, at least, these poems are remarkable: they succeed in enclosing, in small compass, virtually every commonplace of their age and *genre*, the allegorical poem of the Middle Ages. They are both dreams, both dreamed on a May morning. Both use a quasi-religious language; both assemble companies of mythological personalities; both draw up lists of allegorical abstractions. Both, above all other resemblances, are written in that medieval 'poetic diction' which is just as lifeless and conventional as the worst that the eighteenth century can show and which, indeed, in many ways resembles it. 'Fresh anamalit termes celicall' is Dunbar's own phrase for it (praising Chaucer in the *Goldyn Targe*) – 'anamalit' (*enamelled*) is one of his favourite epithets when he writes in this style. 'Naturis nobil fresh anamalyng'; 'anam-

173

alit was the felde wyth all colouris'; 'annamyll it richely with new asur lycht' – these are all from these two poems. And the word is unintentionally appropriate: this diction *is* like enamel, applied from above, rootless, indiscriminate. It abounds in repetitive clichés. 'Quhois[1] armony to heir it wes delyt' says *The Thrissill and the Rois* of the birds' singing, and 'quhat throu the mery foulys armony' answers *The Goldyn Targe*. In the latter also, when 'Omer' and 'Tullius' are praised, it is for their 'lippis suete' and their 'aureate tongis'; Lydgate and Gower, a somewhat dissimilar pair, have 'sugurit lippis and tongis aureate'. In such a diction, fixed and prefabricated, living poetry can hardly be made. Its essential method and fatal effect is to reduce the natural to the artificial, as do these lines of *The Goldyn Targe*, which imprison the living world in the compass of a jeweller's shop:

> The cristall air, the sapher firmament,
> The ruby skyes of the orient,
>> Kest beriall[2] bemes on emerant bewis[3] grene;
> The rosy garth depaynt and redolent
> With purpur, azure, gold, and [4]goulis gent. ...

The modern reader may be reminded of Yeats's cock in *Sailing to Byzantium*, made 'of hammered gold or gold enamelling' – symbol of the dead life of 'artifice', set against the true life of the 'salmon-falls, the mackerel-crowded seas'. Such lines remind one of the 'quaint enamelled eyes' of Milton's flowers in *Lycidas*, and then of Gray's 'Idalia's velvet-green'; and the latter recalls the comment it evoked from Dr Johnson, which will stand as the final judgement on all such writing, be it Augustan or medieval: 'An epithet or metaphor drawn from nature ennobles art; an epithet or metaphor drawn from art degrades nature'.

It is not in such writing that the greatness of Dunbar makes its true contribution, but in his other style, in the 'colloquial, natural, and Scottish'. An analysis of one poem in this style will have to stand for all; I have chosen the *Tretis of the Tua Mariit Wemen and the Wedo* because it is perhaps the finest of all his poems, and it is certainly the most remarkable. There is nothing like it in the language. It cannot be denied, though, that the general reader of the twentieth century may not, at first sight, find it attractive. For this, three reasons may be

1. whose; qu = w, 2. beryl, 3. boughs, 4. beautiful gules.

suggested. The language is, or seems to be, somewhat more 'crabbed' and obscure than that of the average of Dunbar's writings; the alliterative unrhymed metre is strange to modern ears; above all, the tone and intention are apt to be wrongly taken. For the language, it need only be said that in this poem Dunbar is not using the cosmopolitan poetic diction I have glanced at above, but the full colloquial resources of his native Scots. The metre is that alliterative line most familiar to us through *Piers Plowman* and *Sir Gawayne and the Grene Knight*. This poem is one of the latest known examples of the metre; but it is clear that the line survived, as a lively form and not a self-conscious archaism, much later in the North than it did in the South.

The *Tretis* describes a conversation between two married women and a widow; all three, thoroughly tipsy, and increasingly so as the poem proceeds, relate with alcoholic frankness their matrimonial experiences. Marriage, for them, is nothing but a means of securing sexual satisfaction; and all of them are, or have been, bitterly disappointed by their husbands' sexual capacities. The first is married to an old man, the second to a worn-out lecher, and the third, the widow, has had, first, a dotard and, second, a merchant, her inferior in all things but money. The theme of the poem was possibly suggested by the *Wyf of Bathes Prologue*; but the difference between them is radical: the poems differ as their personae differ. Dunbar's women have none of the Wife of Bath's genial tolerance; they are creatures savage in their frustration and primitive in their lust. The whole poem, indeed, under its comic surface, is a terrible creation.

It is also a satirical creation. It cannot be understood unless it is seen to contain a great deal of *parody*; to be, indeed, in a certain sense, a parody as a whole. Two things are parodied: the literary pastoral idealism, so dear to part of the medieval mind and exploited so mechanically (in the allegorical poems) by Dunbar himself, and the great medieval convention of courtliness and courtly love.

The parody of the former is rendered by the poem's setting. It begins and ends with passages, beautiful and lyrical in themselves, evoking the ideal beauty of nature and the 'literary' mood that traditionally accompanied it:

> Appon the Midsummer evin, · mirriest of nichtis,
> I muvit furth allane, · neir as midnicht wes past,

Besyd ane gudlie grein garth, · full of gay flouris,
Hegeit[1], of ane huge hicht, · with hawthorne treis:
Quhairon ane bird, on ane branshe, · so burst out hir notis,
That never ane blythfullar bird · was on the beuche[2] harde:
Quhat throw the sugarat sound · of hir sang glaid,
And throw the savour sanative · of the sueit flouris,
I drew me in derne[3] to the sky · to dirkin[4] efter mirthis;
The dew donkit[5] the daill, · and dynnit[6] the feulis.

(1–10)

So it opens; and it ends in the same 'aureate' style:

The morow myld wes and meik, · the mavis did sing,
And all remuffit[7] the myst, · and the meid smellit;
Silver shouris doune shuke · as the shene cristall,
And berdis shoutit in shaw · with their shill notis.

(513–16)

The language of these passages, with their 'sugarat sound' and 'silver shouris', is clearly akin to the 'anamalit termes' of the two allegorical poems; the word itself appears in the introductory passage: 'nature full nobillie annamalit with flouris'. But the language and the content that come between these framing passages are very different. This is the first wife describing her husband:

I have ane wallifrag[8], ane worme, · ane auld wobat[9] carle,
A waistit wolroun[10], na worth · but wourdes to clatter;
Ane bumbart, ane dron bee, · ane bag full of flewme,
Ane skabbit skarth[11], ane scorpioun, · ane scutarde behind;
To see him scart[12] his awin skyn · grit scunner[13] I think.

(89–93)

So, too, with the looks of the ladies themselves. They, like the landscape, are rendered with stylized idealism, in ironic contrast with the stories they tell:

I saw thre gay ladeis · sit in ane grene arbeir,
All grathit[14] into garlandis · of freshe gudlie flouris;
So glitterit as the gold · wer thair glorius gilt tressis,
Quhill all the gressis did gleme · of the glaid bewis;
Kemmit[15] was thair cleir hair, · and curiouslie shed
Attour thair shulderis doun shyre[16], · syhning full bricht …

1. hedged, 2. branch, 3. secret, 4. listen, 5. moistened, 6. made noise, 7. removed, 8. sloven, 9. caterpillar, 10. boar, 11. cormorant, 12. scratch, 13. disgust, 14. decked, 15. combed, 16. clear.

Of ferliful[1] fyne favour · war thair faceis meik,
All full of [2]flurist fairheid, · as flou is in June;
Quhyt, seimlie, and soft, · as the sweit lillies
New upspred upon spray, · as new spynist[3] rose.

(17–29)

Parody, again, is the opening of the widow's speech, the most out-
rageous and immoral of the three; she begins with the pious unction
of a sermon's exordium:

Now tydis me for to talk; · my taill it is nixt;
God my spreit now inspir · and my speche quykkin,
And send me sentence to say, · substantious and noble;
Sa that my preching may pers · your perverst hertis,
And mak yow mekar to men · in maneris and conditiouns.

(246–50)

With all these parodies, the stage is set for the mockery of courtliness and courtly love. Here the third speaker, the widow, is the main
means of making the satirical effect. She claims for herself the qualities and virtues of courtliness (her claims, of course, are totally nega-
tived by her actual behaviour). She despises her second husband not
only for his amorous feebleness, but also because he is a mere merchant, below her in birth:

The severance wes meikle[4]
Betwix his bastard blude · and my birth noble.

(311–12)

And she claims also the virtue of pity, the proper virtue of the conventional Lady adored by conventional Lover:

Bot mercy in to womanheid · is a mekle vertu,
For never bot in a gentil hert · is generit ony ruth.

(315–16)

The irony of that is given force by the fact that the last line goes
straight to the centre of its target, echoes, and in its context ridicules,
one of the central sayings of courtly love. It derives from Chaucer's
'pity renneth soon in gentil hert'; that comes from Dante's 'amor, che
in cor gentil ratto s'apprende'; both go back to Provence and the
deepest roots of the whole tradition. The satire is both moral and

1. wonderful, 2. blooming beauty, 3. blown, 4. much.

social, for the meaning of 'gentil' hovered between gentle and genteel. It is not only the hypocrisy of one woman that Dunbar is here satirizing; he is commenting also on the gulf between the courtly idealism and the reality of flesh-and-blood women. (The reality itself is caricatured, to match what it exposes; the women are turned into creatures not much more than animals.) It is satire in exactly the spirit of Donne's:

> Love's not as pure, and abstract, as they use
> To say, who have no Mistresse but their Muse

– a collocation which may serve to remind us both that Donne is largely medieval and that the Middle Ages carried within themselves the criticisms of their own extravagances.

What the women represent, positively, is the life of the natural body, rebellious against any restraint, whether of Church or of society. On this the first speaker is the most explicit:

> It is agane the law of lufe, · of kynd, and of nature,
> Togiddir hairtis to strene · that stryveis with uther;
> Birdis hes ane better law · ¹na bernis be meikill,
> That ilk yeir, with new joy, · joyis ane maik,
> And fangis² thame ane freshe feyr³, · unfulyeit⁴, and constant,
> And lattis thair fulyeit feiris · flie quhair thei pleis.
> ⁵Crist gif sic ane consuetude · war in this kith haldin!
>
> (58–64)

Again one is reminded of Donne, of the remarkably close parallel in *Confined Love*:

> Are birds divorced, or are they chidden,
> If they leave their mate, or lie abroad a night?
> Beasts doe no joyntures lose,
> Though they new lovers choose,
> But we are made worse then those.

But, whatever Donne may have felt about it, Dunbar shows no sympathy for the attitude he is dramatically rendering: much less than Chaucer shows for *his* young girl who is married to a dotard, in the *Marchantes Tale*. Chaucer is Shakespearean in his balancing of

1. 'than men, by much', 2. gets, 3. lover, 4. untired, 5. 'If only human beings had a custom like that!'

irony and sympathy; Dunbar, who is a real Scot, fiercer, narrower, more doctrinaire, degrades his women's 'naturalness' to utter animalism. Animal comparisons abound: worm, caterpillar, boar, dronebee, cormorant, scorpion are in the five lines (cited above) with which the first woman begins her description of her husband; and when he makes love, she tells us, he fidgets like a sick cart-horse lusting for a mare ('he fepillis like a farcy · aver that flyrit one a gillot'). The husband of the other wife

> dois as dotit[1] dog · that damys[2] on all bussis[3],
> And liftis his leg apone loft, · thoght he nought list pishe.
> (186–7)

And the widow, having established her sovereignty over her second man, compares herself with a cock crowing in triumph:

> I crew abone that craudone[4], · as cok that wer victour.
> (326)

The women are dominant throughout; the reversal of sex in that line (woman likened to cock) is surely intentional. The men are nothing but the humble (and inadequate) servitors of their lusts: a point that is rammed home by the consistent use of the word 'courage' (what should be the male prerogative) with the meaning of virility – and its equally consistent degradation:

> He has a luke without lust, · and lif without curage.
> (188)

> Wariand[5] oft my wekit kyn · that me away cast
> To sic a [6]craudoune but curage, · that knyt my cler bewte.
> (214–15)

This meaning gives to the ending a particular irony:

> The sweit savour of the sward · and singing of foulis,
> Myght confort ony creatur · of the kyn of Adam,
> And kindill again his curage, · thocht it were [7]cald sloknyt.
> (520–2)

It is a dubious renewal for the 'kin of Adam', whose inadequate 'courage' the whole poem has been exposing. The poetic convention,

1. foolish, 2. makes water, 3. bushes, 4. craven, 5. cursing, 6. craven without, 7. extinguished cold.

a bodiless worshipping of all-pure Lady by adoring Lover, is thus reversed and animalized; the result is not far from the spirit of Swift (the last book of *Gulliver*), but preserved from the anarchy of Swift's negation. The parallel is closer with those passages of *King Lear* which strip mankind down to the 'poor, bare, forked animal' – with lines like these:

> Behold yond simpering dame,
> Whose face between her forks presages snow,
> That minces virtue, and does shake the head
> To hear of pleasure's name –
> The fitchew nor the soiled horse goes to 't,
> With a more riotous appetite ...

Dunbar, like Shakespeare, has his positives; implied in this poem, they are explicit in others. In these lines, for instance (they come from the ode *Of the Nativitie of Christ*):

> Now spring up flouris fra the rute,
> Revert yow upwart naturaly,
> In honour of the blissit frute
> That rais up fro the rose Mary.

By the 'naturaly' of those lines, by their unforced, unselfconscious assimilating of the religious and miraculous Nativity to its natural and seasonal equivalent, the degraded 'law of nature' as preached and practised by the 'tua mariit wemen and the wedo' is judged and condemned. The life of the fields and the life of devotion, in the time of Dunbar, were not yet hostile to each other, for all the strivings of ascetics to make them enemies; but for Burns, some two hundred and fifty years later, the Kirk stood as *opponent* of Nature, a negative and bodiless force in face of which the life of the body was furtive and guilty – or else (the obverse of the same medal) uneasily defiant. Hence, when Dunbar is bawdy, his bawdiness is never distorted by self-consciousness or poisoned by self-justifying, as it is sometimes with Burns. Though Dunbar himself, it would seem, was a dissatisfied, melancholy, restless individual, yet the age he lived in, though standing on the edge of chaos, still held together and held him with it.

Henryson, the man, is known even less than Dunbar. He lived in the second half of the fifteenth century, was 'chief schoolmaster in Dunfermline', and was dead by 1508. His work comprises a number of short poems, mostly devotional, of no great merit; one pastoral (*Robene and Makyne*) of real charm; and two major works, the *Morall Fabillis* and the *Testament of Cresseid*. To these two this study will be confined.

The *Morall Fabillis* consist of thirteen animal-fables. Most, though not all, are taken from Aesop; with the modesty incumbent upon a medieval author, Henryson represents his work as a mere translation, but he is, in fact, as original as Shakespeare: like him, he takes the bare bones and nothing else. The Fables are completely re-created; they emerge as a product conceivable only in the time and place that produced them, in medieval Scotland; and in them, better than in any other work of art, its life is preserved. A first reading will probably pick out the obvious qualities: the life and quickness of narrative, the charm of personal details, and the wealth of discursive comment. But of Henryson as of Chaucer it can be said that the picturesque detail owes its effectiveness to the solidity and seriousness of what it grows from. Henryson's Fables (like La Fontaine's – they deserve the comparison) do more than present types of human beings in animal guises and animals comically behaving like human beings; they build up a total and consistent *society*, both rendered and criticized. The types of humanity are shown in their relationships as well as their individualities; they form the particular pattern of the society that Henryson lived in.

At the basis of this society stands the peasant. Him the Fables observe with detail and accuracy, and with sympathy and anger for the hardness of his lot. Henryson's comment is often political, often stinging in its denunciations of the peasant's oppressors; but it springs from a feeling more primitive than politics. Throughout the Fables the sense of the rural life, the agricultural process, is deeply felt, far more deeply than it is by Dunbar, who has by comparison an urban mind. No one could call Henryson – as one might call, for instance, the author of *Piers Plowman* – a revolutionary mind. His conclusions are thoroughly orthodox: prayer, resignation, and hopes of a better world. He accepts the hierarchical structure of society, and has nothing but contempt for those who would climb above their stations –

La Fontaine, once more, comes to mind, for that conclusion is also his:

> Le monde est plein de gens qui ne sont pas plus sages;
> Tout bourgeois veut bâtir comme les grands seigneurs;
> Tout petit prince a des ambassadeurs;
> Tout marquis veut avoir des pages.

Kindness and common sense, conformity in fundamentals and outspoken criticism of details, acceptance of authority and sympathy with the victims of its abuse: these are Henryson's qualities as a social commentator, and all shot through with a deep, unobtrusive Christianity. The words of the mouse, pleading with the lion –

> Quhen Rigour sittis in the Tribunall,
> The equitie of Law quha may sustene?
> Richt few or nane, but[1] mercie gang betwene,

give the essence of Christian doctrine, that God's mercy outweighs strict justice and is greater than man deserves: the essence which Renaissance and Reformation alike left untouched, to appear in Hamlet's 'use every man after his desert, and who should scape whipping?' and in Isabella's words in *Measure for Measure*:

> Why, all the souls that were were forfeit once,
> And he that might the vantage best have took,
> Found out the remedy.

Here, as elsewhere, there is a real kinship with Chaucer. Henryson leaves an impression somewhat similar to Chaucer's, of a man who has no deep quarrel with his world and no real difference with the ideas of his age, and who did not find it too difficult to love his fellow-creatures, but who was not made complacent, unobservant, or uncritical by his conformity and his tolerance. He is, in fact, the only 'Scottish Chaucerian' who is at all like Chaucer, and he is so by a genuine temperamental affinity much more than by literary discipleship.

The affinity is no less clear, but the discipleship is clearer, when we turn from the Fables to the *Testament of Cresseid*. It is, of course, a platitude of literary criticism that there is no plainer proof of true

---

1. unless.

originality than the ability to borrow and learn from another writer, especially a greater one, without becoming lost in his shadow. As Mr Speirs has observed in his Literary Survey in this volume, Chaucer's great poem is the springboard for Henryson's; the emotional power which Chaucer has given to his heroine and her story is there for Henryson to exploit and develop. This he does, in his own way. He begins with an introduction which is no formal and separate Prologue in the usual medieval mode, but merges with the story in a miracle of artistic skill, and prepares for it with a subtle interplay of resemblances and contrasts and hinted forebodings. The first lines warn us, with the bitter weather foreshadowing the tragic tale:

> Ane doolie[1] sessoun [2]till ane cairfull dyte
> Suld correspond, and be equivalent.
> Richt sa it was quhen I began to wryte
> This tragedie ...

The stars also forbode it; for Venus, whom Cresseid has displeased and by whom she is punished, is dominant in the sky; she rises 'in opposition' to Phoebus, god of tenderness and comfort, as she is to rise against Cresseid. The author would pay his tribute of prayer to her in the fields; but the cold drives him in and his own age restrains him, setting him free from the passions of the young, 'of quhome the blude is flowing in ane rage' (as it flowed in Cresseid and Troilus). So much for the correspondences: then comes the contrast – a picture, delightful in its domestic snugness, of the middle-aged bachelor (so he would seem, for he 'does' for himself), saved, as he hopes, like Horace, from Venus's attentions, making himself comfortable with a fire, a drink, and a book. And the book is Chaucer's poem:

> Writtin be worthie Chaucer glorious
> Of fair Cresseid, and worthie Troilus.

Suave mari magno – it is the Lucretian explanation of why tragedy appeals to us: but Henryson has no Epicurean indifference to the sufferings of others. He is a thoroughly Christian writer, and the *Testament* is one of the most Christian of poems, although (or because) it is quite devoid of preaching. Its keynote is set at once, in the first of the few comments that the author allows himself:

> I have pietie thou suld fall sic mischance.

1. dismal, 2. 'to a tragic tale'.

'Pity' and 'piety' have the same root: in Henryson's language, as in his mind, they are virtually the same. The *Testament* is an exercise in Christian pity for sinners and unfortunates. It has its 'moral', if such is desired: Cresseid, before her punishment, blames the gods:

> O fals Cupide, is name to wyte[1] bot thow

but after it, she recognizes her own responsibility:

> Nane but myself as now I will accuse.

The mood is one of pity and resignation; the language and mode of narrative are appropriately restrained. The poem is a masterpiece in the art of leaving unsaid; its greatest moments are lines or phrases of almost Dantesque bareness and brevity:

> Quhen Diomeid had all his appetyte,
> And mair, fulfillit of this fair ladie ...

The two words 'and mair' suggest a terrible weight of satiety and humiliation. So, in the passage describing the grief of Cresseid and her father, when she has been smitten with leprosy:

> Thus was thair cair aneuch betwix thame twane

the love between the two is very quietly, very movingly realized; her overwhelming shame ('Father, I wald not be kent') and his complete lack of reproachfulness when she comes back to him disgraced:

> 'Welcum to me, thou art full deir ane gest'

are certainly reminiscent – it may be deliberately – of the father's welcome to the prodigal son: but the parallel is not enforced. In all the dramatic moments of the story, the effect is clinched by such restraint and brevity; in the climax of the whole, when Troilus in full knightly splendour ('with greit tryumphe and laude victorious') meets but does not know Cresseid the begging leper, the essence of the episode is given in the plain concluding statement:

> And nevertheless not ane ane uther knew.

This sober tension is now and then relieved: by the vivid and some-

---

1. blame.

times humorous pageant of the seven planets; by an occasional striking detail, such as this line, brilliant in aural and visual beauty:

> Cupide the King ringand ane silver bell

and by one passage, perhaps the only one, in which full eloquence
rises from the prevailing control:

> Nocht is your fairnes bot ane faiding flour,
> Nocht is your famous laud and hie honour
> But wind inflat in uther mennis eiris.
> Your roising reid to rotting sall retour ...

In subtlety of characterization, Henryson does not try, or need, to
rival Chaucer; his heroine is 'given' him by his forerunner, and he
does not try to change her. But his grasp of the original has the flexible sureness of life; he can modify his Cresseid to fit the situation of
his own poem, more utterly tragic than any in Chaucer's, and this he
can do with no awkwardness and no incongruity. Neither dramatic
irony nor psychological insight are beyond his powers when he needs
them. There is irony when the 'chyld' reports to Cresseid that her
father wonders why she is praying so long – 'the goddis wait (*know*)',
says he, 'all your intent full weill' – for the gods have already decided
her fate and awarded her her punishment: she knows it, though her
father does not, yet. And for insight, one may cite the sudden cry
with which she breaks off the making of her 'testament':

> O Diomeid, thou hes baithe Broche and Belt,
> Quhilk Troylus gave me in takning[1]
> Of his trew lufe ...

Such things are enough to avoid the monotony that unrelieved
soberness might bring with it; the poem stands as one of the most
moving, and most completely accomplished, in the canon of medieval
English.

1. token.

MORALITY TRADITION AND
THE INTERLUDES

BY L. A. CORMICAN

St Patrick's College, Ottawa

ANY genuine interest in the Moralities must be based on their intrinsic qualities and not merely on their value as antiquarian documents or as forerunners of the Elizabethan achievement. Modern pro-
ductions of them, especially of *The Summoning of Everyman* and of
The Three Estates, have demonstrated their present-day effectiveness
even to audiences with no special knowledge of the medieval world.
Like *Macbeth*, they do not depend, as plays, on an acceptance of the
beliefs they suppose. By transcending contemporary interests, their
presentation of human nature is of permanent literary and dramatic
value. In one way, the background knowledge necessary to understand them is very small. Those of them which, like *The Three Estates*,
describe contemporary conditions, deal with human frailties and
abuses of wealth and power which are as old as human society. The
most typical, and in some ways the best, of them, *Everyman*, makes
no allusion to contemporary events or persons. The two plays just
mentioned, by representing fairly adequately the varieties and the
common characteristics found within the Morality *genre*, form a
suitable introduction to the whole group.

Drama derives its general qualities from the age in which it is written. The age of the Moralities was one in which religion (with both
its creed of belief and its code of conduct) was an integral part of communal life, and not only influenced work and play, but was itself an
important form of re-creation. Despite surviving elements of paganism, deep strains of coarseness and indecency, and the refusal of many
to follow Christian principles, Christianity was without any serious
rival in its profound and pervasive influence on life. The ordinary
carpenter or weaver (who was a listener rather than a reader) brought
much the same attitude to a sermon as to a Morality; in and out of
church, he was prepared for both learned theological terms and for
the salty, racy language of lively conversation. Like his descendants

today, he preferred stories with a happy ending. But his religion taught him to think in terms of a really conclusive ending, the end of life and of time itself, which ushers in a happy world without end. However prompted the folk may have been in their unhappy lot to look forward to a blissful eternity, their hope did not proceed from mere naïvety or gullibility.

The plays suppose an audience with a fair knowledge of a complex doctrine on the nature of God and of man's relation to him. Far from being merely ingenuous edification, the plays present concretely the ancient problem of the final outcome of man's conduct, of man's attempt to discover and do the right. If they seem over-simplified to the modern reader, that is largely because we find it hard to remember the whole creed of belief from which the code of conduct derives its meaning. A brief reference today to curative drugs or aviation supposes somewhere the existence of a vast knowledge of medicine or physics; in somewhat the same manner, the brief statements in *Everyman* suppose many of the complexities of medieval theology. The basic doctrines are traced firmly and clearly in the opening statements which present God as the sovereign disposer of all things, the sovereign judge of all men. The modern reader may be irked by the frequent references to the 'Messias, King of Jerusalem', to 'God in the high seat celestial'. But these references are integral both to medieval thought and to the structure of the play. Dramatically, they have much the same function as the frequent references to corruption in *Hamlet*, or to ingratitude in *Lear*; they keep alive the central theme – the sense of man's responsibility to a power higher than himself. So complete is the writer's grasp of doctrine that a full commentary would require an extensive treatise in medieval theology; the Biblical references alone are very numerous. The plays as a whole are admirable examples of popularization raised to the level of art.

If we consider the main elements in a play to be plot, character, and thought-content, and the style to be the unifying and vivifying force which gives these three their actual form, then we may say that the morality style derives from the medieval spoken idiom, and the thought-content (to which plot and character are merely subordinate) from the medieval religion. That religion encouraged, and even necessitated, a readiness to face the fact of evil in man (a fact presented concisely in *Everyman*, more expansively in *The Three Estates*). But there is no bleakness or pessimism; even the cynicism of *The Three Estates* is lusty, humorous, and buoyant. For the medieval mind recognized evil in relation to redemption through the action of the man-God. The victory over evil was thought of as achieved not merely by human intelligence or will, but through a powerful divine intervention of which the individual could avail himself as he pleased. What mattered was not the amount of evil that prevailed temporarily, but the power of divine mercy to lead man, even through evil, to a happy eternity where alone results were lasting. And without divine aid, man could achieve nothing. Good Deeds tells Everyman:

> Here I lye, colde in the grounde.
> Thy synnes hath me sore bounde,
> That I can not stere[1].

But once Everyman is led by Knowledge to repent, Good Deeds declares:

> I thank God, now I can walke and go,
> I am delyvered of my sykenesse and wo.
> Therefore with Everyman I wyll go.

The belief in a healing redemption gives to Everyman's remorse of conscience a quality to which we are not accustomed in modern writing. Remorse is not painful or disturbing, but pacifying:

> Thanked be God for his gracyous werke!
> For now I wyll my penaunce begyn;
> This hath rejoysed and lyghted my herte.

It is the implications of divine redemption which also give force to the many appeals to 'saint charity'. Charity was called 'saint' or holy because it was the queen of the virtues, the highest inner force making for man's holiness. The phrase, 'for saint charity', so often repeated and used as the concluding note, was a summary of many aspects of belief, an appeal made in the name of the vast love which God showed men in the redemption and taught men to show one another.

But set against this reliance on redemption is the firm insistence on the inescapable arraignment of man before a judge who cannot be bribed, or swayed by anything but repentance. In spite of the many appeals to the Lady Mary, 'Mother and Maid', and the offices of

1. stir.

Knowledge or Confession, man must carry his own personal and lonely responsibility before God. Death assures Everyman, 'Wete thou well, thou shalt make none attourney'. Not only does Death come equally to all, but he 'makes all equal when he comes'; 'I set not by gold, silver, nor riches,' he says, 'ne by pope, emperor, king, duke, ne princes.' Goods, or temporal possessions, declares that he was merely lent to man for a time, to be eventually taken away, and Everyman reflects that life itself was merely lent to him.

From this general picture of human responsibility and destiny, we can understand the importance attached to Knowledge. It is very different from the scientific knowledge on which we rely so much today. For Everyman, Knowledge is the grasp of the divine law and the divine plan of the universe, in the light of which alone man can properly understand his actions. Knowledge assures Everyman:

> Everyman, I wyll go with the, and be thy gyde,
> In thy moost nede to go by thy syde.

Yet paradoxically, she affirms that she will forsake Everyman at death. For Knowledge is merely faith, one of the divine 'goods' lent to man, to be taken away at death, and transformed into the higher knowledge of the beatific vision, by immediate union with God. The vast and unquestioning trust which the medieval mind placed on faith is indicated by the manner in which Everyman is led to heaven. Knowledge sets the process of salvation in motion by coming of her own accord to Everyman (faith was a gratuitous gift of God, not attainable by man's striving); she then leads Everyman to Confession, the sacraments of Eucharist and Last Anointing, by which he is prepared for reception into heaven. Here particularly, the dramatic action is greatly condensed, supposing in the audience a grasp of the doctrine of the rôle of the sacraments in relation to the individual will.

The condensation is compensated for by the dramatic device of making the forces influencing Everyman into characters in the play. The 'abstractions' of medieval drama (Good Deeds or Kindred) are neither very abstract nor very different from our modern abstractions, 'Big Business', or 'public opinion'. Medieval minds felt the reality of Wantonness or Knowledge as much as we feel the reality of public opinion. Since vice, virtue, and divine providence were accepted as playing important rôles in real life, their transfer to the stage as *dramatis personae* appeared quite natural, and even today does not seem strained or artificial. The psychological handling of these abstractions is undoubtedly simplified but not superficial or mechanical. Not until the better Elizabethans do we find anything definitely superior to the very natural way in which Fellowship and Kindred are led on first to protest that, till their dying day, they will not forsake Everyman, and then to protest, with equal force, that the voyage to death 'would fear a strong man'. Here there is a strong sense of what is 'good stage', as in Goods' pointed reminder to Everyman that if

> I wente with the,
> Thou sholdes fare much the worse for me;
> For bycause on me thou dyd set thy mynde,
> Thy rekenynge I have made blotted and blynde.

The language is indeed quite inadequate to take the audience (or to enable the actor to take the audience) into the inner heart and character of Everyman; there is none of the profound Elizabethan insight into feelings and motives. But such insight would tend to defeat the very purpose of the play, which is to show, not what manner of men we are, but 'how transitory we be all day', how much more important are the eternal than the temporal results of our actions. The aim of the play dictates its dramatic method.

This singleness of aim, growing out of the precision of medieval beliefs, and drawing on the vigour of common speech, helps to determine the characteristics of the style of *Everyman*. Apart from obsolete words, the style is perfectly lucid, and 'speaks' well; it is condensed without becoming obscure, concise without becoming laconic. It has not the finely adapted modulations of later plays, but it has a business-like directness that goes constantly to the point under consideration and, with a minimum of technical terms and at a popular level, keeps in touch with the central view of man's relations to God. It is thus, for all its simplicity, a highly allusive style, and is inimitable because, to imitate it, one would have to re-create a whole popular mentality. The singleness of aim also excludes any preoccupation with style for its own sake, any mere cleverness in the handling of words, such as we find in the Elizabethan puns or in the contrived antitheses of Lyly. In these ways, the play is distinctively medieval, since art was normally not an autonomous activity, but sprang incidentally from an intense interest in religion.

To pass from *Everyman* to *The Three Estates* (by David Lindsay, c. 1540) is to see one of the difficulties of literary history and criticism – that under the one term (e.g. Morality) there may lie very wide difference in treatment and interest. In spite of its length (about nine hours in the Charteris text, and three in the form prepared for the Edinburgh Festival in 1949), it has little more strictly dramatic action than *Everyman*. But in its more deliberate use of irony, in its introduction of popular songs and music, in its greater consciousness of an audience to be amused, we see the beginning of Renaissance, as distinct from medieval, influences.

Yet the play is truly medieval in its blend of the secular with the sacred. The King's first speech is a prayer addressed to the 'Lord of lords, King of Kinges all, unmade Maker' for 'grace and peace perpetual' since his 'days endure but as a dream'. But Wantonness immediately reproves him for 'making such dreary cheer', and goes off to fetch the 'fairest earthly creature that ever was formit by nature', the lady Sensuality. The sacred invocations (*in nomine Domini*, 'by the Trinity', 'by Christ who harried hell') are used ironically to emphasize the lightness with which so many carried their religion. Thus Solace advises the King to have a lusty concubine and to fall to love-making in the name of the Lord. There is a similar ironical touch at the end; Flattery, when Correction has supposedly set all things right, not only assists in the hanging of Deceit and Falsehood, but while his 'companions pay the piper, Flattery slips clean away'. Spirituality, who stands for ecclesiastical power, is made a subject of pointed abuse and ridicule (the play survived only in spite of almost immediate clerical orders that all copies be burnt). Sensuality is banished from Scotland but she begs from Correction 'licence to pass again to Rome', for

> Among the princes of that nation,
> I let you wit my fresh beauty will bloom.

The play falls into two parts which are but poorly unified; the first turns on the struggle between good and evil for control of man, the second on contemporary abuses of power. The two characters who hold the parts together are King Humanity (another version of Everyman, but now presented as a king surrounded by flattering, pandering courtiers who chase away his good advisers) and Divine Correction (who has simply to issue his commands in order to rescue Humanity from the toils of flattery and vice, and to cleanse the realm from extortion and corruption). Correction affects the inner minds of the sinners as little as do policemen dispersing brawlers; his intervention is merely extrinsic and punitive. In spite of the moral inculcations and the variety and intensity of the portrait of vice, *The Three Estates* does not spring directly from moral convictions; it aims at a direct appeal to the audience through witty satire, humorous ridicule, and a realistic presentation of lechery and avarice. The play shows a sure sense of what appeals to the popular mind, as when Poor Man comes from the audience and forestalls Diligence (who is about to make an announcement) with a coarse jest at the value of the play, 'for there is richt little play at my hungry heart'. The play shows a wide command of vocabulary and idiom, and successfully exploits the resources of the acting voice. The great number of characters, the constant and varied use of lively phrases, and the vigorous portrayal of many kinds of human depravity keep interest alive; but it is on burlesque action, clowning (e.g. in the mock-baptism of Falsehood, Deceit, and Flattery), and a language admirably suited to ribaldry that the play relies. Good Counsel and Chastity are ineffectual, while there is real insight and relish in presenting Sensuality and Wantonness. The second part shows the writer more within his range than the first. Particularly in Poor Man and in John the Common-Weal, we get a vivid and searching presentation of the folk, a strong sense of the character and sufferings of the common people, which recalls both *Piers Plowman* and the work of Burns.

The Interludes

The term *Interlude* is used loosely of the sixteenth-century plays prior to the beginnings of English tragedy with *Gorboduc* (c. 1560). While their name suggests short pieces between other entertainments, some of them, like Udall's *Roister Doister* (c. 1540), are almost as long as *Macbeth*. Their themes include science, philosophy, farcical situations, and even stories from the Mysteries; while some deal with religious controversy, none of them show much evidence that the Reformation under Henry VIII deeply disturbed people's ways of thinking.

Many forces made the Interludes a departure from medieval practice. Behind the dramatic movement lay the intertwining of the new position of the monarchy with the tardy arrival of the Renaissance in England. Henry VII not only handed on to Henry VIII the unquestioned supremacy of the king over the nobility, but began to make the royal court an influential artistic as well as administrative centre. The Renaissance was also setting up new relations with the Continent. The Moralities had supposed an England which was part of the European spiritual or religious community; the Interludes began to reintroduce the notion (largely forgotten since Chaucer's time) of England as part of the European cultural community. In that culture, the dominant force in the sixteenth century was no longer a homogeneous, international Christianity. The Renaissance was encouraging a new versatility in art by its emphasis on the pagan Classics (which were variously interpreted by various peoples) and by treating art not as ancillary to religion but as an activity autonomous in its own right; the strong drive towards national churches was making even the religious basis of culture national. The Mysteries and Moralities had, indeed, like Chaucer's work, shown typically English traits, especially the good-humoured satire of which there is relatively little in Continental literature; but the Interludes were drawing more exclusively on non-religious and national sources. The playwrights were often professional scholars from the universities, which were introducing the Classics and paying more attention to music; not only were they experimenting with the use of song in drama (setting a tradition of which Shakespeare richly availed himself), but they were going to Latin comedy for themes and treatment. Their presentation in colleges and in the dining-halls of the nobles indicates the new purposes of the plays – the study of declamation and the Classics, and the catering to learned and aristocratic taste. Lastly, Henry VIII encouraged a new bitterness in anti-clericalism which, while leaving many religious doctrines untouched, was focusing attention much more on religious abuses than on beliefs, and thereby lessening (though not killing) interest in the themes of the Moralities.

All these forces (the new position of the king's court, the separation of art from a religious context, the new trends in scholarship, the new anti-clericalism) helped to make the plays more secular, more worldly, and less other-worldly. This secularism (which had already appeared in the revered masters of Renaissance literature, Petrarch and

Boccaccio, in the fourteenth century) was not simply a direct step towards Elizabethan drama; Marlowe not only helped to restore the patronage of the folk and put serious drama back in the popular theatre, he returned to medieval theology in *Dr Faustus*; Shakespeare made many uses, explicit and implicit, of the attitudes and interests embodied in the Liturgy of Cranmer.

On the whole, however, the Interludes show the constant necessity for dramatic art to seek new forms of appeal and the marked tendency in Renaissance art to assert its own autonomy. While several great figures, especially Dante in Italy and Thomas More in England, had shown that true humanism and traditional Christianity could be combined, the general trend in the sixteenth century was towards a new conception of art as no longer restricted by the requirements of religion, but as free to treat any theme that suited the genius of the artist and his judgement of what he could lead the public to appreciate. Just as the disintegration of feudalism had released new forces in the national life, the break-up of medieval Christianity was the beginning of a new era – one in which the artists, and especially the English playwrights, brought to the human mind the same spirit of exploration of the unknown as Drake and Vasco da Gama brought to the geographical world. To us, who know something of later dramatic achievement, the Interludes may appear awkward in language and amateurish in structure. But they were a series of innovations and experiments both interesting in themselves and valuable in pointing the way for the Elizabethans. Taken along with the Mysteries, Miracles, and Moralities, they help us to observe one of the most interesting and continuous forms of evolution in the whole history of literature – an evolution which, beginning with liturgical worship in mimetic or dialogue form in the early ages of Christianity, can be traced up to the fullest development of dramatic art in the early seventeenth century.

THE POETRY OF WYATT

BY D. W. HARDING

Professor of Psychology, the University of London

FOR those who are not scholars or literary historians the one good reason for reading Wyatt is the enjoyment that his writing can give as poetry. The obstacles to enjoyment are not great. Apart from the language of his period, which is fairly easy to read once variations in spelling and a few archaic words and usages have been grasped, only two difficulties are likely to hinder us. In a small proportion of his poetry the rhythm creates a barrier, one which has been heightened by past misunderstandings and therefore needs some discussion. And, what is probably more serious, the convention of love-poetry that he followed in much of his work may make us think of his poems as artificial exercises, serving a social purpose for his own time but having too little pressure of personal intent to be humanly important four hundred years later.

The contemporary social uses of his verse, as songs for singing and as poems to be passed about among friends, contributed to Wyatt's popularity as a member of Henry VIII's court. His poems were one expression of the high intelligence and culture that found other scope in his diplomatic work (notably in his difficult missions as Henry's ambassador to the Emperor Charles V in Spain and in Paris). They also reflected, for himself and his friends, the moods and outlook induced in him by less agreeable experiences in a court where the King's favour fluctuated and the intrigues of rival factions could bring sudden downfalls. Wyatt himself was twice imprisoned in the Tower, though each time released and eventually restored to royal favour. The second of these arrests followed a shift of power among the factions and the execution of his patron, Thomas Cromwell. The first illustrates another of the hazards and entertainments of the court, for it came with the fall of Anne Boleyn. Tradition suggests that she had been his mistress before her marriage to the King, and Chambers makes out a convincing case for thinking that this was so and that Wyatt was arrested with other suspects whose evidence might be of value.

Wyatt himself, married when he was seventeen, had repudiated his wife about six years later on account of her unfaithfulness. Towards the end of his life (he died at the age of thirty-nine while on a journey in the King's service) his mistress was Elizabeth Darrell, and in his will he left lands to her and their son. He also had a legitimate son, two letters to whom survive, affectionate and full of serious advice. It is against this background of everyday affairs that his poems are to be seen. They reflect not only the literary interests of his day but also the realities of human experience in such a social milieu. It would incapacitate us for serious reading of Wyatt to make the mistake of supposing that his poems belong only to the polish of its public surface or the artificialities of an obsolete code of feeling.

We can best get our bearings by noticing first the conversational quality of much of Wyatt's writing. The Satires – verse-letters giving Wyatt's views of the courtier's life and contemporary moral standards – are, of course, frankly conversational:

> By god, well sayde! But what and if thou wist
> How to bring in as fast as thou doest spend?
> *That would I lerne*, And it shall not be myst
> To tell the how. How hark what I intend. (198)*

The same quality is a more notable achievement in the lyrics, where the conversational tone and the usages of speech are fused remarkably with the 'musical' qualities. The refrains, for instance, often consist of those forcefully rhythmical short phrases that mark the more concentrated, exclamatory moments of everyday speech. So in 102 he warns his friend against letting her eyes betray the fact that she is in love:

> For som ther be of crafete kynde:
> Thowe yow shew no parte of your mynde,
> Sewrlye there iyes ye can not blynde,
>   Therefore take hede!

> For in lyke case there selves hathe bene,
> And thowgt ryght sure none had theym sene,
> But it was not as they did wene,
>   Therefore take hede!

* References are to the numbers of the poems in *Collected Poems of Sir Thomas Wyatt*, edited by Kenneth Muir.

Or poem 111:

> Ys yt possyble
> That so hye debate,
> So sharpe, so sore, and off suche rate,
> Shuld end so sone and was begone so late?
> Is it possyble?

And although Wyatt often uses the vocabulary of the love-conventions – glances from the eye striking to the heart, lutes to complain to, faith and truth and love's service – yet he also makes regular use of everyday experience and everyday words in which to express it:

> What menythe thys? When I lye alone,
> I tosse, I turne, I syghe, I grone;
> My bedd me semys as hard as stone:
>   What menys thys?

> I syghe, I playne contynually;
> The clothes that on my bedd do ly
> Always methynks they lye awry;
>   What menys thys?

> In slumbers oft for fere I quake;
> For hete and cold I burne and shake;
> For lake of slepe my hede dothe ake:
>   What menys thys?   (110)

The same direct handling of real experience in its real setting occurs in poem 37, the famous 'They fle from me ...', when he recalls the times before he was out of favour:

> Thancked be fortune, it hath ben othrewise
> Twenty tymes better; but ons in speciall,
> In thyn arraye after a pleasaunt gyse,
> When her lose gowne from her shoulders did fall,
> And she me caught in her armes long and small;
> And therewithall so swetely did me kysse,
> And softely saide, *dere hert, howe like you this?*

Direct personal statement is the characteristic form of Wyatt's writing; only rarely does he assume a rôle (as in poem 108, where a girl deserted by her lover is speaking). Nor is the habit of personal statement only a convention, for in some of the poems it seems beyond doubt that he intended a serious communication with his friends, using the poem as a means of putting his case or framing his advice in a form that gave it maximum force as effective statement. The strange and interesting poem 152 is an example. Another is 168, addressed from prison to his friend Sir Francis Brian whose political influence might help him, and proclaiming his ill-usage and his continued hope:

> Sure I am, Brian, this wounde shall heale agayne,
> But yet, alas, the scarre shall styll remayne.

Another very interesting example is 93, a reproach to his mistress who has been flirting by eye with someone else:

> And if an iye may save or sleye,
> And stryke more diepe then wepon longe,
> And if an iye by subtil play
> May move on more thenne any tonge,
> How can ye say that I do wronge
> Thus to suspecte withoute deserte?
> For the iye is traitor of the herte ...
>
> And my suspect is without blame,
> For, as ye saye, not only I
> [1]But other moo have demyd the same;
> Thenne is it not jelowsye
> But subtill loke of rekeles iye
> Did raunge to farre to make me smart,
> For the iye is traitor of the hert.

The poem clearly continues an argument, in which Wyatt's reproaches were met by the girl's self-justification and her counter-accusation of his unreasonable jealousy; in the poem he returns to the charge, restating his reproach in the most effective way he can and also trying to restore friendly relations:

> But I your freende shal take it thus,
> Sins you wol soo, as stroke of chaunce;
> And leve furder for to discus
> Wither the stroke did sticke or glaunce ...

1. 'But others as well.'

The references back are to such specific points in the previous argument (including her incautious reproach that he was just like the others in suspecting her) that one cannot think of the poem as merely an exercise in dramatic form; its rôle as a poem for a manuscript book and circulation among friends seems likely to have been secondary to its other purpose as personal communication and personal offering.

*   *   *

Although the conversational aspect of the poetry is important, and appreciated particularly nowadays when the Miltonic convention of poetry has been placed in a longer perspective, it would be misleading to over-emphasize it at the expense of slighting Wyatt's obvious concern with the 'formal' aspects of his poems. His evident zest in developing a great range of skill in the handling of patterns of verbal sound indicates what must have been one of the chief appeals of verse-writing to him; and the results make a great part of his appeal to us.

The use that he makes of refrains is highly characteristic and appears to have been a marked advance on what was usual in the court songs of the time. One of their most usual purposes is to bring about a cumulative forcefulness in the main theme of the poem as the effect of the successive verses increasingly justifies and explains the exclamatory refrain. This happens, for instance, in poem 130:

> Forget not yet the tryde entent
> Of suche a truthe as I have ment,
> My gret travayle so gladly spent
>   Forget not yet.

> Forget not yet when furst began
> The wery lyffe ye know syns whan,
> The sute, the servys none tell can,
>   Forget not yet.

In several poems the refrain also provides an emphatic rhythmical anchorage to which the verse can return after wandering freely through more varied and expressive rhythms. A poem already referred to (111) offers a good example:

Ys yt possible
That eny may fynde
Within on hert so dyverse mynd,
To change or torne as wether and wynd?
Is it possible?

This use of the refrain as part of the rhythmical structure of the poem is allied to the use of an unchanging rhythm at the end of each stanza, for contrast with the rhythm of the other lines. Hallett Smith notes it in a poem (58) where the unchanging rhythm is also the refrain:

To wisshe and want and not obtain,
To seke and [1]sew esse of my pain,
Syns all that ever I do is vain,
    What may it availl me?

He comments that 'this curious difference of effect between the monotonously rhyming first three lines, slow and heavy in their movement, and the rapid energy of the question is carried through to the end …'. Similarly, in poem 84 the first three lines of the stanza give a climbing accelerando to be followed each time by the melancholy slump of the fourth line:

My chaunce doeth so
My wofull case procure,
To offer to my foo
My hert to cure.

*   *   *

Enough has been said, though more examples could be quoted, to put it beyond doubt that Wyatt had an extremely sensitive 'ear' for the effects of rhythm and high skill in managing his words rhythmically. This fact gives the standpoint from which to view the extraordinary history of the editorial and critical handling of Wyatt's rhythms.

Wyatt came at a point when rather simple regularity of metre was just beginning to dominate English verse. Previously it had not done so. The tradition of ballads and carols and the neo-Latin poetry of the *vagantes* established a flowing metrical form, though one that was very varied, and this was the background of those of Wyatt's lyrics that

1. sue ease.

we most readily enjoy.[b] But side by side with this line of metrical form there existed the discursive poetry of the fifteenth century in which regular flowing rhythms played little or no part. This seems to have been part of the rhythmical tradition of the language that went back to the alliterative line with its well-marked pause separating two distinct rhythmical units; it is the tradition that finds a related expression in plainsong, where diverse rhythmical units are divided from one another by pauses and are not intended to flow together in the way that creates regular metre.

Wyatt drew both on the carol tradition and on that of pausing verse, and it is where he used the latter that his editors and readers have found difficulty. Slight traces of the alliterative line are to be seen in his verse occasionally:

> This maketh me at home to hounte and to hawke …
> In lusty lees at libertie I walke. (196)

More important than these vestiges of actual alliterative organization is Wyatt's readiness to combine in one line two differently patterned rhythmical units which have to be held apart by a slight pause in reading. (It would seem that Wyatt or his scribes sometimes used the colon to indicate these pauses, but the punctuation of his verse is erratic and appears not to have been fully studied.) As in Langland's lines, so we have to read with a pause such lines of Wyatt's as

> There was never file · half so well filed * (16)

or

> Syghes ar my foode, drynke are my teares;
> Clynkinge of fetters suche musycke wolde crave;
> Stynke and close ayer away my lyf wears:
> Innocencie · is all the hope I have.
> Rayne, wynde, or wether · I judge by myne eares … (168)

Unfortunately, by the time Wyatt's poetry was printed, in *Tottel's Miscellany* (1557), simple metrical verse had been so universally accepted that Tottel's editor felt justified in changing Wyatt's lines until they would scan in the popular way. Other editors followed his example, including Quiller-Couch in *The Oxford Book of English Verse*.

* Wyatt and his scribes did not use the pause mark. In this and the following quotations it is inserted to indicate a pause that the rhythm seems to demand.

Miss Foxwell in her edition of the poems followed a different but also
mistaken plan: she rightly insisted upon printing the true text, but she
invented an incredibly complicated set of prosodic rules by which to
persuade herself that Wyatt was always writing metrically if only we
could find out how to read him.°

What is quite clear is that the rather trivial changes made by Tottel's
editor cannot by any stretch of the imagination be regarded as beyond
Wyatt's skill; if he had wanted to write in regular metre he would
have done so, and we must assume that he wanted to do something
else. Indeed, no assumption is necessary; the fact happens to be
demonstrated in the poem 'Alas! madame, for stelyng of a kysse'
(44), where we have both Wyatt's early version and his own revisions. The fifth and sixth lines run:

> Then revenge you: and the next way is this:
> An othr kysse shall have my lyffe endid.

Tottel altered the fifth line to

> Revenge you then, the rediest way is this.

But, in fact, Wyatt's version is a revision of what he first wrote, and
what he first wrote was as regular as Tottel:

> Revenge you then and sure ye shall not mysse
> To have my life with an othr ended.

It seems clear that Wyatt deliberately avoided the repetitive thump
of regular metre. In reading him one must be prepared to make
pauses and runs that are usual in speech but are not indicated by any
metrical scheme, and one must sometimes detach a line from the
metre suggested (to metre-habituated ears) by the previous line.
Where it is the last line of a stanza that has in this way to be detached
we can accept the changed rhythm more readily than we can a similar
change in mid-stanza. The line that ends Wyatt's stanza fairly often
presents a rhythm which is vivid by itself and asks no permission of
the previous metre:

> So unwarely was never no man cawght
> With stedefast loke apon a goodly face,
> As I of late: for sodenly, me thowght,
> My hart was torne · owte of hys place.   (122)

and in 91:

> The sonne, the mone doth frowne on the;
> Thow hast darkenes · in daylightes stede,
> As good in grave as soo to be;
> Moost wretched hert, · why art thou not ded?

The forcefulness of many of these pausing lines is beyond doubt. In other lines, especially in the Sonnets (which are conveniently brought together in Miss Foxwell's edition), the rhythm is more defeating, and it must be admitted that puzzles remain about Wyatt's intention. The Sonnets were translated from the Italian, and it seems possible that more efforts of scholarship are needed before we know fully what Wyatt (presumably with the sanction of contemporary readers) was aiming at, and what relation he saw between his translation and native traditions. It may be that some intellectual criterion such as syllable-counting was being allowed to interfere with the direct perception of rhythm. But it seems possible that some of our difficulties arise from expecting one line to flow into the next and both to follow a similar metrical pattern, instead of treating each as standing by itself for rhythmical purposes:

> Like to these unmesurable montayns
> Is my painfull lyff, the burden of Ire[1],
> For of great height be they, and high is my desire,
> And I of teres, and they be full of fontayns.
> Under craggy rockes they have full barren playns;
> Hard thoughtes in me my wofull mynde doeth tyre ...   (33)

Whatever the solution to the puzzle set by some of the lines, we can at least put aside the older idea that Wyatt was groping and fumbling towards a regularity of metre that lack of skill prevented him from achieving. Even if we dislike the lines as Wyatt wrote them, we may be sure that he wrote them because he wanted to and not because he failed to see the possible changes that faced his editors with such irresistible temptation.

* * *

It would be a mistake of proportion if interest in the 'formal' aspects of the verse led us to neglect the significance of Wyatt's poetry as a statement of human experience. The verse would have little be-

1. Probably impetuosity, violence.

yond historical interest if his main object had been to perform technical exercises.

The danger of underrating its importance as an expression of concerns and values still relevant to us is unavoidable if we put the wrong emphasis on the fact that Wyatt wrote within the convention of love-poetry. In particular we may be tempted to dismiss as mere convention the frequent repetition of the love-complaint and the love-plea, often (though by no means always) of a submissive kind that we may feel to be abject. The repetitiveness does include much that is not of great intrinsic interest. Some of it should be attributed to the social function of verse such as Wyatt's in providing entertainment for the court circle, both as songs and as poems to be read (see 142) and copied into the manuscript books in which they have survived (forerunners, apparently, of the long line of 'albums' that were still a big part of educated entertainment in Jane Austen's day).

Social demand of this kind would encourage the circulation of all Wyatt's versions of similar themes. It is, of course, not unusual for a poet to take up the same kind of theme again and again and only occasionally to produce a highly satisfying version of it. We have to pay for King's perfect *Exequy*, for instance, by a very large number of rather dull elegies and laments for the dead; it was a vein that he had to work and it yielded at least one rich nugget. Wyatt's preoccupation was different. His absorbing concern was the relation between men and women. But before observing how he dealt with it we must notice that the convention of the love-lament offered indirect expression to a range of feelings – depression, protest at bad faith, weariness from unrewarded service – that may have arisen from quite other sources, such as the difficulties and disappointments of his diplomatic work, fluctuations in the King's regard for him, and the hazards of his position as a courtier among intriguing rivals. 'Pacyence of all my smart' (118) is characteristic of his mood:

> Pacyence to be content
> With froward fortunes trayn;
> [1]Pacyence to the intent
> Sumwhat to slake my payne;
> I se no Remedy
> But suffer pacyently.

1. 'Patience for the purpose of slightly easing my pain.'

Several of the lines, such as

> Thys is a strange dyssease:
> To serve and never please,

could easily be part of a love-complaint, but there is nothing at all to justify our assuming that in fact it is a love-poem. Similarly, poems 161 and 183 complain of 'Fortune' having turned against him, but in phrases that use some of the conventions of love-poetry; Tottel, in fact, entitles 183 'The lover waileth his changed joyes', though it is not a love-poem. His edition also gives the title 'The lover suspected blameth yll tonges' to 188, which modern editors take to refer to the efforts of Wyatt's enemies to bring about his downfall after the execution of Thomas Cromwell. Open complaint about his public misfortunes, such as those involving his position with the King, might have increased his danger and delayed his return to favour, and it seems understandable that complaints of this sort should take such a deliberately vague form as

> Patiens, for I have wrong,
> And dare not shew whereyn
> Patiens shalbe my song
> Sins truthe can no thing wynne.

The ease with which feelings of melancholy and protest could be assimilated to love-poetry made that convention an inviting outlet of a safely indirect kind for such feelings, wherever they may have arisen.

Yet there can be no doubt of the close association between Wyatt's general tendency to depression and his attitude to women. He belonged to a circle of fashionable and promiscuous people in which the business of court advancement and intrigue for family and faction was combined when possible with the pleasures of sexual attachment. But he gives the impression in his poems of wanting more keenly than most the values which that way of life slighted, notably the values of secure affection, mutual trust, and kindness. In the third Satire (poem 198) he expresses his attitude in one of the pieces of bitter advice he gives for worldly advancement:

> In this also · se you be not Idell:
> Thy nece, thy cosyn, thy sister or thy doghter,

If she be faire, if handsom be her myddell[1],
Yf thy better · hath her love besoght her,
Avaunce his cause and he shall help thy nede.
It is but love: · turne it to a lawghter.

A great part of his poetry is a retort to the attitude of 'It is but
love'. Again and again the poems represent a state of mind in which
happiness and the worth of life are felt to depend upon the sexual love
and affection of a woman. It is worth while examining in full one
poem, fine in itself as well as characteristic of Wyatt, that suggests
something of the relation between his general melancholy and his
attitude to women. It is poem 84.

> All hevy myndes
> Do seke to ese their charge,
> And that that moost theim byndes
> To let at large.
>
> Then why should I
> Hold payne within my hert,
> And may my tune apply
> To ese my smart?

As in many of his poems, one motive for writing is to gain relief for
his melancholy by giving it external expression. Implicitly he asks
for a listener, but it may be, as here, that the ideally sympathetic
listener is best represented by solitude:

> My faithfull lute
> Alone shall here me plaine;
> For els all othre sute
> Is clene in vaine.
>
> For where I sue
> Redresse of all my grieff,
> Lo, they do most eschew
> My hertes relieff.

Up to this point the melancholy and the protest against the lack of
sympathy he finds around him are quite general and may have arisen
from all sorts of causes, as they do in most of us, including sources of

1. Waist.

which we are not clearly conscious. But the convention of love-poetry provides a peg on which to hang the feelings, whether or not unhappy love was their only cause:

> Alas, my dere,
> Have I deserved so,
> That no help may appere
> Of all my wo?
>
> Whome speke I to,
> Unkynd and deff of ere?
> Alas, lo, I go,
> And wot not where.

In the next stanza – very lovely in its combination of varied rhyth-mical flow and heavy rhyme emphasis – he comes back to the nebu-lousness of his distress and his bewilderment at it:

> Where is my thoght?
> Where wanders my desire?
> Where may the thing be soght
> That I require?

Then comes the aspect of conventional love-poetry that means most to him, protest against the betrayal of affection:

> Light in the wynde
> Doth fle all my delight;
> Where trouth and faithfull mynd
> Are put to flyght.

The next stanzas show a momentary return to the sense of not know-ing what it really is that grieves him and then an acceptance of the view that it must be his rejection by the woman and that his appeal to her is useless:

> Who shall me gyve
> Fetherd wynges for to fle,
> The thing that doeth me greve
> That I may se?
>
> Who would go seke
> The cause whereby to playne?
> Who could his foo beseke
> For ese of payne?

My chaunce doeth so
My wofull case procure,
To offer to my foo
My hert to cure.

What hope I then
To have · any redresse?
Of whome or where or when
Who can expresse?

Finally, having in this way inquired a little into his unhappiness and
associated it with his rejection by a woman, he returns to the opening
theme and completes the formal structure of his poem:

No, sins dispaire
Hath set me in this case,
In vain oft in the ayre
To say *Alas*,

I seke nothing
But thus for to discharge
My hert of sore sighing,
To plaine at large;

And with my lute
Sumtyme to ease my pain,
For els all othre sute
Is clene in vain.

The notes most often repeated in Wyatt's love-poetry are the expectation of rebuff and protest at the betrayal of his affection. One
sees this, for example, in poem 143. Frequently, too, there appears a
curiously abject note – seeming to come from something deeper than
the troubadour convention, although no doubt reinforced by that –
expressed in the conviction that his persistent and faithful service
should in justice give him the reward of a woman's love (e.g. poem
57). Whether convention or personal conviction, it runs counter to
our two notions that women's love is as unpredictable and unguidable
as men's and that women equally with men should be 'in love' before

they accept a lover; it suggests something much more like our notion of the love of a mother which can be pleaded for as a 'right'. This aspect of the poetry is probably least acceptable to us at the present time. Whether it reflects a widespread attitude of Wyatt's age is a question for scholarship; it is clear that if it was part of the current convention it was a part that Wyatt personally found it easy to accept and develop. In all probability it reveals his personal attitude, for it is evident that in many of his sentiments about the relations between men and women he could not feel nearly so comfortably ensconced among the fashionable opinions of his time (see, for instance, poem 55).

The salient experiences that Wyatt's love-poetry records are the emotional disturbance of falling in love, his expectation of rebuff, his rather submissive pleading, and his protest and lamentation at betrayal. But this is not the point on which to end one's exploration of his love-poetry, for within the broad outline indicated by these features there are innumerable more finely differentiated responses to particular events and experiences. He records, for instance, in poem 46 the glee he felt when his rival came upon him sitting with the woman they both wanted. There is frequently the remembrance of happier occasions when he was successful in love (e.g. poem 47). He records his feelings about a girl's exclamation of misery at loving him (poem 38). Above all, one must notice the occasional expression of an underlying toughness and endurance not incompatible with his melancholy (read, for instance, poem 91), which carried Wyatt through not only the misfortunes of his love-affairs but the more material troubles of his public life.

His poems were a serious part of active life for an able and sensitive man. They had simple social uses in the entertainment of his friends, they gave him the satisfactions that come from exercising superb craftsmanship and skill, and in the paraphrases and translations they formed part of the welcome his mind gave to Renaissance activity in the other countries of Europe. More intimately they were a means of stating points of view towards incidents in his personal relations with his friends; especially in his relations with the young women of the court circle and the emotional challenges and problems with which they faced him. Still more personally they gave him the relief of putting into disciplined external form the depression and protest with which he responded to much of his experience.

NOTES

a. See Hallett Smith, 'The Art of Sir Thomas Wyatt', *The Huntingdon Library Quarterly*, IX (August 1946).

b. See E. K. Chambers, *Sir Thomas Wyatt and Some Collected Studies*, and E. M. W. Tillyard, *The Poetry of Sir Thomas Wyatt*, who have pointed this out.

c. For a further discussion of his rhythm, see Hallett Smith (above), D. W. Harding, 'The Rhythmical Intention in Wyatt's Poetry', *Scrutiny*, XIV (December 1946); and Alan Swallow, 'The Pentameter Lines in Skelton and Wyatt', *Modern Philology*, XLVIII (August 1950).

SPENSER'S *FAERIE QUEENE*

BY DEREK TRAVERSI

THE true place of Spenser in English literature has been as much ob-
scured as illuminated by his academic reputation. He has been regarded too exclusively as an innovator, as the first great English poet
since Chaucer to mark out new paths, to bequeath a living influence
to future generations. This, however, is only part of the truth. Spenser's influence on Milton and on the romantic poets of the nineteenth
century is, of course, beyond question, although we may reasonably
doubt, whether it was entirely, and in all respects, beneficial; but it is
equally possible, and perhaps not less important, to see *The Faerie
Queene* as a last expression of the great allegorical tradition, which its
author only imperfectly understood, of the Middle Ages. His work,
in other words, represents as much an end as a possible beginning.
To discern the simultaneous presence in Spenser's writings of these
two contrasted aspects is to realize that they mark, in a very true
sense, a turning-point, the burial of one poetic tradition and the birth
of another. And if we conclude, as there are reasons for doing, that
his achievement – in itself beyond question – was in certain respects a
limited one, that it implied the neglect of certain linguistic and emotional resources that had formerly been the natural heritage of English poetry, we shall have reached a more balanced estimate of his true
importance.

Our approach to Spenser must be based, therefore, on a proper
evaluation of his literary origins. His declared literary preferences
barely need recalling. First stimulated to a practical interest in letters
at Cambridge by the humanist scholar Gabriel Harvey, Spenser left
the University to enter the service of the Earl of Leicester and to fall
under the influence of Philip Sidney. Choice and circumstance, in
other words, inclined him as a young writer to the courtly conception of literature which is at once his virtue and his limitation. The
fact, coming at this precise moment, is of decisive importance.
Spenser assumed from the first a set of conventions which, influential
as they were, responded only in part to the necessities of Elizabethan

expression. Having so assumed them, he developed them with out-standing skill and to the limit of their usefulness. But the main line of English literary development, after the writing of *The Faerie Queene*, is only to a secondary degree 'courtly'. Shakespeare's achievement involved a full exploitation, with the new cultivated tendencies assimilated where required, of the vigour of popular speech and dramatic tradition; and this is no more than the reverse of the progressive impoverishment and abstraction imposed by a variety of circumstances upon talented court writers who might have been capable, under conditions, of better things. It was Spenser's fate as a poet to perfect literary forms that, having lost before his day their roots in the past, failed equally to respond adequately to certain needs of the present. This double isolation is, perhaps, the explanation of that least readable of admitted masterpieces, *The Faerie Queene*.

Spenser's peculiar talent and limitation can be recognized from the first in *The Shepheardes Calender*, the set of poems with which, in 1579, he both made his name as a cultivated poet and contributed to a strangely abortive line of literary development. He wrote *The Shepheardes Calender* as a member of the literary circle of Sidney – himself a divided figure, half conventional man of letters, half poet possessed by a curious elegiac pessimism – and immediately before the fall of the circle's powerful patron, the Earl of Leicester. The twelve eclogues which compose the series, conceived after the manner of Theocritus and the tradition he inaugurated, reflect perfectly the peculiar nature of Spenser's inspiration. This is a poetry which contrives to combine, no doubt by design, ambiguity of theme with considerable clarity of expression. On the positive side we have to recognize the achievement of a polished and, within certain limits, varied literary form, understandably attractive after the breakdown during the preceding period of the linguistic and formal standards of the fourteenth century. The achievements of *Piers Plowman* and *Sir Gawayne* had become incomprehensible; that of Chaucer was only partially understood and needed reinterpretation for a different society. These facts must be recognized as the foundations on which Spenser built and which determined the type of poetry he wrote. His language in the *Calender* is normally polished and capable of clear and vivid expression; one has only to compare it, not only with the general run of fifteenth-century verse south of the Scottish border, but with much of the crudity that still passed in more popular circles for poetry, to see why it was valued. Handling this instrument of expression, Spenser was able to achieve political denunciation in an almost Miltonic style (Piers' attack on religious abuses in the *May* eclogue), the sophisticated use of popular song motives (*August*), a 'lofty' style which already anticipates *The Faerie Queene* (Piers again in *October*), the elegiac pessimism of *November*, and the purely decorative use of natural motives in *December*.

The variety exhibited, in other words, is considerable, but always within limits strictly imposed by convention. These limits can be defined in purely literary terms. In writing the poems which compose the *Calender*, Spenser created, or re-created, a poetic speech and the corresponding prosody to suit his purpose. His master in much of this effort was, according to his own acknowledgement, Chaucer, the 'Tityrus' of Colin Clout in the *June* eclogue,

> Who taught me, homely, as I can, to make.

To examine Spenser's relationship to Chaucer, however, as exemplified in *The Shepheardes Calender*, is to realize how the conception of literary tradition has been narrowed in his work. Between the 'homeliness' of Spenser's 'making' and of Chaucer's, there is an essential difference. Chaucer was a poet who, in his own age, united to a remarkable degree the cultivated virtues with a popular strength and directness of expression; we are not aware, as we read him, of any sense of strain underlying this union, any difficulty in bridging the gap between its component elements. In Spenser, from the first, this is not so. His interest in Chaucer is notably antiquarian, almost philological in kind; he picks out words with a Chaucerian ring because they have for him the appeal of a rustic 'homeliness', a simplicity so foreign to himself and to his surroundings as to exercise the fascination of the profoundly different. Here he is elaborating an English subject in 'popular' terms:

> Seest, howe brag yond Bullocke beares,
> So smirke, so smooth, his pricked ears?
> His horns bene as broade as Rainbowe bent,
> His dewelap as lythe as lasse of Kent.
> See how he venteth into the wynd?
> Weenest of love is not hys mynd?

Seemeth thy flocke thy counsell can,
So lustless beene they so weake so wan,
Clothed with cold, and hoary with frost.

(*Februarie*)

This is the voice, not of agricultural simplicity, but of a new so-phistication. Words like 'brag', 'smirke', and 'pricked' have a tradi-tional, popular air about them, but their use suggests a new poetic purpose. They are fastidiously chosen to present to the court a courtly picture of the countryside, and they are set in a rhythm which acts as a decorative frame to the description. They fit the social grace and dignity which an Elizabethan court possessed, and their effect is be-yond question pleasing. But already there is a perilous lack of root in this convention. Those whose way of life has become remote from the real soil cannot be expected to preserve for long the veneer of the soil; and that, translated into social terms, is the meaning of *The Shepheardes Calender*.

This social aspect is, indeed, of considerable importance in esti-mating the nature of Spenser's attachment to literary tradition. The words of his poem, here and in many other passages, are chosen less because they correspond to the needs of direct expression than be-cause they give pleasure by the very fact of contrasting with the language proper to a society aware of its superior cultivation and yet afflicted with the growing sense of an essential lack. This lack is con-nected with developments outside the sphere of literary creation. Spenser belongs, historically speaking, to a generation in which the ideal of the independent humanist, dedicated to the scholarly culti-vation of letters, had finally given way to that of the courtly servant of the absolute monarch; perhaps the execution of Thomas More, some forty years earlier, had marked the decisive moment in this transformation. Be that as it may, after More's death the prospects of humanism, already a movement in some sense abstracted from the traditional sources of literary strength, were profoundly altered. The scholar, absorbed directly into the orbit of power, gave place to the courtier subdued to the purpose and caprices of an absolute master and often engaged in a struggle for survival in which his main weapon was, in a very real sense, flattery of the sovereign. No doubt the liter-ary courtier, accepting these limitations, often gave his work – as Spenser did – a suitable nationalist and 'protestant' turn; no doubt, moreover, these tendencies corresponded to new currents of the times, and those who reflected them were not necessarily insincere in so doing. The fact remains that their work developed a strained, artificial simplicity of its own. The language of such a poem as *The Shepheardes Calender* is that to which the humanist, with courtly artifice imposed upon him, was bound to come; a language eminently suitable for satire (but only in attacking targets recognized to be safe) and equally amenable to the ends of flattery. In a world familiar with the struggle for survival, where a single false step might mean loss of favour and the consequent loss of positions which others were always ready to fill, the conception of literature implied in Spenser's early poems was perfectly at home. It is a sign of his greatness that his own best work is compatible with a profound uneasiness, even a rejection of the indignities of the courtier's life; but this uneasiness is itself coloured by the necessarily artificial mode of its expression.

The Shepheardes Calender was, of course, in Spenser's mind the introduction to another and greater work. Its eclogues were written partly to perfect a style and partly to open the way into the inner circles of court society, at least in its literary manifestations. By a characteristically ironic turn of Fortune, however – and there is nothing abstract or removed from reality in the court poet's pre-occupation with the vagaries of that deity – the publication of the series coincided almost exactly with an exclusion from this society that proved, for Spenser, almost final. In 1580, the Earl of Leicester fell from the royal favour, and his fall affected in varying degree all those who had depended upon his patronage for their place in court circles. In Spenser's case, exclusion took the form of a kind of semi-exile by which he was sent to Ireland as secretary to the Lord Deputy who governed, in the Queen's name, that remote, barbarous, and un-happy island. As is well known, Spenser felt this exclusion (which proved to be, in effect, almost lifelong) deeply, and his emotions, oddly contradictory at different moments and full of barely realized undercurrents, henceforth played a considerable part in his work. The most ambitious product of his exile, written in Ireland and brought to England for publication during two short returns in 1590 and 1595, was *The Faerie Queene*.

The great mass of *The Faerie Queene*, incomplete as it is (for Spenser planned twelve books, of which only six and one fragment of a seventh were written), contains within itself the most varied purposes. This, indeed, is one of the causes of its undeniable failure to convey to most readers a clear sense of underlying unity of intention. Most obviously, the poem sets out to be an English equivalent of the *poema cavalleresco* as cultivated in Italy; Spenser's intention of rivalling, and indeed surpassing, Ariosto and Tasso is obvious. The poem, however, besides standing for a patriotic version of the Arthurian theme and the exaltation of Gloriana, the Virgin Queen (ends which might, in themselves, have been reconciled with the Italian inspiration), contains an element of moral and political allegory which greatly complicates the whole conception. Ariosto laid no claim to allegorical content for the *Orlando Furioso*, and Tasso only attached a symbolic interpretation to the *Gerusalemme Liberata* as an afterthought; but Spenser tried, impossibly, to make it an integral part of his poem. *The Faerie Queene* contains features which make of it a late development of the medieval habit of allegory, elements which obscure its more obvious literary purposes and leave us finally with a sense of chaos. The general impression is that Spenser himself did not understand fully the form he was so determined to use. His allegorical antecedents, indeed, are in great measure abstract and decorative, rather in the line of the *Romaunt of the Rose* than in that, fortified by the strength of concrete reference and popular speech, of Langland. To compare Spenser's poem, strictly as an allegorical construction, with *Piers Plowman* is to be aware of the decay of a convention that had once been valid and had corresponded to a coherent organization of experience[a]. The detailed presentation of Langland's allegory is admittedly full of faults, unwieldy crudities which, when compared with the handling of allegory in the *Divina Commedia*, show that the mental habit on which it is based is already passing through a crisis. The essential habit, however, was still alive. To Langland the idea of seeing a single concrete situation simultaneously under various aspects is still plausible, indeed natural, and the various visions still integrate to form a continuous, significant whole. Piers, the simple ploughman living in an age of grave social stress, can be presented under the guise of Charity, can even be transformed without strain of difficulty into the figure of Christ sacrificed on the Cross, harrowing Hell, and rising again in triumph. The symbol, in short, unites everyday reality with its spiritual context, giving the former its meaning and the latter, through the vivid directness of speech which characterizes the poem, concreteness of expression.

In *The Faerie Queene*, on the other hand, for all its superior finish and polished style, nothing comparable occurs. The allegorical habit of seeing unity beneath diversity is shattered, and little but the mechanical application of abstract meanings remains. The characters and situations of the poem stand, in the mind of each reader, for too many different things: things, moreover, which fail to cohere into a recognizable hierarchy of significances (for hierarchy is a necessary part of the true allegorical outlook) but remain isolated and finally meaningless. According to the original conception, each knight was to have symbolized, in his adventures, the search for perfection through a particular virtue: the Red Cross Knight represents Holiness in search of Truth, Sir Guyon Temperance traditionally conceived, Britomart Chastity, and so forth. In actual fact, however, two things repeatedly happen which are incompatible with any coherent explanation of the separate episodes or with the presence of any continuous pattern of meaning in the poem as a whole. In the first place, the significance of each Knight and his adventures fluctuates, shifting from the moral to the political without attaining the unity that would, in a genuine allegory, have bound together the different levels of vision; the quest of the Red Cross Knight for Truth or Unity (one is not sure which, though clearly the two are related) is mixed with patriotic and political motives only superficially bound to the principal theme. In the second place, the virtues themselves are not bound to one another, fail to respond to any conception of their relative value with reference to one another, or to the common end which is so notably lacking in the conception of the whole poem. No doubt it could be argued that this end was to have been supplied through the figure of Arthur, suitably developed in a final Book as the focal point of the whole structure; but his absence from the completed Cantos makes it hard to believe that he could, at that stage, have exercised any dominating influence on all the scattered earlier themes. Given the definite, though disguised dependence of the whole allegorical scheme upon medieval habits of thought, the result is a structure that has ceased to hold together, a dislocation of what might have been, as in Langland it still was, a varied and coherent unity.

All this, however, though true from a structural standpoint, is not the whole truth about *The Faerie Queene*. If the allegorical outlook no longer lived, as a unifying force, in Spenser's mind, it was still very much alive in some of its parts. Where it most lives, the presence of a very considerable poet can be detected. Such an occasion is the pageant of the Seven Deadly Sins (Book I, Canto iv), where Spenser is at his best in giving life to a traditional theme:

> And by his side rode loathsome Gluttony,
> Deformed creature on a filthie swyne,
> His bellie was up-blowne with luxury,
> And eke with fatnesse swollen were his eyne,
> And like a Crane his necke was long and fyne,
> With which he swallowed up excessive feast,
> For want wherof poore people oft did pyne;
> And all the way, most like a brutish beast,
> He spued up his gorge, that all did him deteast.
>
> In greene vineleaves he was right fitly clad;
> For other clothes he could not weare for heat,
> And on his head an yvie girland had,
> From under which fast trickled downe the sweat;
> Still as he rode, he somwhat still did eate,
> And in his hande did beare a bouzing can,
> Of which he supt so oft, that on his seat
> His drunken corse he scarse upholden can,
> In shape and life more like a monster, than a man.

Here, at least, Spenser gives the lie to Ben Jonson's shrewdly worded charge that in 'affecting the ancients, he writ no language'. The abstract Sin comes to life, in the medieval way, through its concrete representation. The visual quality of the imagination which picks on the eyes, 'swollen' with fatness, and on the grotesque neck, 'long and fyne' like that of a crane with the food visibly proceeding down it, and up again in nausea, the sharp vernacular touch provided by the 'bouzing can' are not in any sense the work of the purely literary poet that Spenser is so often supposed to be; whilst the contrasting reference to the hunger of the poor recalls one of the main social grievances so insistently treated by Langland. The passage belongs to the great tradition of the grotesque, which occupies so important a place in English literature and which has points of contact with Jonson's own treatment of the seamier figures of his comedies. The roots of the tradition are, no doubt, medieval. Realism of a similar kind is apparent in *Piers Plowman*, though still bound there to an organic conception of allegory; here it stands out by its sheer vigour in a poem whose inspiration is in great part decorative, giving the force of concrete reference to one of those pageants of abstractions which so commended themselves to the Renaissance mind.

Only intermittently, however, does *The Faerie Queene* come to life in this particular way. For the most part, it aims at more deliberately 'stylistic' virtues, and it is from these that the poem has derived much of its influence upon later English verse. If, as we have argued, Spenser's early adoption of the pastoral convention implies an effort, more or less imposed by circumstances, to evade a direct approach to delicate realities, the famous 'Spenserian stanza', with its characteristic rhythm, often tends to a similar kind of abstraction. The extraordinary skill and variety with which it is handled, always within the limits of its essential monotony, have no doubt contributed greatly to its reputation; but that monotony itself is the sign of a tendency to divorce rhythm from sense, to reduce verse to a flow of harmonious sound which, however skilful, is more like a decadence than the promise of a fresh beginning. The tendency, of course, is countered in Spenser by the presence of declared purposes of a very different kind, which do not, however, succeed in imposing themselves sufficiently to preserve a genuine unity of style. Certainly nothing more alien to the declared moral intention of his poem could be imagined than some of the most typical stanzas of *The Faerie Queene*.

The stanza, in fact, often seems to give rise – generally when in the process of describing deceit or temptation – to a kind of moral ambiguity. The poem abounds in passages like the description of the House of Morpheus:

> And more, to lulle him in his slumber soft,
> A trickling streame from high rockes tumbling downe,
> And ever-drizling raine upon the loft,
> Mixt with a murmuring winde, much like the sowne
> Of swarming Bees, did cast him in a swowne:
> No other noyse, not peoples troublous cryes,
> As still are wont t'annoy the walled towne,
> Might there be heard; but carelesse Quiet lyes
> Wrapt in eternall silence farre from enemyes.
>
> (Book I, Canto i)

This, again, is anything but negligible poetry. The easy flow and musicality of the rhythm, the contribution of 'ever-drizling raine' and the 'sowne of swarming Bees', with their beautiful marriage of sound to meaning, the bringing of the long verse period easily and without effort to its natural close: all these are typical Spenserian achievements and credit him with a personal voice proceeding from an individual attitude to life. That attitude however, tends in many of its most intimate moments to weariness and abdication. The moral temptation by which the heroes and heroines of *The Faerie Queene* are most persistently beset, and besides which the symbolic dragons and monsters of the poem are so many tedious dummies, is of the kind reflected in the following lines:

> He there does now enjoy eternall rest,
> And happie ease, which thou dost want and crave,
> And further from it dailie wanderest;
> What if some litle paine the passage have,
> That makes fraile flesh to fear the bitter wave?
> Is not short payne well borne, that bringes long ease,
> And layes the soule to sleepe in quiet grave?
> Sleepe after toyle, port after stormie seas,
> Ease after warre, death after life does greatly please.
>
> (Book I, Canto ix)

Needless to say, this does not reflect Spenser's considered reaction to life. Most often, indeed, it is represented, like the languorous pleasures of the flesh, as something to be fought against in the name of a more positive, virile ideal expressed in terms of responsible behaviour, moral self-affirmation. Yet the unity of sentiment and expression which these passages show, and the ease with which the famous stanza adapts itself to this craving for renunciation, are significant. The evidence of style is too powerful, too immediate to be countered even by contrary assertion. With sense and verse movement united in the Spenserian dying fall, the main direction of at least one of the impulses behind the poetry, and one profoundly opposed to the pretensions of *The Faerie Queene* to unity of structure and moral purpose, is apparent.

Feeling of this kind, indeed, based on the abandonment of the positive virtues, tends naturally, in extreme cases, to moral and stylistic disintegration. Spenser's poetry, whilst struggling against this de-

velopment, often illustrates it with peculiar inconsistency. Almost as
typical as the nostalgia we have just discussed, and closely connected
with it, is the sensationalism of the following:

> Ere long they come, where that same wicked wight
> His dwelling has, low in an hollow cave,
> Far underneath a craggie clift ypight,
> Darke, dolefull, drearie, like a greedie grave,
> That still for carrion carcasses doth crave;
> On top whereof aye dwelt the ghastly Owle
> Shrieking his balefull note, which ever drave
> Farre from that haunt all other chearefull fowle;
> And all about it wandring ghostes did wayle and howle.
>
> (Book I, Canto ix)

It is strange to hear the accent of self-conscious melancholy already so
developed in these lines. The setting – the cave with the 'craggie
clift' above it – is thoroughly familiar in the poetry of the romantic
precursors of the eighteenth century; so is the connexion between
darkness in nature and the thought of death. 'Darke, dolefull,
drearie': the artificiality of the inspiration is stressed by the over-
heavy alliteration, taken further in 'greedie grave' and 'carrion
carcasses', whilst over the whole scene, anticipating the emotionally
self-indulgent *Night Thoughts* of a later age, the 'ghastly Owle'
shrieks, inevitably, 'his balefull note'. The wailing 'howle' of
'wandring ghostes' rounds off suitably a passage at once literary and
strained, curiously unsuited to the evocation of the deadly *spiritual*
peril it is supposed to represent. The peril, indeed, if it exists,
proceeds from an important element in the poet's own sensibility.

The Faerie Queene, thus read with an eye to its divergent stylistic
tendencies, in great part belies its own claims to architectural structure and positive content. Its prevailing morality contrasts oddly
with a decorative sensuality that obscures the formal intention and
gives its own kind of life to Spenser's allegorical re-creations. It is
significant that among the most interesting passages of Book III,
which in Spenser's scheme is devoted to Britomart and the virtue of
Chastity, is the sustained and very beautiful description of Adonis'
Garden of Delights. The preceding evocation, similar in spirit, of the
goddess Diana, discovered resting by Venus in the course of her
search for Cupid, is typical:

She having hong upon a bough on high
Her bow and painted quiver, han unlaste
Her silver buskins from her nimble thigh
And her lanke loynes ungirt and brests unbraste,
After her heat the breathing cold to taste;
Her golden lockes, that late in tresses bright
Embreaded were for hindring of her haste,
Now loose about her shoulders hong undight,
And were with sweet Ambrosia all besprinckled light.

(Book III, Canto vi)

The poetic quality of this, and of the whole passage to which it belongs, is not in question. Neither, in itself, is the moral conception of the whole of which it forms a part. That Britomart, the central figure of the Book, represents Married Chastity is, as Professor C. S. Lewis argues[b], true. Nonetheless, the emphasis so persistently laid upon this strain of decorative sensuality seems to point to the presence of a disturbing impulse, to which the symbolic virtue of Britomart provides only a thin counterpart; and for this reason the allegory, as such, fails to keep our attention. The distinctively moralizing strain, when it appears in the same Canto, takes another form. 'All things decay in time, and to their end do draw' we are told, and immediately afterwards the poet draws a wistful contrast between the sources of pleasure and the action of Mutability:

But were it not, that Time their troubler is,
All that in this delightful Garden growes,
Should happie be, and have immortal blis;
For here all plentie, and all pleasure flowes,
And sweet love gentle fits amongst them throwes,
Without fell rancour or fond jealousie.

(Book III, Canto vi)

The intuition is less tragic than sentimental. To the action of time, sensed by Spenser with startling immediacy, the poet, for all his craving for immortality and permanence, can only oppose sensations of their nature impermanent. The 'delightfull Garden', no less than the pastoral convention we have already considered as a typical product of Spenser's society, is make-believe, unreality; its 'immortall blis' is, in fact, no such thing, and the adjective carries no more than a craving for the continuance of 'sweete love', happiness, and 'plentie'.

In theory, of course, *The Faerie Queene* rises from this recognition of impermanence to a moral interpretation capable of imposing itself upon the contradictory impulses revealed; in practice, Spenser's style tends irresistibly to become an instrument of disintegration, furthering the dissolution of the declared moral intention into mere rhythmic flow.

As the poem progresses, however, the moral note, fostered no doubt by personal disappointments and the effects of uncongenial exile, pushes itself rather disagreeably to the fore. As the pretence of allegorical structure collapses almost entirely, and as the tone of the poem becomes increasingly sombre, a new, iron ruthlessness makes itself felt in contrast to courtesy and the craving for idyllic retreat. The outstanding example is the behaviour of Artegall's minion Talus in Book V, which, we are told, represents Spenser's own views about the Irish politics of his time and the way they should be handled:

> Long they her sought, yet nowhere could they finde her,
> That sure they ween'd she was escapt away;
> But Talus, that could like a limehouse winde her,
> And all things secrete wisely could bewray,
> At length found out, whereas she hidden lay
> Under an heape of gold. Thence he her drew
> By the faire lockes, and fowly did array,
> Withouten pitty of her goodly hew,
> That Artegall him selfe her seemlesse plight did rew.
>
> Yet for no pity would he chaunge the course
> Of Justice, which in Talus' hand did lye;
> Who rudely hayld her forth without remorse,
> Still holding up her suppliant hands on hye,
> And kneeling at his feet submissively,
> But he her suppliant hands, those hands of gold,
> And eke her feete, those feete of silver trye,
> Which sought unrighteousnesse, and Justice sold,
> Chopt off, and nayld on high, that all might them behold.
> Her selfe then tooke he by the sclender wast,
> In vain loud crying, and into the flood
> Over the Castell wall adoune her cast,
> And there her drowned in the durty mud.
> But the streame washt away her guilty blood. ...
>
> (Book v, Canto ii)

Once more, the technical mastery (though of a kind quite different from that usually associated with Spenser) is considerable; the very difference testifies to his ability, not always recognized, to compass various and even contrasted styles. The rhymes emphasize the flow of the poet's indignation, and the sharp brutality of 'chopt off' is admirably placed as the culminating point in an effective rhetorical construction. The success, however, calls attention to something fundamentally barbarous in the emotion stressed. The accent falls deliberately on pitilessness, on the supplication (twice insisted on) of the victim, her beauty (suggested in 'faire locks'), and on the physical brutality of the fate which overtakes her. We may at least ask ourselves, whether the motive behind this incident and much else in Book V, is not as much a destructive impulse, born of personal resentment, as the execution of selfless justice it claims to be. Together with Calidore's fruitless effort to put an end permanently to the ravages of the Blatent Beast in Book VI, it throws an interesting light on the spirit in which *The Faerie Queene*, especially in its later parts, was conceived.

That spirit is clearly, on the surface, the reverse of all that we might expect to read into the contemporary court conventions, also incorporated into Spenser's poem in an attempt at epic transformation. The apparent contradiction, however, is an essential part of the feeling of the poem. There are passages from the sixth Book of *The Faerie Queene*, devoted to Courtesy and perhaps the most impregnated with the poet's effort to animate the spirit of court convention, that point the contrast in terms that evidently derive from personal experience. Such is the following (the italics are mine):

> The time was once, in my first prime of yeares,
> When pride of youth forth pricked my desire,
> That I disdained amongst mine equall peares
> To follow sheepe, and shepheardes base attire:
> For further fortune then I would enquire.
> And leaving home, to royall court I sought:
> *Where I did sell myself for yearly hire,*
> *And in the Princes gardin daily wrought:*
> There I beheld such vainenesse as I never thought.
>
> (Book VI, Canto ix)

The presence of strong feeling is surely unmistakable. It finds issue in a sense of 'vainenesse' which prompts a desire to resume the simple life:

> With sight whereof soone cloyd, and long deluded
> With idle hopes, which them do entertaine,
> After I had ten years my self excluded
> From native home, and spent my youth in vaine,
> I gan my follies to my selfe to plaine,
> And this sweet peace, whose lack did there appeare,
> Tho back returning to my sheepe againe,
> I from thenceforth have learn'd to love more deare
> This lowly quiet life, which I inherit here.

No doubt this, if read closely, does not strike us as entirely ingenuous. The return to the 'lowly life', we may reasonably suspect, was forced upon the poet before being accepted by him; without the blasting of his 'idle hopes', the 'vainenesse' which he denounces in court life might well have seemed acceptable enough. But the pathetic accent remains genuine and gives life to an otherwise remote conception.

The rest of Spenser's poetry does not add, in essentials, very much. A number of satirical and occasional poems written at widely different moments in his career – the collection published as *Complaints* in 1591, and *Colin Clouts Come Home Againe* of 1595 – maintain the stylistic qualities of *The Shepheardes Calender*, in some cases matured and affected by the experiences of the intervening years. The two marriage hymns, *Prothalamion* and *Epithalamion*, are splendid pieces of rhetorical decoration in a style of which Spenser was undoubtedly a master. Their skill, in their own kind, is admirable in evoking both sound and colour, and as exercises in literary sensuality dedicated to a conventional purpose they are near perfection. The Platonic *Hymnes*, written at different periods of Spenser's career, might be thought suitable for introducing a deeper philosophic content into his poetry; but, in point of fact, they do no such thing. The pieces abound, indeed, in Platonic phrases, taken out of their philosophic context and embodied into the poems: such phrases as 'soule is forme, and doth the bodie make' (*Hymn of Beautie*), and such commonplaces as –

> Thereof as every earthy thing partakes,
> Or more or lesse by influence divine,
> So it more faire accordingly it makes,
> And the grosse matter of this earthly mine,
> Which clotheth it, thereafter doth refine.

from the same poem, do not seriously claim to communicate a

philosophy but, at best, a rationalized expression of that affirmation of the 'spiritual' in opposition to physical 'dross' which is so marked a characteristic of Spenser's outlook. The structure of these poems corresponds to rhetoric, not to any organization of rational thought. It represents the equivalent, on the allegedly philosophical plane, of the poet's decorative attitude to passion in much of his love-poetry. Within its peculiarly narrow limits it is again almost perfect. One can imagine no development from it in terms of human experience, unless it be the more literary part of Milton's earlier verse up to *Lycidas* and the equally unsubstantial, though more emotional, rhetoric of Shelley's *Adonais*; that is why Spenser's own younger contemporaries, revolting against this abstract, finished perfection, naturally threw up the reaction implied in the poetry of John Donne.

We must conclude, indeed, that Spenser's common designation as the 'poet's poet' can only be accepted with serious reservations. What is most impressive in his style reflects the poet's personal situation, the special conditions of his time, and is therefore largely beyond imitation; what is most easily imitated is the facility, the flow of sound and rhythm. Of the extent of his influence on later writing there can be no doubt, but it is at least questionable whether that influence represented an altogether salutary tendency. The best of Milton is not in the Spenserian polish of his early poems, the best of Keats is not in *The Eve of St Agnes*, nor that of Shelley in *Adonais*; even Tennyson is not at his most interesting or sincere in *The Lotus-Eaters*. The Spenserian tradition, for all its long history, is not in the main line of English poetic development. It produced, within limits, much that we can call perfect, but the true heart of the matter is elsewhere, as we can clearly see if we look beyond him to Chaucer and Langland and the *Sir Gawayne* poet, or to his own near-contemporaries, Shakespeare and Ben Jonson and John Donne.

NOTES

a. On the place of allegory in *Piers Plowman*, see page 132 onwards.
b. C. S. Lewis, *The Allegory of Love*.

ENGLISH ARCHITECTURE IN THE
LATE MIDDLE AGES

BY NIKOLAUS PEVSNER

*Professor of the History of Art, Birkbeck
College, University of London*

WHILE English painting and sculpture of the fourteenth and fifteenth
centuries were steadily looking abroad for inspiration, architecture
was wholly independent. This independence in building style, indeed, dates back much further. The Gothic style was created in the
Ile de France about the middle of the twelfth century; it reached its
moment of classicity in the thirteenth at Chartres, Reims, and Amiens.
This was when Germany, Italy, and Spain took it over – as a startling
innovation, but without understanding its real meaning and implications. By the end of the thirteenth century they had reduced, adapted,
reshaped it into three national Gothics of their own. But England did
the same a hundred years earlier. The Cistercian buildings of the
twelfth century are French, the chancel of Canterbury Cathedral of
1175–c. 85 the design of a Frenchman. But Wells and Lincoln, designed about 1190, are English – English in their preference for
straight-headed chancels rather than the French polygonal ambula-
tories with radiating chapels, English in the balance of verticals by
horizontals which are far more stressed than in France, and English in
the vaults enriched and made heavier by ribs along the ridges and
soon by decorative subsidiary ribs.

Out of these enrichments came, about the year 1290, the Decorated
style, a style of short duration and bewildering originality. No country
on the Continent can show at so early a date so sophisticated and so
luxuriant a treatment of Gothic elements. The pointed arch develops
into the ogee arch; that is, out of the resilient, springy, steep curve of
the thirteenth century grows the undulating, sensuous double curve –
the architectural counterpart of the long, swaying figures in the manu-
scripts. English forms of the early fourteenth century, the flowing
tracery of the windows, the star and grid patterns of the vaulting ribs,
and so on, are often curiously similar to much later German, Span-
ish, and French detail, but by the time these countries had – essentially
independently, it seems – reached them, England had turned to yet

another style, her Perpendicular, which is just as radically opposite to her own preceding Decorated as it is to the flights of fancy in those national Continental late Gothic styles which ran parallel with the English Perpendicular.

The Perpendicular style reached its maturity at the time of Chaucer. It was created, however, as early as about 1330. Its exact place of origin is not clear. The decision lies between the chapter-house of Old St Paul's Cathedral in London and the south transept of the monastery of St Peter (now the Cathedral) at Gloucester. But while questions of origin may be controversial, the character of the new style and its contrast to the Decorated are evident. The contortions of flowing window tracery are replaced by a system based essentially on straight vertical lines. These, as mullions, run right up into the arch of the window, an arch often no longer steeply but depressed pointed ('four-centred'). The mullions are also continued below the windows, forming a blank panelling of the wall below. The motif of panelling more than any other is the hall-mark of Perpendicular decoration. The individual panel consists of two verticals connected by a little arch. In a window such as that at the east end of Gloucester, this motif may, by means of mullions dividing vertically and transoms dividing horizontally, occur as often as eighty times and more. Gloucester Choir, built between 1337 and the fifties, is the paradigm of a Perpendicular interior, all stonework split up into thin, wiry lines meeting at right angles, and all openings large and filled by glass, which if stained was primarily white, yellow, and pale brown, that is, devoid of that ruby and emerald glow which the earlier Gothic style had favoured.

It is a hard, clear, efficient style, powerful but not imaginative, daring in structural matters rather than in inventiveness. The vagaries of the Decorated style are banished, fancy is given asylum only in individual pieces of decoration, such as chantry chapels and screens, and also in the vaults. But even these with their innumerable lierne ribs have patterns as hard and angular as if they were laid out with match-sticks. One exclusively English form of vault was indeed of a fuller and richer character, the fan vault, which, as far as one can see, was also invented at Gloucester. This, while it adds great richness to a room, is structurally just as rational and repetitive as the panel motif. If all the ribs rising from one springing point are given the

Gloucester Cathedral, Interior

same length, the same curvature, and the same distance, a fanlike cone with concave outline will result, and the vault simply consists of a number of these, reaching up from the left and right walls and meeting in the centre. The first surviving example, on a relatively small scale, is the east walk of the cloister at Gloucester, begun after 1351. The courage to take over for the much wider span of a major vault does not seem to have been found earlier than about 1450, when the choir at Sherborne was vaulted.

Sherborne is a monastic church. But amongst the major building work of the late Middle Ages in England, little was done for monasteries. Apart from Sherborne, the rebuilding of Bath Abbey (1495 etc.) and Malvern Priory (c. 1400–60) are worth mentioning, and not much else. Even less was done in cathedrals. After the naves of Winchester (c. 1360–1400) and Canterbury (1378 etc.) had been rebuilt during the second half of the fourteenth century, no major additions were made. The bishops and the abbots had been the chief patrons of the earlier Middle Ages; in the fifteenth century they retreat into the background. Friars' houses, it is true, kept up considerable vitality. The Franciscans or Greyfriars in London had a church begun in 1306 which was nearly 300 feet long. The church of the Austin or White Friars had a length of over 250 feet, that of the Dominicans or Black Friars of about 200. But owing to the universal hatred of the friars at the time of the Reformation, hardly anything that survives is on an impressive scale. Friars' churches were architecturally extremely bare and square – a nave and aisles, and a square chancel divided from the nave by a solid cross wall. The dryness and total lack of imaginative detail fits in well with the character of Perpendicular architecture in general, as exhibited by its major remaining monuments.

The vast majority of these are parish churches. That is perhaps the most important fact of late medieval architecture in England. Not that ambitious parish churches had not existed before, monuments such as Melbourne in Derbyshire of the twelfth century and West Walton in Norfolk of the thirteenth. But it was only with the great prosperity of the wool and cloth trades in the fourteenth and fifteenth that they became common in all districts which benefited from the boom. Sheers, scales, sailing-ships, woolpacks, staplemarks are prominently displayed outside the Lane Aisle at Cullompton Church and the Greenway Aisle at Tiverton Church, both in Devon (1528 and 1517), and in a window of his house at Holme near Newark, close to the little church entirely built by him, John Barton is said to have put up an inscription which ran: 'I thank God and ever shall; It's the sheepe hath paid for all'. John Barton had built a whole church, John Lane an aisle the size of Barton's church. Adding to existing buildings and complete rebuilding went on side by side all over the country. According to this, English parish churches fall clearly into two types, those which by gradual growth have assumed a happy informality of appearance, the favourite hunting-ground for the student eager to discover and distinguish the architectural styles of a long order of generations, and those erected in one go, over a short time, with ample funds, and to one plan. They are as a rule less lovable but more impressive. Their aesthetic values are more pronounced, because aimed at, whereas in the other type they are due to the accident of a new aisle or chapel making an attractive picture with the nave or choir or tower already existing on the site. These new chapels or aisles, if they were not the gift of a merchant, might be given by the lord of the manor, some member of the high aristocracy, such as the fan-vaulted aisle at Ottery St Mary in Devon added to the fourteenth-century church early in the sixteenth century by the Countess of Devon; or by a guild, as for instance at Uxbridge in Middlesex, where the guild of St Mary and St Margaret built a chapel to the south of the church overtowering with its roof the older church and reaching nearly up to the height of the tower. To the church of Holy Trinity at Coventry the Dyers, the Mercers, the Butchers, the Tanners, and the fraternity of Corpus Christi gradually added chapels.

The importance of the guild in the cultural life of the late Middle Ages is familiar. It is said that Norfolk possessed over 900, and the City of York about 180. Edward III accepted membership of the Merchant Taylors of London, and the chief guild of Coventry counted amongst its members Henry IV, the Duke of Bedford, Dick Whittington of London, William Grevel of Chipping Campden, and even Italian merchants. Of guild-halls a number survive in England – for instance, at King's Lynn and Lavenham – though none as splendid as those of the Netherlands. The aisles and chapels of churches were, it is known, used for plenty of secular purposes.

Large parish churches completely rebuilt in the Perpendicular style are chiefly to be found in the areas of the greatest prosperity in the fourteenth and fifteenth centuries – that is, the sheep-farming and cloth-making areas. The north of the country is wanting in them because of the hazards of border warfare, the country immediately round London because of much later rebuilding, and a number of cathedral towns (such as York and Exeter) because of the overpowering presence of the cathedral. Otherwise they can be seen all over East Anglia, into Lincolnshire, Northamptonshire, and Yorkshire, in the West Midlands, the Cotswolds, and all the south-west. They stand in the cities of today, such as Hull and Bristol, in cathedral towns such as Norwich and Wells, in small country towns which were once rich, such as Long Melford and Thaxted, or Northleach and Chipping Campden, or Cullompton, or Oakham; and they stand in villages that are now poor but were then teeming with wealth, all on their own, where the decline of farming and local industry has obliterated the traces of former villages. This is the case, for instance, of Terrington St Clement in north Norfolk, the 'Cathedral of the Marshes'.

Their style has regional peculiarities, but is on the whole the same all over the country. In plan the Perpendicular ideal is no doubt the perfect parallelogram consisting of nave and aisles, west tower embraced by the west bays of the aisles, and chancel and chancel aisles, without anything projecting anywhere, except perhaps the east bay of the chancel with the altar. East and west end have the largest possible windows, and if there are transepts, these also would be made into square glass cages. The nave is divided from the aisles and the chancel from the chancel chapels by slender piers, usually sub-divided into many parallel shafts with shallow grooves between. Forms never swell forward; they are thin and often concave. Capitals as a rule are insignificant and often wholly or partially absent, so that pier mouldings and arch mouldings flow into one. The arcade is tall, a clerestory rises above it, and the aisle windows are large so that the room is amply lit. Little of the mysterious semi-darkness of the earlier Middle Ages survived into the Tudor Age. With the wide and high openings between nave and aisles and the growing width of aisles in relation to naves – in the end they are sometimes of nearly equal width – the impression is created of one room sub-divided, as against the three parallel, but separate, west-east streams of nave and aisles in earlier churches. This unification had its practical use, in connexion with the

232

growing importance of the sermon in the church service, and may well have been suggested to parish churches at first by the large and plain buildings of the friars. Architectural decoration as a rule is sparse. Some may surround the porch or doorway, and some is often applied to what little remains of solid wall surface between the arcade and the clerestory windows. It usually consists of blank tracery panelling not in itself very interesting in design.

Space does not here allow to illustrate more than one parish church. Lavenham in Suffolk has now less than 300 inhabitants; about 1400 it

Lavenham Church, Suffolk, from the South

was wealthy enough to be amongst the seventy towns of England asked by Richard II to lend him money. With the exception of the chancel (of early fourteenth-century date) the church was completely rebuilt during the age of Henry VII and Henry VIII. It is about 175 feet long and to the top of the west tower 141 feet high. Rebuilding was due to apparently undisturbed co-operation between the lords of the manor and the clothiers of the town. The lords of the manor were the de Veres, Earls of Oxford, a family tracing back its origin to a brother-in-law of William the Conqueror and still in possession of their Essex lands in the early seventeenth century. The tower was begun first, with moneys given by Thomas Spring, son of Thomas

Spring, who in 1486 left 300 marks; that is, about £5,000 in terms of value before the First World War, 'ad edificandum campanilem in stepyl ecclesiae'. His merchant's mark can be seen on the plinth. In 1487 another merchant, Aleyn Sexton, left double that sum also for the steeple; in 1493 James Spring £40 (about £1,000). The nave was rebuilt before the tower was completed. In 1494 Rose Grome bequeathed £20 'for the making of an arch', but the bulk of the extensive work on nave and aisles was paid for by John de Vere, the thirteenth Earl. He died in 1513, and his arms appear on the south porch and in the spandrels of the nave arcade. The clerestory windows once showed them (and those of relations) 102 times in the stained glass. The bosses of the timber roof have also de Vere arms, but in conjunction with those recently granted to the Spring family. Helping to build a church was an act pleasant to God, self-praise was not considered to detract from its merit. The age of wholesale indulgences and remission of sins on payment of money could not have strong feelings in favour of anonymity.

The chapels added to the chancel on the south and north sides by the Spring and Branch families about 1525 were chantry chapels, and the purpose of chantry chapels, as they began to be favoured by the mighty and the wealthy in the fourteenth century, was to ensure masses to be said in perpetuity for their own salvation and that of their family or fraternity or guild. Two thousand or more such chapels existed at the end of the Middle Ages. They form the chief Perpendicular enrichment to the cathedrals. The Alcock and the West Chapels at Ely, the Oldham and the Speke Chapels at Exeter, William of Wykeham's chapel at Winchester are only a few picked out at random. Endowments were lavish, and not for the glory of God. Thomas Lord West who died in 1406 left money to Christchurch Priory in Hampshire for 4,500 soul-masses to be recited within six months. On the Spring Chapel at Lavenham an inscription says: 'Orate pro animabus Thomas Spring armigeris et Alice uxoris eius qui istam capellam fieri fecerunt a. dm. MCCCCC vicesimo quarto'. The Branch Chapel has a similar inscription. In 1523 Thomas Spring, son of the other Thomas Spring, had also given £200 (£5,000 today) to the completion of the steeple. A brass in the north aisle also records Alleyn Dister who died in 1534. It says of him in the vernacular tongue: 'A clothir vertuous he was in Lavenham many a year'.

Lavenham Church, Interior

As has been shown, work on the church and work on the tower went on concurrently, and both are indeed equally ambitious. The tower of Lavenham is not specially graceful, but it is sturdy, and a landmark to the glory of the church, the town, and the donors. Towers, indeed, were a special pride of the parish churches in the late Middle Ages – and not only in England. The tallest building of Europe is still the Minster of Ulm in Germany (c. 480 feet), which is a parish church. In England, Louth is 300 feet high, Boston in Lincolnshire 295. At Boston, large as the church is, it appears from some angles almost as an appendix to the steeple. The same effect comes about often, where a church remained in an earlier state and only the tower was rebuilt. Even cathedrals now felt impelled to re-build their crossing towers on the most ambitious scale: Bell Harry at Canterbury is of c. 1490, the crossing tower at Gloucester of c. 1450, that at Durham of c. 1465–90, and so on. In detail, there are as many peculiarities of towers as there are regions of England. Spires are characteristic chiefly of those parts of the eastern Midlands which have their architectural centre in the wealthy Nene valley in North-amptonshire. The absence of spires is, however, characteristic of Eng-lish church towers as a whole, a feature which affects landscape in most countries and impresses the traveller from abroad. At some time in the fourteenth century taste must have changed and the pyramid roofs or the needle-sharp points of such spires as those of Salis-bury and Norwich Cathedrals no longer appealed to the English. That time, one would be inclined to think, must have coincided with the coming of the Perpendicular style. Rectangular crossings of mullions and transoms and straight-ended chancels may well have called for a counterpart in the rectangular outline of towers. They make the whole architectural scenery of England decidedly Perpendicular.

If the west towers are the chief pieces of external display of English parish churches, the timber roofs are their internal glory. No other country of Europe has anything to compare with them. It is true that, on the other hand, England has never had the faith in stone vaulting which existed, for instance, in France. Even cathedrals were ready to put up with timber vaults shaped in imitation of stone. But where the carpenter was allowed to show his skill, he outdid all his Continental fellows. Long traditions of shipbuilding may have contributed to this mastery. Regionally the highest achievements belong to East Anglia. They are based on that construction known as the hammerbeam roof which seems to have been invented in the fourteenth century. Double hammerbeam roofs are by no means rare, and also compound forms where hammerbeams alternate with simple arched braces. The effects are dazzling to the eye, as complex as those of Perpendicular stone vaults with their innumerable lierne ribs, but of a structural solidity and hardness of line which must have been specially congenial to the English. A regional speciality of the south-west are the wagon roofs or cradle roofs, where all rafters, and not only the principal ones, have curved braces so that the result looks like the hulk of a ship upside-down or the hooped awning of a wagon, especially when the interstices between the rafters are filled in with panelling. This is sometimes quite elegantly decorated, but on the whole the roof remains a display of a sturdier craft.

Subtler decoration in timber was lavished on screens. There was a wealth of screens in the Perpendicular parish church which it is hard for us to conceive. The architect, we have seen, provided as few structural divisions as he could possibly be allowed. So the chancel had to be separated from the nave by a screen, known as the rood screen, and chapel had to be divided from chapel by minor screens known as parclose screens. The younger Thomas Spring of Lavenham said in his will in 1523 that he wished to be buried in front of the altar of St Catherine 'where I will be made a Tombe with a Parclose there-about'. In East Anglia screens carry much painting, usually of inferior quality; in Devon they are enriched with the greatest sumptuousness, though even there much of the detail is standardized to a degree un-imaginable in Late Gothic Germany or Spain. The Perpendicular style, may it aim at ever so impressive a display, is not an imaginative style of architecture.

Timber has influenced English church building more than any other material. As for stonework, it has already been said that the best in the country is due to the oölitic limestones of that band which runs diagonally from Somerset to Northamptonshire and the North Sea. Of other kinds of stone which have left a distinguishing mark, only two need be mentioned, granite and flint. The granite of the south-west resulted in buildings of extreme simplicity of detail and only very rarely of crude lavishness (Launceston). Flint, knapped into smoothness one one side, serves to decorate the exterior of porches and such-like pieces of display in East Anglia. Brick, oddly enough, had gone entirely out of use in England from the end of the Roman era to the thirteenth century. It was then reintroduced from Holland, but did not gain recognition as a building material on an equal footing with stone until the fifteenth century. The early Tudor Age at last favoured it even for its proudest palaces. Into its proudest sacred buildings, however, it has nowhere forced its entry.

These proudest sacred buildings of the last medieval century in England are neither cathedrals nor parish churches. They are the Royal chapels built by the kings for their palaces or a favourite church or some other specially favoured foundation. The earliest of them was St Stephen's Chapel in the Palace of Westminster, burnt, alas, in 1834. It was begun in 1292 and completed in the 1350s. According to some, it should be regarded as the cradle of the Perpendicular style. From our present point of view what matters principally is that its exterior, a long plain oblong with large windows and at the four angles thin pinnacled turrets, became the type of the Royal chapels of the fifteenth and early sixteenth centuries. They are the following: Eton College Chapel begun in 1441, King's College Chapel at Cambridge begun in 1446 but completed only in 1515, St George's Chapel at Windsor begun in 1474, and the chantry chapel of Henry VII at the east end of Westminster Abbey built by Henry VIII in 1503–19. All these have in common with the parish churches an extreme simplicity of plan. What distinguishes them more than anything else is their stone vaults. That at Windsor is of the lierne rib type and as elaborate as the most elaborate in cathedrals. At King's College a similar vault was, it seems, projected, but when, finally, in the years 1508 to 1515, it came to the completion of the chapel, a fan-vault was substituted, on the pattern of Sherborne (and the east end of Peterborough which immediately precedes Cambridge). The result is one of the most splendid impressions the lastest Gothic style has to offer anywhere in Europe. The building is extremely long in relation to its width. The low side chapels running all the way along on both sides are screened or walled off so as not to interfere with that spatial unity which the Perpendicular style wished to create. Above these screens or walls are windows of five lights each filling the wall space almost completely. Their closely set mullions descend into the screens below so that the whole of the wall is covered with slender uprights. But the fan-vault lies massive on them and restores the balance of vertical and horizontal. That a balance could also be achieved between an intended luxuriance and such standardized elements as the window tracery and the fans with their narrow ribs and uniform panelling is much more astonishing. Decoration, apart from these ever-recurring motifs, is crisp and skilful though decidedly hard. It consists chiefly of coats-of-arms and beasts as supporters. An excessive emphasis on heraldry is characteristically English, also in the parish church and the manor-house. It is as significant socially as aesthetically. The social implications need not here be discussed, aesthetically it shows the same preference for relatively unimaginative over more fanciful forms as we have seen in architecture proper.

King's College Chapel formed part of the foundation at Cambridge of a King's College by Henry VI. He, in his so-called testament of 1448, intended it to be 'in large fourme, clene and substantial, settyng a parte superfluite of too great curious workes of enteille and besy moulding'. Henry VIII, typically enough, did not abide by this advice. It yet is one of the truest contemporary descriptions of the character of English Perpendicular which we possess. King's College, in spite of the postulated plainness of execution, was to be on a grander scale than any Cambridge College before, grander even than William of Wykeham's New College at Oxford, the largest and architecturally most unified college then in existence. William of Wykeham had founded it, in conjunction with his new school at Winchester, in 1379. Eton College, founded in 1440, played the same part relative to King's College. The educational aspects of these foundations do not concern us here, although the fact that the munificence of bishops, kings, queens, and noblemen now endowed colleges to train men of secular as well as clerical achievements clearly forms a parallel to the gradually growing importance of secular architecture in England in competition with the religious architecture which had, down to the later thirteenth century, so indubitably prevailed. The parallelism goes even further. The very layout of the medieval college, especially at Cambridge with its gatehouse, courtyard, hall, high table, and kitchens, is a reflection of the layout of the contemporary manor-house.

The manor-house is the most significant creation of late medieval

King's College Chapel, Cambridge, Interior

domestic architecture in England. There was, in spite of the Wars of the Roses, far more security inside the country than there had been before, and so the castle began to open its façades into large windows, and concurrently to open its plan from the compactness of military requirements to the freedom and comforts of a less restricted life. Not that the castle of the twelfth and thirteenth centuries had been necessarily less spacious within its thick walls. Moreover, it is a mistake to think that the medieval castle in general had the keep as its principal living-quarters. That is not so. We have evidence of independent Norman halls in the bailey of a castle (Richmond, Yorkshire) and at least one completely surviving twelfth-century hall (Oakham, Rutland). In the thirteenth century such halls were sometimes architecturally of an elegance matching that of Early English cathedrals. The Hall of the Bishops and Coints Palatine of Durham at Bishop Auckland (now the chapel of the bishop's palace) is the finest surviving example. Such halls had aisles, and it was only in the fourteenth century that developments in the construction of timber roofs allowed for large halls to be built without inner supports. Westminster Hall, the hall of the Kings of England, is the grandest of all, over 238 feet long, 69 feet wide, and over 80 feet high, with a splendid hammerbeam roof. The date is 1393–1400. By that time England had already created, for less representational and more domestic purposes, a type of house with the hall as its nucleus, which is characteristic of the country and of the time. It seems to differ from other countries. It is the type with a hall and a porch leading into a passage divided from the hall proper by a wooden screen. On the other side of this screen passage, three doors lead into buttery, corridor to the kitchen lying farther back, and pantry. Kitchens were large apartments with hearth-openings of considerable size. Some were planned with great ingenuity, notably the monastic kitchen of the prior and monks of Durham Cathedral, built about 1370, and provided with a rib-vault of strangely moorish character. The halls had either a big chimney on one side, or an open fire in the middle, ventilated through a louvre in the roof. At the far end of the hall, away from the smells of the kitchen and the draughts of the screen passage was the high table, and at one end of this a door to the principal staircase which led up to the solar or parlour or withdrawing-room. Privacy in the house was improving during the fourteenth century, and already Langland in *Piers*

Plowman could complain that meals were no longer taken by the lord and lady in the hall.

> Now hath each riche a reule · to eten by hym-selve
> In a prye-parloure, · for pore mennes sake,
> Or in a chambre with a chymney, · and leve the chief halle.

There are no specially lavish chimney-pieces preserved of the fourteenth century, but that in the Bishop's Palace at Exeter of about 1480 can vie with the most ambitious on the Continent. Another enrichment of the hall, however, can be traced back to John of Gaunt's time at least, the bay-window at the high-table end. This survives in the splendid hall at Kenilworth. Kenilworth is one of the most precious survivals of fourteenth-century domestic display. A little earlier

Haddon Hall, Derbyshire

are the ranges containing hall and adjuncts at Haddon and Penshurst. Haddon was the house of the Vernons, members of the high nobility, Penshurst was built by John Poulteney, a merchant and four times mayor of London. The magnificence which the hall of a merchant's house could display even inside the City of London is exemplified by Crosby Hall which once stood in Bishopsgate and was later re-erected in Chelsea.

Parallel with the rise in the wealth and status of the merchants and the power of their guilds goes a similar development in the standing of the best masons. The first on whose life and circumstances we are well informed is Henry Yevele who was one of the leading members of the London guild in 1356, and a few years later became Master of the King's Works in the Palace of Westminster and the Tower. He was the mason of Westminster Hall and the nave of Westminster Abbey and very probably of the nave of Canterbury Cathedral. Much else was built to his design or, as it was then called, his 'devyse', though more has been attributed to him than can be justified. He was

Penshurst Place, Kent

one of the two Wardens of London Bridge and owned property in London and estates on the Isle of Purbeck and in Essex. He must have known Chaucer well who was made Clerk of the King's Works in 1389, and as a sign of the social rank which he attained it may be quoted that he appears as a guest for dinner at William of Wykeham's London house in 1393 together with Lord Ponynges, the rector of his own parish church in the City, and others. As for later masons we know many of their names, and many outstanding works of the Early Tudor decades can be attributed to known designers. Mr John Harvey has lately collected much information on them. The completion of King's College Chapel at Cambridge was due to John Wastell, who also designed Bell Harry at Cambridge. Hampton Court and Cardinal College were in the hands of Henry Redman. The brothers Robert and William Vertue designed first the vaults of Bath Abbey and then Henry VII's Chapel at Westminster Abbey. Their names are worth recording, as all these leading works of about 1500 show considerable originality, ingeniousness, and sense of beauty.

There was evidently no division of work between ecclesiastical and secular specialists. A man like Henry Yevele was responsible for churches as well as houses, and also for castles. As regards castles, the

Bodiam Castle, Sussex

late Middle Ages in England went on to build new ones, at least in those regions in which no political security had yet been accomplished. They were designed along the lines laid down by the most representational Edwardian castles and paralleled in France and Italy. Castles, that is to say, remained symmetrical and monumental. There are chiefly two types, both tall and square from outside, with battlements and machicolations, and with angle towers or turrets. The one has an inner courtyard, the other is solid. It is not certain to which of the two Sir Gawayne's castle belongs, but it clearly belongs to one of them. Of the first type, the most spectacular English example is Bodiam in Sussex, for which the King granted his licence in 1386; of the second, Warkworth in Northumberland, where the date of the licence is 1377.

The second is indeed a speciality of the Scottish border. In the south –
except for the chain of castles built by Henry VIII against the French
along the south coast from Sandwich to Falmouth – the castle by the
beginning of the Tudor Age had disappeared, and Henry VIII's
castles are in characteristic ways different from those of the Middle
Ages. They are low and squat, for defence against cannon and for
mounting cannon, and they are planned in new symmetrical shapes
with three-, four-, or six-lobed bastions surrounding a higher core.
The designing engineers looked to Italy for technique and pattern.

The Age of Henry VIII saw indeed the introduction into England
of a fashion of alien ornamentation, developed as part of a new architectural style in Italy during the fifteenth century. But what there had
been, the visual expression of a new system of thought, was in the
North no more than a fashion of ornament at the courts. Renaissance
laws of proportion could not be appreciated for a long time, but
Renaissance symmetry of planning could be linked up with existing
indigenous tendencies. Thus castles ever since Harlech and Beaumaris
had sometimes been strictly symmetrical. The principle was now applied to the country house, first to its façade, then, occasionally even to
elements in its plan. As one approaches Hampton Court, one sees a
front with two identical wings projecting at the sides, and a central
gatehouse. The first courtyard which one then enters is also symmetrical, and the second gatehouse lies in axis with the first. Then,
however, in the inner court the symmetry is broken, and the Hall
placed on the left side with nothing to balance it on the right. In
Wolsey's Cardinal College at Oxford, later to be renamed Christ
Church, the same is to be found, a symmetrical outer façade, a
hundred and fifty years later completed by Christopher Wren's Tom
Tower, and then a large quadrangle with the Hall placed asymmetric-
ally. Cardinal College was begun in 1525, Hampton Court in 1514.
Both were intended by Wolsey to be the grandest of their kind in the
country. 'Why come ye not to Court?' wrote Skelton,

> To wyche court?
> To the Kynges Courte?
> Or to Hampton Court?
> Nay, to the Kynges Courte,
> But Hampton Court
> Hath the preemynence.

Hampton Court was indeed planned on a scale leaving behind even Chambord. It tried to vie with France also in another respect, though only feebly. It was the first country house in England to incorporate details in the new Italian style. On the turrets of the gatehouses are majolica medallions with busts of Roman Emperors in naturalistic foliage and flower wreaths. The subject was alien, and the ornament, so different from the bossy stylized leaves in which the Perpendicular style excelled, was alien too. It is indeed known that Giovanni da Maiano, a Tuscan sculptor, was paid for these medallions. The date is

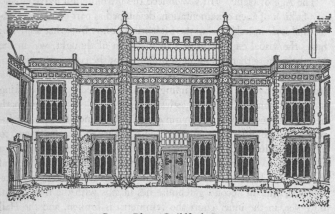

Sutton Place, Guildford, Surrey

1521. Earlier still is the date of the tomb of Henry VII in Westminster by Pietro Torrigiani. The contract was made in 1512, and that year marks the arrival of the Italian fashion. But there is only one work of architecture built under Henry VIII to which the term Renaissance can be applied for better than ornamental reasons: Sutton Place in Surrey – near London and the court.

At Sutton Place, which was built in 1523–7, the new ideals for once affect the plan, that is, the essence of the building. A central gatehouse, in a wing now demolished, led into an inner courtyard. The hall lies at the far end and its entrance is in axis with the former gatehouse. In fact, the whole hall front is a symmetrical composition, so much so that the bay-window at the high-table end is matched on the side of the offices by an identical bay-window without any functional justification. This seems the first time in England that an imposed evenness of design interferes with considerations of use. The next time the same principle turns up is at Kirby Hall in 1570, that is, in the fullness of the Elizabethan style. The front of Sutton Place has in other respects also a remarkably Elizabethan appearance. All windows are large, transomed, and straight-headed, and thereby create a grid of

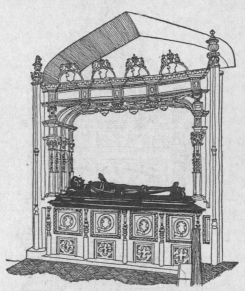

Tomb of Henry Lord Marney, Layer Marney Church,
typical of the 1520s

uprights and horizontals over the whole façade which heralds the system of Hardwick Hall at the end of the century.

'Hardwick Hall – more window than wall.' More window than wall had already been the principle of the Perpendicular style, in church buildings as well as such halls as Hampton Court. Symmetry also and Italian detail had already come in under Henry VIII. What, then, distinguishes the Later from the Earlier Tudor style? It is partly a matter of straight development. Symmetry was the exception at the beginning – such famous houses as Compton Wynyates, about 1520, have none of it – in Elizabethan days it was the rule. The demand for imposed form as a prerequisite of beauty also became universal only under Elizabeth. Italian details similarly were rare and very superficially applied at the beginning, and handled with ease and consider-

Tomb of Sir William Sharington at Lacock Abbey, Wiltshire, typical of the 1550s

able freedom later. Ease and freedom in this case were by no means interchangeable expressions. Ease had to be acquired first, before liberties could be taken.

The Italian style as more than an ornamental fashion applied to details was introduced into England by a small group of leading men of the Protectorate, Somerset and then Northumberland, and a few courtiers around them. Old Somerset House in the Strand of 1546–9 had, on the French example, windows with pediments, a balustrade all along the top, and in the centre a triple entrance with detached columns, a motif derived from Roman triumphal arches. Somerset's protégé, Sir William Sharington, at Lacock Abbey in Wiltshire, before 1553, installed two stone tables in a tower which, from their style, could be found just as well in Italy or the Netherlands. Sharington was also in touch with Northumberland, and Northumberland on his part paid in 1550 for a painter called John Shute to go and study up-to-date architecture in Italy. Shute came back and in 1563 published his *First and Chief Groundes of Architecture*, the earliest book of architectural theory in England. In the book he calls himself 'paynter and archytecte'. That also was new.

The appearance of the architect, as opposed to the mason, marks the beginning of the modern age as clearly as the appearance of the orders of columns which are Shute's object in his book. His treatment is far from correct. There is still much confusion dating from a Gothic past, but there is also a robust exuberance of fancy which is neither Gothic nor Italian. It has to be called Elizabethan.

The Elizabethan style as such cannot be treated here. It clearly belongs to a new chapter in English civilization. What characterizes Elizabethan architecture is the mixture of Perpendicular and Italo-Franco-Renaissance elements. The individual motifs, especially in houses in intimate connexion with the court, are usually of the second, but the spirit in which they are used is of the first kind. The result is far from harmonious, and nearly always far from elegant. But it is robust and original, and, with all its solecisms and mannerisms, wholly illustrative of the spirit of Elizabethan England.

PART
IV

AN ANTHOLOGY
OF MEDIEVAL POEMS

EDITED BY FRANCIS BERRY

★ Editorial titles

INTRODUCTION

This first volume of *The Pelican Guide to English Literature* differs from all the succeeding volumes in that it consists not only of critical essays, but also of an anthology of poems drawn from the period. The simple reason for including this anthology (which makes the book an unusual one by any standard) is to enable people to read some of the poetry which the essays have been discussing. As we said in the General Introduction, the success of this whole venture depends on the degree to which people go to the literature itself. But the literature with which this volume is concerned is not easy to go to – indeed, much of it is virtually inaccessible to the general reader. Either the local library will have no copy of, for instance, *Sir Gawayne* or of the *First Shepherds' Play* from the Towneley Mystery Cycle; or, if the library has a copy of *Sir Gawayne*, the general reader will be hardly any nearer reading the poem since he will find it reproduced in a script that includes extinct characters and sigla. In which case the earlier essays might have aroused the reader's interest in this great poem to no purpose.

It thus seemed imperative to provide the general reader with a substantial anthology containing some of the main poems discussed earlier, and to provide them in an intelligible form. In this way the volume becomes an introduction in the full sense.

Choice of Poems

The anthology has been chosen from the best and most interesting English verse of the Middle Ages which has been hitherto more or less inaccessible to the general reader. It is this consideration of accessibility which accounts for the fact that the anthology contains no Chaucer or Dunbar or Henryson, nothing from *Everyman*, and no short lyrics and carols and ballads. It is the criterion of merit that ruled out even a token representation of some kinds of verse, such as the chronicles, or rhymed axioms, or metrical expositons of dogma, or verse whose chief interest is linguistic or historical. As a compromise, however, *Sir Orfeo* has been included though it is accessible.

With merit and inaccessibility as the main tests, the poems were chosen as representing a wide variety of kind; romance, poetry, allegory, works intended primarily for entertainment, works intended primarily for moral instruction, poems chiefly of French background and inspiration, poems chiefly of native (often provincial) background and inspiration, narrative, drama, verse in rhyme and accent, and verse in the old alliterative rhythm, are all represented.

But any attempt to represent the entire period (virtually the eleventh to the fifteenth centuries) was impossible because of the need to make the selection intelligible to the general reader, a consideration which has in fact confined the selection to the late thirteenth to the fifteenth centuries. Fortunately, for present purposes, the best post-conquest verse does belong to the fourteenth century (or has survived only in texts of that century), and the Miracle plays have survived only in fifteenth-century transcripts. Whereas the general reader can grasp most verse of the fourteenth century after only a little practice and familiarity (though *Sir Gawayne*, because of its dialect and many words of Norse origin, is still hard), he would be discouraged by such earlier poems as *The Owl and the Nightingale*, unless it were to be virtually transformed from the original.

A final consideration, in compiling this anthology, has been to offer *complete* poems or parts of poems. It was essential, for instance, to give at least some of *Piers Plowman*, though impossible to give it all. Hence a single but complete episode from B text has been chosen, in our opinion one that is unsurpassed of its kind by Langland. Similarly, complete stories from Mannyng and Gower have been given; and a complete play from the York Mystery Cycle.

What is offered then, is an anthology of the best inaccessible poetry mainly of the fourteenth century, and readers may be interested to know that this is the *only* anthology of its kind.

Editing the Texts

With the general reader in mind, the controlling principle in editing the texts has been to produce a version which is as easy as possible to follow *while keeping editorial interference to the minimum*. To this end the extinct character and sigla, such as þ, ð, ȝ, have been replaced by their nearest modern equivalents or combinations; and there has been a general substitution of our modern *i, v,* and *wh* for such older signs as *ȝ, j, u,* and *hw*.

The main aim has been neither 'translation' nor 'modernization' (both of which are distortions of the original), but what might be called 'normalization' – offering the poems as they are with only a discreet normalizing of the spelling, punctuation, lineation, etc., where this makes the difference between the reader's comprehension and frustration. None the less, where the older spelling has some significance or is readily intelligible, it has been left alone. Moreover, the poems included vary considerably in their linguistic difficulty from the hard *Sir Gawayne* and Langland to the easy Gower and *Roberd of Cisyle* (where the earliest extant text is later than the composition of the poem and so, probably, is already a 'normalization' to some extent); for this reason, the degree of editorial attention has varied from poem to poem, without any attempt to impose editorial consistency on the anthology as a whole.

In all the alliterative poems in this anthology, a point has been inserted to indicate the rhythmic break in each line, thus:

In the monethe of Maye · when mirthes bene fele,
And the sesone of somere · when softe bene the wedres ...

For a discussion of the rhythm of the alliterative line, see pp. 134 and 150 in this volume.

Each poem has been glossed as a separate unit; as a general rule difficult words have been glossed at the foot of the page on their first three appearances. But again this rule has been treated inconsistently, and some words have been glossed fewer times and some many more than this, depending on their obscurity and unfamiliar appearance. As a further help to the reader, a literal translation of the first dozen or so lines of each poem has been provided. However, the reader is best advised not to interrupt a first general impression of the poem by a crippling zeal to understand every word as it occurs, but rather to take a good deal for granted as he would if he were hearing for the first time a poem in an unfamiliar dialect.

Brief notes on authorship, etc., are given at the end of each poem.

A Note on Pronunciation

It is worth keeping in mind, while reading, that English spelling at this period was much more nearly phonetic than it is now (pronunciation having changed greatly, while spelling has not). So every letter (or group of letters like *th* or *gh*) must be taken to represent a sound: in a word like knight, both the *k* and the *gh* were pronounced, the *gh* much as in the present-day Scots pronunciation of night. As in Scots, too, *r* in all positions was slightly trilled; and the final *e* had, very often, the value we give to the *-er* in a word like rather. For the rest, the short vowels should be pronounced as in the north of England today; while, of the long ones, *ā* had its value as in our word father, *i* as in machine, and *ū* (spelt *ou*) as in rude. The long vowels *ē* and *ō* (often indicated by doubling – *ee*, *oo*) had each two varieties of pronunciation which give even specialists trouble: perhaps the modern reader need only remember to give words which contain them – the words 'mete' (*meet*) and 'fote' (*feet*), for instance – genuine *ē* and *ō* sounds, that is, to pronounce 'mete' much like our word mate, and 'fore' and 'mode' (*mood*) with something like the vowel of our word moat.

ACKNOWLEDGEMENTS

The Editor would like to acknowledge his indebtedness to his editorial predecessors, particularly for help he has received from consulting the E.E.T.S. editions of *Sir Gawayne and the Grene Knight*, the *First Shepherds' Play*, and *Robert Mannyng* (by F. J. Furnivall); and of *Piers Plowman*; Mr Kenneth Sisam's *Fourteenth Century Verse and Prose* (for *Sir Orfeo*); the Roxburghe Club Editions and the late Sir I. Gollancz for the *Parlement of the Thre Ages* and *Wynnere and Wastoure*; the E.E.T.S. edition of Gower; and the Clarendon Press for the Toulmin Smith edition of the York Play.

*

The Wicche, the Bagge and the Bisshop

There was a wicche, and made a bagge,
A bely of lethyr, a grete swagge.
She sigaldryd so thys bagge-bely
That hit yede and soke mennys ky,
5 At evene, and at morw tide,
In here pasture, other ellys be-side.
Long hyt yede aboute fast,
Til hit was parceyved at the last.
Than al the godemen of the toune,
10 Byfore the bysshop dyden here somoune;
They dyden the bagge with here bere,
To wete what she shuld answere.
Hit was shewyd byfore the bisshop,
That she dide to goo swich a melk-slop,
15 Thurgh wycchecraft and misaventure,
To sugke here keyn in here pasture.

The Witch, The Bag and the Bishop

There was a witch, and she made a bag,
A belly of leather, a great swag,
She so contrived this belly-bag
That it walked about and sucked men's cattle
5 *At evening, and in the morning tide,*
At their pasture, or elsewhere.
Long it walked about and fast,
Till it was perceived at last.
Then all the goodmen of the town
10 *Before the bishop did the witch summon;*
They caused her to bring the bag with her
To see what she would answer.
It was shown before the bishop
How the witch caused to walk such a milk-slop,
15 *Through witchcraft and through misadventure,*
To suck their cattle in their pasture.

257

The bisshop merveyled, and other mo,
How that she might [1]do hit go.
'Dame,' seyd the bysshop, 'do thy quentyse[2],
20 And late us se how hit shal ryse.'
Thys wycche here charme began to sey,
[3]The slop ros up, and yede the weye.
The bysshop seyd, 'thys have we seyn;
[4]Do hit now to lygge ageyn.'
25 The wycche dede al at hys wylle:
She made the slop agen lygge stylle.
The bisshop made a clerk than write
Al that she seyd, mochel and lite,
And alle how she made here went;
30 The bysshop tharto gaf gode entent.
'Than,' seyde the bisshop, 'now shal I,
As thou hast do, do thy maystry[5].'
The bisshop bygan the charme to rede,
And as she dyde, he dyde in dede;
35 He seyd and dede every deyl,
Ryght as she dede, he dede as weyl.
The sloppe lay stille, as hit ded wore,
For him ne ros hit never the more.
'Why,' seyd he, 'wil hit nat ryse?
40 And I have do the same wyse,
And seyd the wurdys, lesse ne mo,
And for my seying wil hit nat go?'
'Nay,' she seyd, 'why shuld hit so?
Ye beleve nat as I do.
45 Wulde ye beleve my wurdys as I,
Hit shulde a go, [6]and sokum ky.'
He seyd, 'than faileth noght but belevyng.'
She seyd, 'that helpeth al my thing;
And so hit is for oure lawe,
50 [7]Beleve is more than the sawe.
For, thou mayst sey what thou wilt,

1. 'make it walk', 2. tricks, 3. 'The bag rose up, and took its way',
4. 'Cause it now to lie still again', 5. mystery, achievement, 6. and suck
cows, 7. belief counts more than the actual formula used.

But thou beleve hyt, ellys is alle spilt.
Alle that I seyd, I beleve hyt weyl,
My beleve[1] hath do the dede every deyl.'
55 The bisshop comaundyd that she shuld noght
Beleve ne wurche as she had wroght.

Here now we wyte,[2] beleve wil make
There the wurde no might may take.
The bisshop seyd the wurdys echoun[3],
60 But, beleve theryn hadde he noun[4].
Nomore shall hit avayle thee
That belevest not there[5] beleve shulde be.

from *Handlyng Synne*

1. belief, 2. it is the belief (and not the actual words of the charm) that does the trick, 3. each one, 4. none, 5. where.

ROBERT MANNYNG OF BOURNE

*

The Cursed Daunsers

Karolles, wrastlinges, or somour games,
Whoso ever haunteth any swiche shames
In cherche, other in chercheyerd,
Of sacrilage he may be aferd;
5 Or enterludes, or singinge,
Or tabure bete, or other pypinge,
Alle swiche thing forbodin is
Whyle the prest stondeth at messe.
Alle swyche to every gode preste is lothe,
10 And sunner wyl he make hym wroth
Than he wyl, that hath no wit,
Ne undyrstondeth nat Holy Writ.
And specyaly at hyghe times
Karolles to singe and rede rymes
15 Noght in none holy stedes,
That myght disturble the prestes bedes:

___

The Cursed Dancers

Carols,[1] wrestlings, or summer games,
Whosoever practises any such shameful pastimes
In church, or in churchyard,
Of (the commission of the sin of) sacrilege he may be afraid;
5 *Or interludes, or singing,*
Or tabor-beating or piping –
Every such thing is forbidden
While the priest is standing at mass.
All such to every good priest is hateful,
10 *And will more quickly make the priest furious*
Than it will make the unlearned angry
Who do not understand Holy Writ.
And especially on occasions of the great feasts of the Church
Carols to sing and to speak rhymes
15 *Should not be done in sacred places*
Where it might disturb the priest's prayers;

1. Not our Christmas carols but popular dances accompanied by song.

Or if he were in orysun[1]
Or any outher devociun:
[2]Sacrylage is alle hyt tolde,
20   This and [3]many other folde.
      But for to leve, in cherche to daunce,
I shal yow telle a ful grete chaunce[4],
And I trow the most that fel
Is sothe as the gospel;
25   And fel this chaunce in this londe,
In Ingland, as I undyrstonde;
In a kinge's time that hight Edward
Fel this chaunce that was so hard.
      Hit[5] was uppon a Crystemesse nyght
30   That twelve folys[6] a karolle dyght[7],
In wodehed[8], as hit were in cuntek[9]
They come to a tounne men calle Colbek.
The cherche of the tounne that they do come
Is of Seynt Magne, that suffred martyrdome;
35   Of Seynt Bukcestre hit is also –
Seynt Magne's Suster – that they come to.
Here[10] names of alle thus fonde I write,
And as I wote now shul ye wyte:
Here lodesman[11], that made hem glew,
40   Thus is wryte, [12]he hyghte Gerlew.
Twey maydens were in here coveyne[13],
Mayden Merswynde andWybessyne.
Alle these come thedyr for that enchesone[14]
Of the prestes doghtyr of the tounne.
45   The prest hight Robert, as I kan ame;
Azone hight hys son by name;
His doghter, that these men wulde have,
Thus is wryte, that she hight Ave.
[15]Ech oune consented to o wyl

1. prayer, 2. 'it is all proclaimed sacrilege', 3. 'much else besides',
4. event, happening, 5. it, 6. fools, 7. arranged, 8. mad audacity, 9. strife,
10. their, 11. guide, ringleader, 12. 'he was called Gerlew', 13. company,
14. on account of, 15. All the dancers agreed as to who should go to the
priest's house to invite his daughter – Ave – out to join them.

50   Who shuld go Ave oute to tyl:
They graunted ech one out to sende
Both Wybessyne and Merswynde.
      These wommen yede and tolled her oute
With hem to karolle the cherche aboute.

55   Bevune ordeyned here carolling;
Gerlew endyted what they shuld sing.
Thys is the carolle that they sunge,
As telleth the Latin tunge:
      [1]*'Equitabat Bevo per siluam frondosam,*
60   *Ducebat secum Merswyndam formosam.*
      Quid stamus? cur non imus?'
'By the leved wode rode Bevolyne,
Wyth hym he ledde feyre Mersyne.
Why stonde we? why go we noght?'

65   This is the karolle that Gerlew wroght.
This songe sunge they in the chercheyerd –
Of foly were they no thing aferd –
Unto[2] the matines were alle done,
And the messe shuld byginne sone.

70   The preste him revest to beginne messe,
And they ne left therfore never the lesse,
But daunsed furthe as they bygan,
For alle the messe they ne blan[3].

      The preste, that stode at the autere[4],
75   And herd her[5] noyse and her bere[6],
Fro the auter down he nam,
And to the cherche porche he cam,
And seyd 'On Goddes behalve, I yow forbede
That ye no lenger do swich dede!

80   But cometh in, on feyre manere,
Goddes servise for to here,
And doth at Crystyn mennys lawe;
Karolleth no more, for Crysty's awe!
Wurschyppeth Hym with all youre myght
85   That of the Virgine was bore this nyght.'

1. A translation of this carol immediately follows in the text, 2. until,
3. ceased (to dance), 4. altar, 5. their, 6. behaviour.

For alle hys bydding lefte they noght,
But daunsed furth, as they thoght.
The preste tharefor was sore agreved;
He preyd God that he on belevid,
90   And for Seynt Magne, that he wulde so werche –
(In whos wurschyp sette was the cherche)
That swich a veniaunce[1] were on hem sent,
[2]Are they oute of that stede were went,
That they might ever right so wende
95   Unto that time twelvemonth ende;
(In the Latyne that I fonde thore
He seyth nat 'twelvemonth' but 'evermore');
He cursed hem there alsaume[3]
As they karoled on here gaume[4].

100   As sone as the preste hadde so spoke
Every hand in outher so fast was loke
That no man might with no wundyr
That twelvemonthe parte hem asundyr.

The preste gede in, whan thys was done,
105   And commaunded his sone Azone
That he shulde go swithe[5] aftyr Ave,
Oute of that karolle algate[6] to have.
But al to late that wurde was seyd,
For on hem alle was the veniaunce leyd.

110   Azone wende[7] weyl for to spede;
Unto the karolle as swythe he gede,
His sistyr by the arme he hente,
And the arme fro the body wente.
Men wundred alle that there wore,
115   And merveyle mowe ye here more,
For, sethen[8] he had the arme in hand,
[9]The body yede furth karoland
And nother the body ne the arme
Bledde never blode, colde ne warme,
120   But was as drye, with al the haunche,

1. vengeance, 2. 'Ere they out of that place had gone', 3. altogether,
4. their game, 5. quickly, 6. by all means, 7. thought, 8. after, 9. 'The
body went on carolling'.

As of a stok were rive a braunche.
  Azone to hys fadyr went,
And broght him a sory present:
'Loke, fadyr,' he seyd, 'and have hit here,
125 The arme of thy doghtyr dere,
That was myn owne sister Ave,
That I wende I myght have safe.
Thy cursyng now sene hit ys
With veniaunce on thy owne flessh.
130 Felliche[1] thou cursedest, and over sone;
Thou askedest veniaunce, – thou hast thy bone[2].'

   You thar[3] nat aske if there was wo
Wyth the preste, and with many mo;
The prest, that cursed for that daunce,
135 On some of hys fel harde chaunce.
He toke hys doghtyr arme forlorn
And byryed hit on the morn;
The nexte day the arme of Ave
He fonde hit ligging[4] above the grave.
140 He byryed hit on anouther day,
And eft above the grave hit lay.
The thridde[5] tyme he byryed hit,
And eft was hit kast oute of the pit.
The prest wulde byrye hyt no more,
145 He dredde the veniaunce ferly sore.
Into the cherche he bare the arme,
For drede and doute of more harme,
He ordeyned hit for to be
That every man might with eye hit se.
150   These men that gede so karolland,
Alle that yere, hand in hand,
They never oute of that stede gede,
[6]Ne none might hem thenne lede.
There[7] the cursyng fyrst bygan,
155 In that place aboute they ran,
That never ne felt they no werines –

1. savagely, 2. boon, 3. need, 4. lying, 5. third, 6. 'Nor none might them thence lead', 7. where.

As many bodyes for going dos –
Ne mete ete, ne drank drinke,
Ne slepte onely a–lepy[1] winke.
160   Night ne day, they wist of none,
What hit was come, whan hit was gone;
Frost ne snogh, haile ne reyne,
Of colde ne hete, felte they no peyne;
Heere[2] ne nailes never grewe,
165   Ne solowed[3] clothes, ne turned hewe;
Thundyr ne lightning did hem no dere,
Goddys mercy ded hit from hem were[4]; –
But sunge that songe that the woe wroght:
      'Why stonde we? why go we noght?'
170   What man shuld thyr be in this lyve
That ne wulde hit see and thedyr drive?
The Emperoure Henry come fro Rome
For to see this harde dome[5].
Whan he hem say[6], he wepte sore
175   For the mischefe that he sagh thore.
[7]He ded come wrightes for to make
Covering over hem, for tempest sake.
But that they wroght, hit was in veyn,
For hit come to no certeyn,
180   [8]For that they sette on oo day
On the t'outher downe hit lay.
Ones, twyys, thryys, thus they wroght,
And alle here making was for noght.
Might no covering hyle hem fro colde
185   Tyl time of mercy that Cryst wolde.
      Time of grace fyl thurgh His myght
At the twelvemonth ende, on the Yole nyght.
The same houre that the prest hem banned[9],
The same oure atwynne[10] they woned;
190   That houre that he cursed hem ynne,
The same oure they gede atwynne:

1. a single, 2. hair, 3. soiled, 4. ward off, 5. severe judgement, 6. sees,
7. 'he ordered carpenters to come', 8. 'For that which they set up on one day',
9. cursed, 10. apart.

And as in twinkelyng of an eye
Into the cherche gun they flye,
And on the pavement they fyl alle downe
195 As they had be dede, or fal in a swone.
  Thre days, stil, they lay ech one,
That none steryd, other[1] flesshe or bone,
And at the thre days ende
To life God graunted hem to wende.
200 They sette hem upp, and spak apert
To the parisshe prest, syre Robert:
'Thou art ensample and enchesun[2]
Of oure long confusyun;
Thou maker art of oure travayle,
205 That is to many grete mervayle:
And thy traveyle shalt thou sone ende,
For to thy long home sone shalt thou wende.'
  [3]Alle they rise that yche tyde
But Ave, – she lay dede beside.
210 Grete sorowe had here fadyr, here brother,
Merveyle and drede had alle outher;
I trow no drede of soule dede,
But with pyne was broght the body dede.
The fyrst man was the fadyr, the prest,
215 That deyd aftyr the doghtyr nest[4].
This iche arme, that was of Ave,
That none myght leye in grave,
The Emperoure did a vessel werche
To do hit yn, and hange in the cherche,
220 That alle men myght see hit and knawe,
And thenk on the chaunce when men hit sawe.
  [5]These men, that hadde go thus karolland
Alle the yere, fast hand in hand,
Thogh that they were than asunder
225 Yet alle the world spake of hem wonder:
That same hopping that they fyrst yede,

---

1. cither, 2. cause, 3. 'All rise together that same time Except Ave',
4. next, 5. The dancers though released from their circle are condemned to
hop about singly ever afterwards.

That daunce yede they thurgh land and lede,
And, as they ne myght fyrst be unbounde,
So efte togedyr myght they never be founde,
230 Ne myght they never come ageyn
Togedyr to oo[1] stede certeyn.
    Foure gede to the courte of Rome,
And ever hopping aboute they nome,
With sundyr lepys[2] come they thedyr,
235 But they come never efte togedyr.
Here clothes ne roted, ne nailes grewe,
Ne heere ne wax, no solowed hewe,
Ne never hadde they amendement,
That we herde, at any corseynt,
240   But at the virgine Seynt Edyght,
There was he botened, Teodright[3],
On oure Lady day, in lenten tyde,
As he slepte here toumbe besyde.
There he had his medycyne
245   At Seynt Edyght, the holy virgine.
    Bruning[4], the bisshope of seynt Tolous
Wrote this tale so merveylous;
Setthe was his name of more renoun,
Men called him the pope Leoun.
250   This at the court of Rome they wite,
And in the kronykeles hit is write
In many stedys beyounde the see,
More than is in this cuntre.
Tharfor men seye, an weyl is trowed,
255 'The nere the cherche, the fyrther fro God.'
    So fare men here by this tale,
Some holde hit but a trotevale[5],
In other stedys hit is ful dere
And for grete merveyle they wyl hyt here.
260 A tale hit is of feyre shewing,
Ensample and drede agens cursing.

1. one, 2. several leaps, 3. None of the dancers was remedied (*botened*) of his curse save one, Theodric, at the behest of Saint Edyght at whose tomb he slept, 4. Bruno, 5. idle yarn.

This tale I tolde you to make you aferde,
In cherche to karolle, or in chercheyerde,
Namely agens the prestys wylle:
265   Leveth whan he biddeth you be stille.

NOTE

The Wicche, the Bagge and the Bisshop and *The Cursed Daunsers* (editor's titles) are two extracts from Robert Mannyng's *Handlyng Synne*, which was begun, he tells us, in 1303. Mannyng was probably a native of Bourne, Lincolnshire, and was certainly a member of the Gilbertine priory at Sixhill, near Sempring-ham.

    Handlyng Synne is an English version of William of Wadington's *Manuel de Pechiez*, and its purpose and scope are identical with those of its original: it is a handbook on moral theology – the different kinds of sins, and how to avoid them, diversified by 'cautionary tales'. It is in these 'cautionary tales' that much of the excellence and power of Mannyng's work lies.

ANONYMOUS

*

Sir Orfeo

Orfeo was a king
In Inglond, an highe lording,
A stalworth man and hardi bo,
Large and curteys he was also.
His fader was comen of King Pluto,
And his moder of Quene Iuno,
That sum time were as godes i-hold,
For aventours that thai dede and told.
Orpheo most of ony thing
Lovede the gle of harpyng;
Syker was every gode harpoure
Of hym to have moche honoure.
Hymself loved for to harpe,
And layde theron his wittes scharpe.
He lernid so, ther nothing was
A better harper in no plas.

_____

Sir Orfeo

Orfeo was a king
In England, a great nobleman,
A man both stalwart and bold,
Liberal and courtly he was also.
His father was descended from King Pluto,
And his mother from Queen Juno,
Who once upon a time were regarded as gods,
On account of the adventures they performed and related.
Orfeo more than anything else
Loved the joy of harp-playing;
Hence was every good harper
Sure to receive much honour from him.
He himself loved to perform on the harp,
And gave his sharp wits to that skill.
He learnt so well indeed that there was not at all
A better harper anywhere.

In the world was never man born
That ever Orpheo sat byforn
And he myght of his harpyng[1] here
20   He schulde thinke that he were
In one of the joys of Paradys,
Suche joy and melody in his harpyng is.
    This king sojournd in Traciens
That was a cite of noble defens,
25   [2]For Winchester was cleped tho
Traciens withouten no.
The king hadde a quen of priis[3]
That was y-cleped Dame Herodis,
The fairest levedi,[4] for the nones,
30   That might gon on bodi and bones,
Ful of love and of godenisse.
Ac[5] no man may telle hir fairnise.
    Bifel so in the comessing[6] of May,
When miry and hot is the day,
35   And away beeth winter-schours,
And every feld is ful of flours,
And blosme breme[7] on every bough
Overal wexeth miry enow,
This ich quen, Dame Herodis,
40   Tok two maidens of priis,
And went in an undrentide[8]
To play bi an orchard side,
To see the floures sprede and spring,
And to hear the foules sing.
45   They sett hem down al thre
Under a fair ympe-tre[9],
And wel sone this fair quene
Fel on slepe upon the grene.
The maidens durst hir nought awake
50   Bot lete hir ligge[10] and rest take.
So she slepe till afternone

1. i.e. Orfeo's harping. 2. 'For Winchester was called then Thrace without contradiction', 3. price, excellence, 4. lady, 5. but, 6. progress, 7. glorious blossoms, 8. i.e. about mid-morning, 9. orchard-tree, 10. lie.

[1]That undertide was al y-done.
Ac as sone as she gan awake,
She cried and lothly bere[2] gan make,
55 She froted hir honden and hir fet,
And crached[3] hir visage – it bled wete –
Hir riche robe hye al torett,
And was reveysed[4] out of hir witt.
The two maidens hir biside
60 No durst with hir no leng abide
Bot ourn[5] to the palays ful right,
And tolde bothe squier and knight
[6]That her quen a-wede wold,
And bad hem go and hir at-hold.
65 Knightes urn[7], and levidis, also,
Damisels sexti and mo,
In the orchard to the quen hie[8] come,
And her up in her[9] armes nome[10],
And brought hir to bed atte last,
70 And held hir there fine fast;
Ac ever she held in a cry
And wold up and away.
　　When Orfeo herd that tiding,
Never him nas werse fer no thing,
75 He come with knightes ten
To chaumber right bifor the quene,
And biheld, and seyd with grete pitie:
[11]'O lef liif, what is te,
That ever yete hast ben so stille,
80 And now gredest[12] wonder shille?
Thi bodi, that was so white y-core,
With thine nailes is al o-tore,
Allas! thy rode[13], that was so red,
Is al wan as thou were ded.
85 And also thine fingres smale,

1. 'when the morningtide was quite passed', 2. clamour, 3. scratched,
4 carried away, 5. ran, 6. 'That their queen would go mad', 7. ran,
8. they, 9. their, 10. took, 11. 'O dear life, what ails thee?', 12. criest out,
13. young face.

Be–th al blody and al pale.
Allas! thy lovesom eyen two
Loketh so man doth on his foe.
A! dame, Ich biseche merci.

90   Lete ben al this reweful cry,
And tel me what thee is, and how,
And what thing may thee help now.'
    Tho[1] lay she stille atte last,
And gan to wepe swithe fast

95   And seyd thus the king to:
'Allas! my lord, Sir Orfeo,
Seththen[2] we first togider were,
Ones wroth never we nere
Bot ever Ich have y-loved thee

100   As mi lif, and so thou me.
[3]Ac now we mot delen a-two;
Do thy best, for I mot go.'
    'Allas!' quath he, 'forlorn Ich-am.
Whider wiltow go, and to wham?

105   Whider thou gost, ich wil with thee,
And whider I go, thou schalt with me.'
    'Nay, nay, sir, that nought nis.
Ich wil thee telle al how it is:
As ich lay this undertide,

110   And slepe under our orchard-side,
Ther come to me two fair knightes,
Wele y-armed al to rightes,
And bad me comen an heighing[4]
And speke with her[5] lord the king.

115   And ich answerd at wordes bold,
I durst nought, no I nold.
Thay priked[6] ogain as thay might drive;
[7]Tho com her king also blive,
With an hundred knightes and mo,

120   And damisels an hundred also,
Al on snowe-white stedes;

1. then, 2. since, 3. 'But now we must part', 4. in haste, 5. their,
6. rode fast, 7. 'Then came their king also straightaway.'

As white as milke were here wedes;
I no seighe never yete bifore
So fair creatours ycore[1].

125　　The king hadde a croun on hed,
It nas of silver, no of gold red,
Ac[2] it was of a precious ston,
As bright as the sonne it schon.
And as son as he to me cam,

130　　Wold ich, nold ich, he me nam[3],
And made me with him ride
Opon a palfray bi his side
And brought me to his palays,
Wele atird in ech ways.

135　　And schewed me castels and tours,
Rivers, forestes, frith[4] with flours,
And his riche stedes echon.
And seththen[5] me brought ogain hom
Into our own orchard,

140　　And said to me thus afterward:
[6]"Loke, dame, to-morwe that'ou be
Right here under this ympe-tre,
And than thou schalt with ous go,
And live with ous evermo;

145　　[7]And if thou makest ous ylet,
Whar thou be – thou worst yfet
And totore thine limes al,
That nothing help thee no schal;
And though thou be-est so totorn

150　　[8]Yete thou worst with ous y-born".'
　　　　When King Orfeo herd this cas,
'O we!' quath he, 'allas, allas!
Lever me were to lete mi lif
Than thus to lese the Quen mi wif!'

155　　He asked conseil at ech man

---

1. excellent, 2. but, 3. 'he seized me', 4. woodland, 5. afterwards,
6. 'See to it, lady, that you are here to-morrow', 7. 'And if you resist, Be-
ware – you will be fetched, And all your limbs torn apart', 8. 'Yet you will be
borne away with us'.

Ac[1] no man him help no can.
  A-morwe the undertide is come,
And Orfeo hath his armes y-nome[2],
And wele ten hundred knightes with him
160   Ech y-armed stout and grim:
And with the Quen wenten he
Right unto that ympe-tre.
Thai made scheltrom[3] in ech a side,
And sayd thai wold there abide
165   And die ther everichon,
Er the Quen schuld fram hem gon.
[4]Ac yete amiddes hem ful right
The Quen was away y-tuight,
With fairi forth ynome.
170   Men wist never wher she was bicome.
  Tho[5] was ther crying, wepe and wo.
The king into his chaumber is go
And oft swoned upon the ston,
And made swiche dole and swiche mon
175   That neighe his lif was y-spent.
Ther was non amendement.
  He cleped togider his barouns,
Erls, lordes of renouns:
And when thay al y-comen were,
180   'Lordinges,' he said, 'bifor you here
Ich ordainy min heighe steward
To wite[6] my kingdom afterward:
In my stede ben he shal,
To kepe my londes over al.
185   For, now ic-have mi Quen y-lore[7],
The fairest levedi that ever was bore,
Never eft I nil no woman se.
Into wildernes ich wil te[8],
And live ther evermore
190   With wilde bestes in holtes hore[9].

1. but, 2. taken up, 3. drawn ranks, 4. 'But yet the Queen was drawn away from amidst them, taken away by fairy power', 5. then, 6. look after, 7. lost, 8. go, 9. grey woods.

And when ye understood that I be spent,
Make you than a parlement
And chese you a newe king.
Now doth your best with al my thing.'

195   Tho was ther wepeing in the halle,
And grete cry among hem alle,
Un-nethe[1] might old or yong
For wepeing speke a word with tong.
Thay kneled a-down al y-fere[2]
200   And prayd him, if his wille were,
That he no schuld nought fram hem go.
'Do way!' quath he, 'it shal be so.'
    Al his kingdom he forsoke
Bot a slavin[3] on him he toke.
205   He no hadde kirtel no hode,
Shert, ne no nother gode.
Bot his harp he tok algate[4],
And dede him barfot out atte gate.
No man most with him go.
210   O way! what ther was wepe and wo,
When he, that hadde ben King with croun,
Went so poverlich out of toun!
Thurgh wode and over heth
Into the wildernes he geth.
215   Nothing he finds that him is ays[5]
Bot ever he liveth in gret malais.
[6]He that hadde y-werd the fowe and gris
And on bed the purper bis,
Now on hard hethe he lith,
220   With leves and gresse he him writh.
He that hadde had castels and tours,
River, forest, frith with flours,
Now, whan it comence to snewe and frese,
This King mot make his bed in mese[7].
225   He that y-hade knightes of pris

1. scarcely, 2. together, 3. a pilgrim's mantle, 4. at any rate, 5. ease,
6. 'He who had worn the vari-coloured pelt and grey fur And in bed fine
linen', 7. moss.

Bifor him kneland, and levedis,
Now seth he nothing that him liketh,
Bot wilde wormes bi him striketh.
He that had y-hade plente
230 Of mete and drink, of ech deynte,
Now may he al day digge and wrote[1]
Er he finde his fille of rote.
In somer he liveth bi wild frut
[2]And berien bot gode lite.
235 In winter may he nothing finde
Bot rote, grases, and the rinde.
Al his bodi was oway dwine
[3]For missays, and al tochine.
Lord! who may telle the sore
240 This king sufferd ten yere and more?
His here of his berd, blac and rowe[4],
To his girdelstede was growe.
His harp, whereon was al his gle,
He hidde in an holwe tre;
245 And, when the weder was clere and bright,
He toke his harp to him wel right,
And harped at his owhen wille.
Into alle the wode the soun gan shille
That alle the wilde bestes that ther be-th
250 For joye abouten him thai teth[5];
And alle the foules that ther were
Come and sete on ech a brere
To here his harping a-fine
So miche melody was therin.
255 And when he his harping lete wold[6],
No best by him abide nold.
He might se him bisides,
Oft in hot undertides[7],
The king o'fairy with his rout
260 Com to hunt him al about
With dim cri and bloweing,

1. root (verb), 2. 'And berries but of little worth', 3. 'On account of hardships, and all scarred', 4. rough, 5. draw near, 6. would cease, 7. mornings.

And houndes also with him berking.
Ac no best thay no nome,
No never he nist whider thay bicome.
265 And other while he might him se
    [1]As a gret ost bi him te
    Wele atourned ten hundred knightes,
    Ech y-armed to his rightes,
    Of cuntenaunce stout and fers,
270 With many desplaid baners,
    And ech his swerd y-drawe hold,
    Ac never he nist whider thay wold.
    And other while he seighe other thing:
    Knightes and levedies com daunceing
275 In queynt atire, gisely[2],
    Queynt pas[3] and softly;
    Tabours and trumpes yede hem by,
    And al maner menstraci.
    And on a day he seighe him biside
280 Sexti levedis on hors ride,
    Gentil and iolif as brid on ris[4], –
    Nought a man amonges hem ther nis.
    And ech a faucoun on hond bere,
    And riden a-hawking by a rivere.
285 Of game thay founde wel gode haunt,
    Maulardes, hayroun, and cormeraunt;
    The foules of the water ariseth,
    The faucouns hem wele deviseth –
    Ech faucoun his prey slough.
290 That seighe Orfeo, and lough[5];
    'Parfay!' quath he, 'ther is fair game,
    Thider ich wil, bi Godes name!
    Ich was y-won[6] swiche werk to se.'
    He aros, and thider gan te.
295 To a levedi he was y-come,
    Biheld, and hath wele undernome[7],

1. A great host approaches him of a thousand well-accoutred knights,
2. skilfully, 3. elegant steps, 4. bird on spray, 5. laughed, 6. accustomed,
7. understood, recognized.

And se-th by al thing that it is –
His owhen Quen, Dam Herodis.
Yern[1] he biheld hir, and she him eke,
300   Ac noither to other a word no speke.
For messais[2] that she on him seighe,
That had ben so riche and so heighe,
The teres fel out of her eiye.
The other levedis this y-seighe,
305   And maked hir oway to ride,
She most with him no lenger abide.
   'Allas!' quath he, 'now me is wo.
Whil nil deth now me slo?
Allas! wreche, that I no might
310   Die now after this sight!
Allas! to long last my lif,
When I no dar nought with mi wif,
[3]No hie to me, a word speke.
Allas! why nil min hert breke?
315   Parfay!' quath he, 'tide wat bitide[4],
Whider so his levedies ride,
The selve way i-chil streche;
Of lif ne deth me no reche[5].'
   His slavin[6] he dede on also spac[7],
320   And hange his harp opon his bac,
And had wel gode wil to gon –
He no spard noither stub no ston.
In at a roche the levedis rideth,
And he after, and nought abideth.
325   When he was in the roche y-go,
Wele thre mile other mo,
He com into a fair cuntray,
As bright so sonne on somers day,
Smothe and plain and al grene,
330   Hille no dale nas ther non y-sene.
Amidde the lond a castel he sighe,
Riche and regal, and wonder heighe.

1. eagerly, 2. signs of misfortune, 3. 'nor she to me', 4. come what may,
5. 'I care not', 6. pilgrim's mantle, 7. quickly.

Al the utmost wal
Was clere and shine as cristal.
335 An hundred tours ther were about,
Degiselich[1], and batailed stout;
The butras com out of the diche,
Of rede gold y-arched riche;
The [2]vousour was a-wowed al
340 Of each maner divers animal.
Within ther were wide wones[3]
Al of precious stones.
The werst piler on to biholde
Was al of burnist gold.
345 Al that lond was ever light,
For when it schuld be therk and night,
The riche stones light gonne[4]
As bright as doth at none the sonne.
No man may telle, no thinke in thought
350 The riche werk that ther was wrought;
By al thing him think that it is
The proude court of Paradis.

In this castel the levedis alight.
He wold in after, yif he might.
355 Orfeo knokketh atte gate.
The porter was redi therate
And asked what he wold have y-do.
'Parfay!' quat he, 'ich-am a minstrel, lo!
To solas thi lord with my gle,
360 Yif his swete wille be.'
The porter undede the gate anon,
And lete him into the castel gon.

Than he gan behild about al,
[5]And seighe a foule liggeand within the wal
365 Of folk that were thider y-brought,
And thought dede, and nare nought.
Sum stode withouten hade[6],
And sum non armes nade,

1. wonderful, 2. 'vaulting was all carved', 3. halls, 4. did light, 5. 'And saw a crowd lying within the wall', 6. head.

PART FOUR

| | And sum thurch the bodi hadde wounde, |
|370| And sum lay wode[1], y-bounde. |

And sum thurch the bodi hadde wounde,
370 And sum lay wode[1], y-bounde.
And sum armed on hors sete,
And sum a-strangled as thay ete,
And sum were in water adreynt,
And sum with fire al forschreynt[2];
375 Wives ther lay on childbedde,
Sum ded, and sum awedde;
And wonder fele[3] ther lay bisides,
Right as they slepe her undertides[4].
Eche was thus in this warld y-nome,
380 With fairi thider y-come.
Ther he seighe his owhen wif,
Dame Herodis, his lef lif,
Slepe under an ympe-tre.
By her clothes he knewe that it was she.

385   And when he hadde bihold this mervails alle,
He went into the kinges halle.
Than seighe he ther a semly sight, –
A tabernacle[5] blisseful and bright.
Therein her[6] maister king sete,
390 And her quen fair and swete.
Her crounes, her[6] clothes, schine so bright,
That unnethe[7] bihold he hem might.
  When he hadde biholden al that thing,
He kneled adoun bifor the king.
395 'O lord,' he seyd, 'yif it thy wille were,
Mi menstraci thou shust y-hear.'
The king answered: 'What man artow,
That art hider y-comen now?
[8]Ich, no non that is with me,
400 No sent never after the.
Seththen that ich here regni gan,
I no fond never so folehardi man
That hider to ous durst wende,

1. mad, 2. smothered, 3. a marvellous number, 4. 'just as they sleep their noonday sleep', 5. pavilion, 6. their, 7. scarcely, 8. 'I, nor none with me, ever sent for thee'.

[1]Bot that ich him wald of sende.'

405   'Lord,' quath he, 'trowe ful wel,
I nam bot a pouer menstrel;
And, sir, it is the maner of ous
To seche many a lordes hous.
Thei[2] we nought welcom no be,
410   Yete we mot proferi forth our gle.'

Bifor the king he sat a-down,
And tok his harp, so miry of soun,
And tempreth his harp, as he wele can,
And blisseful notes he ther gan,
415   That al that in the palays were
Com to him for to here,
And liggeth a-down to his fete,
Hem thenketh his melody so swete.
The king herkneth and sitt ful stille,
420   To here his gle he hath gode wille;
Gode bourde[3] he hadd of his gle,
The riche quen also hadde she.

When he hadde stint his harping
Than seyd to him the king:
425   'Menstrel, me liketh wele thy gle.
Now aske of me what it be,
Largelich ich wil thee pay.
Now speke, and tow might asay.'
'Sir,' he seyd, 'ich biseche thee
430   That thou woldest give me
That ich levedi, bright on ble[4],
That slepeth under the impe-tre.'
'Nay,' quath the king, 'that nought nere!
A sori couple of you it were,
435   For thou art lene, rowe, and blac,
And she is lovesum, withouten lac[5];
A lothlich thing it were forthi
To sen hir in thi compayni!'
'O sir,' he seyd, 'gentil king,

1. 'unless I had sent for him', 2. though, 3. entertainment, 4. of con-
plexion, 5. spot.

440 Yete were it a wele fouler thing
To here a lesing[1] of thy mouthe.
So, sir, as ye seyd nouthe[2]
What ich wold aski, have I schold,
And nedes thou most thy word hold.'

445 The king seyd: 'Seththen it is so,
Take hir by the hond, and go:
Of hir ich wil that thou be blithe.'
    He kneled a-doun, and thonked him swithe.
His wif he tok by the hond,

450 And dede him swithe out of that lond,
And went him out of that thede[3], –
Right as he come the way he yede.
    So long he hath the way y-nome,
To Winchester he is y-come

455 That was his owhen cite.
Ac no man knewe that it was he.
No forther than the tounes ende
[4]For knoweleche no durst wende,
Bot with a begger, in bilt[5] ful narwe,

460 Ther he tok his herbawe,
To him and to his owhen wif,
As a minstrel of pouer lif,
And asked tidinges of that lond,
And who the kingdom held in hond.

465 The pouer begger in his cote
Tol him everich a grot;
How her quen was stole oway
Ten yer gon with fairy;
And how her king en exile yede,

470 Bot no man nist in wiche thede;
And how the steward the lond gan hold;
And other many thinges him told.
    A-morwe, ogain nonetide,
He maked his wif ther abide.

475 The begger's clothes he borwed anon,

---

1. falsehood, 2. just now, 3. land, 4. 'for fear of being known he dared not go', 5. dwelling.

And heng his harp his rigge[1] opon,
And went him into that cite,
That men might him bihold and se.
Erls and barouns bold,
480   Burgays and levedis him gan bihold.
'Lo!' thay seyd, 'swiche a man!
How long the hair hongeth him opan!
Lo, how his berd hongeth to his kne!
He is y-clongen[2] also a tre!'
485   And as he yede in the strete,
With his steward he gan mete,
And loude he sett on him a crie:
'Sir steward,' he seyd, 'merci!
Ich-am an harpour of hethenisse[3];
490   Help me now in this destresse!'
The steward seyd: 'Com with me, come.
Of that ichave thou shalt have some.
Everich gode harpour is welcom me to,
For my lordes love Sir Orfeo.'
495   In the castel the steward sat atte mete,
And many lording was by him sete.
Ther were trompours and tabourers,
Harpours fele, and crouders[4].
Miche melody they maked alle,
500   And Orfeo sat stille in the halle
And herketh. When they ben al stille,
He toke his harp and tempred shille[5],
The blissefulest notes he harped there
That ever any man y-herd with ere.
505   Ech man liked wele his gle.
The steward biheld and gan yse[6],
And knewe the harp als blive[7].
'Menstrel,' he seyd, 'so mot thou thrive,
Where hadest'ow this harp, and how?
510   I pray that thou me telle now.'
'Lord,' quath he, 'in uncouthe thede[8],

---

1. back, 2. withered, 3. from pagan lands, 4. fiddlers, 5. clearly,
6. scrutinize, 7. straightaway, 8. land.

Thurch a wildernes as I yede,
Ther I founde in a dale
With lyouns a man totorn smale,
515 And wolves him frete with teth so sharp.
Bi him I fond this ich harp.
Wele ten yere it is y-go.'
'O,' quath the steward, 'now is me wo!
That was my lord Sir Orfeo.
520 Allas! wreche, what shal I do,
That have swiche a lord y-lore?
A way! that ich was y-bore!
That him was so hard grace y-yarked[1]
And so vile deth y-marked!'
525   A-down he fel a-swon to grounde.
His barouns him tok up in that stounde,
And telleth him how it geth –
It is no bot of manes deth.
    King Orfeo knewe wele by than
530 His steward was a trewe man
And loved him as he aught to do,
And stont up and seyt thus: 'Lo,
Steward, herkne now this thing.
Yif ich were Orfeo the king,
535 And hadde y-suffred ful yore
In wildernisse miche sore,
And hadde y-won my quen oway
Out of the lond of fairy,
And hadde y-brought the levedi hende[2]
540 Right here to the tounes ende,
And with a begger her in y-nome[3],
And were miself hider y-come,
Pouerlich to thee, thus stille,
For to asay thy gode wille,
545 And ich founde thee thus trewe,
Thou no shust it never rewe.
Sikerlich, for love or ay,
Thou shust be king after my day.

1. ordained, 2. gracious, 3. lodged.

And yif thou of my deth hadest ben blithe,
550 Thou shust have voided also swithe.'
   Thou al tho that therin sete
That it was King Orfeo undergete[1],
And the steward him wele knewe.
Over and over the bord he threwe,
555 And fel a-down to his fet.
So dede everich lord that ther sete,
And al thay seyd at o crying:
'Ye beth our lord, sir, and our king!'
Glad they were of his live.
560 To chaumber thay ladde him also bilive[2],
And bathed him, and shaved his berd,
And 'tired him as a king apert.
And seththen with gret processioun
That brought the quen into the toun
565 With al maner menstraci.
Lord! ther was grete melody!
For joie thay wepe with her eiye,
That hem so sounde y-comen seighe.
   Now King Orfeo newe coround is,
570 And his quen Dame Herodis,
And lived long afterward.
And seththen was king the steward.
   Harpours in Bretaine[3] after than
Herd how this mervaile bigan,
575 And made herof a lay of gode likeing,
And nempned it after the king:
That lay 'Orfeo' is y-hote:
God is the lay, swete is the note.
   Thus com Sir Orfeo out of his care.
580 God graunt ous alle wele to fare.

1. understood, 2. quickly, 3. Brittany.

[See over]

NOTE

Sir Orfeo, which is in a southern dialect, is preserved in three MSS., of which the earliest dates from the early fourteenth century, not long after the poem's composition.

The closing lines of *Sir Orfeo* refer to Brittany as the place where the 'lay' first developed. It is therefore assumed, though no such original has been found, that our poem is a translation from the French. It has been suggested that the prowess of the disguised Orfeo with the harp conceals a folk-memory of Alfred's reputed venture into the Danish camp in the shape of a minstrel.

ANONYMOUS

*

Roberd of Cisyle

Princes proude that ben in pres,
I wil you telle thing, not les!
In Sicily was a noble king,
Fair and strong and sumdel young.
He hadde a brother in grete Rome,
Pope of alle Cristendome;
Another he hadde in Alemayne
Emperour, that Sarsynes wroughte payne.
The king was hote King Roberd,
Never man ne wiste him ferd.
He was king of gret honour
For that he was conquerour.
In al the worlde nas his per,
King ne prince, fer no ner.
And, for he was of chivalrie flour,
His brother was made Emperour,

5

10

15

King Robert of Sicily

Proud noblemen here assembled,
I shall tell you all a tale:
In Sicily dwelt a noble king,
Handsome and strong and somewhat young.
He had one brother in great Rome
Who was Pope of all Christendom;
He had another brother in Germany
Who was Emperor and inflicted pain on the Saracens.
The king was named King Robert,
No man ever knew him to be afraid.
He was a king of great honour
Because he was such a conqueror.
In all the world there was not his equal —
Neither king nor prince — far nor near.
And, because he was the flower of chivalry,
His brother was created Emperor,

5

10

15

287

His other brother Godes Vikere[1],
Pope of Rome, as I seide ere.
The pope was hote Pope Urban:
20   He was good to God and man.
The emperour was hote Valemounde:
A strenger werrour[2] nas non founde
After his brother of Sicily.
Of whom that I schal telle a while.
25   The kyng thoughte, he hadde no per
In al the worlde, fer no ner;
And in his thought he hadde pride
[3]For he was nounpeer in ech a side.
At midsomer, a seynt Johnes night,
30   The king to cherche com ful right,
Forto heere his evensong.
Him thoughte, he dwelled ther ful long!
He thoughte more in worldes honour,
Than in Crist, our saveour.
35   In 'Magnificat' he herde a vers,
He made a clerk hit him rehers,
In langage of his owne tonge,
In Latin he nyste[4], what they songe.
The vers was this, I telle thee:
40   [5]'Deposuit potentes de sede,
Et exaltavit humiles.'
This was the vers, withoute les.
The clerk seide anone right:
'Sire, such is Godes might,
45   That he may maken heighe lowe
And lowe heighe in litel throwe.
God may do, withoute lie,
His wil in twinkling of an eye.'
The kyng seide with herte unstable:
50   'Al your song is false and fable!
What man hath such pouwer,

1. deputy, 2. defender, warrior, 3. 'Because he was unequalled anywhere',
4. did not know, 5. 'He hath put down the mighty from their seat And hath
exalted the humble'.

288

Me to bringe lowe in daunger?
I am flour of chivalrye,
Min enemys I may distrye;
55 No man liveth in no londe
That me may with strength withstonde.
Than is this a song of nought!'
This errour he hadde in thought.
And in his thought a slep him tok
60 In his pulpit[1], as seith the bok.
Whan that evenson was al don,
[2]A kyng i-like him out gan gon,
And alle men with him gan wende,
King Roberd lafte out of mende[3].
65 The newe kyng was, as I you telle,
Godes angel, his pride to felle.
The angel in halle joye made,
And alle men of him were glade.
The kyng wakede, that lay in cherche,
70 His men he thoughte wo to werche,
For he was laft ther alon,
And derk night him fell uppon.
He gan crie after his men,
Ther nas non, tha spak agen.
75 But the sexteyn atten ende
Of the cherche to him gan wende,
And seide: 'What dost thou nouthe her,
Thou false thef, thou losenger[4]?
Thou art her with felonye,
80 Holy cherche to robbeye.'
He seyde: 'Foule gadeling[5],
I am no thef, I am a king!
Opene the cherche-dore anon,
That I mowe to mi paleys gon!'
85 The sexteyn thoughte anon with than,
That he was sum wod[6] man,

1. The Cathedral throne of the king, 2. An angel in the guise of King Robert left the church with the real king's retainers, 3. mind, 4. false speaker, flatterer, 5. vagabond, 6. mad.

And wolde, the cherche delyvered were
Of him, for he hadde fere;
And openede the cherche-dore in haste.
90 The king bigan to renne out faste,
As a man, that was wod[1].
At his paleys gate he stod,
[2]And heet the porter Gadeling,
And bad him come in hie-ing,
95 Anon the gates up to do.
The porter seide: 'who clepeth so?'
He onswerde anon tho:
'Thou schalt witen, ar I go:
Thi kyng I am; thou schalt knowe
100 In prison thou schalt ligge[3] lowe
And ben honged and to-drawe
As a traytour bi the lawe.
Thou schalt wel wite, I am king.
Open the gates, gadeling!'
105 The porter seide: 'So mot I thee!'
The king is mid his meyne[4];
Wel I wot, withoute doute,
The kyng nis not now withoute.'
The porter com into halle,
110 Bifore the king[5] a-knes gan falle
And seide: 'Ther is atte gate
A nice fool y-come late.
He seith, he is lord and king
And clept me foule gadeling.
115 Lord, what wil ye, that I do?
Lete him in or lete him go?'
The angel seide right in haste:
'Do him come in swithe faste!
For mi fol[6] I wile him make,
120 Forte[7] he the name of king forsake.'
The porter com to the gate,
Him he called in, to late!

1. mad, 2. 'And called the porter Lazy Good-for-Nothing, And ordered
him to come at once', 3. lie, 4. company, 5. i.e. the angel, 6. fool, 7. unless.

He smot the porter, whan he com in,
That blod barst out of mouth and chin.
125   The porter yeld him his travayle,
Him smot agen, withoute fayle,
That nose and mouth barst a blod;
Thanne he semed almost wod.
The porter and his men in haste,
130   Kyng Roberd in a podel[1] caste:
Unsemely made his body than
That he nas lik non other man,
And brought him bifore the newe king;
And seide: 'Lord, this gadelyng
135   Me hath smite withoute desert.
He seith, he is our king apert.
This harlot oughte for his sawe
Ben y-honged and to-drawe;
For he seith non other word,
140   But that he is bothe kyng and lord.'
The angel seide to king Roberd:
'Thou art a fol, that art nought ferd[2]
Mi men to do such vilenye;
Thy gilt thou most nede abye.
145   What art thou?' seide the angel.
Quath Roberd: 'Thou salt wite wel,
That I am king and king wil be,
With wronge thou hast mi dignite.
The pope of Rome is mi brother
150   And the emperour min other;
Thei wil me wreke, for soth to telle,
I wot, they nylle nought longe dwelle.'
'Thou art mi fol,' seide the angel,
'Thou schalt be schoren[3] everichdel,
155   Like a fol, a fol to be,
Wher is now thi dignite?
Thi counseyler shal ben an ape,
[4]And o clothyng you worth y-shape.

1. puddle, 2. afraid, 3. shorn, 4. 'And in the same clothing you shall
be dressed.'

I shal him clothen as thi brother,
160 Of o clothyng – hit is non other;
He schal be thin owne fere[1],
Sum wit of him thou might lere.
Houndes, how to hit bifalle,
Shulen ete with thee in halle;
165 Thou schalt eten on the grounde;
Thin assayour[2] schal ben an hound,
To assaye thi mete bifore thee.
Wher is now thy dignite?'
He het[3] a barbur him bifore,
170 That as a fol he shulde be schore,
Al around i-like a frere
An honde-brede[4] bove either ear,
And on his croune made a crois.
He gan crie and make nois.
175 He swor, they shulde alle abye,
That him dyde such vileynye,
And ever he seide, he was lord,
And eche man scorned him for that word,
And eche man seide, he was wod,
180 That proved wel, he couthe no good.
For he wende in none wise,
That God almighty couthe devise,
Him to bringe to lower stat:
[5]With o draught he was chekmat!
185 With houndes every night he lay,
And ofte he cried welaway
That he ever was y-bore,
For he was a man forlore.
Ther nas in court grom ne page,
190 That of the kyng ne made rage.
For no man ne mighte him knowe,
He was defigured in a throwe,
So lowe ere that was never king.
Allas, here was a delful thing,

1. companion, 2. food-taster, 3. summoned, 4. hand's breadth, 5. 'With
one move he was checkmate!'

195   That him sholde for his pride
      Such hap among his men bitide!
      Hunger and thirst he hadde grete,
      For he ne moste no mete ete,
      But houndes eten of his disch,
200   Whether hit were flesh or fish.
      He was to dethe nigh y-brought
      For hunger, ere he might eten ought
      With houndes, that ben in halle.
      How mighte him hardore bifalle?
205   And whan hit nolde non other be,
      He eet with houndes gret plente.
      The angel was king, him thoughte long.
      In his time was never wrong,
      Tricherye ne falshede ne go gyle
210   Don in the londe of Sicily.
      Alle gode ther was gret plente,
      Among men love and charite.
      In his time was never strif
      Bitwene man and his wif;
215   Eche man loved wel other,
      Beter love nas never of brother.
      Thanne was that a joyful thing,
      In londe to have such a king.
      King he was thre yer and more,
220   Roberd yede[1] as man forlore[2].

      Suththe hit fel uppon a day,
      A litel bifore the moneth of May,
      Sire Valemound, the emperour,
      Sente lettres of gret honour
225   To his brother, of Sicil king,
      And bad him come withoute letting
      That they mighte be bothe y-some[3]
      With here[4] brother, pope of Rome.
      Him thoughte long, they were at-winne[5];

1. underwent, 2. abandoned, 3. together, 4. their, 5. parted from each other.

230   He bad him lete for no winne,
         That he nere of good aray
         In Rome an holy Thoresday.
         The angel welcomede the messagers
         And gaf hem clothes riche of pers[1],
235   Furred alle with ermyne,
         In Cristendom is non so fyne;
         And al was couched mid perre[2],
         Beter was non in cristiante.
         Such cloth, and hit were to dighte,
240   Al Cristendom hit make ne mighte;
         Of that wondrede al that lond,
         How that cloth was wrought with hond;
         Wher such cloth was to selle,
         Ne who hit made, couthe no man telle.
245   The messagers wente with the king
         To grete Rome withoute letting.
         The fol Roberd also went,
         Clothed in lodly[3] garnement
         With foxes tailes rive aboute,
250   Men might him knowen in the route.
         The angel was clothed al in whit,
         Nas never seyghe such samite;
         And al was couched mid perles riche,
         Never man seigh none hem liche.
255   Al whit atire was and stede,
         The stede was fair, ther he gede.
         So fair a stede, as he on rod,
         Nas never man that ever bistrod.
         The angel com to Rome sone,
260   [4]Real as fel a kyng to done;
         So real kyng com never in Rome,
         Alle men wondred whethen he come.
         His men were realliche dight,
         Here richess can seye no wight
265   Of clothes, gyrdeles and other thing;

1. Persian blue, 2. precious stones, 3. loathsome, 4. 'Royally as befell a king'.

Everich squyer thoughte a king.
And alle ride of riche aray,
But king Roberd, as I you say.
Alle men on him gon pike[1],
270   For he rod al other unlike.
An ape rod of his clothing,
In tokne he was underling.
The pope and the emperour also
And other lordes many mo
275   Welcomed the angel as for king
And made joye of his coming.
These thre bretheren made cumfort,
The angel was brother mad bi sort.
Wel was the pope and the emperour,
280   That hadde a brother of such honour.

Forth com sterte king Roberd
As fol and man that nas nought ferd,
And cried with ful egre[2] speche
To his bretheren, to [3]don him wreche
285   Of him, that hath with queynte gyle
His croune and lond of Sicily.
The pope, ne the emperour, nother,
The fol ne knew nought for here brother.
Tho was he more fol i-holde,
290   More than ere a thousend folde;
To cleyme such a brotherhede
Hit was holde a foles dede.
King Roberd bigan to make care,
Moche more than he dide ere,
295   Whan his bretheren nolde him knowe:
'Allas,' quath he, 'now am I lowe.'
For he hoped bi eny thing,
His bretheren wolde ha mad him king;
And whan his hope was al ago,
300   He seide allas and weilawo.
He seide allas that he was bore,

1. stare, 2. bitter, 3. 'do him vengeance'.

For he was a man forlore.
He seide allas that he was mad,
For of his life he was al sad.
305 Allas, allas was al his song,
His hair he tar, his hondes wrong,
And ever he seide allas allas.
And thanne he thoughte on his trespas.
He thoughte on Nabugodonosore[1],
310 A noble kyng, was him bifore.
In al the world nas his per,
Forte acounte, fer no ner.
With him was Sire Olyferne[2],
Prince of knightes stout and stern.
315 Olyferne swor evermor
Bi God Nabugodonosor,
And seide ther nas no God in londe
But Nabugodonosor was glad,
That he the name of God had,
320 And loved Olyferne the more;
And seththe[3] hit greved hem bothe sore.
Olyferne deyed in dolour,
He was slaye in harde shour[4];
Nabugodonosor lyvede in desert,
325 Dorst he nowher ben apert;
Fyftene yer he lived thare
With rotes, gras and evel fare.
And al of moss his clothing was;
Al com that bi Godes grace!
330 He cried merci with delful chere,
God him restored, as he was ere.
'Now am Ich in such a cas,
And wel worse than he was.
Whan God gaf me such honour,
335 That I was cleped conquerour,
In every lond of cristendome

---

1. Nebuchadnezzer, v. *Daniel* iv., 2. Holofernes, v. *Judith* iv., 3. afterwards, 4. battle-blow. Judith killed him.

Of me men speke wel y-lome;
And seide, nowher was mi per
In al the worlde, fer no ner.
340   For that name I hadde pride,
As angels that gonne from joye glide.
And in twinkling of an eye
[1]God binam here maystrye.
So hath he min, for mi gylt,
345   Now am I wel lowe y-pilt.
And that is right that I so be,
Lord, on thi fol thou have pite.
I hadde an errour in min herte,
And that errour doth me smerte.
350   Lord, I leved[2] nought on thee,
Lord on thi fol thou have pite.
Holy writ I hadde in dispyt,
For that is reved[3] mi delyt,
For that is right, a fol I be,
355   Lord, on thi fol thou have pite.
Lord, I am thi creature,
This wo is right that I endure,
And wel more yif hit may be,
Lord, on thi fol thou have pite.
360   Blisful Marie to thee I crye,
As thou art ful of cortesye,
Preye thi sone, that deyed for me,
On me his fol he have pite.
Blisful Marie, ful of grace,
365   To thee I knowe mi trespas;
Prey thi sone, for love of thee,
On me, his fol, he have pite.'
He seide no more allas, allas,
But thanked Crist of his grace;
370   And thus he gan himself stille
And thanked Crist mid goode wille[4].

---

1. 'God took away their mastery', 2. believed, 3. taken away, 4. i.e. a
properly disposed elective will.

The pope, emperour and king
Five wikes maden here dwelling;
Whan five wikes were agon,
375 To here owne lond they wolde anon,
Bothe emperour and king.
Ther was a fair departing,
The angel com to Sicily,
He and his men, in a while.
380 Whan he com into halle,
The fool anon he bad forth calle.
He seide: 'Fol, artow king?'
'Nay, sire,' quath he, 'withoute lesing[1].'
'What artow?' seide the angel.
385 'Sire, a fol, that wot I wel,
And more than fol, yif hit may be;
Kep I non other dignite.'
The angel into chaumbre went,
And after the fol anon he sent.
390 He bad his men out of chaumbre gon,
Ther lafte nomo but he alon,
And the fol that stod him bi.
To him he seide: 'thou hast mercy!
Thenk, thou were lowe y-pylt,
395 And al was for thin owne gylt,
A fol thou were to hevene king,
Therfore thou art an underling,
God hath forgive thi misdede,
Ever herafter thou him drede.
400 I am an angel of renoun,
Y-sent to kepe thi regioun;
More joye me shal falle
In hevene among mi feren alle
In an houre of a day
405 Than in erthe, I thee say,
In an hundred thousend yer,
Theigh al the world, fer and ner,
Were min at mi liking.

1. lying.

298

I am an angel, thou art kyng!'
410 He went in twinkling of an eye,
No more of him ther nas seghe.
King Roberd com into halle,
His men he bad anon forth calle,
And alle were at his wille,
415 As to her lord, as hit was skille.
He loved God and holicherche,
And ever he thoughte wel to werche.
He regned after two yer and more
And loved God and his lore.
420 The angel gaf him in warning
Of the time of his dying.
Whan time com to deye son,
He let write hit right anon,
How God mid his mochel might
425 Made him lowe, as hit was right.
This storie he sente everichdel
To his bretheren, under his sel,
And the time, whan he shulde deye,
That time he deyed as he gan seye.
430 Al this is write withoute lie,
At Rome to ben in memorye,
At seinte Petres cherche, I knowe.
And thus is Godes might y-sowe,
That heyghe be lowe, theigh hit ben ille,
435 And lowe heighe, at Godes wille.
Crist, that for us gan deye,
In his kineriche[1] let us ben heighe,
Evermore to ben above,
Ther is joye, cumfort and love. Amen.

1. kingdom.

NOTE

Roberd of Cisyle was written before 1370 in the south-east Midlands. It is preserved in three fourteenth- and five fifteenth-century MSS. It is really a pious legend rather than a romance.

ANONYMOUS

*

The Parlement of the Thre Ages

PROLOGUE

In the monethe of Maye · when mirthes bene fele,
And the sesone of somere · when softe bene the wedres,
Als I went to the wodde · my werdes to dreghe,
In-to the shawes my-selfe · a shotte me to gete
5 At ane hert or ane hynde, · happen as it myghte:
And as Dryghtyn the day · drove frome the heven,
Als I habade on a banke · be a bryme syde,
There the gryse was grene, · growen with floures —
The primrose, the pervynke, · and piliole the riche —
10 The dewe appon dayses · donkede full faire,
Burgons and blossoms · and braunches full swete,
And the mery mystes · full myldely gane falle:
The cukkowe, the cowschote, · kene were thay bothen
And the throstills full throly · threpen in the bankes,

The Debate between the Three Ages of Man

PROLOGUE

In the month of May when pleasures are many,
And the season of summer when gentle are the weathers,
As I went to the wood my chances to try,
Into the thickets to get me a shot
5 *At a hart or a hind, happen as it might:*
And as God drove the day from the sky,
As I tarried on a bank by a river-side,
Where the grass was green, grown with flowers —
The primrose, the periwinkle, and the rich wild-thyme —
10 *The dew upon the daisies was fairly dank,*
Buds and blossoms and branches most delightful,
And the pleasant mists full mildly began to fall:
The cuckoo, the wood-pigeon, active were they both,
And the thrushes full boldly competed on the banks,

300

15   And iche foule in that frythe[1] · faynere[2] than other
     That the derke was done · and the day lightenede:
     Hertys and hyndes · on hillys thay goven[3],
     The foxe and the filmarte[4] · they flede to the erthe,
     The hare [5]hurkles by hawes, · and harde thedir drives,
20   And [6]ferkes faste to hir fourme · and fatills hir to sitt.
     Als I stode in that stede[7] · on stalkynge I thoghte;
     Bothe my body and my bowe · I buskede[8] with leves;
     And turnede to-wardes a tree · and tariede there a while;
     And als I lokede to a launde[9] · a littill me be-syde,
25   I seghe ane hert with [10]ane hede, · ane heghe for the nones;
     Alle unburneshede was the beme, · full borely[11] the mydle,
     With iche feetur[12] as thi fote, · [13]for-frayed in the greves,
     With auntlers on aythere syde · egheliche[14] longe;
     The ryalls full richely[15] · [16]raughten frome the myddes,
30   With surryals[17] full semely · appon sydes twayne;
     And he [18]assommet and sett · of six and of fyve,
     And ther-to borely[19] and brode · and of body grete,
     And a coloppe[20] for a kynge, · cache hym who myghte.
     [21]Bot there sewet him a sowre · that servet hym full yerne,
35   That woke and warned him · when the winde failede,
     [22]That none so sleghe in his slepe · with sleghte sholde him dere,
     [23]And went the wayes him by-fore · when any wothe tyde.
     My lyame[24] than full lightly · lete I doun falle,
     And to the bole of a birche · [25]my berselett I cowchide;
40   I waited wisely the wynde · by waggynge of leves,
     Stalkede full stilly · no stickes to breke,
     And crepite to a crabtre · and coverede me ther-undere.
     Then I bende up my bowe · and bownede[26] me to shote,

1. wood, 2. more eager, 3. betook themselves, 4. polecat, 5. 'squats by hedges, and vigorously hastens thither', 6. 'presses straight to her bed and prepares her ...', 7. place, 8. camouflaged, 9. stretch of ground, 10. 'a head of horns, a high one indeed', 11. strong, 12. line, 13. 'rubbed in the grooves', 14. terribly, 15. nobly, 16. 'extended from the centre', 17. crown antlers, 18. 'was full-grown and of age about six or five', 19. tall, 20. dish, 21. 'But there accompanied him (the stag) a sorrel (a four-year old buck) that served the stag zealously', 22. 'so that no hunter should attack him in his sleep', 23. The buck 'preceded him along the ways when any harm threatened', 24. leash, 25. 'my hound I made to couch', 26. prepared.

Tighte up my tilere[1] · and [2]taysede at the hert.

45 [3]Bot the sowre that him sewet · sett up the nese,
And waittede wittyly abowte · and windide full yerne.
Then I moste stonde als I stode · and stirre no fote ferrere,
For had I mintid[4] or movede · or made any synys,
Alle my layke hade bene loste · that I hade longe waittede.

50 Bot gnattes gretely me grevede · and [5]gnewen myn eghne.
And he [6]stotayde and stelkett · and starede full brode.
[7]Bot at the laste he loutted doun · and laughte till his mete,
And I hallede to the hokes · and the hert smote,
And happenid that I hitt him · by-hynde the lefte sholdire,

55 That the blode braste owte · appon bothe the sydes:
And he balkede and brayed · and brushede thurgh the greves,
As alle had hurlede on ane hepe · that [8]in the holte longede.
And some the sowre that him sewet · resorte to his feris[9],
And thay, forfrayede of his fare, · to the fellys[10] thay hyen.

60 And I heyde to my hounde · and hent him up sone,
And louset my lyame · and lete him umbycaste[11].
The breris and the brakens · were blody by-ronnen,
And he assentis to that sewte · and seches him aftire,
There he was crepyde in-to a krage · and croushede to the erthe;

65 Dede als a dore-nayle · doun was he fallen.
And I him hent by the hede · and heryett him uttire[12],
[13]Turned his troches and tachede · thaym in-to the erthe,
[14]Kest up that keudart · and kutt off his tonge,
Brayde out his bowells · my berselett[15] to fede;

70 And I sliste[16] him at the assaye[17] · to see how me semyde,
And he was floreshede full faire · of two fyngere brode.

---

1. handle of a cross-bow, 2. stretched the bow-string, 3. 'But the sorrel
buck that accompanied the stag threw up his nose, And waited knowingly
about and sniffed the scent strenuously', 4. made a gesture, 5. 'gnawed my
eyes', 6. hesitated and moved slowly, 7. 'But finally he bowed his head
down and took up his food, And I hauled to the hooks (of the cross-bow) and
smote the hart', 8. in the wood abode, 9. companions, 10. mountains,
11. seek around, 12. '... and dragged him out', 13. 'Turned his smaller tines
and inserted them into the earth', 14. 'Turned over that rogue', 15. hound,
16. sliced, 17. a test of the fatness of the deer.

I chese to the chawylls[1] · chefe to be-gynn,
And ritte doun at a rase · reghte to the tayle,
And than the herbere[2] anone · aftir I makede,
75   I raughte the righte legge by-fore, · ritt in ther-aftir,
And so fro legge to legge · I lepe thaym aboute,
And the felle fro the fete · fayre I departede,
And flewe it doun with my fiste · faste to the rigge[3];
I tighte oute my trenchore · and toke off the sholdires,
80   Cuttede corbyn's bone · and kest it a-waye;
I slitte him full sleghely, · and slyppede in my fyngere,
Lesse the poynte sholde perche[4] · the pawnche or the guttys:
I soughte owte my sewet[5] · and semblete it to-gedre,
And pullede owte the pawnche · and put it in an hole:
85   I grippede owte the guttes · and graythede thaym be-syde,
And than the nombles[6] anone · name[7] I there-aftire,
Rent up fro the rigge · reghte to the myddis;
And than the fourches full fayre · I fonge fro the sydes,
And chynede him chefely, · and choppede off the nekke,
90   And the hede and the haulse[8] · homelyde[9] in sondree;
The fete of the fourche · I feste thurgh the sydis,
And hevede alle in-to ane hole · and hidde it with ferne,
With hethe and with hore mosse · hilde it about,
That no fostere of the fee[10] · sholde fynde it ther-aftir;
95   Hid the hornes and hede · in ane hologhe oke,
That no hunte sholde it hent · ne have it in sighte.
[11]I foundede faste there-fro · for ferde to be wryghede,
And sett me oute on a syde · to see how it chevede[12],
[13]To wayte it from wylde swyne · that wyse bene of nesse.
100   And als I satte in my sette · the sone was so warme,
[14]And I for slepeles was slome · and slomerde a while,
And there me dremed, in that dowte, · a full dreghe sweuynn[15],
And what I seghe in my saule · the sothe I shall telle.

1. jowels. The reader can compare this account with the description of the 'breaking of the deer' in *Sir Gawayne and the Grene Knight* (see pp. 391–2), 2. gullet, 3. back, 4. pierce, 5. suet about the kidneys, 6. entrails, 7. took, 8. neck, 9. cut, 10. royal forester, for the stag had been poached, 11. 'I set off quickly from there for fear of discovery', 12. turned out, 13. 'To guard it from wild swine that are cunning of scent', 14. 'And I for lack of sleep was heavy', 15. a very long dream.

I

[1]I seghe thre thro men · threpden full yerne
105 And moteden of myche-whate · and maden thaym full
      tale.
And ye will, ledys[2], me listen · ane littille-while,
I shall reken thaire araye · redely for sothe,
And to youe nevern[3] thaire names · naytly there-aftire.
The firste was a ferse freke,[4] · fayrere than thies othire,
110 [5]A bolde beryn on a blonke · bownne for to ryde,
A hathelle[6] on ane heghe horse · with hawke appon hande.
He was balghe[7] in the breste · and brode in the sholdirs,
His axles[8] and his armes · were eghe-liche longe,
And in the medill als a mayden · menskfully[9] shapen.
115 Longe legges, and large, · and lele[10] for to shewe,
He streghte him in his sterapis · and strode up-rightes.
He ne hade no hode ne no hatte · bot his here one,
A chaplet on his chefe-lere[11], · chosen for the nones,
Raylede alle with rede rose, · richeste of floures,
120 With trayfoyles and trueloves · of full triede perles,
With a chefe charebocle[12] · chosen in the myddes.
He was gerede alle in grene, · alle with golde by-wevede,
Embroddirde alle with besanttes[13] · and beralles full riche.
His colere with calsydoynnes · clustrede full thikke,
125 With many dyamandes full dere · dighte on his sleves.
The semys with saphirs · sett were full many,
With emeraudes and amatistes · appon iche side,
With full riche rubyes · raylede by the hemmes;
The price of that perry[14] · were worthe poundes full many.
130 His sadill was of sykamoure · that he satt inn,
His bridell alle of brente golde · with silke brayden raynes,
His trapoure[15] was of tartaryne[16], · that traylede to the erthe,

1. 'I saw (in my sleep) three urgent men who debated among each other
very eagerly, And discussed a great deal and they opposed each other',
2. men, 3. name (verb), 4. a fierce fellow, 5. 'A bold man on a horse prepared for riding', 6. man, 7. rounded, 8. shoulders, 9. handsomely, 10. attractive, 11. hair, 12. carbuncle, 13. small round gold ornaments, coins,
14. outfit of precious stones, 15. saddle-cloth, 16. silk of Tartary.

[1]And he throly was threven · of thritty yere of elde,
And ther-to yonge and yape[2], · and Youthe was his name;
135 And the semelyest segge[3] · that I seghe ever.

II

The seconde segge in his sete · satte at his ese,
[4]A renke alle in rosette · that rowmly was shapyn;
In a golyone[5] of graye · girde in the myddes,
And iche bagge in his bosome · bettir than othere.
140 On his golde and his gude · gretly he mousede[6].
His renttes and his reches · rekened he full ofte,
[7]Of mukking, of marleling, · and mendynge of houses,
Of benes[8] of his bondemen, · of benefetis many,
Of presanntes of polayle[9], · of purfilis[10] als,
145 Of purches of ploughe-londes, · of parkes full faire,
Of profettis of his pastours, · that his purse mendis,
Of stiewardes, of storrours[11], · stirkes[12] to bye,
Of clerkes of countours, · his courtes to holde,
And alle his witt in this werlde · was on his wele one.
150 Him semyde, for to see to, · of sexty yere elde,
And ther-fore men in his marche[13] · Medill-elde[14] him callede.

III

The thirde was a laythe lede[15] · lenyde on his syde,
[16]A beryne bownn alle in blake, · with bedis in his hande;
Croked and courbede[17], · encrampeshett for elde.
155 Alle disfygured was his face, · and fadit his hewe,
His berde and browes · were blanchede full whitte,
And the hare on his hede · hewede of the same,
He was ballede and blynde · and all babirlippede,
Totheles and tenefull[18], · I tell youe for sothe,
160 And ever he momelide and ment[19] · and mercy he askede,

1. 'And he excellently was thriven of thirty years of age', 2. frisk, 3. man,
4. 'A fellow all in russet who corpulently was shaped', 5. tunic, 6. mused,
7. 'Of manuring, of dressing land with marl', 8. requests, 9. poultry,
10. edgings for garments, 11. storers, 12. bullocks, 13. district, 14. Middle-
Age, 15. repulsive man, 16. 'A fellow arrayed all in black ...', 17. doubled
up, 18. querulous, 19. moaned.

And cried kenely on Criste, · and his crede sayde,
With sawtries[1] full sere tymes, · to sayntes in heven.
Envyous and angrye, · and Elde was his name.
[2]I helde him be my hapynge · a hundrethe yeris of age,
165 And bot his cruche and his couche · he carede for no more.
Now hafe I rekkende you theire araye, · redely the sothe,
And also namede you thaire names · naytly there-aftire,
And now thaire carpynge[3] I shall kythe, · knowe it if
        youe liste.

IV

Now this gome[4] alle in grene · so gayly attyrede,
170 This hathelle on this heghe horse, · with hawke on his fiste,
He was yonge and yape · and yernynge to armes,
[5]And pleynede him on paramoure · and peteuosely syghede.
He sett him up in his sadill · and seyde theis wordes:
'My lady, my leman[6], · that I hafe luffede ever,
175 My wele and my wirchip, · in werlde where thou dwellys,
My playstere[7] of paramours, · with pappis full swete,
Alle my hope and my hele, · myn herte es thyn ownn!
[8]I by-hete thee a heste, · and heghely I a-vowe,
There shall no hode ne no hatt · on my hede sitt,
180 Till that I joyntly with a gesserante[9] · justede[10] hafe ones
And done dedis for thi love, · doghety in armes.'

V

Bot then this gome alle in graye[11] · greved with this wordes,
And sayde, 'felowe, be my faythe · thou fonnes[12] full yerne,
For alle fantome and foly · that thou with faris.
185 Where es the londe and the lythe[13] · that thou arte lorde over?
For alle thy ryalle araye, · renttis hase thou none.
Ne for thi pompe and thi pride, · penyes bot fewe.
For alle thi golde and thi gude · glows on this clothes,

1. psalteries, psalms, 2. 'I held him by my estimate to be a hundred years of age', 3. their argument among themselves, 4. man, 5. 'And lamented about his mistress', 6. beloved one, 7. salve, 8. 'I avow thee a promise', 9. coat of mail, 10. jousted, 11. i.e. Middle-Age, 12. speakest stupidly, 13. dependants, tenants.

[1]And thou hafe caughte thi kaple, · thou cares for no fothire.
190 [2]Bye thee stirkes with thi stede, · and stalles thaym make;
Thi bridell of brent golde · wolde bullokes thee gete;
The pryce of thi perrye · wolde purches thee londes;
[3]And wonne, wy, in thi witt, · for wele-neghe thou spilles.'

VI

Than the gome alle in grene · greved full sore,
195 And sayd, 'sir, be my soule, · thi consell es feble.
Bot[4] thi golde and thi gude · thou hase no god ells!
For, be the lorde and the laye[5] · that I leve inne,
And by the Gode that me gaffe · goste and soule,
[6]Me were levere on this launde · lengen a while,
200 Stoken in my stele-wede, · on my stede bakke,
Harde haspede in my helme · and in my here-wedys[7],
With a grim-grounded glayfe[8] · graythely in myn honde,
And see a kene knyghte come · and cowpe with my-selven,
That I myghte halde that I hafe highte · and heghely avowede,
205 And parfourme my profers · and proven my strengthes,
Than alle the golde and the gude · that thoue gatt ever,
Than alle the londe and the lythe · that thoue arte lorde over;
And ryde to a revere[9] · redily there-aftir,
With hawkes full hawtayne[10] · that heghe willen flye,
210 And when the fewlis[11] bene founden, · fawkoneres hyenn
To lache oute thaire lessches[12] · and lowsen thaym sone,
[13]And heppyn of thaire caprons, · and casten fro honde,
And than the hawteste[14] in haste · hyghes to the towre,
With theire bellys so brighte · blethely thay ryngen,
215 And there they hoven appon heghte, · as it were heven
angelles.
Then the fawkoners full fersely · to floodes thay hyen,
To the revere with thaire roddes · to rere up[15] the fewles,

1. 'So long as you have your horse in hand you care for nothing else',
2. 'Buy bullocks with (the price of) your horse', 3. 'And live, man, with
your brains, for now you talk nonsense', 4. except for, 5. faith, 6. 'I would
rather remain a while on this land, Clad in my steel coat, on my horse's back',
7. war garments, 8. spear, 9. river, hawking course, 10. proud, 11. birds,
12. leashes, 13. 'And slip off their hoods', 14. proudest, 15. beat up.

[1]Sowsshes thaym full serely · to serven thaire hawkes.
That [2]tercelettes full tayttely · telys[3] down stryken,
220 [4]Laners and lanerettis · lightten to thes endes,
Metyn with the maulerdes[5] · and many down striken.
Fawkons thay founden · freely to lighte,
With *Hoo!* and *Howghe!* to the heron · thay hitten him
full ofte,
Buffetyn him, betyn him, · and brynges him to sege,
225 And saylen him full serely · and sesyn him there–aftire.
Then fawkoners full fersely · founden tham aftire,
To helpen thaire hawkes · thay hyen thaym full yerne,
For the bitt of his bill · bitterly he strikes.
They knelyn down on theire knees · and krepyn full lowe,
230 Wynnen to his wynges · and wrythen thaym to–gedire,
Brosten the bones and brekyn · thaym in sondire,
[6]Puttis oute with a penn · the pyth on his glove,
And quopes[7] thaym to the querrye · that quelled him to the
dethe.
[8]He quysses thaym and quotes thaym, · quyppeys[9] full lowde,
235 [10]Cheres thaym full chefely · ecchekkes to leve;
Than henntis[11] thaym on honde · and hodes thaym ther–aftire,
[12]Couples up theire cowers · thaire caprons to holde,
[13]Louppes in thaire lesses · thorowe vertwells of silvere;
Than he laches to his luyre[14], · and lokes to his horse,
240 And lepis upe on the lefte syde, · [15]als the laghe askes.
[16]Portours full pristly · putten upe the fowlis,
And taryen for theire tercelettis · that tenyn[17] thaym full ofte.
For some chosen [18] to the echecheke, · thoghe some chefe
bettire.
Spanyells full spedily · thay spryngen abowte,

1. 'Strike them up vigorously', 2. 'falcons full nimbly', 3. teals, 4. Male
and female falcons, 5. mallards, 6. 'Puts out with a quill the marrow on his
glove', 7. whoops, 8. The falconer cries and calls to his falcons, 9. whips,
10. The falconer 'encourages his falcons especially to abandon false scents',
11. receives, 12. he draws the braces which open and close the hood (*capron*)
behind, 13. 'Loops their leashes through the silver rings' (which, attached to
the jesses, had the owner's name engraved on them), 14. lure, 15. 'as the
law requires', 16. 'Carriers full readily', 17. tease, 18. 'to pursue inferior
game, while others achieve better'.

245   [1]Be-dagged for dowkynge · when digges ben enewede.
      And than kayre[2] to the courte · that I come fro,
      With ladys full lovely · to lappyn in myn armes,
      And clyp thaym and kysse thaym · and comforthe myn hert;
      And than with damesels dere · to daunsen in thaire chambirs;
250   Riche Romance to rede, · and rekken the sothe
      Of kempes[3] and of conquerours, · of kynges full noblee,
      How thay wirchipe and welthe · wanne[4] in thaire lyves.
      With renkes in ryotte · to revelle in haulle,
      With coundythes and carolles[5] · and compaynyes sere,
255   [6]And chese me to the chesse · that chefe es of gamnes.
      And this es life for to lede · while I shalle lyfe here.
      And thou with wandrynge and woo · shalte wake for thi
        gudes,
      [7]And be thou dolven and dede, · thi dole shall be shorte,
      And he that thou leste luffes · shall layke him there-with,
260   And spend that thou sparede, · the devyll spede him ells!'
      Than this renke alle in rosett · rothelede thies wordes:
      He sayde, 'thryfte and thou have threpid · this thirtene
        wynter.
      I seghe wele samples bene sothe · that sayde bene full yore:
      [8]*Fole es that with foles delys.* · Flyte we no lengare!'

VII

265   [9]Than this beryn alle in blake · bownnes him to speke,
      And sayde, 'sirres, by my soule, · sottes bene ye bothe.
      [10]Bot will ye hendely me herken · ane hande-while,
      And I shalle stynte your stryffe · and stillen your threpe.
      I sett ensample bi my-selfe, · and seke it no forthire:
270   While I was yonge in my youthe · and yape[11] of my dedys,

---

1. 'Bedraggled on account of the soaking when the ducklings (which they retrieved) were driven into the water', 2. proceed, 3. warriors, 4. won, 5. songs and dances, 6. 'And betake me to chess', 7. 'And when you are dead and buried your wealth won't last long, And he whom you like least shall amuse himself with it, And spend what you hoarded', 8. *Fool is that deals with fools. Let us squabble no longer!*', 9. 'Then this man all in black (Old) gets ready to speak', 10. 'But if you will kindly listen to me for a short space, I shall silence your strife and quieten your contest', 11. sprightly.

I was als everrous[1] in armes · as outher of youre-selven,
[2]And as styffe in a stourre · on my stede bake,
And as gaye in my gere · als any gome ells,
And as lelly by-luffede · with ladyes and maydens.
275 My likame[3] was lovely · as lothe nowe to shewe,
And as myche wirchip I wane · i-wis as ye bothen.
[4]And aftir irkede me with this, · and ese was me levere,
Als man in his medill elde · his makande[5] wolde have.
Than I mukkede and marlede · and made up my houses,
280 And purcheste me plough-londes · and pastures full noble;
Gatte gude and golde · full gaynly to honde;
Reches and renttes · were ryfe to my-selven.
Bot elde undire-yode[6] me · are[7] I laste wiste,
And alle disfegurede my face · and fadide my hewe,
285 Bothe my browes and my berde · blaunchede full whitte,
[8]And when he sotted my syghte, · than sowed myn hert,
Croked me, cowrbed me, · encrampeshet myn hondes,
That I ne may hefe tham to my hede, · ne noghte helpe
        my-selven,
Ne stale[9] stonden on my fete, · bot I my staffe have.
290 Makes youre mirrours bi me, · men, bi youre trouthe;
This shadowe in my shewere[10] · shunte[11] ye no while.
And now es dethe at my dore · that I drede moste.
I ne wot wiche daye, ne when, · ne whate tyme he comes,
Ne whedir-wardes, ne whare, · ne whatte to do aftire.
295 But man modyere[12] than I, · men on this molde[13],
Hafe passed the passe · that I shall passe sone;
[14]And I shall neven you the names · of Nyne of the Beste
That ever wy in this werlde · wiste appon erthe,
That were conquerours full kene · and kiddeste[15] of other.

[Here follow 330 lines in which the poet catalogues the exploits of the Nine Worthies.]

1. eager. 2. 'And as bold in a contest on my horse's back', 3. body,
4. 'And later this irked me and I came to prefer ease', 5. comfort, 6. under-
mined, 7. ere, before, 8. 'And when he bleared my sight, then it made sore
my heart', 9. firmly, 10. mirror, 11. avoid, 12. more excellent, 13. earth,
14. 'And I shall give you the names of Nine of the Best That ever man in this
world knew', 15. most renowned.

XXI

631 Sythen doughtynes when dede comes · ne dare noghte
     habyde,
    Ne dethe wondes for no witt · to wende where him lykes,
    And thereto paramours and pride · puttes he full lowe
    Ne there es reches ne rent · may rawnsone your lives,
635 Ne noghte es sekire[1] to youre-selfe · in certayne bot dethe,
    And he es so uncertayne · that sodaynly he comes,
    Me thynke the wele of this werlde · worthes to noghte,
    Ecclesiastes the clerke · declares in his booke
   [2]*Vanitas vanitatum et omnia vanitas,*
640 That alle es vaynest of vanytes, · and vanyte es alle;
    For-thi amendes youre mysse · whills ye are men here,
    Quia in inferno nulla est redempcio;
    For in helle es no helpe, · I hete you for sothe;
    Als God in his gospelle · graythely you teches,
645 *Ite ostendite vos sacerdotibus,*
    Go shryve you full shirle[3], · and shewe you to prestis;
    Et ecce omnia sunt vobis,
    And that ye wronge have wroghte · shall worthen[4] full
     clene.
    Thou man in thi Medill Elde, · hafe mynde whate I saye!
650 I am thi sire and thou my sone, · the sothe for to telle,
    And he the sone of thi-self, · that sittis on the stede,
    For Elde es sire of Midill Elde, · and Midill-elde of Youthe:
    And haves gud daye, for now I go; · to grave moste me
     wende;
    Dethe dynges on my dore, · I dare no lengare byde.'

655   When I[5] had lenged and layne · a full longe while,
    I herde a bogle[6] on a bonke · be blowen full loude,
    And I wakkened therwith · and waytted me umbe[7].
    Than the sone was sett · and syled[8] full loughe[9];

---

1. surer, 2. after each line of Latin, the translation follows, 3. purely,
4. be made, 5. i.e. the deer-stalker of the Prologue, 6. bugle, 7. about,
8. glided, 9. low.

And I founded appon fote · and ferkede towards townn.
660   And in the monethe of Maye · thies mirthes me tydde,
    [1]Als I shurted me in a shelfe · in the shawes faire,
    And belde[2] me in the birches · with bewes[3] full smale,
    And lugede[4] me in the leves, · that lighte were and grene.
    There, dere Drightyne, this daye · dele us of this blysse,
665   And Marie, that es mylde quene, · amende us of synn!
                            Amen Amen.

Thus endes THE THRE AGES

1. 'As I amused myself in a seat in the fair thickets', 2. built, 3. boughs, 4. lodged.

NOTE

The Parlement of the Thre Ages, by a Western man, is almost certainly by the same author as *Wynnere and Wastoure*; they contain similar passages, are written in the same style, and they follow the same convention of a debate.

ANONYMOUS

*

Wynnere and Wastoure

Here begynnes a Tretys and god shorte Refreyte
by-twixe Wynnere and Wastoure

PROLOGUE

Sythen that Bretayne was biggede, · and Bruyttus it aughte,
Thurgh the takynge of Troye · with tresone with-inn,
There hathe selcouthes bene sene · in seere kynges tymes,
But never so many as nowe · by the nynde dele.
5   For nowe alle es Witt and Wylle · that we with delyn,
Wyli wordes and slee, · and icheon wryeth othere.
Wyse wordes with-inn · that writen were never:
'Dare never no westren wy, · while this werlde lasteth,
Send his sone south-warde · to se ne to here,
10   That he ne shall holden by-hynde · when he hore eld es.'
For-thi sayde was a sawe · of Salomon the wyse –
It hyeghte harde appone honde, · hope I no nother –

Winner and Waster

Here begins a Treatise and good short Debate
between Winner and Waster

PROLOGUE

Since that Britain was founded, and Brutus possessed it,
Through the taking of Troy by treason within,
There have strange things been seen during many kings' times,
But never so many as now by the ninth part.
5   *For now all is Wit and Will that we deal in,*
Wily words and sly, and each one betrays the other.
Wise words within that written were never:
'Dare no western man, while this world lasts,
Send his son southward to see or to hear,
10   *But rather he shall keep him behind at home when he is hoar of age,'.*
Therefore was said a saying of Solomon the wise –
It comes hard at hand, I expected it not otherwise –

'When wawes[1] waxen shall wilde, · and walles bene doun,
And hares appon herthe-stones · shall [2]hurcle in hire fourme,
15 And eke boyes of no blode, · with boste and with pryde,
Shall wedde ladyes in londe, · and lede at hir will,
Thene dredfull domesdaye · it draweth neghe aftir.'
Bot who-so sadly[3] will see · and the sothe telle,
Say it [4]newely will neghe, · or es neghe here.
20 Whylome[5] were lordes in londe · that loved in thaire
     hertis
To here makers of myrthes, · that matirs couthe fynde.
And now es no frenchipe [6]on fere · bot fayntnesse of hert
Ne redde in no romance · that ever renke[7] herde.
Bot now a childe appon chere, · with-owtten chin-wedys[8],
25 That never wroghte thurgh witt · three wordes to-gedire,
Fro[9] he can jangle als a jaye, · and japes[10] can tell,
He shall be levede[11] and lovede · and lett[12] of a while
Wele more than the man · [13]that makes hym-selven.
Bot[14] never the lattere at the laste, · when [15]ledys bene knawen,
30 Werk witnesse will bere · who wirche kane beste.

FITT I

Bot I shall tell you a tale · that me by-tyde ones,
Als[16] I went in the weste, · wandrynge my one,
Bi a bonke of a bourne[17], · bryghte was the sone,
[18]Undir a worthiliche wodde, · by a wale medewe:
35 Fele[19] floures gan folde · ther[20] my fote steppede.
I layde myn hede on ane hill, · ane hawthorne be-syde:
The throstills full throly[21] · they threpe to-gedire,
Hipped up heghwalles[22] · fro heselis[23] tyll othire,
Bernacles[24] with thayre billes · on barkes thay roungen,
40 The jay janglede on heghe; · [25]jarmede the foles;
The bourne full bremly[26] rane · the bankes by-twene.

---

1. waves, 2. 'crouch on their lairs', 3. seriously, 4. draws near, 5. once,
6. in company, 7. man, 8. chin-weeds, i.e. a beard, 9. because, 10. jests,
11. believed, 12. esteemed, 13. 'who really makes true songs', 14. nevertheless, 15. 'men are known' (for what they are), 16. as, 17. river, 18. 'Under a
fair wood, by a pleasant meadow', 19. many, 20. where, 21. actively, 22.
woodpeckers, 23. hazels, 24. wild geese, 25. 'chanted the birds', 26. noisily.

[1]So ruyde were the roughe stremys, · and raughten so heghe,
That it was neghande nyghte · or I nappe myghte,
For dyn of the depe watir, · [2]and dadillyng of fewllys.
45   Bot as I laye at the laste, · [3]than lowked myn eghne,
And I was swythe in a sweven · sweped be-lyve.
Me thoghte I was in the werlde, · I ne wiste in whate ende,
On a loveliche lande · that was ylike grene,
That laye [4]loken by a lawe · the lengthe of a myle.
50   In aythere holte was ane here[5] · in hawberkes full brighte,
Harde hattes appon hedes · and helmys with crestys,
Brayden[6] owte thaire baners, · bown for to mete
Shoven owte of the shawes[7], · in shiltrons[8] they felle;
And bot the lengthe of a launde · thies ledes by-twene[9].
55   And als I prayed for the pese[10] · till the prynce come,
For he was worthiere in witt · than any wy ells,
[11]For to ridde and to rede · and to rewlyn the wrothe
That aythere here appon hethe · had un-till othere.
At the creste of a clyffe · a caban was rerede,
60   Alle raylede with rede · the rofe and the sydes,
With Inglisse besantes[12] full brighte, · betyn of golde,
And ichone gayly umby-gone[13] · with garters of Inde,
And iche a gartare of golde · gerede full riche.
Then were thies wordes in the webbe · [14]werped of he,
65   Payntted of plunket[15], · and poyntes by-twene,
That were fourmed full fayre · appon freshe lettres,
And alle was it one sawe, · appon Inglisse tonge,
[16]*Hethyng have the hathell · that any harme thynkes.*

Now the kyng of this kythe[17], · kepe hym oure Lorde!
70   Upon heghe on the holt[18] · ane hathell[19] up stondes,

1. 'So sounded the boisterous stream and reached so high, That it was approaching night before I could sleep', 2. 'and chattering of birds', 3. 'then closed my eyes, And I was truly in a dream assailed quickly', 4. enclosed by a hill, 5. army, 6. unfurled, 7. thickets, 8. squadrons, 9. i.e. these opposing groups of men, 10. peace, 11. 'To part and to reconcile and to govern the anger That each army upon the heath had to the other', 12. small round gold ornaments. English besant, possibly the 'noble', a coin, 13. surrounded, 14. 'worked above them', 15. blue, 16. 'Scorn have the man who thinks any malice', 17. country, 18. woodland, 19. man.

Wroghte als a wodwyse[1], · alle in wrethyn lokkes[2],
With ane helme on his hede, · ane hatte appon lofte,
And on heghe on the hatte · ane hatefull beste,
A lighte lebarde[3] and a longe, · lokande full kene,

75 Yarked[4] alle of yalowe golde · in full yape[5] wyse.
[6]Bot that that hillede the helme · by-hynde in the nekke,
Was casten full clenly · in quarteres foure:
Two with flowres of Fraunce · be-fore and be-hynde,
And two other of Inglonde · with sex irous bestes,

80 Thre leberdes on lofte, · and thre on-lowe undir;
At iche a cornere a knoppe · of full clene perle,
Tasselde of tuly[7] silke, · tuttynge[8] out fayre.
And by the cabane I knewe · the knyghte that I see,
And thoghte to wiete[9], or I went, · wondres ynewe.

85 And als I waytted with-inn · I was warre[10] sone
Of a comliche kynge · crowned with golde.
Sett on a silken bynche, · with septure in honde,
One of the lovelyeste ledis[11], · who-so loveth hym in hert,
That ever segge undir sonn · sawe with his eghne[12].

90 This kynge was comliche clade · in kirtill and mantill,
Bery-brown as his berde, · [13]brouderde with fewlys,
Fawkons of fyne golde, · flakerande[14] with wynges,
And ichone bare in ble[15], · blewe als me thoghte,
A grete gartare of Inde · gerede ful riche.

95 Full gayly was that grete lorde · girde in the myddis,
A brighte belte of ble, · broudirde with fewles,
With drakes and with dukkes, · daderande[16] tham semede,
For ferdnes of fawcons fete, · [17]less fawked thay were.
And ever I sayd to my-selfe, · 'full selly[18] me thynke

100 Bot if[19] this renke[20] to the revere · ryde umbestounde.'
The kyng biddeth a beryn[21] · by hym that stondeth,
One of the ferlyeste frekes[22], · that faylede hym never:

1. satyr, 2. curled locks, 3. leopard, 4. made, 5. lively, 6. 'But that which hid the helm behind at the neck', 7. tile-coloured, red, 8. protruding, 9. know, experience, 10. aware, 11. men, 12. eyes, 13. 'embroidered with birds', 14. flapping, 15. colour, 16. trembling, 17. 'lest they were pounced on by falcons', 18. strange, 19. unless, 20. man, 21. baron, 22. most excellent men.

[1]'Thynke I dubbede thee knyghte · with dynttis to dele!
105　Wende wightly thy waye · my willes to kythe.
　　Go bidd thou yondere bolde batell · that on the bent hoves,
　　That they never neghe · nerre to-gedires;
　　For if thay strike one stroke, · stynte thay ne thynken.'
　　'I serve, lorde,' said the lede, · 'while my life dures.'
　　He dothe hym doun on the bonke, · and dwellys a while,
110　Whils he busked and bown was · on his beste wyse.
　　He laped his legges in yren · to the lawe bones,
　　With pysayne and with pawnce · polishede full clene,
　　With brases of broun stele · brauden ful thikke,
　　With plates buklede at the bakke · the body to yeme[2],
115　With a jupown[3] full juste, · joynede by the sydes;
　　A brod chechun[4] at the bakke; · the breste had another;
　　Thre wynges in-with, · wroghte in the kynde,
　　Umbygon with a gold wyre. · When I that gome[5] knewe,
　　What, he was yongeste of yeris, · and yapeste[6] of witt,
120　That any wy in this werlde · wiste of his age!
　　He brake a braunche in his hande, · and brawndeshet it
　　　　swythe.
　　Trynes on a grete trotte, · and takes his waye
　　There[7] bothe thies ferdes[8] folke · in the felde hoves.

　　Sayd, 'loo, the kyng of this kyth, · (ther kepe hym oure
　　　　Lorde!)
125　Sendes byddyng by me, · als hym beste lyketh,
　　That no beryn[9] be so bolde, · [10]on bothe his two eghne,
　　Ones to strike one stroke, · ne stirre none nerre,
　　To lede rowte in his rewme,[11] · so ryall to thynke
　　Pertly with powere · his pese to disturbe.
130　For this es the usage here · and ever shall worthe[12] –
　　If any beryn be so bolde · with banere for to ryde

1. 'Remember, I dubbed thee knight in order to deal blows! Go manfully
your way to make known my will. Tell yonder embattled forces that on the
field abide, That they are not to approach nearer together; For if they begin
striking, they will never cease,' 2. protect, 3. jupon, a tunic worn under or
above the armour, 4. a broad escutcheon, 5. man, 6. sharpest, 7. where,
8. armies', 9. warrior, baron, 10. 'on both his two eyes' – an oath, 11. realm,
12. be.

With-inn the kydde kyngdome, · [1]bot the kynge one,
That he shall losse the londe · and his lyfe aftir.
Bot sen ye knowe noghte this kythe[2] · ne the kynges ryght,
135 He will forgiffe you this guilt · of his grace one.
Full wyde hafe I walked · [3]wyes amonges,
Bot sawe I never siche a syghte, · segges[4], with myn eghne;
For here es alle the folke of Fraunce · ferdede be-syde,
Of Lorreyne, of Lumbardye, · and of Lawe Spayne;
140 Wyes of Westwale, · [5]that in were dwellen;
Of Inglonde, of Irlonde, · Estirlinges full many,
That are stuffede in stele, · strokes to dele.
And yondere a banere of blake · [6]that on the bent hoves,
[7]With thre bulles of ble white · brouden with-inn,
145 And iche one hase of henppe · hynged a corde,
Seled with a sade lede. · I say als me thynkes –
[8]That hede es of holy kirke, · I hope he be there,
Alle ferse to the fighte · with the folke that he ledis.
Another banere es up-brayde · with a bende of grene,
150 With thre hedis white-herede · with howes[9] on lofte,
Croked full craftyly, · and kembid in the nekke: –
Thies are ledis of this londe · that shold oure lawes yeme,
That thynken to dele this daye · with dynttis full many[10].
I holde hym bot a fole that fightis · whils flyttynge[11] may
helpe,
155 When he hase founden his frende · that fayled hym never.

The thirde banere on bent[12] · es of blee whitte,
[13]With sexe galegs, I see, · of sable with-inn,
And iche one has a brown brase[14] · with bokeles twayne,
Thies are Sayn Franceys folke, · [15]that sayen 'alle shall fey
worth.'

1. 'except the king only', 2. custom, 3. 'among men', 4. men, 5. 'that
dwell in a state of war', 6. 'that on the field stands', 7. 'With three bulls of
white colour embroidered within, And each one has hanging a cord of hemp
Sealed with a heavy lead seal', 8. 'I presume (hope) that he who is head of
Holy Church is there', 9. hoods, 10. The three white-haired heads on the
banner probably signify the judiciary, 11. debate, parley, 12. on field,
13. 'With six galoshes, I see, of sable within', 14. brace, strap, 15. 'who
preach "all shall pass to death".'

160 They aren so ferse and so freshe · that feghten bot seldom.
I wote wele for Wynnynge[1] · they wentten fro home.
His purse weghethe full wele · that wanne thaym alle hedire.

The fourte banere on the bent · es brayde appon lofte,
[2]With bothe the brerdes of blake, · a balle in the myddes
165 Reghte siche as the sone es · in the someris tyde,
When moste es the maze[3] · on Missomer Even.
Thynkes Domynyke[4] this daye · with dynttis to dele?
With many a blesenande[5] beryn · his banere es stuffede.
[6]And sythen the pope es so priste · thies Prechours to helpe,
170 And Fraunceys with his folke · [7]es forced besyde,
And alle the ledis of the lande · ledith thurgh witt,
There es no man appon molde · to machen thaym agayne,
Ne gete no grace appon grounde, · undir God hym-selven.

And yitt es the fyfte appon the folde · the faireste of tham
   alle –
175 A brighte banere of blee whitte · with three boar-hedis;
Be any crafte that I kan · Carmes[8] thaym semyth,
For thay are the ledis that love · oure Lady to serve.
If I sholde say the sothe, · it semys no nothire,
Bot that the freris[9] with othere folke · shall the felde wynn[10].

180 The sexte[11] es of sendell · (and so are thay alle),
[12]Whitte als the whalles bone, · who-so the sothe tellys,
With beltys of blake, · bocled to-gedir,
The poyntes pared off rownde, · the pendants a-waye,
And alle the lethire appon lofte · that on-lowe hengeth,
185 Shynethe for sharpynynge · of the shavynge iren –
The Ordire of the Austyns[13], · for oughte that I wene,
For by the blusshe[14] of the belte · the banere I knewe!

1. i.e. gain and getting, 2. 'With both the borders of black, a ball in the
midst Just as the sun is in the summer-time', 3. madness, 4. For the black-
bordered banner signifies the presence of the Dominicans, 5. shining, 6. 'And
since the pope is so forward to help these Preachers', 7. 'is also supplied with
forces', 8. Carmelites, 9. friars, 10. hold, 11. the sixth banner, 12. 'White
as the whale's bone', 13. Augustinians, 14. look.

And othere synes I see, · sett appon lofte,
Some witnesse of wolle, · and some of wyne tounnes,
190 And other of merchandes merkes, · so many and so thikke,
That I ne wote in my witt, · for alle this werlde riche,
Whatt segge[1] under the sonne · can the sowme[2] rekken.
[3]And sekere on that other syde · are sadde men of armes,
Bolde squires of blode, · bowemen many,
195 That, if thay strike one stroke, · stynt thay ne thynken,
Till owthir here[4] appon hethe · be hewen to dethe.

For-thi[5] I bid you bothe · that thaym hedir broghte
That ye wend with me, · are[6] any wrake falle,
To oure comely kyng · [7]that this kythe owethe.
200 [8]And, fro he wiete wittirly · where the wronge ristyth,
Thare nowthir wy be wrothe · to wriche als he demeth.'
Of ayther rowte ther rode oute · a renke[9], als me thoghte,
Knyghtis full comly · on coursers attyred,
And sayden, 'Sir Sandisman[10], · sele[11] thee be-tyde!
205 Well knowe we the kyng; · he clothes us bothe,
And has us fosterde and fedde · this fyve and twenty wyn-
tere.
Now fare thou by-fore, · and we shall folowe aftire.'
And now are thaire brydells up-brayde, · and bown[12] on
thaire wayes.
Thay lighten doun at the launde, · and leven thaire stedis,
210 Kayren[13] up at the clyffe, · and on knees fallyn.
The kynge henttis[14] tham by the handes, · and hetys tham
to ryse,
And sayde, 'Welcomes, heres[15], · [16]as hyne of oure house
bothen.'
The kynge waytted on wyde, · and the wyne askede:
[17]Beryns broghte it anone · in bolles of silvere.

1. man, 2. sum, 3. 'And secure on the other side are serious men of
arms', 4. the other army, 5. therefore, 6. before, 7. 'who this land owns',
8. 'And, as soon as the King knows entirely where the wrong rests, Let neither
of them be wrathful to do as he judges', 9. champion (here spokesman),
10. Sir Messenger, 11. bliss, 12. proceed, 13. go, 14. takes, 15. gentlemen,
16. 'as retainers of our house both', 17. 'Men brought it (the wine) along
soon in bowls of silver'.

215   Me thoghte I[1] sowpped so sadly[2] · it sowrede[3] bothe myn
        eghne.
        And he that wilnes of this werke · to wete any forthire,
        Full[4] freshely and faste! · for here a fitt endes.

FITT II

        Bot than kerpede[5] the kynge, sayd, · [6]‘kythe what ye hatten,
        And whi the hates aren so hote · youre hertis by-twene.
220   [7]If I shall deme you this day, · dothe me to here.’
        ‘Now certys, lorde,’ sayde that one, · ‘the sothe for to telle,
        [8]I hatt Wynnere, a wy · that alle this werlde helpis,
        For I ledes cane lere, · thurgh ledyng of witt.
        Thoo that spedfully will spare, · and spende not to grete[9],
225   Lyve appon littill-whattes[10], · I lufe hem the bettir.
        [11]Witt wiendes me with, · and wysses me faire;
        Aye when I gadir my gudes, · than glades myn hert.
        Bot this felle false thefe[12] · that by-fore youe standes
        Thynkes to strike or[13] he styntt, · and stroye[14] me for ever.
230   Alle that I wynn thurgh witt · he wastes thurgh pryde;
        I gedir, I glene, · and he lattys goo sone;
        I pryke and I pryne, · and he the purse opynes.
        Why hase this cayteffe no care · how men corne sellen?
        [15]His londes liggen alle ley, · his lomes aren solde,
235   Downn bene his dowfehouses[16], · drye ben his poles[17];
        The devyll wounder the wele[18] · he weldys at home,
        Bot hungere and heghe horses · and houndes full kene!
        [19]Safe a sparthe and a spere · sparrede in ane hyrne,
        A bronde at his bede-hede, · biddes he no nother
240   Bot a cuttede-capill to cayre · with to his frendes.

---

1. I = the poet, 2. intently, 3. bleared, 4. fill up – this to the poet's
audience, 5. spoke, 6. ‘make known what you are called’, 7. ‘If I shall judge
you to-day, cause me to hear’, 8. ‘I am Winner, a man that all this world helps,
For I can teach people, through leading of wit’, 9. too much, 10. little,
11. ‘Wit accompanies me and guides me well’, 12. i.e. the Waster, 13. before,
14. destroy, 15. ‘His lands lie all fallow, his tools are sold’, 16. dove-cotes,
17. pools, 18. wealth, 19. ‘Except a halberd and a spear hid away in a corner,
A sword at his bed's-head, he asks for nothing else Except a gelding to ride to his
friends’.

Then will he boste with his brande, · and braundeshe hym
   ofte,
This wikkede weryed thefe, · that Wastoure men calles,
That, if he life may longe, · this lande will he stroye.
[1]For-thi deme us this daye – · for Drightyn's love in heven –
245   To fighte furthe with oure folke · to owthire fey worthe.'

'Yee, Wynnere,' quod Wastoure, · 'thi wordes are hye.
Bot I shall tell thee a tale · [2]that tene shall thee better
When thou haste waltered and went · and wakede alle the
   nyghte,
[3]And iche a wy in this werlde · that wonnes thee abowte,
250   And hase werpede[4] thy wyde houses · full of wolle sakkes –
The bemys benden at the rofe, · siche bakone there hynges,
Stuffed are sterlynges[5] · undere stelen boundes –
What sholde [6]worthe of that wele, · if no waste come?
Some rote, some ruste, · some ratons[7] fede.
255   Let by thy cramynge of thi kystes[8], · for Cristis lufe of heven!
Late the peple and the pore · hafe parte of thi silvere;
For if thou wydwhare[9] sholde walke, · and waytten thee
   sothe,
[10]Thou sholdeste reme for rewthe, · in siche ryfe bene the pore.
For, and thou lengare thus lufe, · leve[11] thou no nother,
260   Thou shall be hanged in helle · for that thou here spareste:
For siche a synn haste thou solde · thi soule in-to helle,
And there es ever wellande woo, · worlde with-owtten ende.'
'Late be thi worde, Wastoure,' · quod Wynnere the riche.
'Thou melleste[12] of a matter, · thou madiste it thi-selven,
265   With thi sturte and thi stryffe · thou stroyeste[13] up my gudes:
In wrastlinge and in wakynge · in wynteres nyghttis,
In outtrage, in unthrifte, · in angarte[14] of pryde.
There es no wele[15] in this werlde · to wasshen thyn handes
That ne es gyffen and grounden · are[16] thou it getyn have.

1. 'Therefore decide this day – for God's love – that we fight on with our
supporters to our end', 2. 'that shall trouble thee more When thou hast tossed
and turned', 3. 'and each man ... that lives with thee', 4. stored, 5. pounds
sterling, 6. 'come of that wealth', 7. rats, 8. chests, 9. far and wide,
10. 'Thou shouldst weep for pity, in such numbers be the poor', 11. believe,
12. speakest, 13. destroyest, 14. arrogance, 15. wealth, 16. ere.

270 Thou ledis renkes in thy route · wele rychely attyrede;
Some hafe girdills of golde, · that more gude coste
Than all the faire fre londe · that ye by-fore haden.
Ye folowe noghte youre fadirs · that fosteredc you alle
A kynde herveste to cache, · and cornes to wynn,
275 For the colde wyntter and the kene · with clengande frostes
[1]Sythen dropeles drye · in the ded monethe.
And thou wolle thee to the taverne, · by-fore the toune-hede,
Eche beryne redy withe a bolle · to blerren thyn eghne,
Hete thee[2] whatte thou have shalte, · and whatt thyn hert
lykes –
280 Wyfe, wedowe, or wenche, · what wonnes there aboute.
Then es there bott "fille in!" and "feche forthe!" · [3]Florence
to shewe,
"Wee-hee", and "worthe up", · wordes ynewe.
Bot when this wele es a-waye, · the wyne moste be payede
fore.
[4]Than lympis youe weddis to laye, · or youre londe selle.
285 For siche wikked werkes, · wery thee oure Lorde!
And for-thi God laughte[5] that He lovede, · and levede[6] that
other.
[7]Iche freke on felde ogh · the ferdere be to wirche.
Teche thy men for to tille · and tynnen thyn feldes;
Rayse up thi rent-houses, · ryme up[8] thi yerdes,
290 Outhere[9] hafe as thou haste done, · and hope aftir werse –
That es firste the faylynge of fode, · and than the fire aftir,
To brene[10] thee alle at a birre[11], · for thi bale[12] dedis:
The more colde es to come, · als me a clerke tolde.'

'Yee, Wynnere,' quod Wastoure, · 'thi wordes are vayne.
295 With oure festes and oure fare · we feden the pore;
It es plesynge to the Prynce · that paradyse wroghte.
When Cristes peple hath parte · hym payes alle the better

1. 'Afterwards dropless drought in the dead months', 2. 'order yourself',
3. 'So as to make Florence (the barmaid) show herself', 4. 'Then happens you
must give bonds, or your land sell', 5. took to himself, 6. left, 7. 'Each man
ought to be more eager to work on the land', 8. open up, 9. otherwise,
10. burn, 11. blast, 12. evil.

Then here ben hodirde[1] and hidde · and happede in cofers,
That it no sonn may see · thurgh seven wyntter ones.
300 [2]Outhir it freres feche · when thou fey worthes
To payntten with thaire pelers, · or pergett with thaire
walles.
Thi sone and thi sektours[3], · ichone sewes[4] othere;
[5]Maken dale aftir thi daye, · for thou durste never
Mawngery ne myndale, · ne never myrthe lovediste.
305 A dale[6] aftir thi daye · dose thee no mare
Than a lighte lanterne · late appone nyghte,
When it es borne at thi bakke, · beryn, be my trouthe.
Now wolde God that it were · [7]als I wisse couthe –
That thou, Wynnere, thou wriche[8], · and Wanhope[9], thi
brothir,
310 [10]And eke ymbryne dayes, · and evenes of sayntes,
The Frydaye and his fere · on the ferrere syde,
Were drownede in the depe see · there never droghte come!
And Dedly Synn for thayre dede · were endityde with
twelve[11];
[12]And thies beryns on the bynches · with biggins on-lofte
315 That bene knowen and kydde[13] · for clerkes of the beste,
Als gude als Arestotle, · or Austyn the wyse,
[14]That alle shent were those shalkes, · and Scharshull[15] itwiste,
That saide I prikkede with powere · his pese[16] to distourbe!
For-thi, comely kynge, · that oure case heris,
320 Late us swythe with oure swerdes · swyngen to-gedirs,
For now I se it es full sothe · that sayde es full yore –
"The richere of ranke wele, · the rathere will drede:
The more havande[17] that he hathe, · the more of hert feble."

1. covered up, 2. 'Or the friars make off with it when you die, And paint
their pillars, or plaster their walls', 3. executors, 4. sues, 5. 'Distribute
charity after thy day, for thou durst never Hold feast nor wake', 6. a gift
to charity (from his estate), 7. 'as I could arrange it', 8. wretch, 9. Despair,
10. 'And also ember days and saints' vigils, Good Friday and Holy Saturday
Were drowned in the deep sea where ...', 11. 'indicted by twelve' (of a
jury)' 12. 'And these law-lords in the benches with coifs' (*biggins* for MS.
howes supplied by I. Gollancz), 13. reputed, 14. 'Would that all those
fellows were shamed', 15. William Scharshull was a Justice of the King's
Bench in 1333, 16. peace, 17. having.

Bot than this wrechede Wynnere · full wrothely he lukes[1],

325 Sayse, 'this es spedles speche · to speken thies wordes!

Loo, hou weryed Wastoure, · that wyde-whare es knawenn,

[2]Ne es nothir kaysser, ne kynge, · ne knyghte that thee folowes,

Barone, ne bachelere, · ne beryn that thou loveste,

Bot foure felawes or fyve, · that thee fayth owes;

330 And thou shall dighte[3] thaym to dyne · with dayntethes so many

That iche a wy in this werlde · may wepyn for sorowe.

The bore's hede shall be broghte · with bayes appon lofte,

Buk-tayles full brode · in brothes there be-syde,

Venyson with the frymentes[4], · and fesanttes full riche,

335 Baken mete ther-by · on the borde sett,

Chewettes of chopped fleshe, · charbiande[5] fewlis,

[6]And iche a segge that I see · has sexe mens doke.

If this were nedles note, · anothir come aftir, –

Roste with the riche sewes[7], · and the ryalle spyces,

340 Kiddes cleven by the rigge[8], · quartered swannes,

Tartes of ten inche, · that tenys[9] myn hert

To see the borde over-brade · with blasande[10] dishes,

[11]Als it were a rayled rode · with rynges and stones.

The third mese[12] to me · were mervelle to rekken,

345 For alle es Martynmesse mete · that I with moste dele,

Noghte bot worttes[13] with the fleshe, · with-owt wilde fowle,

Save ane hene[14] to hym · that the house owethe[15].

[16]And ye will hafe birdes bownn · on a broche riche,

Barnakes and buturs · and many billed snyppes,

350 Larkes and lyngwhittes[17], · lapped in sogoure[18],

Wodcockes and wodwales[19], · full wellande hote,

Teeles and titmoyses[20] , · to take what youe lykes;

Caudels of conynges[21], · and custadis swete,

Dayntyes and dishe-metis, · that ful dere coste,

---

1. looks, 1. 'There is neither kaiser, nor king ...', 3. invite, 4. frumenty, 5. grilled, 6. 'And each man that I see has the portion of six men', 7. sauce, 8. spine, 9. sorrows, 10. shining, 11. 'As it were a rood decorated with rings and stones', 12. mess, dish, 13. vegetables, 14. hen, 15. owns, 16. 'While you will have birds prepared on a costly spit, Geese and bitterns ...' 17. linnets, 18. sugar, 19. woodpeckers, 20. blue-tits, 21. rabbits.

355　　Mawmene[1] that men clepen, · your mawes to fill,
　　　　Twelve mese[2] at a merke, · by-twen twa men,
　　　　[3]Thoghe bot brynneth for bale · your bowells with-in.
　　　　[4]Me tenyth at your trompers, · thay tounen so heghe
　　　　That iche a gome in the gate · goullyng may here;
360　　Than wil thay say to tham-selfe, · as thay samen[5] ryden,
　　　　Ye hafe no myster[6] of the helpe · of the heven kyng.
　　　　[7]Thus are ye scorned by skyll, · and shent theraftir,
　　　　That rechen for a repaste · a rawnsom of silver.
　　　　　　Bot ones I herd in a haule · of a herdman's tong –
365　　"Better were meles many · than a mery nyghte." '
　　　　And he that wilnes of this werke · for to wete forther,
　　　　Full freshely and faste, · for here a fit endes.

FITT III

　　　　'Yee, Wynnere,' quod Wastour, · 'I wote well my-selven
　　　　[8]What sall lympe of the lede, · within a lite yeris.
370　　Then the pure plente of corne · that the peple sowes,
　　　　That God will graunte, of his grace, · to growe on the erthe,
　　　　Ay to appaire[9] the pris, · that it passe nott too hye,
　　　　Shal make thee to waxe wod[10] · for wanhope[11] in erthe,
　　　　(To hope aftir anharde yere) · to honge the-selven[12].
375　　[13]Woldeste thou haf lordis to lyfe · as laddes on fote?
　　　　Prelates als prestes · that the parishen yemes?
　　　　Prowde marchandes of pris, · as pedders in towns?
　　　　[14]Late lordes lyfe als tham liste, · laddes as tham falles, –
　　　　Thay the bacon and beefe, · thay boturs[15] and swannes,
380　　Thay the roughe of the rye, · thay the rede whete
　　　　Thay the grewell gray, · and thay the gude sewes[16];

1. a rich dish, 2. dishes, 3. 'Though your bowels for bale may burn within', 4. 'I quail at your trumpeters, they sound so high That every man on the road their braying may hear', 5. together, 6. need, 7. 'Thus are you scorned by right reason and shamed afterwards, That give for a repast a ransom of silver', 8. 'What shall happen to the people within a few years', 9. impair, 10. mad, 11. despair, 12. Waster declares that Winner desires a dearth and a rise in prices – with the ensuing social disturbance – so that he can hoard and profiteer, 13. 'Do you want lords to live like foot-boys? Prelates like parish priests?', 14. 'While lords can afford delicacies, the common people have to put up with bacon and beef', 15. bitterns, 16. sauce.

[1]And thes may the peple hafe parte, · in povert that standes,
Sum gud morsell of mete · to mend with thair chere.
If fewlis flye shold forthe, · and fongen[2] be never,
385 And wild bestis in the wodde · wone[3] al thair lyve,
And fishes flete in the flode, · [4]and ichone frete other,
[5]Ane henne at ane halpeny · by halfe yeris ende,
Shold not a ladde be in londe · a lorde for to serve.
This wate thou full wele · witterly thee-selven,
390 Who so wele shal wyn, · a wastour moste he fynde,
For if he greves one gome, · it gladdes another.'
'Now,' quod Wynner to Wastour, · 'me wondirs in hert
Of thies poure penyles men · that pelour[6] will by,
Sadills of sendale, · with sercles full riche.
395 Lesse that he wrethe[7] your wifes, · thaire willes to folowe,
Ye sellyn wodd[8] aftir wodde · in a wale[9] tyme,
Bothe the oke and the asshe · and all that ther growes;
The spyres[10] and the yonge sprynge[11] · ye spare to your children
And sayne God will grant it his grace · to grow at the laste,
400 For to shadewe your sones; · bot the shame es your ownn.
Nedeles save ye the soyle, · for sell it ye thynken.
Your forfadirs were fayne, · when any frende come,
[12]For to shake to the shawe, · and shewe hym the estres,
In iche holt that they had · ane hare for to fynde,
405 Bryng to the brode lande · bukkes ynewe[13],
[14]To lache and to late good, · to lightten thaire hertis.
Now es it sett and solde, · my sorowe es the more,
Wasted alle wilfully, · your wyfes to paye.
That are[15] had lordes in londe · and ladyes riche,
410 [16]Now are thay nysottes of the new gett, · so wysely attyred,
With side slabbande[17] sleves, · sleght to[18] the grounde,

1. 'So may the people who stand in poverty have a share', 2. captured, 3. live, i.e. without reduction by man's hand, 4. 'and each eat the other', 5. A hen would be worth only a halfpenny and there would be no lads available for service, 6. furs, 7. make angry, 8. wood, 9. short, 10. sprouts, 11. saplings, 12. 'to go to the thickets and show him the coverts', 13. enough, 14. 'To catch and to let go', 15. formerly, 16. 'Now are they puppets in the new style, so fantastically attired', 17. trailing, 18. straight down.

[1]Ourlede all umbtourne · with ermyn aboute,
That as harde es, I hope[2], · to handil in the derne[3],
Als a cely symple wenche · that never silke wroghte.
415   Bot who-so lukes on hir, · oure Lady of Heven,
How sho fled for ferd · ferre out of hir kythe,
Appon ane amblande asse, · with-owtten more pride,
Safe[4] a barne in hir barme, · and a broken heltre[5]
That Joseph held in hys hande, · [6]that hend for to yeme.
420 [7]All-thofe sho walt al this werlde · hir wedes wer pore
For to gyf ensample of siche, · for to shewe other
For to leve pompe and pride, · that poverte eschewes.'

Than this Wastour wrothly · [8]werped up his eghne,
And said, 'thou Wynnere, thou wriche, · me wondirs in hert
425 What hafe oure clothes coste thee, · caytef, to by,
That thou shal birdes[9] up-brayd · of thaire bright wedis,
Sythen that we vouche-safe · that the silver payen.
It lyes wele for a lede · his leman[10] to fynde,
Aftir hir faire chere · to forthir hir herte.
430 Then will sho love hym lelely[11] · as hir lyfe one,
Make hym bolde and bown[12] · with brandes to smytte,
  [13]To shonn shenchipe and shame · ther shalkes are gadird.
And if my peple ben prode, · me payes alle the better
To see tham faire and free · to-fore with myn eghne.
435 And ye negardes[14], appon nyghte, · ye nappe never harde,
  [15]Raxillen at your routtlyng, · raysen your hurdies;
Bedene ye wayte on the wedir, · then wery[16] ye the while,
That ye hade hightilde[17] up your houses, · and your hyne[18]
   arayed.
For-thi, Wynnere, with wronge · thou wastes thi tyme
440 For gode day ne glade · getys thou never.
The Devyll at this dede-day · shal delyn[19] thi gudis,

---

1. 'Bordered all round', 2. think, 3. dark, 4. except, 5. halter, 6. 'that
high one to protect', 7. 'Although she rules all this world, her clothes were
poor', 8. 'cast up his eyes', 9. ladies, 10. sweetheart, 11. loyally, 12. ready,
13. 'To shun ignominy and shame where men are gathered', 14. niggards,
15. 'Are restless in your snoring, raise your buttocks, Continually keep watch
on the weather', 16. curse, 17. repaired, 18. servants, 19. part.

The thou woldest that it ware[1], · wyn[2] thay it never;
[3]The skathill sectours · shall severe tham aboute,
And thou hafe helle full hotte · for that thou here saved.
445 [4]Thou tast no tent on a tale · that tolde was full yore:
"I holde hym madde that mournes[5] · his make for to wyn;
Hent[6] hit that hit haf shal, · and hold hit his wile;
Take the coppe[7] as it comes, · the case as it falles;
[8]For who-so lyfe may lengeste · lympes to feche
450 Woodd that he waste shall, · to warmen his helys,
Ferrere[9] than his fadir dide · by fyvetene myle."
Now kan I carpe no more. · Bot, Sir Kyng, by the trouthe,
Deme us where we dwell shall; · me thynke the day hyes.
Yit harde sore es myn herte, · and harmes me more
455 Ever to see in my syghte · that I in soule hate.'

The kynge lovely lokes · on the ledis twayne,
Says, 'blynnes[10], beryns, of your brethe · and of youre brothe
     wordes,
And I shal deme you this day · where ye dwelle shall.
Aythere[11] lede in a lond · ther[12] he es loved moste.
460 Wende, Wynnere, the waye · over the wale[13] stremys,
Passe forthe by Paris · to the Pope of Rome:
The cardynalls ken thee wele, · will kepe thee ful faire,
And make thi sydes in silken · shetys to lygge,
And fede thee and foster thee · and forthir thyn hert,
465 [14]As leefe to worthen wode · as thee to wrethe ones.
Bot loke, lede, be thi lyfe, · when I lettres sende,
That thou hy thee to me home · on horse or on fote;
And when I knowe thou will come, · [15]he shall cayre uttire,
And lenge with another lede, · till thou thi lefe lache;
470 For thof[16] thou bide in this burgh · to thi beryinge-day,
With hym falles thee never · a fote for to strecche.

1. keep, 2. acquire, 3. 'The harmful executors', 4. 'Thou payest no
heed to a tale', 5. worries, 6. sieze, 7. cup, 8. 'For who may live
longest is likely to fetch ...', 9. further, 10. cease, 11. both, 12. where,
13. quick, 14. 'As willing to go mad as to make you once angry', 15. 'he
shall take his departure, And tarry with another man until thou take leave',
16. though.

And thou, Wastoure, I will · that thou wonne ther[1] ever
Ther moste waste es of wele[2] · and wynges untill.
[3]Chese thee forthe in-to the Chepe, · a chambre thou rere,
475   Loke the wyndowe be wyde, · and wayte thee aboute,
Where any berande potener[4] · thurgh the burgh passe;
[5]Teche hym to the tonne · till he tayte worthe,
Doo hym drynk al nyghte · that he dry be at morow;
Sythen[6] ken hym to the Crete[7] · to comforth his vaynes;
480   Brynge hym to Bred Strete, · bikken with thi fynger,
Shew hym of fatt shepe · sholdirs ynewe[8],
Hotte for the hyngry, · a hen other twayne,
Sett hym softe on a sete, · and sythen send aftir,
Bryng out of the burgh · the best thou may fynde,
485   And luke thi knave hafe a knoke · both he the clothe spred;
Bot late hym paye or[9] he passe, · and pik hym so clene
That fynd a peny in his purse, · and put owte his eghe.
When that es dronken and don, · dwell ther no longer,
Bot teche hym owt of the townn, · to trotte aftir more.
490   Then passe to the Pultrie, · the peple thee knowes,
And ken wele the katour[10] · to knawen the fode,
The herons, the hasteletz[11], · the hennes wele served,
The pertrikes[12], the plovers, · the other pulled byrddes,
[13]The albus, the osulles, · the egretes dere.
495   The more thee wastis the wele, · the better the Wynner lykes,
And wayte to me, thou Wynnere, · if thou wilt wele chese[14],
When I wende appon werre · my wyes[15] to lede;
For at the proude paleys · of Parys the riche
I thynk to do it in ded, · and dub thee to knyghte,
500   And giff giftes full grete · of golde and of silver
To ledis of my legyance · that lufen me in hert,
And sythen kayren as I come, · with knyghtis that me foloen,
To the kirke of Colayne[16] · [17]ther the kynges ligges ...

---

1. where, 2. wealth, 3. 'Sct thee forth into Cheapside', 4. purse,
5. 'Teach him (the way) to the tun till he becomes tight', 6. afterwards,
7. wine of Crete, 8. enough, 9. before, 10. caterer, 11. joints of meat
roastcd on spits, 12. partridges, 13. 'The bullfinches, the ouzels, the egrets
expensive', 14. choose, 15. men, soldiers, 16. Cologne, 17. 'where the
Three Kings lie'.

NOTE

Wynnere and Wastoure, by a Western man, is almost certainly by the same author as *Parlement of the Thre Ages*: they contain similar passages, are written in the same style, and they follow the same convention of a debate. The date of *Wynnere and Wastoure* is thought to be 1352, for it contains a reference to Edward III being in the twenty-fifth year of his reign.

WILLIAM LANGLAND

*

Christ's Dying and Descent into Hell

Wolleward and wete-shoed · went I forth after,
As a reccheles renke · that of no wo reccheth
And yede forth lyke a lorel · al my lyf-tyme,
Tyl I wex wery of the worlde · and wilned eft to slepe,
5   And lened me to a lenten · and longe tyme I slepte:
And of Crystes passioun and penaunce, · the peple that of-
    raughte –
Reste me there, and rutte faste · til *ramis-palmarum* –
Of gerlis and of *Gloria laus* · gretly me dremed,
And how *osanna* by orgonye · olde folke songen.
10 One semblable to the Samaritan · and some-del to Piers the
    Plowman,
Barefote on an asse bakke, · botelees cam prykye,
Wyth-oute spores other spere – · spakliche he loked,
As is the kynde of a knyghte · that cometh to be dubbed,

Christ's Dying and Descent into Hell

Wool-garbed and wet-shod went I forth after,
As a careless fellow that of no woe considers,
And went forth like a tramp all my life-time,
Until I grew tired of the world and wanted again to sleep,
5   *And then I lay down till Lent and long time I slept:*
And I dreamed of Christ's passion and penance, the effects that these wrought
    on people –
I slept there and snored fast until Palm Sunday –
Of children and Gloria Laus I dreamed much,
And of how old folks sang Hosannah to musical instruments.
10 *One resembling the Samaritan and also like Piers the Plowman,*
Barefooted on an ass's back bootless came riding,
Without spurs and without spear – sprightly he looked
Like the kind of knight that comes to be dubbed,

To geten hem gylte spores · or ¹galoches ycouped.
15 Thanne was Faith in a fenestre · and cryde *a, fili David*
As doth an heraud² of armes · whan auntrous³ cometh to
justes.
Olde Juwes of Jerusalem · for Joye their songen,
⁴*Benedictus qui venit in nomine domini.*

⁵Thanne I frayned at Faith · what al that fare be-mente,
20 And who sholde jouste in Jherusalem · 'Jesus,' he seyde,
⁶'And fecche that the fende claymeth · Piers fruit the Plowman.'
'Is Piers in this place?' quod I · and he preynte⁷ on me,
⁸'This Jesus of his gentrice · wole juste in Piers armes,
In his helme and in his haberion · *humana natura*;
25 That Cryst be nought biknowe⁹ here · ¹⁰for *consummatus deus*,
¹¹In Piers paltok the Plowman · this priker shal ryde;
¹²For no dynte shal hym dere · as in *deitate patris*.'
'Who shal Juste with Jesus?' quod I · 'Juwes or scribes?'
'Nay,' quod he, 'the foule fende · and Fals–dome and Deth.
30 Deth seith he shal fordo · and adown bringe
Al that liveth or loketh · in londe or in watere.
Lyf seyth that he likth¹³ · and leyth his lif to wedde¹⁴,
That for al that Deth can do · with-in thre dayes,
¹⁵To walke and fecche fro the fende · Piers fruite the Plowman,
35 And legge it there hym lyketh · and Lucifer bynde,
And forbete and adown brynge · bale and deth for evere:
*O mors ero mors tua!*¹⁶

1. gaily-cut shoes, 2. herald, 3. adventurous (knights), 4. 'Blessed is he
that cometh in the name of the Lord', 5. 'Then I enquired of Faith what all
that to-do meant, And who meant to joust ...', 6. Jesus intends to 'redeem
what the Fiend claims – the fruit of Piers the Plowman'. Piers = Humanity,
7. glanced, 8. 'This Jesus of his gentility will joust in Piers' arms, In his helm
and in his habergeon – in his Human Nature', 9. known, 10. because his
Godhead is temporarily suspended, 11. 'in Piers the Plowman's jacket this
champion will ride', 12. 'For no blow shall assail him in his divine aspect', 13. Life says that Death lies, 14. to pledge, 15. Life declares that he
will rescue the Fruit (Piers) and place it where he wants and that he (Life)
'will bind Lucifer, and will thrash and destroy sorrow and death for ever',
16. 'O Death I will be your death'.

Thanne cam *Pilatus* with moche peple, · *sedens pro tri-
　　bunati[1],
To se how doughtilich Deth sholde do · and deme her
　　botheres righte[2].

40　The Juwes and the Justice · ageine Jesu thei were,
And al her courte on hym cryde · *Crucifige* sharpe.
Tho put him forth a piloure · bifor Pilat, and seyde,
'This Iseus of oure Jewes temple · japed and dispised,
To fordone[3] it on o day · and in thre dayes after

45　Edefye it eft newe · – here he stant that seyde it –
And yit maken it as moche · in al manere poyntes,
Bothe as longe and as large · bi loft and by grounde.'
'*Crucifige*!' quod a cacchepolle[4] · 'I warante hym a wicche!'
'*Tolle, tolle*!' quod an other · and toke of kene thornes,

50　And bigan of kene thorne · a gerelande to make,
And sette it sore on his hed · and seyde in envye,
[5]'*Ave, rabby*!' quod that ribaude · and threw redes at hym,
Nailled hym with thre nailles · naked on the rode,
And poysoun on a pole · thei put up to his lippes,

55　And bede hym drynke his deth-yuel[6] · his dayes were ydone.
'And yif that thou sotil[7] be · help now thi-selven,
If thow be Cryst, and kynges sone · come downe of[8] the rode;
[9]Thanne shul we leve that Lyf thee loveth · and wil nought
　　lete thee deye!'
'*Consummatum est*,' quod Cryst · and somsed forto swowe[10]

60　Pitousliche and pale · as a prisoun[11] that deyeth:
The lorde of lyf and of lighte · tho[12] leyed his eyen togideres.
The daye for dred with-drowe · and derke bicam the sonne,
The wal wagged and clef · and al the worlde quaved.
Ded men for that dyne · come out of depe graves,

65　And tolde whi that tempest · so longe tyme dured:
'For a bitter bataille' · the ded bodye sayde;
'Lyf and Deth in this derknesse · her one fordoth her other.

1. 'sitting on the judgement seat', 2. 'and judge the right of both' – Life
and Death, 3. destroy, 4. a bumptious petty official, 5. ' "Hail, Rabbi,"
said that ruffian and hurled advice at him', 6. death-drink, 7. subtle, 8. from
the cross, 9. 'Then shall we believe that Life loves thee ...', 10. swoon,
11. prisoner, 12. then.

[1]Shal no wighte wite witterly · who shal have the maystrye
Er Sondey aboute sonne-rysyng' · [2]and sank with that til
erthe.

70   Some seyde that he was goddes sone · that so faire deyde,
         [3]Vere filius erat iste, etc.
And somme saide he was a wicche · 'good is that we assaye,
Where he be ded or nought ded · doun er he be taken.'
    Two theves also · tholed[4] deth that tyme,

75   Uppon a crosse bisydes Cryst – · so was the comune lawe.
A cacchepole cam forth · and craked bothe her legges,
And her armes after · of eyther of tho theves.
Ac was no boy so bolde · goddes body to touche;
For he was knyghte and kynges sone · [5]kynde forgaf that tyme,

80   That non harlot were so hardy · to leyne hande uppon hym.
Ac there cam forth a knyghte · with a kene spere ygrounde.
Highte Longeus, as the lettre telleth · and longe had lore his
sighte[6].

Bifor Pilat and other peple · in the place he hoved[7];
Maugre his many tethe · he was made that tyme

85   To take the spere in his honde · and justen with Iesus;
For alle thei were unhardy · that hoved on hors or stode,
To touche hym or to taste hym · or take hym down of rode.
But this blynde bacheler thanne · bar hym thorught he herte;
The blode spronge down by the spere · and unspered the
knightes eyen[8].

90   Thanne fel the knighte upon his knees · and cryed hym
mercy –
'Ageyne my wille it was, lorde · to wounde yow so sore!'
He seighed and sayde · 'sore it me athynketh;
For the dede that I have done · I do me in youre grace:
Have on me rewth, rightful Jesu!' · and right with that he
wept.

95   Thanne gan Faith felly[9] · the fals Jewes dispise,
Called hem caytives, · acursed for evere

1. 'No one shall finally know ...', 2. 'and then sank (the dead body) back
to earth', 3. 'Truly this man was [the Son of God]', 4. suffered, 5. Nature
ordained, 6. Legend tells that Longeus was blind, 7. halted, 8. Longeus'
sight was healed by the blood he drew from Christ's side, 9. fiercely.

For this foule vileinie: · [1]'Veniaunce to yow alle!
To do the blynde bete hym ybounde · it was a boyes conseille.
Cursed caitive! · knighthod was it nevere
100 To misdo a ded body · by day or by nyghte.
The gree[2] yit hath he geten · for al his grete wounde.
For youre champioun chivaler · chief knyght of yow alle,
[3]Yelt hym recreaunt rennyng · right at Jesus wille.
For be this derkenesse ydo · his deth worth[4] avenged,
105 And ye, lordeynes, han ylost · for Lyf shal have the
maistrie,
And youre fraunchise, that fre was · fallen is in thraldome,
And ye, cherles, and yowre children · chieve[5] shal ye nevre,
Ne have lordship in londe · ne no londe tilie,
But al bareyne be · and usurye usen,
110 Which is lyf that oure lorde · in alle lawes acurseth.
Now yowre good dayes ar done · as Danyel prophecyed,
Whan Cryst cam, of her kyngdom · the croune shulde cesse;
Cum veniat sanctus sanctorum, cessabit unxio vestra.'
[6]What for fere of this ferly · and of the fals Juwes,
115 I drowe me in that derkenesse · to *descendit ad inferna.*
And there I sawe sothely · *secundum scripturas,*
Out of the west coste · a wenche, as me thoughte,
Cam walkynge in the way · to-helle-ward she loked.
[7]Mercy hight that mayde, · a meke thynge with-alle,
120 A ful benygne buirde, · and boxome of speche.
Her suster, as it semed, · cam softly walkynge,
Evene out of the est · and westward she loked.
A ful comely creature · Treuth she highte,
For the vertue that hir folwed · aferd was she nevere.
125 [8]Whan this maydenes mette · Mercy and Treuth,
Eyther axed other · of this grete wonder,
Of the dyne and of the derknesse · and how the daye rowed,

1. 'Vengeance on you all! To make the blind man beat him when tied
and helpless was a knave's advice', 2. prize of victory, 3. 'Yields himself
as recreant when running at tilt against', 4. be, 5. prosper, 6. The dreamer
now descends in vision to the underworld. 7. 'Mercy was the name of that
maid', 8. 'When these maidens Mercy and Truth met Each asked the
other'.

And which a lighte and a leme[1] · lay befor helle.
'Ich have ferly[2] of this fare · in feith,' seyde Treuth,
130 'And am wendyng to wite · what this wonder meneth.'
'Have no merveille,' quod Mercy · 'myrthe it bytokneth.'
A mayden that hatte Marye · and moder with-out felyng[2]
Of any kynnes creature · conceyved thorw speche
And grace of the holygoste; · wex grete with childe;
135 With-outen wem · in-to this worlde she brought hym;
And that my tale be trewe · I take god to witnesse.
Sith this barn was bore · ben thritti winter passed;
Which deyde and deth tholed[4] · this day aboute mydday.
And that is cause of this clips[5] · that closeth now the sonne,
140 In meninge that man shal · fro merkenesse be drawe,
The while this lighte and this leme · shal Lucyfer ablende[6].
For patriarkes and prophetes · han preched her-of often,
That man shal man save · thorw a maydenes helpe,
[7]And that was tynt thorw tre · tree shal it wynne,
145 And that deth doun broughte · deth shal releve.'
'That thow tellest,' quod Treuth · 'is but a tale of Waltrot![8]
[9]For Adam and Eve, · and Abraham, with other
Patriarkes and prophetes · that in peyne liggen,
Leve thow nevere that yone lighte · hem alofte brynge,
150 Ne have hem out of helle · (holde thi tonge, Mercy!
It is but a trufle that thow tellest, · I, Treuth, wote the sothe)
For that is ones in helle · out cometh it nevere;
Job the prophete, patriarke · reproveth thi sawes,
[10]Quia in inferno nulla est redempcio.'
155 Thanne Mercy ful myldly · mouthed thise wordes,

1. gleam. For this beam of light that appears in limbo after the death of
Christ, the reader is referred to the Towneley 'Harrowing of Hell' Miracle
Play in the easily obtainable *Everyman and Other Interludes* (Dent). Langland's
Passus and the Miracle plays have many features in common. It is probable
that Langland saw, and was deeply impressed by, performances of Miracle
plays, 2. wonder, 3. touch, 4. suffered, 5. eclipse, 6. blind, 7. 'And
that which was lost through a tree (in Eden) shall be restored through a tree
(on Calvary), And that which Death brought down shall be lifted up again
by Death', 8. a piece of nonsense, 9. Truth declares that the patriarchs
and prophets believe 'Once in hell then never out', 10. 'For in hell there
is no redemption.'

'Thorw experience,' quod she · 'I hope[1] thei shal be saved.
[2]For venym for-doth venym · and that I prove by resoun.
For of alle veynmes · foulest is the scorpioun,
May no medcyne helpe · the place there he stingeth,
160   Tyl he be ded and do ther-to · the ivel he destroyeth,
The fyrst venymouste · thorw venym of hym-self.
So shal this deth for-do · I dar my lyf legge,
Al that Deth fordyd furste · thorw the develles entysynge[3];
And right as thorw gyle · man was bigyled,
165   So shal grace that bigan · make a good sleighte;
          [4]*Ars ut artem falleret.*'
'Now suffre we,' seyde Treuth · 'I se, as me thinketh,
Out of the nippe of the north · [5]nought ful fer hennes,
Rightwisnesse come rennynge; · reste we the while;
170   For she wrote more than we; · she was er we bothe.'
'That is soth,' seyde Mercy · 'and I se here bi southe,
Love hath coveyted hir longe; · leve I none other
But she sent hir some lettre · what this lighte bymeneth[6],
That over-hoveth helle thus; · she us shal telle.'
175   Whan Pees, in pacience yclothed, · approched nere hem
              tweyne,
Rightwisnesse her reverenced · for her riche clothyng,
And preyed Pees to telle hir · to what place she wolde,
And in her gat garnementz · whom she grete thoughte?
'My wille is to wende,' quod she · 'and welcome hem alle,
180   That many day myghte I noughte se · for merkenesse of
              synne.
Adam and Eve · and other moo in helle,
Moyses and many mo · mercy shal have;
And I shal daunce ther-to: · do thow so, sustre!
For[7] Jesus justed wel · joye bygynneth dawe[8];
185   [9]*Ad vesperum demorabitur fletus, et ad matutinum leticia.*

---

1. confidently expect, 2. Mercy expresses the belief that poison neutralized
the effect of poison, and that the only cure for a scorpion's sting is the application of a dead scorpion to the wound it has caused, 3. enticing, 4. 'That a
trick might defeat a trick', 5. Not very far hence, 6. 'what this light (now
shining in hell) means', 7. because, 8. dawn, 9. 'Misery endureth for a night,
but joy cometh in the morning'.

338

Love, that is my lemman[1], · suche lettres me sente,
That Mercy, my sustre, and I · mankynde shulde save;
[2]And that god hath forgiven · and graunted me, Pees, and
    Mercy,
To be mannes meynpernoure · for evere-more after.
190   Lo! here the patent!'[3] quod Pees: · '*in pace in idipsum* –
And that this dede shal dure – · *dormiam et requiescam*.'
   'What, ravestow?' quod Rightwisenesse, · 'or thow art
    right dronke?
[4]Levestow that yonde lighte · unlouke myghte helle,
And save mannes soule? · sustre, wene it nevre!
195   At the bygynnynge, god · gaf the dome hym-selve,
That Adam and Eve · and alle that hem suwed[5]
Shulde deye doune righte · and dwelle in pyne after,
If that thei touched a tre · and the fruite eten.
Adam afterward, · ageines his defence,
200   [6]Frette of that fruit · and forsoke, as it were,
The love of oure lorde · and his lore bothe;
And folwed that the Fende taughte · and his felawes wille,
Ageines resoun. I, Rightwisnesse, · recorde thus with treuth
That her[7] peyne be perpetual · and no preyere hem helpe.
205   For-thi late hem chewe as thei chose · and chyde we nought,
    sustres,
For it is botelees bale[8] · the bite that thei eten.'
   'And I shal preve,'[9] quod Pees · 'her [10]peyne mote have
   ende,
[11]And wo in-to wel · mowe wende atte laste,
For had thei wist of no wo · wel had thei noughte knowen.
210   For no wighte wote what wel is · that nevere wo suffred,
Ne what is hote hunger · that had nevere defaute.
If no nyghte ne were · no man, as I leve,
Shuld wite witterly · what day is to mene;

1. sweetheart, 2. 'And that God has finally given and granted me, Peace, and Mercy, to be mankind's guarantors for ever', 3. She shows, and quotes from, the document, 4. 'Believest thou that yon light could unlock mighty hell And save man's soul?', 5. followed, 6. eat, 7. their, 8. remediless misery, 9. Peace shall prove to the contrary …, 10. their, 11. 'And that woe into well-being might change at the last, For had they not experienced woe, they could not have recognized well-being'.

Shulde nevere righte riche man · that liveth in reste and ese
215 Wyte what wo is · ne were the deth of kynde[1].
So god that bygan al · of his good wille
Bycam man of a mayde · mankynde to save,
And suffred to be solde · to see the sorwe of deyinge,
The which unknitteth al care · and comsynge is of reste,
220 [2]For til *modicum* mete with us, · I may it wel avowe,
Wote no wighte, as I wene · what is ynough to mene.
    For-thi god of his goodnesse · the fyrste gome Adam
Sette hym in solace · and in sovereigne myrthe;
And sith he suffred hym synne[3], · sorwe to fele,
225 To wite what wel was, · kyndelich to knowe it.
And after [4]god auntred hym-self · and toke Adames kynde,
To wyte what he hath suffred · in thre sondri places,
Bothe in hevene, and in erthe · and now til helle he thynketh,
To wite what al wo is · that wote of al Joye.
230 So it shal fare bi this folke · her foly and her synne
Shall lere hem what langour is · and lisse with-outen ende.
Wote no wighte what werre is · there that pees regneth,
Ne what is witterly wel · til weyllowey[5] hym teche.'
    Thanne was there a wighte · with two brode eyen.
235 [6]Boke highte that beupere · a bolde man of speche.
'By godes body,' quod this Boke · 'I wil bere witnesse,
That tho this barne was ybore · there blased a sterre,
That alle the wyse[7] of this worlde · in o witte acordeden,
That such a barne was borne · in Bethleem citee,
240 That mannes soule sholde save · and synne destroye.
And all the elementz,' quod the Boke · 'her-of bereth witnesse.
That he was god that al wroughte · the walkene[8] firste
    shewed;
Tho that weren in hevene · token *stella comata*,
And tendeden[9] hir as a torche · to reverence his birthe;
245 The lyghte folwed the lorde · in-to the lowe erthe.

1. 'Were there not death from natural causes', 2. No man knows what a *sufficiency* of anything is until he has experienced *in*sufficiency, 3. God allowed Adam to sin and experience sorrow in order that he might know what well-being was through its deprivation, 4. 'God ventured himself and took Adam's nature', 5. misery, 6. the name of this man was Book, 7. wise man, 8. sky, 9. attended, followed.

That water witnessed that he was god · for he went on it;
Peter the apostel · parceyved his gait,
And as he went on the water · wel hym knewe, and seyde,
    Iube me venire ad te super aquas[1].

250 [2]And lo! how the sonne gan louke · her lighte in her-self,
Whan she seye hym suffre · that sonne and se made!
The erthe for hevynesse · that he wolde suffre,
Quaked as quikke thinge · and al biquashte[3] the roche!
Lo! helle mighte noughte holde · but opened tho god tholed,

255 And lete oute Symonde's sones · to seen hym hange on rode.
[4]And now shal Lucifer leve it · thowgh hym loth thinke;
For Jesus as a gyaunt · with a gyn cometh yonde
To breke and to bete a-doun · all that ben a-gayns hym.
And I, Boke, wil be brent · but Jesus rise to lyve,

260 In all myghtes of man · and his moder gladie,
And conforte al his kynne · and out of care brynge,
[5]And al the Juwen joye · unjoignen and unlouken;
And but thei reverencen his rode · and his resurexioun,
And bileve on a new lawe · be lost lyf and soule.'

265 'Suffre we,' seide Treuth · [6]'I here and se bothe,
How a spirit speketh to helle · and bit unspere the gatis:
    Attollite portas, etc.'[7]
A voice loude in that lighte · to Lucifer cryeth,
'Prynces of this place · unpinneth and unlouketh!

270 For here cometh with croune · that kynge is of glorie.'
Thanne syked[8] Sathan · and seyde to hem alle,
[9]'Such a lyghte, ageines owre leve, · Lazar is fette.
Care and combraunce · is comen to us alle.

275 If this kynge come in · mankynde wil he fecche,
And lede it ther hym lyketh · and lyghtlych[10] me bynde.

1. 'Bid me come unto thee on the water', 2. 'And lo! how the sun began to lock her light into herself when she saw Christ suffer', 3. shattered in two the rocks, 4. The meaning is: Now even Lucifer, however reluctantly, is compelled to believe in the divinity of Christ, 5. 'And to all the Jews (i.e. the patriarchs and prophets who are waiting in hell for their deliverance) release and unlock joy', 6. 'I both hear and see How a spirit speaks to hell and bids unspar the gates' (See *Everyman and Other Interludes*, Dent, p. 145), 7. 'Lift up your gates ...', 8. complained sighingly, 9. 'Such a light as this once, without our leave, fetched Lazarus (from my keep)', 10. lightly – i.e. easily.

Patriarkes and prophetes · han parled her-of longe,
That such a lorde and a lyghte · shulde lede hem all hennes.'
'Listeneth,' quod Lucifer · 'for I this lorde knowe,
Bothe this lorde and this lighte; · is longe ago I knewe hym.
280 [1]May no deth hym dere · ne no develes queyntise,
And where he wil, is his waye; · ac war hym of the perilcs;
If he reve me my righte · he robbeth me by maistrye.
For by right and bi resoun · tho renkes[2] that ben here
Bodye and soule ben myne · bothe gode and ille.
285 For hym-self sayde, · that sire is of hevene,
Yif Adam ete the apple · alle shulde deye,
And dwelle with us develes; · this thretynge he made,
And he, that sothenesse is, · seyde thise wordes.
And sitthen I seised · sevene hundreth wyntre,
290 I leve that lawe nil naughte · lete hym the leest.'
'That is sothe,' seyde Sathan · 'but I me sore drede,
For thow gete hem with gyle · and his gardyne breke,
And in semblaunce of a serpent · sat on the appeltre,
And eggedest hem to ete · Eve by hir-selve,
295 And toldest hir a tale · of tresoun were the wordes;
And so thow haddest hem oute · and hider atte laste.
It is noughte graythely geten · there gyle is the rote.'
'For god wil nought be bigiled' · quod Gobelyn, 'ne bi-
japed[3];
We have no trewe title to hem · for thorwgh tresoun were
thei dampned.'
300 'Certes, I drede me,' quod the devel · 'leste treuth wil hem
fecche.
This thretty wynter, as I wene · hath he[4] gone and preched;
I have assailled hym with synne · and some tyme yasked
Where he were god or goddes sone? · he gaf me shorte
answere.
And thus hath he trolled forth · this two and thretty wynter,
305 And whan I seighe it was so · slepyng, I went
To warne Pilate's wyf · [5]what dones man was Jesus;
For Juwes hateden hym · and han done hym to deth.

1. 'No death can damage him, nor no devils' cunning,' 2. men, 3. be-
fooled, 4. Christ, 5. 'What sort of man Jesus was'.

I wolde have lengthed his lyf · for I leved[1], yif he deyede,
That his soule wolde suffre · no synne in his syghte.
310 [2]For the body, whil it on bones yede, · aboute was evere
To save men fram synne · yif hem-self wolde.
And now I se where a soule · cometh hiderward seyllynge[3]
With glorie and with grete lighte – · god it is, I wote wel.
[4]I rede we flee,' quod he · 'faste alle hennes;
315 For us were better noughte be · than biden his syghte.
For thi lesynges[5], Lucifer · loste is al oure praye.
Firste thorw the we fellen · fro hevene so heighe;
For we leved thi lesynges, · we loupen oute alle with the,
And now for thi last lesynge · ylore[6] we have Adam,
320 [7]And al oure lordeship, I leve, · a londe and a water;
        [8]*Nunc princeps huius mundi eicietur foras.*'
    [9]Efte the lighte bad unlouke, · and Lucifer answered,
'What lorde artow?' quod Lucifer · [10]*quis est iste?*'
'*Rex glorie*' · the lighte sone seide,
325 'And lorde of myghte and of mayne · and al manere vertues;
        dominus virtutum.
    Dukes of this dim place · anon undo this gates,
    That Cryst may come in · the kynges sone of hevene!'
    And with that breth helle brake · with Beliales barres;
    [11]For any wye or warde · wide opene the gatis.
330 Patriarkes and prophetes, · [12]*populus in tenebris.*
    Songen seynt Johanes songe · '*ecce agnus dei*'.
    Lucyfer loke ne myghte · [13]so lyghte hym ableynte;
    And tho that oure lorde loved · in-to his lighte he laughte,
    And seyde to Sathan, 'lo! here · my soule to amendes
335 For alle synneful soules · to save tho that ben worthy.
    Mine they be and of me · I may the bette hem clayme.
    Al-though resoun recorde, · and right of my-self,

1. believed, 2. Christ while alive on earth was busy in saving men from
sin, 3. sailing, 4. 'I suggest we flee', 5. falsehoods, 6. lost, 7. 'And all our
dominion, I think, both on land and on water', 8. 'Now shall the prince of
this world be cast out', 9. 'After the light bade Open' (Christ's body rests in
the grave until the resurrection. And the light, which so disturbed hell, is his
Soul), 10. 'Who is there?' 'The King of Glory', 11. 'Despite efforts of man
or gatekeeper wide opened the gates', 12. 'a people in the shadows ... behold
the lamb of God', 13. 'The light so blinded him'.

That if thei ete the apple · alle shulde deye,
I bihyghte[1] hem nought here · helle for evere.
340 [2]For the dede that thei dede · thi deceyte it made.
With gyle thow hem gete · agayne al resoun.
For in my paleys, paradys, · in persone of an addre,
Falseliche thow fettest there · thynge that I loved.
[3]Thus ylike a lusarde · with a lady visage,
345 Thevelich thow me robbedest; · the olde lawe graunteth
That gylours[4] be bigiled · and that is gode resoun;
     [5]*Dentem pro dente, et oculum pro oculo.*
Ergo, soule shal soule quite, · and synne to synne wende,
And al that man hath mysdo · I, man, wyl amende.
350 Membre for membre · bi the olde lawe was amendes,
And lyf for lyf also · and by that lawe I clayme it,
Adam and al his issue · at my wille her-after.
And that deth in hem fordid · my deth shal releve,
And bothe quikke and quite · that queynte was thorw synne;
355 And that grace gyle destruye · good feith it asketh.
So leve it noughte, Lucifer, · againe the lawe I fecche hem,
[6]But bi right and by resoun · raunceoun here my lyges;
     [7]*Non veni solvere legem, sed adimplere.*
Thow fettest myne in my place · ageines al resoun,
360 Falseliche and felounelich; · gode faith me it taughte,
To recoure[8] hem thorw raunceoun · and bi no resoun elles,
So that with gyle thow gete · thorw garce it is ywone.
Thow, Lucyfer, in lyknesse of a leode · that lorde am of hevene,
Graciousliche thi gyle have quitte · go gyle ageine gyle!
365 [9]And as Adam and alle · thorw a tre deyden,
Adam and all thorwe a tree · shal torne ageine to lyve;
And gyle is bigyled · and in his gyle fallen:
     [10]*Et cecidit in foveam quam fecit.*

---

1. directed, 2. 'It was on account of thy deceit that they did the deed for
which they died', 3. 'Thus like a lizard with a lady's face.' This was a frequent
pictorial representation, in the Middle Ages, of the Tempter, 4. deceivers,
5. 'A tooth for a tooth, and an eye for an eye', 6. 'But (I) by right and by
reason ransom here my lieges', 7. 'I am come not to destroy the Law but to
fulfil it', 8. recover, 9. 'And as Adam and all through a tree died, Adam and
all – through a tree (the Cross) shall turn again to life; And guile is outwitted,
and sunk in his cunning', 10. 'He that diggeth a pit shall fall into it'.

Now bygynneth thi gyle · ageyne the to tourne,
370 And my grace to growe · ay gretter and wyder,
¹The bitternesse that thow hast browe · brouke it thi-selven,
That art doctour of deth – · drynke that thow madest!
    For I, that am lorde of lyf, · love is my drynke,
And for that drynke to-day · I deyde upon erthe.
375 ²I faughte so – me threstes yet – · for mannes soule sake,
May no drynke me moiste, · ne my thruste³ slake,
Tyl the vendage falle · in the vale of Josephath,
That I drynke righte ripe must · *resureccio mortuorum*,
And thannes shal I come as a kynge · crouned with angeles,
380 And han out of helle · alle mennes soules.
    Fendes and fendekynes⁴ · bifor me shulle stande,
And be at my biddynge · where so evre me lyketh.
And to be merciable to man · thanne my kynde⁵ it asketh;
For we beth bretheren of blode · but noughte in baptesme
    alle.
385 Ac alle that beth myne hole bretheren · in blode and in
    baptesme,
Shal noughte be dampned to the deth · that is with-outen
    ende;
    ⁶*Tibi soli peccavi, etc.*
It is nought used in erthe · to hangen a feloun
Ofter than ones · though he were a tretour.
390 And yif the kynge of that kyngedome · come in that tyme,
There the feloun thole⁷ sholde · deth or otherwyse,
Lawe wolde, he geve hym lyf · if he loked on hym.
And I, that am kynge of kynges · shal come such a tyme,
There dome to the deth, · dampneth al wikked;
395 And gif lawe wil I loke on hem · it lithe in my grace,
Whether thei deye or deye noughte · for that thei deden
    ille.
Be it any thinge aboughte · the boldenesse of her synnes,
I may do mercy thorw rightwisnesse · and alle my wordes
    trewe.

1. 'The bitterness which thou hast brewed – enjoy it yourself', 2. 'I fought so – I thirst yet – for the sake of man's soul', 3. thirst, 4. minor devils, 5. nature, 6. 'To thee alone have I sinned', 7. suffer.

And though holiwrit wil that I be wroke · of them that
deden ille.
400   *¹Nullum malum inpunitum, etc.*
Thei shul be clensed clereliche · and wasshen of her synnes
In my prisoun purgatorie · till *parce* it hote,
And my mercy shal be shewed · to manye of my bretheren.
For blode may suffre blode · bothe hungry and akale,
405 Ac blode may nought se blode · blede, but hym rewe.'
         ²Audivi archana verba, que non licet homini loqui. –
'Ac my rightwisnesse and right · shal reulen al helle,
And mercy al mankynde · bifor me in hevene.
For I were an unkynde kynge · but I my kynde holpe,
410 And namelich at such a nede · ther nedes helpe bihoveth;
         ³Non intres in iudicium cum servo tuo, domine.
Thus bi lawe,' quod oure lorde · 'lede I wil fro hennes
Tho that me loved · and leved in my comynge.
And for thi lesynge, Lucifer, · *⁴that thow lowe til Eve,*
415 Thow shalt abye it bittre' – · and bonde hym with cheynes.
Astaroth and al the route · hidden hem in hernes⁵,
They dorste noughte loke on oure lorde · the boldest of hem
alle,
But leten hym lede forth what hym lyked · and lete what
hym liste.
     Many hundreth of angeles · harpeden and songen,
420   *⁶Culpat caro, purgat caro: regnat deus dei caro.*
Thanne piped pees · of poysye a note,
⁷*'Clarior est solito post maxima nebula phebus,*
Post inimicitias clarior est et amor.
After sharpe shoures,' quod Pees · 'moste shene is the
sonne;
425 Is no weder warmer · than after watery cloudes.
Be no love levere · ne lever frendes,
Than after werre and wo · whan Love and Pees be maistres.

1. 'No evil shall go unpunished', 2. 'I have heard secret words, which it
is not allowed man to repeat ...', 3. 'Enter thou not into judgement with
thy servant, O Lord', 4. 'Because thou laughed at Eve ...', 5. corners,
6. 'The flesh sins, the flesh redeems [from sin], the flesh of God reigns as God',
7. Paraphrase: 'The darkest hour before the dawn'.

Was nevere werre in this worlde · ne wykkednesse so kene,
That ne Love, and hym luste · to laughynge ne broughte,
430 And Pees thorw pacience · alle perilles stopped.'
'Trewes,' quod Treuth · 'thow tellest us soth, bi Jesus!
Clippe we in covenaunt · and ech of us cusse[1] other!'
'And lete no peple,' quod Pees · 'perceyve that we
    chydde!
For impossible is no thyng · to hym that is almyghty.'
435 'Thow seist soth,' seyde Ryghtwisnesse · and reverentlich
    hir kyste,
Pees, and Pees here · *per secula seculorum*.
      [2]*Misericordia et veritas obviaverunt sibi; iusticia et pax*
        osculate sunt.
Treuth tromped tho, and songe · '*Te deum laudamus*';
And thanne luted Love · in a loude note,
440   [3]*Ecce quam bonum et quam iocundum, etc.*
Tyl the daye dawed · this damaiseles daunced,
That men rongen to the resurexioun · and right with that I
    waked,
And called Kitte my wyf · and Kalote my doughter –
'Ariseth and reverenceth · goddes resurrexioun,
445 And crepeth to the crosse on knees – and kisseth if for a juwel!
For goddes blissed body · it bar for oure bote,
And it afereth the fende · for suche is the myghte,
May no grysly gost · glyde there it shadweth!'

           from *Piers Plowman*, Passus xviii, B Text.

1. embrace ... kiss, 2. 'Mercy and Truth are met together; Justice and Peace
have kissed each other', 3. 'Behold how good and joyful it is ...'.

NOTE

Piers Plowman, which tradition and a few scraps of documentary evidence
attribute to William Langland (or de Langland), is preserved in a large number of MSS. of the fourteenth and fifteenth centuries. These MSS. fall into
three groups representing three successive versions of the poem. The evidence
suggests that the poem in its first version (the A Text) was written about 1362,

and was then revised, expanded, and enormously extended to result in B Text (dated c. 1377), and again revised and enlarged – though on a smaller scale – to result in its final form (the C Text) by about 1393.

Passus xviii in B Text (its equivalent in C Text is Passus xxi) deals with Christ's Passion and Death and Descent into Hell and His Harrowing of Hell – the extraction of the souls of the Prophets and Patriarchs who are now delivered from the penalty of Original Sin by Christ's death. The scriptural authority for the Descent into Hell is contained in the *Gospel of Nicodemus*, but Langland may well have witnessed the episode acted in the contemporary cycles of Miracle plays.

ANONYMOUS

*

Sir Gawayne and the Grene Knight

I

Sithen the sege and the assaut · was cesed at Troye,
The borgh brittened and brent · to brondes and askes,
The tulk[1] that the trammes · of tresoun ther wroght
Was tried for his tricherie, · the trewest on erthe.
5   Hit was Ennias the athel · and his highe kynde,
That sithen depreced provinces, · and patrounes bicome
Welneghe of all the wele · in the West Iles.
Fro riche Romulus to Rome · ricchis him swythe
(With gret bobbaunce that burghe · he biges upon first,
10 And nevenes hit his aune nome, · as hit now hat),
Ticius to Tuskan turnes · and teldes biginnes,
Langaberde in Lumbardie · liftes up homes,

――――――――

Sir Gawain and the Green Knight

I

After the siege and the assault had ceased at Troy,
The town destroyed and burnt to brands and ashes,
The man that the schemes of treason there wrought
Was tried for his treachery, the truest on earth.
5   *It was Aeneas the nobleman and his high kindred,*
Who afterwards subdued provinces, and patrons became
Of well nigh all the wealth of the Western Isles.
After noble Romulus to Rome goes forthwith
(With great show of pomp that town he establishes at first,
10 *And gives it his own name, as it now has),*
Ticius turns to Tuscany and founds houses,
Longbeard in Lombardy raises homes,

1. One of the poet's many words for 'man'. In the lines that follow the medieval belief that the descendants of Aeneas – the survivor of Troy's destruction – became the founders of the Western kingdom, is set out.

And fer over the French flod · Felix Brutus
On mony bonkkes[1] ful brode · Bretayn he settes
        with winne[2],
15   Where werre and wrake[3] and wonder
    [4]Bi sythes has wont therinne,
    And oft bothe blysse and blunder
    [5]Ful skete has skifted sinne.

20 Ande when this Bretayn was bigged[6] · bi this burn[7] rich,
[8]Bolde bredden therinne, · baret that lofden,
In mony [9]turned time · tene that wroghten.
Mo ferlies[10] on this folde[11] · han fallen here oft
Then in any other that I wot, · sin that ilk time.
25 Bot of alle that here bult[12] · of Bretaygne kinges
Ay was Arthur the hendest[13], · as I haf herde telle.
[14]Forthi an aunter in erde · I attle to schawe,
That a selly[15] in sight · summe men hit holden,
And an outtrage awenture[16] · of Arthure's wonderes.
30 If ye wil listen this laye · bot on littel while,
I schal telle hit astit, · [17]as I in toun herde,
        with tonge,
    As hit is stad and stoken
    In story stif and stronge,
35   With lel lettres loken,
    In londe so has ben longe.

This king lay at Camilot · upon Krystmasse
With mony luflych lorde, · ledes[18] of the best,
Rekenly of the Rounde Table · alle tho rich brether,
40 With rich revel oright · and rechles merthes.

1. hillsides, 2. joy, 3. woe, 4. 'At times have dwelt therein', 5. 'Very swiftly have alternated since', 6. established, 7. knight, 8. 'Brave fellows were bred there, that loved fighting', 9. time past, 10. marvellous happenings, 11. earth, 12. dwelt, 13. noblest, 14. 'Therefore an adventure on earth I intend to show', 15. marvel, 16. surprising adventure, 17. '... with my tongue, as I heard it in town, (that is) As it (the adventure) is set forth and secured In firm and strong narrative, With letters faithfully interlocked (i.e. in alliterative verse), As in the old custom in the country', 18. 'men of the best'.

Ther tournayed tulkes[1] · by times ful mony,
Justed ful jolile · thise gentile knightes,
[2]Sithen kayred to the court · caroles to make.
For ther the fest was i-like · ful fiften dayes,
45   With alle the mete and the mirthe · that men couthe avyse;
Such glaum[3] and gle · glorious to here,
Dere din upon day, · daunsing on nyghtes,
Al was hap upon heghe · in halles and chambres
With lordes and ladies, · as levest him thoght.
50   With alle the wele of the worlde · [4]thay woned ther samen,
The most kid[5] knightes · under Kryste's selven,
And the lovelokkest ladies · that ever lif haden,
And he the comlokest king · that the court haldes;
For al was this faire folk · in her[6] first age,
55   on sille[7],
            The hapnest under heven,
            King highest mon of wille;
            Hit were now gret nie[8] to neven[9]
            So hardy a here[10] on hille.

60   Wyle New Yer was so yep[11] · that hit was newe cummen,
That day doubble on the dais · was the douth[12] served,
Fro the king was cummen · with knightes into the halle,
The chauntre of the chapel · cheved[13] to an ende.
Loude crye was ther kest · of clerkes and other,
65   Noël nayted[14] onewe, · nevened ful ofte;
And sithen riche[15] forth runnen · to reche hondeselle[16],
Yeayed[17] year's-giftes on high, · yelde hem bi hond,
Debated busily · aboute tho giftes;
Ladies laghed ful loude, · thogh thay lost haden,
70   And he that wan was not wrothe, · that may ye wel trawe.
Alle this mirthe thay maden · to the mete[18] time.
When thay had waschen worthily · thay wenten to sete,

---

1. men, 2. 'Afterwards proceeded to the court to make dances', 3. noise,
4. 'they abode there together', 5. famous, 6. their, 7. in the hall, 8. difficulty, 9. name, 10. company, 11. sharp, 12. company, 13. came, 14. celebrated, 15. courtiers, 16. gifts of the season, 17. proclaimed, 18. meal (or
meat) time.

[1]The best burne ay abof, · as hit best semed,
Quene Guenore[2], ful gay, · [3] graythed in the myddes,
75   Dressed on the dere dais, · dubbed al aboute,
Smal sendal[4] bisides, · a selure[5] hir over
Of tried tolouse, · of tars tapites[6] innoghe,
That were enbrawded and beten · with the best gemmes
That might be preved of prys · with penyes to buy,
80   in daye.
        The comlokest to discrye
        Ther glent with eyen gray,
        A semloker that ever he see
        Soth moght no man say.

85   Bot Arthure wolde not ete · til al were served,
He was so joly of his joyfnes, · and sumwhat childgered[7]:
His lif liked hym light, · he lovied the lasse
Auther to longe lye · or to longe sitte,
So busied him his yonge blod · and his brain wylde.
90   And also an other maner · meved[8] him eke
That he thurgh nobelay had nomen[9], · he wolde never ete
Upon such a dere day, · er hym devised were
Of sum aventurus thing · an uncouthe tale,
Of sum main mervayle, · that he might trawe,
95   Of alderes, of armes · of other aventurus,
Other sum segg[10] him bisoght · of sum siker knight
To joine with him in Justing, · in joparde to lay,
Lede lif for lif, · leve eachon other,
As fortune wolde fulsun[11] hom, · the fairer to have.
100   This was kinges countenaunce · where he in court were,
At each farand fest · among his fre meny
            in halle.
        Therefore of face so fere
        He stightles[12] stif in stalle,
105   Ful yep in that New Yere
        Much mirthe he was with alle.

1. the best man in the most dignified seat, 2. Guinevere, Arthur's queen,
3. seated in the midst, 4. silk, 5. canopy, 6. tapestry of rich silk, 7. boyish,
8. moved, 9. undertaken, 10. man, 11. help, 12. stands motionless.

Thus ther stondes in stale[1] · the stif king hisselven,
Talkkande bifore the highe table · of trifles ful hende.
There gode Gawan was graythed · Gwenore biside,
110 And Agravain a la Dur Main · on that other side sittes,
Bothe the kinges sistersunes · and ful siker knightes;
Bishop Bawdewyn abof · bigines the table,
And Ywan, Urin son, · ette with himselven:
Thise were dight on the dais · and derworthly served,
115 And sithen mony siker segge[2] · at the sidbordes.
Then the first course come · with crakkyng of trumpes,
With mony baner ful bright · that therbi henged,
Newe nakryn noise · with the noble pipes,
Wylde werbles · and wight wakned lote[3],
120 That mony hert ful highe · hef at her touches.
Dayntes driven therwith · of ful dere metes,
Foysoun of the fresche, · and on so fele[4] dishes
That pine to finde the place · the peple biforne
For to sette the silveren · that sere sewes[5] halden
125   on clothe. ·
        Eache lede[6] as he loved himselve
        Ther laght[7] withouten lothe;
        Ay two had dishes twelve,
        Good ber and bright wyn bothe.

130 Now wyl I of hor servise · say you no more,
For each wight may wel wit · no want that ther were.
An other noise ful newe · neghed bilive[8],
That the lude might haf leve · liflode to cach.
For unethe[9] was the noise · not a whyle cesed,
135 And the first course in the court · kindely served,
[10]Ther hales in at the halle dor · an aghlich maister,
On the most on the molde[11] · on mesure highe;
[12]Fro the swyre to the swange · so sware and so thik,
And his lindes[13] and his limbes · so longe and so grete,

---

1. seat, 2. men, 3. sound, 4. many, 5. various stews, 6. lord, 7. helped himself, 8. quickly, 9. hardly, 10. While they were merrily feasting 'there crashes in through the hall door a (huge and) terrifying fellow', 11. earth, 12. 'From the neck to the waist so stout and so thick', 13. loins.

140   Half etayn[1] in erde · I hope that he were,
         Bot mon most I algate · minn[2] him to bene,
         And that the meriest in his muckel · that might ride;
         For of bak and of brest · al were his bodi sturne,
         Both his wombe and his wast · were worthily smale,
145   And alle his fetures folyande, · in forme that he hade,
               ful clene;
               For wonder of his hue men hade,
               Set in his semblaunt sene;
               [3]He ferde as freke were fade,
150   And overal enker grene.

         [4]Ande al graythed in grene · this gome and his wedes:
         A strait cote ful streght, · that stek on his sides,
         A mere mantile abof, · mensked withinne
         With pelure pured apert, · the pane ful clene
155   With blythe blaunner ful bright, · and his hode bothe,
         That was layt fro his lokkes · and laide on his schulderes;
         Heme[5] wel-haled hose · of that same grene,
         That spenet on his sparlyr[6], · and clene spures under
         Of bright golde, upon silk bordes · barred ful ryche,
160   And scholes under schankes · there the schalk[7] rides;
         And alle his vesture virayly · was clene verdure[8],
         Bothe the barres of his belt · and other blythe stones,
         That were richely rayled · in his aray clene
         Aboutte himself and his sadel, · upon silk werkes,
165   [9]That were to tor for to telle · of trifles the halve
         That were enbrauded abof, · with briddes and flyes,
         With gay gaudi of grene[10], · the golde ay inmiddes.
         The pendauntes of his payttrure[11], · the proude copure,
         His molaynes, and alle the metail · anamayld[12] was thenne,
170   The steropes that he stod on · stained of the same,

---

1. giant; *Hope* has the sense of 'suppose', 2. nevertheless believe, 3. He fared as a fearless man And (was in colour) bright green all over, 4. And all decked in green this man – and his clothes were green, 5. neat, 6. calves (of legs), 7. man (its meaning here is not far from the modern 'bloke'), 8. bright green, 9. 'that were too cumbersome to enumerate', 10. his green garments were embroidered with figures of birds and butterflies, 11. a war-horse's neck covering, 12. enamelled.

And his arsouns al after · and his athel sturtes[1],
That ever glemered and glent · al of grene stones;
The fole[2] that he ferkkes on · fyn of that ilke,
    certain,
175   A grene hors gret and thikke,
        A stede ful stif to straine,
        In brawden bridle quik –
        To the gome[3] he was ful gain.

Wel gay was this gome · gered in grene,
180 And the here of his hed · of his hors swete[4].
  [5]Faire fannand fax · umbefoldes his schulderes;
A much berd as a busk · over his brest henges,
That with his highlich here · that of his hed reches
Was evesed al umbetorne · abof his elbowes,
185 That half his armes ther-under · were halched in the wyse
Of a kynges capados[6] · that closes his swyre[7];
The mane of that main[8] hors · much to hit lyke,
Wel cresped and cemmed, · with knottes ful mony
Folden in with fildore[9] · aboute the fayre grene
190 Ay a herle[10] of the hair, · an other of golde;
The tayl and his topping · twinnen of a sute,
And bounden bothe with a bande · of a bright grene,
Dubbed with ful dere stones, · as the dok[11] lasted,
Sithen thrawen[12] with a thwong · a thwarle[13] knot alofte,
195 Ther mony belles ful bright · of brende golde rungen.
  [14]Such a fole upon folde · ne freke that him ride
Was never sene in that sale · with sight er that time,
    with eye.
        He loked as layt[15] so light,
200   So sayd al that him see;
        Hit semed as no mon might
      [16]Under his dinttes drye.

1. splendid pieces of saddle harness, 2. horse, 3. man, 4. to match, 5. 'fair fanning hair surrounds his shoulders', 6. cape or tippet, 7. neck, 8. huge, 9. gold thread, 10. strand, 11. tail, 12. twisted, 13. tight, 14. 'Such a horse upon earth no fellow that rides him', 15. lightning, 16. 'under his blows survive'.

Whether hade he no helme · ne hawbergh nauther,
Ne no pisan[1] ne no plate · that pented to armes,
205 Ne no shafte ne no shelde · to shuve[2] ne to smite,
Bot in his on honde · he hade a hollyn bobbe[3],
That is grattest in grene · when groves ar bare,
And an axe in his other, · [4]a hoge and unmete,
[5]A spetos sparthe to expoun · in spelle, whoso might.
210 The hede of an elnyarde · the large lenkthe hade,
The grain al of grene stele · and of golde hewen,
The bit burnist bright, · with a brode edge
As wel shapen to schere · as sharp rasores.
The stele[6] of a stif staf · the sturne hit bi gripte,
215 That was wounden with iron · to the wandes ende,
And al bigraven with grene · in gravios werkes;
A lace lapped aboute · that louked at the hede,
And so after the helme · halched ful ofte,
Wyth tried tasseles therto · tacched innoghe
220 On botouns of the bright grene · brayden ful ryche.
This hathel[7] heldes him in · and the halle entres,
Drivande to the high dais, · dut he no wothe,
Hailsed[8] he never one, · bot heghe[9] he over loked.
The first word that he warp[10], · 'Wher is', he said,
225 'The governour of this ging?[11] · Gladly I wolde
See that segg in sight, · and with himself speke
      rasoun.'
            To knightes he kest his eye,
            And reled him up and doun;
230   He stemmed, and con studie
            Who walt ther most renoun.

Ther was loking on lenthe · the lude[12] to beholde,
For each mon had mervayle · what hit mene might,
That a hathel and a horse · might such a hue lach[13],
235 As growe grene as the gres · and grener hit semed

1. piece of metal attached to helmet, 2. shove, 3. holly branch, 4. a huge and immeasurable (one), 5. 'A sharp battle-axe to describe …', 6. stem shaft, 7. man, 8. greeted by embracing, 9. high, 10. flung out, 11. gang or company, 12. man, 13. take (they marvelled how 'a man and a horse could assume such a colour').

Then grene aumail[1] on golde · glowande brighter.
Al studied that ther stod, · and stalked him nerre
With al the wonder of the worlde · what he worch schulde.
For fele sellies[2] had they sen, · bot such never are[3];
240   Forthi[4] for fantoum and fayrye · the folk there hit demed.
Therfore to answare was arghe[5] · mony athel freke,
[6]And al stouned at his steven · and stonstil seten
In a swoghe silence · thurgh the sale riche;
As al were slipped upon slepe · [7]so slaked hor lotes
245   in highe –
          I deme hit not al for doute,
          Bot sum for cortaysye –
          Bot let him that al shulde loute
          Cast unto that wighe.

250   Thenn Arthour bifore the high dais · that aventure biholdes,
And rekenly him reverenced, · for rad was he never,
And said, 'Wighe, · welcum iwis to this place,
The hede of this ostel · Arthour I hat;
Light luflich adoun · and lenge, I thee praye,
255   And what-so thy wille is · we shal wit after.'
'Nay, as help me,' quoth the hathel, · 'he that on highe sittes,
[8]To wone any whyle in this won, · hit was not myn ernde;
Bot for the los[9] of thee, lede, · is lift up so highe,
And thy bourg and thy burnes[10] · best ar holden,
260   Stifest under stel-gere · on stedes to ride,
The wightest[11] and the worthiest · of the worldes kinde,
Preve for to play with · in other pure laykes[12],
And here is kidde cortaysie, · as I haf herd carp,
And that has wained me hider, · iwis, at this time,
265   Ye may be seker[13] bi this braunch · that I bere here
That I passe as in pes[14], · and no plight seche;
For had I founded in fere · in fighting wise,
I have a hauberghe at home · and a helme bothe,

1. enamel, 2. many marvels, 3. before, 4. therefore, 5. afraid, 6.' And
all astonished at his voice and stone-still sat', 7. 'So ceased their words',
8. 'To remain for any length of time in this place was not my purpose',
9. fame, 10. men, 11. manliest, 12. sports, 13. re-assured, 14. peace.

A shelde and a sharp spere, · shinande bright,
270 Ande other weppenes to welde, · I wene wel, als.
¹Bot for I wolde no were, · my wedes ar softer.
Bot if thou be so bold · as alle burnes tellen,
Thou wil grant me godly · the gomen² that I ask
bi right.'
275 Arthour con answare,
And said, 'Sir cortais knight,
If thou crave batail bare,
Here failes thou not to fight'.

'Nay, fraist³ I no fight, · in faith I thee telle,
280 ⁴Hit arn aboute on this bench · bot berdles childer.
If I were hasped in armes · on a heghe stede,
Here is no mon me to match, · for mightes so wayke.
Forthi I crave in this court · a Cristemas gomen,
For hit is Yule and Newe Yer, · and here are yep mony:
285 If any so hardy in this hous · holdes hymselven,
Be so bolde in his blod, · brain in his hede,
That dar stifly strike · a strok for an other,
I shal gif him of my gift · this giserne⁵ riche,
This ax, that is hevie innogh, · to hondele as him likes,
290 And I shal bide the first bur⁶ · as bare as I sitte
⁷If any freke be so felle · to fonde that I telle,
Lepe lightly me to, · and lach this weppen,
I quit-claime hit for ever, · kepe hit as his auen,
And I shal stonde hym a strok, · stif on this flet⁸;
295 Elles thou wil dight me the dom · to dele him an other,
barlay⁹,
And yet gif him respite,
A twelmonith and a day;
Now highe, and let se tite
300 Dar any herinne oght say¹⁰.'

1. 'But because I intend no battle ...', 2. sport, 3. crave, 4. 'There are
about on this bench only beardless children', 5. battle-axe, 6. blow, 7.' If
any fellow be so plucky as to test what I say', 8. floor, 9. an exclamation
of obscure origin and meaning, 10. The Green Knight's offer is this: Is there
any man here who will borrow my axe and give me a blow with it on the
condition that I return the blow in a year and a day's time?

If he hem stouned upon first, · stiller were thanne
Alle the heredmen in halle, · the high and the lowe.
[1]The renk on his rounce · him ruched in his sadel,
And runischly[2] his rede eyen · he reled aboute,

305   Bende his bresed browes, · blicande grene,
Wayved his berde for to waite · who-so wolde rise.
When non wolde kepe him with carp · he coghed ful highe,
Ande rimed him ful richley, · and right him to speke:
'What, is this Arthure's hous,' · quoth the hathel thenne,

310   [3]'That al the rous rennes of · thurgh rialmes so mony?
Where is now your surquidrie[4] · and your conquestes,
Your grindellayk[5] and your greme[6], · and your grete wordes?
Now is the revel and the renoun · of the Rounde Table
Overwalt with a worde · of one wighes speche,

315   For al dares for drede · withoute dint schewed!'
With this he laghes so loude · that the lorde greved;
The blod shot for sham · into his shire[7] face
                    and lere;
                He wex as wroth as winde,
320   So did alle that ther were.
                The kyng as kene bi kinde
                Then stod that stif mon nere,

And saide, 'Hathel, by heven, · thin asking is nis,
And as thou foly has fraist, · finde thee behoves.
325   I know no gome that is gast · of thy grete wordes;
Gif me now thy geserne[8], · upon Godes halve,
And I shal bathen[9] thy bone[10] · that thou boden habbes.'
Lightly lepes he hym to, · and laght at his honde.
Then feersly that other freke · upon fote lightis.

330   Now has Arthur his axe, · and the halme gripes,
And sturnely stures hit aboute, · that strike with hit thoght.
The stif mon him bifore · stod upon hight,
Herre[11] then ani in the hous · by the hede and more.

1. 'The chap (Green Knight) on his mount then swayed himself about
in the saddle', 2. violently, 3. 'That all the fame, which spreads through
so many realms, is about?', 4. pride, 5. fierceness, 6. anger, 7. bright,
8. battle-axe, 9. grant, 10. boon, 11. higher.

With sturne chere ther he stod · he stroked his berde,
335 And with a countenaunce drighe · he drogh doun his cote,
No more mate ne dismaid · for his main dintes
Then any burne upon bench · hade broght him to drink
of wine.
[1]Gawan, that sate bi the quene,
340 To the king he can encline,
'I beseche now with sawes sene
This melly mot be mine'.

'Wolde ye, worthilych lorde,' · quoth Wawan[2] to the
king,
'Bid me bowe[3] fro this benche, · and stonde by you there,
345 That I withoute vilanie · might voide this table,
And that my legge lady · liked not ille,
I wolde com to your counseil · bifore your cort riche.
For me think hit not semly, · as hit is soth knawen,
Ther such an asking is hevened · so highe in your sale,
350 Thagh ye yourself be talentif[4] · to take hit to yourselven,
Whil mony so bolde you aboute · upon bench sitten,
That under heven, I hope · non hay-erer[5] of wille,
Ne better bodies on bent · ther baret[6] is rered.
I am the wakkest, I wot, · and of wit feblest,
355 And les lur[7] of my lif, · who laites the sothe,
Bot for as much as ye ar min em[8] · I am only to praise,
No bounte bot your blod · I in my bode knowe;
And sithen this note is so nis, · that noght hit yow falles,
And I have frained hit at yow first, · foldes hit to me,
360 And if I carp not comlily, · let all this cort rich
bout blame.'
[9]Riche togeder con roun,
And sithen thay redden alle same
To rid the king with croun,
365 And gif Gawayne the game.

1. Gawain asks Arthur's permission to undertake the challenge instead,
2. *Wawan, Walwain*, etc. – variants of Gawain, 3. bend (his course), 4. desir-
ous, 5. more warlike, 6. contest, 7. loss, 8. uncle, 9. 'The nobles consulted
one another …'.

Then comaunded the king · the knight for to rise;
And he ful radly upros, · and ruchched[1] him faire,
Kneled doun bifore the king, · and caches that weppen;
And he luflily hit him laft, · and lifte up his honde,
370 And gef him Goddes blessing, · and gladly him biddes
That his hert and his honde · shulde hardi be bothe.
'Kepe thee, cosin,' quoth the king, · 'that thou on kirf[2] sette,
And if thou redes him right, · redly I trowe
That thou schal biden the bur[3] · that he schal bede after'.
375 Gawayne gets to the gome · with giserne in honde,
And he baldly hym bides, · he baist never the helder.
Then carppes to Sir Gawayne · the knight in the grene,
[4]'Refourme we oure forwardes, · er we firre passe.
First I ethe thee, hathel, · [5]how that thou hattes
380 That thou me telle truly, · as I tryst may'.
'In god faith,' quoth the goode knight, · [6]'Gawayne I hatte,
That bede thee this buffet, · what-so bifalles after,
And at this time twelmonith · take at thee an other
With what weppen so thou wilt, · and with no wigh elles
385   on live'.
        That other onswares again,
        'Sir Gawayne, so mot I thrive,
        As I am ferly fain
        This dint that thou shal drive'.

390 'Bigog,' quoth the Grene Knight, · 'Sir Gawayne, me likes
[7]That I shal fange at thy fust · that I haf fraist here.
And thou has redily rehersed, · bi resoun ful trewe,
Clanly al the covenaunt · that I the kinge asked,
[8]Saf that thou shal siker me, · segge, bi thi trawthe,
395 That thou schal seche me thiself, · where-so thou hopes
I may be funde upon folde[9], · and foch[10] thee such wages
As thou deles me to-day · bifore this douthe[11] riche.'
'Where shulde I wale thee,' quoth Gavan, · 'where is thy place?

---

1. proceeded, 2. cutting, 3. blow, 4. 'Let us set out conditions before
we go any farther', 5. 'What you are called', 6. 'Gawain is my name',
7. 'That I shall take at thy hand (fist)', 8. 'Except thou shalt assure me, man,
by thy truth', 9. earth, 10. receive, 11. company.

I wot never where thou wonies[1], · bi him that me wroght,
400 Ne I know not thee, knight, · thy cort ne thi name.
Bot teche me truly thereto, · and telle me howe thou hattes[2],
And I shal ware alle my wit · to winne me theder,
And that I swere thee for sothe, · and by my seker traweth.'
'That is innogh in Newe Yer, · hit nedes no more,'
405 Quoth the gome in the grene · to Gawayne the hende[3],
'Yif I thee telle trewly, · when I thee tape have
And thou me smothely has smiten, · smartly I thee teche
Of my hous and my home · and min owen nome,
Then may thou fraist[4] my fare · and forwardes[5] holde;
410 And if I spende no speche, · thenne spedes thou the better,
For thou may leng in thy londe · and layt no firre –
                    bot slokes![6]
        Ta now thy grimme tole to the,
        And let se how thou knokes.'
415   'Gladly, sir, for sothe',
        Quoth Gawayne; his ax he strokes.

The Grene Knight upon grounde · graythely him dresses,
A littel lut[7] with the hede, · the lere[8] he discoveres,
His longe lovelich lokkes · he laid over his croun,
420 Let the naked neck · to the note[9] schewe.
Gavan gripped to his ax, · and gederes hit on hight,
The kay[10] fot on the fold · he before sette,
Let hit doun lightly · light on the naked,
[11]That the sharp of the shalk · shindered the bones,
425 And shrank thurgh the shire grece[12], · and scade hit in twinne,
That the bit of the broun stel · bot on the grounde.
[13]The faire hede fro the halce · hit to the erthe,
That fele hit foined with her fete, · there hit forth roled;
The blod brayd fro the body, · that blikked on the grene;

---

1. dwellest, 2. thou callest thyself, 3. handsome, 4. inquire, 5. terms of agreement, 6. but enough!, 7. bow or dip, 8. flesh, 9. business, 10. left, 11. 'So that the edge sundered the (neck) bones of the man', 12. fat, 13. 'The fair head from the neck hit on the ground, (So) that many thrust at it with their feet where it forth rolled'.

430   [1]And nawther faltered ne fel · the freke never the helder,
       Bot stithly he start forth · upon stif schonkes,
       And runischly he raght out, · there as renkkes stoden,
       Laght to his lufly hed, · and lift hit up sone;
       And sithen bowes to his blonk, · the bridel he cachches,
435   Steppes into stelbawe · and strides alofte,
       And his hede by the here · in his honde haldes;
       [2]And as sadly the segge hym · in his sadel sette
       As non unhap had him ailed, · thagh hedles he were
               in stedde.
440   He braide his bluk aboute,
             That ugly bodi that bledde;
             Moni on of him had doute,
             Bi that his resouns were redde.

       For the hede in his honde · he haldes up even,
445   Toward the derrest on the dais · he dresses the face,
       And hit lifte up the eye-liddes · and loked ful brode,
       And meled[3] thus much with his muthe, · as ye may now here:
       'Loke, Gawayne, thou be graythe[4] · to go as thou hettes,
       [5]And latye as lelly til thou me, · lude, finde,
450   As thou has hette in this halle, · herande thise knightes,
       To the Grene Chapel thou chose · I charge thee to fotte[6]
       Such a dunt[7] as thou has dalt – · disserved thou habbes –
       To be yederly yolden · on New Yere's morn.
       The Knight of the Grene Chapel · men knowen me mony;
455   Forthi me for to finde if thou fraistes, · failes thou never:
       Therefore com, other[8] recreaunt · be calde the behoves.'
       With a runisch rout · the reines he tornes,
       Halled out at the hal dor, · his hed in his hande,
       That the fyr of the flint · [9]flaghe fro fole hoves.

1. 'And the man neither faltered nor fell in spite of his beheading, But abruptly started forth on stiff legs, And violently he rushed to where the people stood around, Caught up his lovely head and brandished it up on high, And carries it towards his horse, catches hold of the bridle', 2. 'seats himself in the saddle firmly, As though no mishap had befallen him – in spite of being headless', 3. spoke, 4. prompt, 5. 'And seek faithfully till you – lord – find me.', 6. fetch, 7. blow, 8. otherwise, 9. 'flew from the horse's hooves'.

460 To what kith he becom · knewe non there,
Never more then thay wiste · fram whethen he was wonnen.
What thenne?
The king and Gawen there
At that grene thay laghe and grenne,
465 Yet breved[1] was hit ful bare
A mervail among tho menne.

Thogh Arther the hende king · at hert hade wonder,
He let no semblaunt be sene, · bot saide ful highe
To the comlich quene · with cortais speche,
470 'Dere dame, to-day · demay you never;
Wel bycommes such craft · upon Cristmasse,
Layking[2] of enterludes, · to laghe and to sing,
Among thise kinde caroles · of knightes and ladies.
Never the less to my mete · I may me wel dres,
475 For I haf sen a selly[3], · I may not forsake.'
He glent upon Sir Gawen, · and fainly he saide,
'Now sir, heng up thin ax, · that has innogh hewen';
And hit was don abof the dais · on doser[4] to henge,
There alle men for mervail · might on hit loke,
480 And bi trewe title therof · to telle the wonder.
Thenne thay bowed to a borde · this burnes togeder,
The king and the gode knight, · and kene men hem served
Of alle dainties double, · as derrest might falle;
With alle maner of mete · and minstralci bothe,
485 With wele walt thay that day, · til worthed an ende
in londe.
Now thenk wel, Sir Gawayne,
For wothe[5] that thou ne wonde
This aventure for to frain
490 That thou has tan on honde.

<hr>

1. set down, 2. playing, 3. wonder, 4. wall-tapestry, 5. danger.

II

This hanselle[1] has Arthur · of aventures on first
In yonge yer, for he yerned · yelping[2] to here.
Thagh him wordes were wane[3] · when thay to sete wenten,
Now ar thay stoken of sturne werk, · stafful[4] her hond.
495 Gawayne was glad to beginne · those gomnes in halle,
Bot thagh the ende be hevy, · haf ye no wonder;
For thagh men ben mery in minde · when thay han main
        drink,
  [5]A yere yernes ful yerne, · and yeldes never like,
The forme to the finisment · foldes ful selden.
500 Forthi this Yol[6] overyede, · and the yere after,
And eche sesoun serlepes[7] · sued after other:
After Cristenmasse · com the crabbed lentoun,
That fraistes[8] flesh with the fishe · and fode more simple;
Bot thenne the weder óf the worlde · with winter hit threpes,
505 Colde clenges adoun, · cloudes upliften,
Sheer shedes the rain · in showres ful warme,
Falles upon faire flat, · flowres there schewen,
Bothe groundes and the greves[9] · grene ar her wedes,
  [10]Brides busken to bilde, · and bremlich singen
510 For solace of the softe somer · that sues therafter
                bi bonk;
            And blossumes bolne to blowe
            Bi rawes[11] rich and ronk,
            Then notes noble innoghe
515   Ar herde in wod so wlonk.

After, the sesoun of somer · with the soft windes,
When Zeferus sifles himself · on sedes and erbes;
Wela winne is the wort[12] · that waxes theroute,
When the donkande[13] dewe · dropes of the leves,
520 To bide a blisful blusch · of the bright sunne.

1. New Year's gift, 2. brave enterprises, 3. lacking, 4. cram-full, 5. 'A
year passes quickly, and yields never the same, The beginning (of the year)
seldom matches its end', 6. Yule, 7. in turn, 8. makes trial of, 9. groves,
10. 'Birds hasten to build and splendidly sing', 11. rows, 12. plant, 13.
moistening.

Bot then highes hervest, · and hardenes him sone,
Warnes him for the winter · to wax ful ripe;
He drives with droght · the dust for to rise,
Fro the face of the folde[1] · to flye ful highe;
525 Wrothe winde of the welkin · wrasteles with the sunne,
The leves lancen fro the linde[2] · and lighten on the grounde,
And al grayes the gres[3] · that grene was ere;
Thenne al ripes and rotes[4] · that ros upon first,
And thus yirnes the yere · in yisterdayes mony,
530 And winter windes again, · as the worlde askes,
          no fage[5],
        Til Meghelmas mone
        Was cumen with winter wage;
        Then thenkkes Gawayne ful sone
535   Of his [6]anious viage.

Yet whyl Al-hal-day · with Arther he lenges;
And he made a fare on that fest · for the frekes[7] sake,
With much revel and riche · of the Rounde Table.
Knightes ful cortais · and comlich ladies
540 [8]Al for luf of that lede · in longinge thay were,
Bot never the less ne the later · thay nevened[9] bot merthe:
Mony joyless for that gentle · japes ther maden.
[10]For aftter mete with mourning · he meles to his eme,
And spekes of his passage, · and pertly he saide,
545 'Now, lege lorde of my lif, · leve I you ask;
Ye knowe the cost of this case, · kepe I no more
To telle you tenes[11] therof, · never bot trifel;
Bot I am boun to the bur[12] · barely to-morne
To sech the gome of the grene, · as God wil me wisse'.
550 Thenne the best of the burg · bowed[13] togeder,
Aywan, and Errik, · and other ful mony,
Sir Doddinaval de Savage, · the duk of Clarence,
Launcelot, and Lionel, · and Lucan the gode,

---

1. earth, 2. tree, 3. grass, 4. decays, 5. in truth, 6. troublesome journey,
7. knights, 8. 'All for love of that knight (Gawain) in longing they were',
9. mentioned, 10. 'For after meat with sorrow Gawain speaks with his
uncle,' 11. sufferings, 12. blow, 13. turned.

Sir Boos, and Sir Bidver, · big men bothe,
555 And mony other menskful, · with Mador de la Port.
Alle this compayny of court · com the kyng nerre
For to counseil the knight, · with care at her hert.
¹There was much derve doel · driven in the sale,
That so worthy as Wawan² · shudde wende on that ernde³,
560 To drighe⁴ a delful dint, · and dele no more
         with bronde.
       The knight mad ay god chere,
       And seyde, 'What shuld I wonde?
       Of destines derf⁵ and dere
565   What may mon do bot fonde?'⁶

He dowelles ther al that day, · and dresses on the morn,
Askes erly his armes, · and alle were thay broght.
⁷First a tule tapit · tight over the flet,
And miche was the gild gere · that glent theralofte;
570 The stif mon steppes theron, · and the stel hondeles,
Dubbed in a dublet · of a dere tars,
And sithen a crafty capados, · closed aloft,
That with a bright blaunner · was bounden withinne.
Thenne set thay the sabatouns · upon the segge fotes,
575 His leges lapped in stel · with luflich greves,
With polaines piched therto, · policed ful clene,
Aboute his knes knaged · with knotes of golde;
Queme cuissewes then, · that coyntlich closed
His thik thrawen thighes, · with thwonges to tachched;
580 And sithen the brawden bryne · of bright stel ringes
Um-beweved⁸ that wigh · upon wlonk stuffe,
And wel bornyst brace · upon his bothe armes,
With gode couters and gay, · and gloves of plate,
And alle the godlich gere · that him gain shulde
585   that tide;

1. 'There was much severe lamentation made in the hall', 2. Gawain,
3. undertaking, 4. suffer, 5. arduous, 6. attempt, 7. The arming of Gawain.
The reader need not, however, concern himself with the *precise* meaning of
the terminology – with which this passage abounds – of medieval personal
armament, 8. enveloped.

With riche cote-armure,
His gold spores spend with pride,
Gurde with a bront ful sure
With silk sain umbe his syde.

590   When he was hasped in armes, · his harnays was riche:
The lest lachet other loupe · lemed[1] of golde.
So harnayst as he was · he herknes[2] his masse,
Offred and honoured · at the heghe auter[3].
Sithen he comes to the king · and to his cort-feres,
595   [4]Laches lufly his leve · at lordes and ladies;
And thay him kist and conveyed, · bikende him to Kryst.
[5]Bi that was Gringolet graith, · and gurde with a sadel
That glemed ful gayly · with mony golde frenges,
Aywhere nailet[6] ful newe, · for that note riched;
600   The bridel barred aboute, · with bright golde bounden;
The apparail of the payttrure · and of the proude skirtes,
The cropore and the covertor, · acroded with the arsoundes[7];
And al was railed on red · riche golde nailes,
That al glitered and glent · as glem of the sunne.
605   Thenne hentes[8] he the helme, · and hastily hit kisses,
That was stapled stifly, · and stoffed withinne.
Hit was highe on his hede, · hasped bihinde,
With a lightly urysoun[9] · over the aventayle[10],
Enbrawden and bounded · with the best gemmes
610   On brode silkin borde, · and briddes on semes,
[11]As papiayes painted · perning bitwene,
Tortors and trulofes · entailed so thik
[12]As many burde thereboute · had ben seven winter
in toune.
615   The cercle was more o prys
        That umbeclipped his croun,

1. shone, 2. hears, 3. high altar, 4. 'Takes lovingly his leave from lords and ladies', 5. 'By that time Gringolet (the name of Gawain's horse) was prepared, and ...', 6. studded with ornamental nails, 7. saddle-bows, 8. seizes, 9. band or streamer of silk, 10. the mouthpiece of the helmet, 11. 'likewise butterflies painted preening between, Turtledoves and doves', 12. *As ... toune*. The suggestion is that many maidens must have been engaged – and for a long time (seven winters) – on such an elaborate piece of embroidery.

Of diamauntes a devis
That bothe were bright and broun.

Then they shewed him the shelde, · that was of shir goules
620 With the pentangel[1] depaint · of pure golde hues.
He braides hit by the bauderik[2], · aboute the hals[3] kestes,
That bisemed the segge · semlily faire.
And why the pentangel apendes · to that prince noble
I am intent you to telle, · thogh tray hit me shulde:
625 Hit is a signe that Salamon · set sumwhile
In bitokning of trawthe, · bi title that hit habbes,
For hit is a figure that haldes · five pointes,
And eche line umbelappes · and loukes in other,
And aywhere hit is endeles; · and Englich hit callen
630 Overal, as I here, · the endeles knot[4].
Forthy hit acordes to this knight · and to his cler armes,
For ay faithful in five · and sere five sithes
Gawan was for gode knawen, · and as golde pured,
Voided of eche vilany, · [5]with vertues ennourned
635   in mote;
Forthy the pentangel newe
He ber in shelde and cote,

1. The pentagon painted on Gawain's shield is an emblem signifying perfection. 2. baldrick. 3. neck. 4. The emblem on the front of Gawain's shield was like this:

It is 'endless' in that (like a circle but unlike a straight line) it can be continuously traced with the finger. On the interior of the shield is an image of the Blessed Virgin. The modern mind has lost the faculty of enjoying and apprehending pictorial emblems. Consequently it is perhaps more important that we should – by an exercise of the will – understand the nature of our loss, than merely unravel the various significances of the pentagon. 5. 'And adorned with virtues in the castle'.

As tulk[1] of tale most trewe
And gentilest knight of lote.

640   First he was funden fautles · in his five wittes,
And efte failed never the freke[2] · in his five fingres,
And alle his afiaunce upon folde · was in the five woundes
That Cryst kaght on the croys, · as the crede telles;
And where-so-ever this mon · in melly[3] was stad,
645   His thro thoght was in that, · thurgh alle other thinges,
[4]That alle his fersnes he feng · at the five joyes
That the hende heven quene · had of hir childe;
At this cause the knight · comliche hade
In the more half of his shelde · hir image depaynted,
650   That when he blushed therto · his belde never payred.
The fift five that I finde · that the frek used
Was fraunchise and felawschyp · forbe al thing,
His clannes and his cortaysie · croked were never,
And pite, that passes alle poyntes, · thise pure five
655   Were harder happed on that hathel · then on any other.
Now alle these five sithes, for sothe, · were fetled on thus
     knight,
And ech one halched in other, · that non ende hade,
And fiched upon five pointes, · that faild never,
Ne samned never in no side, · ne sundred nouther,
660   Withouten ende at any noke[5] · aiwhere, I finde,
Wherever the gomen bigan, · or glod to an ende.
Therfore on his shene shelde · shapen was the knot
Ryally with red golde · upon rede goules,
That is the pure pentaungel · with the peple called
665   with lore.
      Now graithed is Gawayne gay,
      And laght his launce right thore,
      And gef hem alle goud day,
      He wende for ever more.

1. man, 2. man, 3. battle, 4. 'All his fierce courage he derived from the five joys Which the gracious Queen of Heaven had of her Child; Therefore the knight had fittingly On the larger half (the inside) of his shield painted her image, So that when he gazed on it his courage never defaulted', 5. nook.

670   He spered the sted with the spures · and sprong on his way,
       So stif[1] that the ston-fyr · stroke out therafter.
       Al that seye that semly · sicked in hert,
      [2]And sayde sothly al same · scggcs til other,
       Carande[3] for that comly: · 'Bi Kryst, hit is scathe
675   That thou, leude, shal be lost, · that art of lif noble!
      [4]To finde his fere upon folde, · in faith, is not ethe.
       Warloker[5] to haf wrought · had more wit bene,
       And haf dight yonder dere · a duk to have worthed;
       A lowande[6] leder of ledes · in londe him wel semes,
680   And so had better haf ben · then britned to noght,
      [7]Hadet with an alvisch mon · for angardes pride.
       Who knew ever any king · such counsel to take
       As knightes in cavelaciouns · on Cristmasse gomnes!'
       Wel much was the warme water · that waltered of eyen,
685   When that semly sire · soght fro tho wones
               thad daye.
            He made non abode,
            Bot wightly went his way;
            Mony whilesome way he rode,
690   The bok as I herde say.

       Now rides this renk · thurgh the realme of Logres,
       Sir Gavan, on Godes halve, · thagh him no gomen thoght.
       Oft leudless alone · he lenges on nightes
       Ther he fonde noght him before · the fare that he liked.
695   [8]Hade he no fere bot his folc · bi frithes and downes,
       Ne no gome but God · bi gate wyth to karp,
       Til that he neghed ful neghe · into the Northe Wales.
       Alle the iles of Anglesay · on left half he haldes,
       And fares over the fordes · by the forlondes,

---

1. violently, 2. 'And said in fact together each man to the other,' 3. Pity-ing, 4. 'To find his equal on earth, in faith, is not easy', 5. more cautiously, 6. very able – even brilliant. (It would have been wiser to have made Gawain an administrator instead of dispatching him on such a perilous mission.), 7. 'Be-headed by an elvish man for the sake of pride', 8. 'Had no companion except his horse by friths and downs, Nor no one except God to chat with on the way.' Gawain, of course, is journeying alone to keep his appointment with the Green Knight at the Green Chapel.

700   Over at the Holy Hede, · til he hade eft bonk
       In the wildrenesse of Wyrale; · wonde ther bot lite
       That auther God other gome · with goud hert lovied.
       [1]And ay he frained, as he ferde, · at frekes that he met,
       If thay hade herde any karp · of a Knight Grene,
705   In any grounde theraboute, · of the Grene Chapel;
       And al nikked him with nay, · that never in her live
       Thay seye never no segge · that was of suche hewes
                   of grene.
           The knight tok gates straunge
710   In mony a bonk unbene,
           His cher ful oft con chaunge
           That chapel er he might sene.

       Mony clif he overclambe · in contrayes straunge,
       Fer floten fro his frendes · fremedly he rides.
715   [2]At eche warthe other water · ther the wighe passed
       He fonde a foo him before, · bot ferly hit were,
       And that so foule and so felle · that feght him behode.
       So mony mervayl bi mount · ther the mon findes,
       Hit were to tore for to telle · of the tenthe dole.
720   Sumwhile with wormes[3] he werres, · and with wolves als,
       Sumwhile with wodwos[4], · that woned in the knarres[5],
       Bothe with bulles and beres, · and bores otherwhile,
       And etaines[6], that him anelede · of the heghe felle;
       [7]Nade he ben dughty and drighe, · and Drighten had served,
725   Douteless he hade ben ded · and dreped[8] ful ofte.
       For werre wrathed him not so much, · that winter was wors,
       When the colde cler water · fro the cloudes shadde,
       And fres[9] er hit falle might · to the fale[10] erthe;
       Ner slain with the slete · he sleped in his yrnes[11]
730   Mo nightes then innoghe · in naked rokkes,
       Ther as clatcrande fro the crest · the colde borne rennes,

---

1. 'And always he inquired, as he journeyed, of men that he met If they had heard any talk of a Green Knight', 2. Every ford that he had to wade was guarded by a foe whom he had to tackle, 3. serpents, 4. satyrs, 5. rocks, 6. giants, 7. 'Had he not been doughty and tough, and God had served', 8. trounced, 9. froze, 10. pale, faded, 11. irons, i.e. his armour.

And henged heghe over his hede · in hard iise-ikkles[1].
Thus in peril and paine · and plites ful harde
Bi contray cayres this knight, · til Kristmasse even,
735   al one;
      The knight wel that tide
      To Mary made his mone,
      That ho[2] him red to ride
      And wisse him to sum wone.

740 Bi a mounte on the morne · merily he rides
Into a forest ful dep, · that ferly was wilde,
Highe hilles on eche a halve, · and holtwodes under
Of hore oakes ful hoge · a hundreth togeder;
The hasel and the hawthorne · were harled[3] al samen,
745 With roghe raged mosse · railed aywhere,
With mony briddes unblithe · upon bare twiges,
That pitosly ther piped · for pyne of the colde.
The gome upon Gringolet · glides hem under,
Thurgh mony misy and mire, · mon al him one,
750 [4]Carande for his costes, · lest he ne kever shulde
To se the servise of that Sire, · that on that self night
Of a burde[5] was borne · oure baret[6] to quelle.
And therfore siking he saide, · 'I beseche the, lorde,
And Mary, that is mildest · moder so dere,
755 Of sum herber ther heghly · I might here masse,
Ande thy matines to-morne, · mekely I ask,
And therto prestly I pray · my *pater* and *ave*
      and crede'.
      He rode in his prayere,
760   And cried for his misdede,
      He sained him in sithes sere,
      And sayde 'Cros Kryst me spede?'

Nade he sained himself, · segge, bot thrye,
Er he was war in the wod · of a won in a mote[7],

1. icicles, 2. she, 3. tangled, 4. 'Concerned over his religious duties lest he should not manage To see the service (i.e. attend Christmas mass) ...' 5. lady, 6. strife, 7. 'A dwelling (set) in a moat'.

765 Abof a launde, on a lawe, – loken under boghes
Of mony borelich bole · aboute bi the diches:
A castel the comlokest · that ever knight aghte,
Piched on a prayere[1], · a park al aboute,
With a piked palays · pined ful thik,
770 That umbetewe mony tre · mo then two mile.
That holde on that on side · the hathel avised,
As hit shemered and schon · thurgh the shire okes;
Thenne has he hendly off his helme, · and heghly he thonkes
Jesus and sain Gilian, · that gentile ar bothe,
775 That cortaisly had him kidde[2], · and his cry herkened.
'Now bone hostel,' cothe the burne, · 'I beseche you yette!'
Thenne gerdes he to Gringolet · with the gilt heles,
And he ful chauncely has chosen · to the chef gate,
That broght brebly the burne · to the brige ende
780   in haste.
        The brige was breme upbrayde,
        The gates wer stoken faste,
        The walles were wel arayed,
        Hit dut no windes blaste.

785 The burne bode on bonk, · that on blonk hoved,
Of the depe double dich · that drof to the place;
The walle wod in the water · wonderly depe,
Ande eft a ful huge heght · hit haled up on lofte
Of harde hewen ston · up to the tables,
790 Enbaned under the abatailment · in the best lawe;
And sithen garites[3] ful gaye · gered bitwene,
With mony luflich loupe · that louked ful clene:
A better barbican that burne · blushed upon never.
And innermore he behelde · that halle ful highe,
795 [4]Toures telded bitwene, · trochet ful thik,
Faire filioles that fighed, · and ferlyly long,
With corvon coprounes · craftily sleghe.
Chalkwhyt chimnees · ther ches he innoghe
Upon bastel roves, · that blenked ful whyte;

1. meadow, 2. shown, 3. look-out turrets, 4. 'Turrets erected at intervals, thickly pinnacled, Fair spires that fitted, marvellously long, With ornamental tops craftily wrought.'

800   So mony pinakle paintet · was poudred aywhere,
        Among the castel carneles[1] · clambred to thik,
        That pared out of papure · purely hit semed[2].
        The fre freke on the fole · hit fayr innoghe thoght,
        If he might kever to com · the cloyster withinne,
805   To herber in that hostel · whyl halyday lested,
                  avinant.
              He calde, and sone ther com
              A porter pure plesaunt,
              On the wal his ernd he nome,
810   And hailsed the knight erraunt.

        'Gode sir,' quoth Gawayne, · 'woldes thou go myn ernde
        To the hegh lorde of this hous, · herber to crave?'
        'Ye, Peter,' quoth the porter, · 'and purely I trowee
        That ye be, wighe, welcum · to won while yow likes.'
815   Then yede that wighe · again swithe,
        And folke frely him with, · to fonge[3] the knight.
        Thay let doun the grete draght[4] · and derely out yeden,
        And kneled doun on her[5] knes · upon the colde erthe
        To welcum this ilk wigh · as worthy hom[6] thoght;
820   They yolden him the brode yate, · yarked up wide,
      [7]And he hem raised rekenly, · and rod over the brigge.
        Sere segges him sesed · by sadel whel he light,
        And sithen stabeled his stede · stif men innoghe.
        Knightes and squieres · comen doun thenne
825   For to bring this buurne · with blis into halle.
        When he lef up his helme, · ther highed innoghe
        For to hent hit at his honde, · the hende to serven;
        His bronde and his blasoun · bothe thay token.
        Then hailsed he ful hendly · tho hatheles echone,
830   And mony proud mon ther pressed · that prince to honour.

1. embrasures among the battlements, 2. The building, which Sir Gawain sees, with its elaborate ornamentation of pinnacles and 'chalk-white chimneys', is typical of late fourteenth-century architecture, 3. receive, 4. drawbridge, 5. their, 6. them, 7. And Gawain caused the retainers, who were kneeling in obeisance, to stand up again promptly. He crosses the drawbridge, is handsomely received by knights and squires and relieved by them of his armour, and is finally welcomed by the lord of the castle.

Alle hasped in his hegh wede · to halle thay him wonnen,
Ther faire fire upon flet · fersely brenned.
Thenne the lorde of the lede · loutes fro his chambre
For to mete with menske[1] · the mon on the flor;
835 He saide, 'Ye ar welcum · to welde as you likes;
That here is, al is youre awen, · to have at youre wille
and welde'.
'Graunt mercy,' quoth Gawayne,
'Ther Krist hit you foryelde;'
840 As frekes that semed fain
Ayther other in armes con felde.

Gawayne [2]glight on the gome · that godly him gret,
And thught hit a bolde burne · that the burgh aghte[3],
A huge hathel for the nones, · and of highe elde[4];
845 Brode, bright, was his berde, · and al bever-hewed,
Sturne, stif on the strithe · on stalworth shonkes,
Felle face as the fire, · and fre of his speche;
And wel him semed, for sothe, · as the segge thught,
To lede a lortschip in lee[5] · of leudes ful gode.
850 The lorde him charred to a chambre, · and chefly cumaundes
To deliver him a leude, · hym lowly to serve;
And there were boun at his bode · burnes innoghe,
That broght him to a bright boure, · ther bedding was noble,
Of cortines of clene silk · with cler golde hemmes,
855 And covertores ful curious · with comlich panes,
Of bright blaunmer above · embrawded bisides,
Rudeles rennande on ropes, · red golde ringes,
[6]Tapites tight to the wowe · of tuly and tars,
And under fete, on the flet, · of folyande sute.
860 Ther he was dispoiled, · with speches of merthe,
The burn of his bruny, · and of his bright wedes.
Riche robes ful rad · renkkes him broghten,
For to charge, and to chaunge, · and chose of the best.
Sone as he one hent, · and happed therinne,
865 That sete on him semly · with sailande skirtes,

1. honour, 2. 'glanced at the fellow', 3. 'that the castle possessed', 4. advanced age, 5. peace and security, 6. 'Tapestries tied to the walls'.

The ver by his visage · verayly hit semed
Welnegh to eche hathel, · alle on hewes,
Lowande and lufly · alle his limmes under,
That a comloker knight · never Krist made
870   hem thoght.
            Whethen in worlde he were,
            Hit semed as he moght
            Be prince withouten pere
            In felde ther felle men foght.

875   A cheyer[1] bifore the chemne, · wher charcole brenned,
      Was graythed for Sir Gawayne · graythely with clothes,
      Whyssines[2] upon queldepointes[3] · that koint wer bothe;
      And thenne a mere mantile · was on that mon cast
      Of a broun bleeaunt, · enbrauded ful riche,
880   And faire furred withinne · with felles of the best, –
      Alle of ermin inurnde, · his hode of the same.
      And he sete in that settel · semlich riche,
      And a-chaufed[4] him chefly, · and thenne his cher mended.
      Sone was telded up a tabil, · on trestels ful faire,
885   Clad with a clene clothe, · that cler whit shewed,
      Sanap and salure[5], · and silverin spones.
      The wighe wesche as his wylle, · and went to his mete.
      Segges him served · semly innoghe,
      [6]With sere sewes and sete, · sesounde of the best,
890   Double-felde, as hit falles, · and fele kin fisches;
      Summe baken in bred, · summe brad on the gledes[7],
      Summe sothen, summe in sewe, · savered with spices,
      [8]And ay sawes so sleye · that the segge liked.
      The freke calde hit a fest · ful frely and ofte
895   Ful hendely, when alle the hatheles · rehayted him at once
                  as hende:
            'This penaunce now ye take,
            And eft hit shal amende'.
            That mon much merthe con make,
900   For wyn in his hed that wende.

1. chair,   2. cushions,   3. quilted coverings,   4. warmed (himself),
5. covering-cloth and salt-cellar,   6. 'with several and excellent soups',   7.
glowing embers,   8. 'and also sauces so cunning.'

[1]Thenne was spied and spured · upon spare wise,
Bi privy pointes of that prince, · put to himselven,
That he beknew cortaisly · of the court that he were,
That athel Arthure the hende, · haldes him one,
905   That is the riche ryal king · of the Rounde Table;
And hit was Wawen himself · that in that won sittes,
Comen to that Kristmasse, · as case him then limped.
When the lorde hade lerned · that he the leude hade,
Loude laghed the therat, · so lef hit him thoght,
910   And alle the men in that mote · maden much joye
To apeare in his presence · prestly that time,
That alle prys and prowess · and pured thewes
Apendes to his persoun, · and praised is ever,
Byfore alle men upon molde · his mensk is the most.
915   Ech segge ful softly · sayde to his fere:
'Now shal we semlich · se sleghtes of thewes
And the teccheles termes · of talking noble,
Which spede is in speche, · unspurd may we lerne,
Sin we half fonged that fine · fader of nuture;
920   God has geven us his grace · godly for sothe,
That such a gest as Gawayne · grauntes us to have,
When burnes blythe · of his burthe shal sitte
           and singe.
      In menyng of maneres mere
925   This burne now shal us bring,
      I hope that may him here
      Shal lerne of luf-making.'

By that the diner was done, · and the dere up[2],
Hit was negh at the night · neghed the time;
930   Chaplaines to the chapeles · chosen the gate[3],
Rungen ful richely, · right as thay shulden,
To the hersum evensong[4] · of the highe tide.

1. They enquire of Gawain whether he is one of King Arthur's knights
and, when they learn that their guest is no other than Gawain, they are delighted and are confident of learning from him the latest and most refined
ways of love-making. 2. and the noble man risen from the table. 3. took
their way. 4. devout evensong.

The lorde loutes therto, · and the lady als,
Into a comly closet[1] · cointly ho entres.
935 Gawayne glides ful gay, · and gos theder sone;
[2]The lorde laches him by the lappe · and ledes him to sitte,
And couthly him knowes, · and calles him his nome,
And saide he was the welcomest · wighe of the worlde;
And he him thonkked throly, · and ayther halched[3] other,
940 And seten soberly samen · the servise while.
Thenne list the lady · to loke on the knight,
[4]Whenne com ho of hir closet · with mony cler burdes,
Ho was the fairest in felle, · of fleshe and of lyre,
And of compass and colour, · and costes of all other,
945 [5]And wener then Wenore, · as the wighe thoght.
He ches thurgh the chaunsel · to cheriche that hende.
[6]An other lady hir lad · bi the lyft honde,
That was alder then ho, · an auncian hit semed,
And heghly honoured · with hatheles aboute.
950 Bot unlike on to loke · tho ladies were,
For if the yonge was yep, · yolwe was that other;
Riche red on that on · rayled aywhere,
Rugh ronkled chekes · that other on rolled;
Kerchofes of that on · with mony cler perles,
955 Hir brest and hir bright throte · bare displayed,
Shom shyrer than snawe · that shedes on hilles;
That other with a gorger · was gered over the swire[7],
Climbled over hir blake chin · with chalkwhite vailes,
Hir frount folden in silk, · enfoubled aywhere,
960 Toret and treieted · with trifles aboute,
That noght was bare of that burde · bot the blake browes,
The tweyne eyen and the nase, · the naked lippes,
And those were soure to see · and sellyly blered;
A mensk lady on molde · mon may hir calle!
965   for Gode!

1. a closed pew, 2. 'The lord takes him by the lapel and leads him to sit',
3. embraced, 4. 'When she (ho) came from her closed pew with many fresh
ladies', 5. 'And fairer than Guinevere as the man thought', 6. The mistress of
the castle leads another woman by the hand – a filthy old hag, much unlike
the other. The succeeding lines continue the contrast, 7. neck.

Hir body was short and thik,
Hir buttokes balg and brode,
More likkerwis on to lik
Was that sho hade on lode!

970 [1]When Gawayne glyght on that gay, · that graciously loked,
With leve laght of the lorde · he went hem againes;
The alder he hailses, · heldande ful lowe,
The loveloker he lappes · a littel in armes,
He kisses hir comlyly, · and knightly he meles;

975 Thay kallen him of aquointaunce, · and he hit quick askes
To be her servaunt sothly, · if hemself liked.
Thay tan him bitwene hem, · with talking hym leden
To chambre, to chemne, · and chefly thay asken
Spices, that unsparely men · speded hom to bring,

980 And the winnelich wine · therwith eche time.
The lorde luflich aloft · lepes ful ofte,
Minned merthe to be made · upon mony sithes,
Hent heghly of his hode, · and on a spere henged,
And waved hom to winne · the worchip therof,

985 That most mirthe might meve · that Cristenmas while –
'And I shal fonde, bi my faith, · to filter[2] with the best,
Er me wont the wede · with help of my frendes'.
Thus with laughande lotes · the lorde hit lait makes,
For to glade Sir Gawayne · with gomnes in halle

990 that night,
Til that hit was time
The lord comaundet light;
Sir Gawen his leve con nime
And to his bed him dight.

995 On the morne, as eche mon · mines that time
That Drighten[3] for oure destine · to deye was borne,
Wele waxes in eche a won · in worlde for his sake;

1. Gawain, with permission of the lord, greets the elder of the two women and then holds the young and beautiful one in his arms for a short time and kisses her. Then all adjourn for Christmas games. 2. to press forward among, contend with. (The lord of the castle will take part in the games.), 3. God.

So did hit there on that day · thurgh daintes mony:
Bothe at mes and at mele · messes ful quaint
1000 Derf men upon dais · drest of the best.
The olde auncian eif · heghest ho sittes;
The lorde lufly her · by lent, as I trowe;
¹Gawayne and the gay burde · togeder thay seten,
Even inmiddes, as the messe · metely come,
1005 And sithen thurgh al the sale², · as hem best semed,
Bi eche grome at his degre · graythely was served.
Ther was mete, ther was mirthe, · ther was much joye,
That for to telle therof · hit me tene were,
And to pointe hit yet · I pined me paraventure;
1010 Bot yet I wot that Wawen · and the wale burde
Such comfort of her³ compaynye · caghten togeder
Thurgh her dere daliaunce · of her derne wordes,
With clene cortais carp⁴ · closed fro filthe;
And hor play was passande · eche prince gomen,
1015   in vayres⁵.
          Trumpes and nakeris,
          Much pipyng ther repaires;
          Eche mon tented his,
          And thay two tented thaires.

1020 Much dut was ther driven · that day and that other,
And the third as thro · thronge in therafter;
The joye of sain John's day · was gentile to here,
And was the last of the layk · leudes ther thoghten.
Ther werd gestes to go · upon the gray morne,
1025 Forthy wonderly thay woke, · and the win dronken,
Daunsed ful dreghly · with dere caroles;
⁶At the last, when hit was late, · thay lachen her leve,
Echon to wende on his way · that was wighe stronge.
Gawayne gef him god day, · the god mon him lachches,
1030 Ledes him to his awen chambre, · the chimne byside,

1. 'Gawain and the pretty lady sat together' (while the lord sat with the
old hag), 2. hall, 3. their (their mutual), 4. conversation, 5. in truth,
indeed, 6. The season's festivities over, the guests depart and Gawain goes
to his room, where his host asks him to stay longer.

And there he drawes him on driye, · and derely him thonkkes
Of the winne worschip · that he him wayved hade,
As to honour his house · on that highe tide,
And enbelise his burgh · with his bele chere.

1035 'I-wisse sir, whil I leve, · me worthes the better
That Gawayne has ben my gest · at Goddes awen fest'.
'Grant merci, sir,' quoth Gawayne, · 'in god fayth hit is youres,
Al the honour is your awen – · the heghe King you yelde!
And I am wighe at your wille · to worch youre hest,

1040 As I am halden therto, · in highe and in lowe,
        bi right.'
        The lorde fast can him paine
        To holde lenger the knight;
        To hym answares Gawayne,
1045   Bi non way that he might.

Then frained the freke · ful faire at himselven
What derve dede had him driven · at that dere time
So kenly fro the kinges kourt · to kaire al his one,
Er the halidayes holly · were halet out of toun.

1050 'For sothe, sir,' quoth the segge, · 'ye sain bot the trawthe,
A heghe ernde[1] and a hasty · me hade fro tho wones,
For I am sumned myselfe · to sech to a place,
I ne wot in worlde whederwarde · to wende hit to finde;
I nolde bot if I hit negh might · on New Yeres morne,

1055 For alle the londe inwith Logres, · so me oure lorde help!
Forthy, sir, this enquest · I require you here,
That ye me telle with trawthe · if ever ye tale herde
Of the Grene Chapel, · where hit on grounde stondes,
And of the Knight that hit kepes, · of colour of Grene.

1060 Ther was stabled bi statut · a steven[2] us betwene
To mete that mon at that mere, · if I might last;
And of that ilk New Yere · bot neked now wontes,
And I wolde loke on that lede, · if God me let wolde,
Gladloker, bi Goddes Son, · then any god welde!

1065 Forthi, I-wisse, bi youre wille · wende me bihoves,
Naf I now to busy · bot bare thre dayes,

1. errand, 2. tryst.

And me als fain to falle feye · as faily of min ernde.'
[1]Thenne laghande quoth the lorde, · 'Now leng thee behoves,
For I shal teche you to that terme · bi the tymes ende,
1070 The Grene Chapayle upon grounde · greve you no more;
Bot ye shal be in youre bed, · burne, at thin ese,
While forth dayes, and ferk · on the first of the Yere,
And cum to that merk at midmorn, · to make what you likes
in spenne.
1075   Dowelles[2] while New Yeres Daye,
         And ris, and raykes thenne,
         Mon shal you sette in waye,
         Hit is not two mile henne.'
Thenne was Gawayne ful glad, · and gomenly he laghed, –
1080 'Now I thonk you thrivandely · thurgh alle other thinge,
Now acheved is my chaunce, · I shal at your wille
Dowelle, and elles · do what ye demen'.
Thenne sesed him the sire, · and set him biside,
[3]Let the ladies be fette · to like hem the better;
1085 Ther was seme solace · by hemself stille;
The lorde let for luf · lotes so miry,
[4]As wigh that wolde of his witc, · ne wist what he might.
Thenne he carped to the knight · criande loude,
'Ye han demed to do · the dede that I bidde;
1090 Wil ye halde this hes · here at this ones?'
'Ye, sir, for sothe,' · said the segge true;
'Whyl I bide in youre borghe, · be bain to youre hest.'
'For ye haf travayled,' quoth the tulk, · 'towen fro ferre,
And sithen waked me with, · ye arn not wel warist
1095 Nauther of sostnaunce ne of slepe · sothly I knowe;
[5]Ye shal lenge in your lofte, · and lie in your ese
To-morn while the messewhile, · and to mete wende
When ye wyl, with my wyf, · that with you shal sitte

1. The lord promises Gawain that he will see he does not miss his appointment at the Green Chapel if he remains a guest until New Year's Day, 2. dwell,
3. The lord 'Ordered the ladies be brought to please him the more', 4. 'Like
a man who was about to go out of his mind and knew not what he was
doing', 5. Until he sets out in his quest Gawain is to lie in bed at his ease
and recuperate his strength.

And comfort you with compayny, · ¹til I to cort torne,
1100   ye lende;
     And I shal erly rise,
     On hunting wil I wende.'
     Gawain grantes alle thise,
     Him heldande, as the hende.

1105 'Yet firre,' quoth the freke, · 'a forwarde² we make:
 ³What-so-ever I winne in the wod · hit worthes to youres,
And what chek so ye acheve · chaunge me therforne.
Swete, swap we so, · sware with trawthe,
Whether, leude, so limp · 'lere other better.'
1110 'Bi God,' quoth Gawayne the gode,' · 'I grant thertille,
And that you list for to layke · lef hit me thinkes.'
'Who bringes us this beverage, · this bargayn is maked':
So saide the lorde of that lede · thay laghed ech one,
Thay dronken and daylyeden · and dalten untitel,
1115 Thise lordes and ladies, · while that hem liked;
And sithen with frenkisch fare · and fele faire lotes
Thay stoden and stemed · and stilly speken,
Kisten ful comlyly · ⁵and kaghten her leve.
With mony leude ful light · and lemande torches
1120 Eche burne to his bed · was broght at the laste,
         ful softe.
     To bed er yet thay yede,
     Recorded covenauntes ofte;
     The olde lorde of that leude
1125   Couthe wel halde layk alofte.

1. 'Until I return home you stay where you are', 2. pact, 3. 'Whatso-ever I win in the wilds (while out hunting) belongs to you, (So) whatever you get (while remaining in the castle at ease) you give to me in exchange. 4. 'for better or worse', 5. 'and took their leave (of each other)'.

III

Ful erly bifore the day · the folk uprisen,
Gestes that go wolde · hor gromes thay calden,
And thay busken up bilive[1] · blonkkes[2] to sadel,
Tyffen her takles, · trussen her males,
1130 Richen hem the richest, · to ride alle arayde,
    [3]Lepen up lightly, · lachen her brideles,
Eche wighe on his way · wher him wel liked.
The leve lorde of the londe · was not the last
Arayed for the riding, · with renkkes ful mony;
1135 Ete a sop hastily, · when he hade herde masse,
With bugle to bent-felde · he buskes bilive;
By that any daylight · lemed upon erthe,
He with his hatheles · on highe horsses weren.
Thenne thise cacheres[4] that couthe · coupled hor houndes,
1140 Unclosed the kenel dore · and calde hem theroute,
Blewe bigly in bugles · thre bare mote;
Braches bayed therfore · and breme noise maked,
And thay chastised and charred · on chasing that went,
A hundreth of hunteres, · as I haf herde telle,
1145   of the best.
      [5]To tristors vewters yod,
      Couples huntes of kest;
      Ther ros for blastes gode
      Gret rurd[6] in that forest.

1150 At the first quethe[7] of the quest · quaked the wylde;
Der drof in the dale, · doted for drede,
Highed to the highe, · bot heterly thay were
    [8]Restayed with the stabile, · that stoutly ascried.
Thay let the herttes haf the gate, · with the highe hedes,
1155 The breme bukkes also, · with hor brode paumes;
For the fre lorde hade defende · in fermisoun time[9]
That ther shulde no mon meve · to the male dere.

1. quickly, 2. horses, 3. 'Lept up (on their steeds) lightly, caught up their bridles', 4. kennel-men, 5. 'To stations the dog-keepers went ...', 6. uproar, 7. outcry, 8. 'Restrained by the cordon of beaters', 9. in the close-season.

The hindes were halden in · with *Hay!* and *War!*
The does driven with gret din · to the depe slades;
1160 Ther might mon se, as thay slipte, · slenting of arwes
[1]At eche wende under wande · wapped a flone –
That bigly bote on the broun · with ful brode hedes.
What! thay brayen, and bleden, · bi bonkkes thay deyen.
And ay rachches[2] in a res · radly hem folwes,
1165 Hunteres with highe horne · hasted hem after
With such a crakkande cry · as kliffes hade brusten;
What wilde so atwaped · wighes that shotten
Was al toraced and rent · at the resayt.
Bi thay were tened at the highe · and taysed to the wattres.
1170 The ledes were so lerned · at the lowe tristeres,
And the grehoundes so grete, · that geten hem bilive,
And hem to-filched, as fast · as frekes might loke,
                    ther right.
          The lorde for blis abloy
1175   Ful oft con launce and light,
          And drof that day with joy
          Thus to the derk night.

Thus laykes[3] this lorde · by linde-wodes eves,
[4]And Gawayne the god mon · in gay bed liges,
1180 Lurkkes whil the daylight · lemed on the wowes,
Under covertour ful clere, · cortined aboute;
And as in slomering he slode, · sleyly he herde
A littel din at his dor, · and derfly upon;
And he heves up his hed · out of the clothes,
1185 A corner of the cortin · he caght up a littel,
And waites warly thiderwarde · what hit be might.
Hit was the ladi, · lofliest to beholde,
That drow the dor after hir · ful dernly and stille,
And bowed towarde the bed; · and the burne[5] shammed,
1190 And layde him down listily, · and let as he slepte.
And ho stepped stilly · and stel to his bedde,

---

1. 'At each turning in the wood sped an arrow', 2. hounds, 3. sports, 'larks', 4. While the lord is out hunting, Gawain lies in his comfortable bed, 'concealed while the daylight gleams on the walls', 5. the man.

Kest up the cortin · and creped withinne,
And set hir ful softly · on the bed-side,
And lenged there selly longe, · to loke when he wakened.
1195 The lede lay lurked · a ful longe while,
Compast in his concience · to what that case might
Meve other amount: · to mervaile him thoght.
Bot yet he sayde in himself, · 'More semly hit were
To aspye with my spelle · in space what ho wolde'.
1200 Then he wakenede, and wroth[1], · and to hir warde torned,
And unlouked his eye-lyddes · and let as him wondered,
[2]And sayned him, as bi his saye · the saver to worthe,
    with hande.
    With chinne and cheke ful swete,
1205   Bothe white and red in blande[3],
    [4]Ful lufly con ho lete
    With lyppes smal laghande.

'God moroun, Sir Gawayne,' · saide that gay lady,
'Ye ar a sleper unslye, · that mon may slide hider;
1210 [5]Now are ye tan astit! · Bot true us may shape,
I shal binde you in your bedde, · that be ye trayst!':
[6]Al laghande the lady · lanced tho bourdes.
'Goud moroun, gay,' · quoth Gawayne the blythe,
'Me shal worthe at your wille, · and that me wel likes,
1215 For I yelde me yederly, · and yeye[7] after grace,
And that is the best, be my dome, · for me bihoves nede';
And thus he bourded again[8] · with mony a blithe laghter.
'Bot wolde ye, lady lovely, · then leve me grante,
[9]And deprece your prisoun, · and pray him to rise,
1220 I wolde bowe[10] of this bed, · and busk me better,
[11]I shulde kever the more comfort · to karp you with.'
'Nay for sothe, beau sir,' · said that swete,
'Ye shal not rise of your bedde, · I rich you better,

1. stretched himself, 2. 'And signed himself (i.e. crossed himself), so as to be safer by his prayers', 3. mingling, 4. 'Very charmingly she conducted herself with her delicate laughing lips', 5. 'Now you are captured straight-away!', 6. 'All laughing, the lady uttered these jests', 7. cry eagerly for, 8. jested again in return, 9. 'And release your prisoner', 10. leave, 11. 'I should obtain more comfort (were I risen from my bed) for chatting with you'.

I shal happe you here · that other half als,
1225 And sithen carp with my knight · that I caght have;
For I wene wel, i-wisse, · Sir Wowen ye are,
That alle the worlde worchipes, · where-so ye ride;
Your honour, your hendelayk · is hendely praised
With lordes, with ladies, · with alle that lyf bere.
1230 And now ye are here, i-wisse, · [1]and we bot oure one;
My lorde and his ledes · ar on lenthe faren,
Other burnes in her bedde, · and my burdes als,
The dor drawen and dit · with a derf haspe;
And sithen I have in this hous · him that al likes,
1235 I shal ware my while wel, · while hit lastes,
                    with tale.
            [2]Ye are welcum to my cors,
            Youre awen won to wale,
            Me behoves of fine force
1240   Your servaunt be, and shale.'

'In god faith,' quoth Gawayne, · 'gain hit me thinkkes,
Thagh I be not now he · that ye of speken;
To reche to such reverence · as ye reherce here
I am wighe unworthy, · I wot wel myselven.
1245 Bi God, I were glad, · and you god thoght,
At sawe other at servyce · that I sette might
To the plesaunce of your pris, – · hit were a pure joye.'
'In god faith, Sir Gawayne,' · quoth the gay lady,
'The pris and the prowes · that pleses al other,
1250 If I hit lakked, other set at light, · hit were littel dainte;
Bot hit ar ladies innoghe · [3]that lever wer nouthe
Haf thee, hende, in hor holde, · as I thee habbe here,
To daly with derely · your daynte wordes,
Kever hem[4] comfort · and colen her cares,
1255 Then much of the garisoun[5] · other golde that thay haven.
Bot I love that ilke lorde · that the lifte haldes,
I haf hit holly in my honde · that al desires,
                    thurghe grace.'

1. 'And we are by ourselves', 2. 'You are welcome to my body'; but
Gawain manages to resist her advances whilst remaining courteous, 3. 'Whom
it would delight more now', 4. obtain themselves, 5. treasure.

Sho made him so gret chere,
1260   That was so fair of face,
The knight with speches skere
Answered to eche a case.

[1]'Madame,' quoth the miry mon, · 'Mary you yelde,
For I haf founden, in god faith, · youre fraunchis nobelle;
1265   And other ful much of other folk · fongen hor dedes,
Bot the daynte that thay delen · for my disert nysen[2];
Hit is the worchip of yourself, · that noght bot wel connes.'
'Bi Mary,' quoth the menskful, · 'me think hit an other;
For were I worth al the wone · of wymmen alive,
1270   And al the wele of the worlde · were in my honde,
And I shulde chepen and chose · to cheve me a lorde,
For the costes that I haf knowen · upon thee, knight, here,
Of bewte and debonerte · and blythe semblaunt,
And that I haf er herkkened · and halde hit here truee,
1275   Ther shulde no freke upon folde · bifore you be chosen.'
'I-wisse, worthy,' quoth the wighe, · 'ye haf waled wel better,
Bot I am proude of the pris · that ye put on me,
And, soberly your servaunt, · my soverayn I holde you,
And youre knight I becom, · and Krist you foryelde.'
1280   Thus thay meled of muchwhat · til midmorn paste,
And ay the lady let lik · as him loved mich;
[3]The freke ferde with defence, · and feted ful faire.
Thagh ho were burde brightest, · the burne in minde hade,
The lasse luf in his lode · for lur that he soght
1285   boute hone;
The dunte that schulde him deve,
And nedes hit most be done.
The lady thenn spek of leve,
He granted hir ful sone.

1290   Thenne ho[4] gef him god day, · and with a glent laghed,

1. The sense of the following is that Gawain, while remaining chaste,
pledges himself to be the lady's knight. 2. exaggerate. 3. 'The man adopted
the tactics of defence and yet behaved very graciously. Though she were the
fairest woman, the man had love less in mind on his journey because of the
harm he soght ...' (i.e. the Green Knight's blow). 4. she.

And as he stod, ho stonied him · with ful stor wordes:
'Now he that spedes eche spech · this disport yelde you!
[1]Bot that ye be Gawayne, · hit gots in minde'.
'Wherfore?' quoth the freke, · and freshly he askes,
1295   Ferde lest he hade failed · in fourme of his castes;
Bot the burde him blessed, · and bi this skil sayde:
'So god as Gawayne · gainly is halden,
And cortaysye is closed · so clene in himselven,
Couth not lightly haf lenged · so long with a lady,
1300   Bot he had craved a cosse, · bi his courtaysye,
Bi sum touch of summe trifle · at sum tales ende'.
Then quoth Wowen: 'I-wisse, · worthe as you likes;
I shal kisse at your comaundement, · as a knight falles,
And fire, lest he displese you, · so plede hit no more'.
1305   Ho comes nerre with that, · and caches him in armes,
Loutes luflich adoun · and the leude kisses.
Thay comly bikennen · to Kryst ayther other;
Ho dos hir forth at the dore · withouten din more;
And he riches him to rise · and rapes him sone,
1310   Clepes to his chamberlayn, · chose his wede,
Bowes forth, when he was boun, · blithely to masse;
And thenne he meved to his mete · that menskly him keped,
And made myry al day, · til the mone rised,
           with game.
1315   [2]Was never freke fayrer fonge
        Bitwene two so dingne dame,
        The alder and the yonge;
        Much solace set thay same.

And ay the lorde of the londe · is lent on his gamnes,
1320   To hunt in holtes and hethe · at hindes barayne,
Such a sowme[3] he ther slowe · bi that the sunne heldet,
Of does and of other dere, · to deme were wonder.
Thenne fersly thay flokked · in folk at the laste,

1. She pretends to believe that the man could not be Gawain, for Gawain – the prince of courtesy – would assuredly have craved a kiss from a lady on some pretext or other; Gawain gives her what she thus hints for. 2. 'Was never fellow better situated Between two such worthy females, The older and the young ...'. Meanwhile the lord of the castle is out hunting deer, 3. number.

And quikly of the quelled dere · a querray[1] thay maked.
1325 The best boghed therto · with burnes innoghe,
Gedered the grattest · of gres that ther were,
And didden hem derely undo · as the dede askes;
Serched hem at the asay · summe that ther were,
Two fingeres thay fonde · of the fowlest of alle;
1330 Sithen they slit the slot, · sesed the erber,
Shaved with a sharp knif, · and the shyre knitten;
Sithen ritte thay the foure limmes, · and rent of the hide,
Then brek thay the bale, – the baules out token,
Listily forlancing, · and bere of the knot;
1335 Thay griped to the gargulun, · and graithely departed
The wesaunt fro the wint-hole, · and walt out the guttes;
Then sher thay out the schulderes · with her sharp knives,
Haled hem by a littel hole, · to have hole sides;
Sithen britned thay the brest, · and braiden hit in twinne,
1340 And eft at the gargulun · bigines on thenne,
Rives hit up radly, · right to the bight,
Voides out the avanters, · and veraily therafter
Alle the rimes by the ribbes · radly thay lance;
So ride thay of by resoun · bi the rigge bones,
1345 Evenden to the haunche, · that henged alle samen,
And heven hit up al hole, · and hewen hit of there,
And that thay neme for the noumbles, · bi nome, as I trowe,
       by kinde;
     Bi the bight al of the thighes
1350   The lappes thay lance bihinde;
     To hewe hit in two thay highes,
     Bi the bakbon to unbinde.

1. a single heap or stack of all the deer killed. Then follows an account of the 'breaking up' of the animals killed, in which the technical names for the different parts of the animals are used. After this operation each member of the hunt receives his part of the deer, his perquisite, according to rule. This ceremonial distribution extends to the hounds who are thrown the liver, lights, paunch-skins together with morsels of bread soaked in the animals' blood. The whole episode in truth presents a *ritual* (as does the arming of Gawain in Fitt One) and it is as a ritual that the reader should understand it rather than that he should labour after the modern equivalents for the anatomical details of the slain deer.

Bothe the hede and the hals · thay hewen of thenne,
And sithen sunder thay the sides · swift from the chine,
1355 And the corbeles fee · thay kest in a greve;
Thenn thurled thay ayther thik side · thurgh bi the ribbe,
And henged thenne ayther · bi hoghes of the fourches,
Eche freke for his fee, · as falles for to have.
Upon a felle of the faire best · fede thay thair houndes
1360 With the liver and the lightes, · the lether of the paunches,
And bred bathed in blod · blende ther-amonges.
Baldely thay blew pris, · bayed thair rachches,
Sithen fonge thay her fleshe, · folden to home,
Strakande ful stoutly · mony stif motes.
1365 Bi that the daylight was done · the douthe was al wonen
Into the comly castel, · ther the knight bides
                    ful stille.
              With blis and bright fyr bette.
              The lorde is comen thertylle;
1370   When Gawayne with him mette,
              Ther was bot wele at wille.

Thenne comaunded the lorde in that sale · [1]to samen alle the
     meny,
Bothe the ladies on loghe[2] · to light with her burdes
Bifore alle the folk on the flette[3], · frekes he beddes
1375 Veraily his venisoun · to fech him biforne.
And al godly in gomen · Gawayne he called,
Teches him to the tales · of ful tait bestes,
    [4]Shewes him the shyree grece · shorne upon ribbes.
'How payes you this play? · Haf I pris wonnen?
1380 Have I thrivandely thonk · thurgh my craft served?'
'Yea i-wisse,' quoth that other wighe, · 'here is waith fairest
That I se this seven yere · in sesoun of winter.'
'And al I gif you, Gawayne,' · quoth the gome thenne,

1. 'To assemble all the company', 2. down to the hall, 3. on the floor,
4. The lord of the castle shows Gawain his kill and inquires if it is not
time to exchange their day's earnings with each other as had been bargained.
Hence Gawain takes the kill, and gives the lord the kiss which he had had
from the lady.

'For by acorde of covenaynt · ye crave hit as your awen.'
1385 'This is soth,' quoth the segge, · 'I say you that ilke:
That I haf worthily wonnen · this wones withinne,
I-wisse with as god wille · hit worthes to youres.'
He hasppes his faire hals · his armes withinne,
And kisses him as comlyly · as he couthe awyse:
1390 ''Tas you there my chevicaunce, · I cheved no more;
I vouche hit saf fynly, · thagh feler hit were.'
'Hit is god,' quoth the god mon, · 'grant mercy therfore.
Hit may be such, hit is the better, · and ye me breve wolde
¹Where ye wan this ilk wele · bi witte of yorselven?'
1395 'That was not forward,' quoth he, · 'frayst me no more
For ye haf tan that you tides, · trawe ye non other
ye mowe.'
Thay laghed, and made hem blithe,
With lotes that were to lowe.
1400 To soper thay yede as-swithe,
With daintes new innowe.

And sithen by the chimne · in chamber thay seten,
Wighes the walle² wyn · weghed to hem oft,
And efte in her bourding³ · ⁴thay baythen in the morn
1405 To fille the same forwardes · that thay bifore maden:
Wat chaunce so bitides · hor chevisaunce to chaunge,
What newes so thay nome, · at naght when thay metten.
Thay acorded of the covenauntes · bifore the court alle;
The beverage was broght forth · in bourde at that time,
1410 Thenne thay lovelich leghten · leve at the last,
Eche burne to his bedde · busked bilive.
Bi that the coke hade crowen · and cakled bot thrise,
The lorde was lopen of his bedde, · the leudes ech one;
So that the mete and the masse · was metely delivered,
1415 The douthe⁵ dressed to the wod, · er any day sprenged,
to chace;

1. 'Where won you this bounty? By your own wit?' 'That was not included in the bargain (to tell the source of our day's gains)', replied Gawain,
2. excellent, 3. (in their) joking, 4. They agreed to repeat the bargain for
to-morrow, i.e. to exchange their day's earnings, 5. company.

Hegh with hunte and hornes
Thurgh plaines thay passe in space,
Uncoupled among tho thornes
1420 Raches[1] that ran on race.

Sone thay calle of a quest · in a ker[2] side,
The hunt rehayted the houndes · that hit first minged,
Wilde wordes him warp · with a wrast noice;
The houndes that hit herde · hastid thider swithe,
1425 And fellen as fast to the fuyt[3], · fourty at ones;
[4]Thenne such a glaver ande glam · of gedered rachches
Ros, that the rocheres · rungen aboute;
Hunteres hem hardened · with horne and with muthe.
Then al in a semble · sweyed togeder,
1430 [5]Bitwene a flosche in that frith · and a foo cragge;
In a knot bi a cliffe, · at the kerre side,
Ther as the rogh rocher · unridely was fallen,
Thay ferden to the findyng, · and frekes hem after;
Thay umbekesten[6] the knarre · and the knot bothe,
1435 Wighes, while they wisten wel · withinne hem hit were,
The best that ther breved was · with the blodhoundes.
Thenne thay beten on the buskes, · and bede him uprise,
And he unsoundily out soght · segges overthwert;
On the sellokest swin[7] · swenged out there,
1440 Long sithen fro the sounder · that wight forolde,
[8]For he was breme, · bor alther grattest,
Ful grimme when he gronied, · thenne greved mony,
For thre at the first thrast[9] · he thright[10] to the erthe,
And sped forth good sped · boute spit more.
1445 This other halowed *highe!* ful high, · and *hay! hay!* cried,
Haden hornes to mouthe, · heterly rechated[11];
Mony was the miry mouthe · of men and of houndes
That buskkes after this bor · with bost and with noise
to quelle.

1. hounds, 2. thicket, 3. track, 4. '... such an uproar and din from gathered hounds', 5. 'Between a pool in that wood and a fearful cliff-edge', 6. searched all about, 7. 'The hugest of wild boars', 8. 'For he was broad-beamed, a boar of the hugest sort', 9. thrust, 10. pushed, 11. vigorously sounded the 'assemble together' (signal on the horn).

1450   Ful oft he bides the baye,
        And maimes the mute inn melle[1];
        He hurtes of the houndes, and thay
        Ful gomerly yaule and yelle.

Shalkes[2] to shote at him · showen to thenne,
1455 Haled to him of her arewes, · hitten him oft;
  [3]Bot the pointes paired at the pith · that pight in his sheldes,
And the barbes of his browe · bit non wolde,
Thagh the shaven shaft · shindered in peces;
The hede hipped ayain · were-so-ever hit hitte.
1460 Bot when the dintes him dered · of her drighe strokes,
Then, brainwod[4] for bate, · on burnes he rases,
Hurtes hem ful heterly · wher he forth highes,
And mony arghed[5] therat, · and on lite drogen[6].
Bot the lorde on a light horse · launces him after,
1465 As burne bolde upon bent · his bugle he blowes,
He rechated, and rode · thurgh rones ful thik,
Suande[7] this wilde swyn · til the sunne shafted.
This day with this ilk dede · thay driven on this wise,
While oure luflich lede · lys in his bedde,
1470 Gawayne graithely at home, · in geres ful riche
              of hewe.
          The lady noght forgate,
          Com to him to salve,
          Ful erly ho was him at
1475   [8]His mode for to remue.

Ho[9] commes to the cortin, · and at the knight totes[10].
Sir Wawen her welcumed · worthy on first,
And ho him yeldes ayain, · ful yerne of hir wordes,
Settes hir sofly by his syde, · and swithely ho laghes,
1480 And with a luflich loke · ho laide him thise wordes:
'Sir, yif ye be Wawen, · wonder me thynkkes,
Wighe that is so wel wrast · alway to god,
And connes not of compaynye · the costes undertake,

---

1. in the midst, 2. men, 3. 'But the points (of the arrows) turned at the toughness embedded in his shoulders', 4. mad for prey, 5. were afraid, 6. backwards retreated, 7. chasing, 8. 'his mood to alter', 9. she, 10. peeps.

And if mon kennes you hom to knowe, · [1]ye kest hom of
  your minde;

1485 [2]Thou has forgeten yederly · that yisterday I taghtte
  By alder-truest token · of talk that I couthe.'
  'What is that?' quoth the wighe, · 'I-wisse I wot never;
  If hit be sothe that ye breve, · the blame is min awen.'
  [3]'Yet I kende you of kissing,' · quoth the clere thenne,

1490 'Where-so countenaunce is couthe, · quikly to claime,
  That bicumes eche a knight · that cortaysy uses.'
  'Do way,' quoth that derf mon, · 'my dere, that speche,
  For that durst I not do, · lest I denayed were;
  If I were werned, I were wrang, · I-wisse, if I profered.'

1495 'Ma fay,' quoth the mere wyf[4], · 'ye may not be werned,
  [5]Ye ar stif innoghe to constrayne · with strenkthe, yif you lykes,
  Yif any were so vilanous · that you devaye wolde.'
  'Ye, be God,' quoth Gawayne, · 'good is your speche,
  Bot threte is unthrivande · in thede ther I lende,

1500 And eche gift that is geven · not with goud wille.
  I am at your comaundement, · to kisse when you likes,
  Ye may lach when you list, · and leve when you thinkkes,
    in space.'
      The lady loutes adoun,
1505   And comlyly kisses his face,
      Much speche thay ther expoun
      Of druries[6] greme and grace.

'I woled wit at you, wighe,' · that worthy ther saide,

1. 'you cast him out of your mind', 2. 'You have forgotten what I taught
you yesterday By the very truest token of the kind of conversation that I am
able to manage' – the allusiveness is deliberate. See next footnote, 3. ' "Nevertheless I taught you something about kissing," said the beautiful (lady) then'.
She implies that a knight should claim a kiss as a point of elegant manners,
4. merry woman, 5. 'You are strong enough to take a kiss by force, if you
liked, If there were any woman so loutish as to refuse you.' After this exchange
of gay and subtle humour the lady wins – she kisses him, 6. love's, 7. in the
passage that follows the lady taunts him. Gawain is young, sprightly, and alert,
and the practice of love is the most essential of all accomplishments. Yet here
she has come to sit by his bed-side for the second time running and Gawain
gives no sign of having any prowess whatever in love-making. He *ought* to
teach a young girl a trick or two, while her husband is away.

'And you wrathed not therwith, · what were the skille,
1510 That so yong and so yepe, · as ye at this time,
So cortayse, so knightyly, · as ye ar knowen oute –
And of alle chevalry to chose, · the chef thing alosed
Is the lel laik of luf, · the lettrure of armes;
For to telle of this teveling · of this true knightes,
1515 Hit is the titelet token, · and tixt of her werkkes,
How ledes for her lele luf · hor lives han auntered,
Endured for her drury · dulful stoundes,
And after wenged with her walour · and voyded her care,
And broght blisse into boure · with bountees hor awen –
1520 And ye ar knight comlokest · kid of your elde,
Your worde and your worchip · walkes aywhere,
And I haf seten by yourself · here sere twies,
Yet herde I never of your hed · helde no wordes
That ever longed to luf, · lasse ne more;
1525 And ye, that ar so cortays · and coint of your hetes,
Oghe to a yonke think · yern to shewe
And teche sum tokenes · of trueluf craftes.
Why! ar ye lewed, · that alle the los weldes?
Other elles ye demen me to dille · your daliaunce to herken?
1530   For shame!
         I com hider sengel, and sitte
         To lerne at you sum game;
         Dos, teches me of your witte,
         Whil my lorde is fro hame.'

1535 'In goud faithe,' quoth Gawayne, · 'God you foryelde!
Gret is the gode gle, · and gomen to me huge,
That so worthy as ye · wolde winne hidere,
And pine you with so pouer a mon, · as play with your knight
With anyskynnes countenaunce, · hit keveres me ese;
1540 Bot to take the torvayle to myself · to trueluf expoun,
And touche the temes of tixt · and tales of armes
To you that, I wot wel, · weldes more slight
Of that art, bi the half, · or a hundreth of seche
As I am, other ever shal, · in erde wer I leve,
1545 Hit were a fole felefolde, · my fre, by my trawthe.

I wolde youre wilning · worche at my might,
As I am highly bihalden, · and evermore wille
Be servaunt to yourselven, · so save me drighten!'
Thus him frained that fre, · and fondet him ofte,
1550 For to haf wonnen him to woghe[1], · what-so sho thought
    elles;
Bot he defended him so fair · that no faut semed,
Ne non evel on nawther halve, · nawther thay wisten
      bot blysse.
    Thay laghed and laiked longe;
1555   At the last sho con him kisse,
    Hir leve faire con sho fonge
    And went hir waye, I-wisse.

[2]Then ruthes him the renk, · and rises to the masse,
And sithen hor diner was dight · and derely served.
1560 The lede with the ladies · laiked alle day,
Bot the lorde[3] over the londes · launced ful ofte,
Sues his uncely swyn, · that swinges bi the bonkkes
And bote the best of his braches · the bakkes in sunder
Wher he bode in his bay, · tel bawemen hit breken,
1565 [4]And madee him mawgref his hed · for to mue utter,
So felle flones ther flete · when the folk gedered.
Bot yet the stiffest to start · bi stoundes he made,
Til at the last he was so mat · he might no more renne,
Bot in the hast that he might · he to a hole winnes
1570 Of a rasse bi a rokk · ther rennes the boerne.
He gete the bonk at his bak, · bigines to scrape,
The frothe femed at his mouth · unfaire bi the wikes,
Whettes his white tusches; · with him then irked
Alle the burnes[5] so bolde · that him by stoden

---

1. sin. Gawain avoids sin and, at the same time, avoids giving offence to the lady's feelings. They have a gay, good-humoured talk and then she kisses him and departs, 2. 'Then the man bestirs himself ...', 3. The lord of the castle meanwhile 'pursues his ferocious pig, which lurches by the banks, And bites the best of his hounds' backs in sunder', 4. 'And forced him – despite his head – to move out into the open, So fell the swift arrows there ...', 5. men (the hunters).

1575 To nye him on-ferum[1], · bot neghe him non durst
           for wothe;
        He hade hurt so mony biforne
        That al thught thenne ful lothe
        Be more with his tusches torne,
1580   [2]That breme was and brainwod bothe.

Til the knight com himself, · kachande his blonk[3],
Sees him bide at the bay, · his burnes biside;
[4]He lights luflich adoun, · leves his corsour,
Braides out a bright bront, · and bigly forth strides,
1585 Foundes fast thurgh the forth · wer the felle[5] bides.
The wilde was war of the wighe · with weppen in honde,
[6]Hef highly the here, · so hetterly he fnast
That fele ferde for the freke, · lest felle him the worre.
The swyn settes him out · on the segge even.
1590 That the burne and the bor · were bothe upon hepes
In the wightest of the water. · The worre hade that other,
For the mon merkkes him wel, · as thay mette first,
Set sadly the sharp · in the slot even,
Hit him up to the hult, · that the hert shindered,
1595 And he yarrande him yelde, · and yed over the water
           ful tyt.
        A hundreth houndes him hent,
        That bremely con him bite,
        Burnes him broght to bent,
1600   And dogges to dethe endite.

There was blawing of prys · in mony breme horne,
Heghe halowing on highe · with hatheles that might;
Brachetes bayed that best, · as bidden the maysteres
Of that chargeaunt chace · that were chef huntes,
1605 Thenne a wighe that was wys · upon wodcraftes
To unlace this bor · lufly biginnes.

1. at a distance, 2. 'That (the boar) was both randy and mad', 3. steed,
4. 'He alights easily, leaves his horse, Draws out a bright sword ...', 5. brute,
6. '(The boar) raised up his bristles, so savagely he snorted That many men
(the hunters) feared for the man, lest the man got the worst of it (in the fight).'
But the man does, in fact, succeed in stabbing the boar to the hult.

First he hewes of his hed · and on highe settes,
And sithen rendes him al roghe · bi the rygge after,
[1]Braydes out the boweles, · brennes hom on glede,
1610 With bred blent therwith · his braches rewardes.
Sithen he britnes out the brawen · in bright brode cheldes,
And has out the hastlettes, · as hightly bisemes;
And yet hem halches al hole · the halves togeder,
And sithen on a stif stange · stoutly hem henges.
1615 Now with this ilk swyn · thay swengen to home;
The bores hed was borne · bifore the burnes selven
That him forferde in the forthe · thurgh forse of his honde
so stronge.
Til he see Sir Gawayne
1620 In halle him thoght ful longe;
He calde, and he com gayn
His fees ther for to fonge.

The lorde ful lowde with lote, · and laghed myry,
When he see Sir Gawayne. · With solace he spekes.
1625 The goude ladies were geten, · and gedered the meiny[2].
He schewes hem[3] the scheldes, · and shapes hem the tale
Of the largesse and the lenthe, · the lithernes[4] alse
Of the were of the wilde swyn · in wod wer he fled.
That other knight ful comly · comended his dedes,
1630 And praised hit as gret prys · that he proved hade,
For suche a brawne of a best, · the bolde burne sayde,
Ne such sides of a swyn · segh he never are.
Thenne hondeled thay the hoge hed, · the hende mon hit
praysed,
And let lodly therat · the lorde for to here.
1635 'Now, Gawayne,' quoth the god mon, · 'this gomen is
your awen
Bi fyn forwarde and faste, · faithely ye knowe.'

---

1. The hounds receive their perquisite – the boar's bowels mixed with
bread heated. The rest of the boar is then broken up, and the hunters return
home, the head of the slain animal borne before the lord (of the castle) who
had killed him. On arrival, he calls for Gawain so that they may exchange
their day's earnings as agreed, 2. company, 3. them, 4. bestial ferocity.

'Hit is sothe,' quoth the segge, · 'and as siker true
Alle my get I shal you gif · again, bi my trawthe.'
[1]He hent the hathel aboute the halse, · and hendely him kisses,
1640 And eftersones of the same · he served him there.
'Now ar we even,' quoth the hathel, · 'in this eventide
Of alle the covenauntes that we knit, · sithen I com hider,
              bi lawe.'
              The lorde sayde, 'Bi saynt Gile,
1645   Ye ar the best that I knowe!
              [2]Ye ben riche in a while,
              Such chaffer an ye drowe!'

Thenne thay teldet tables · trestels alofte,
Kesten clothes upon; · clere light thenne
1650 Wakned bi wowes[3], · waxen torches.
Segges sette and served · in sale al aboute;
Much glam and gle · glent up therinne
Aboute the fire upon flet, · [4]and on fele wyse
At the soper and after, · mony athel songes,
1655 As coundutes of Krystmasse · and caroles newe
With al the manerly merthe · that mon may of telle,
And ever oure luflich knight · the lady bisyde.
Such semblaunt to that segge · semly ho[5] made
With stille stollen countenaunce, · that stalworth to plese,
1660 That al forwondered was the wighe, · and wroth with
              himselven,
              [6]Bot he nolde not for his nurture · nurne hir ayaynes,
Bot dalt with hir al in dainte, · how-se-ever the dede turned
              towrast.
              When thay hade played in halle
1665   As longe as hor wille hom last,
              To chambre he con him calle,
              And to the chemne thay past.

1. Gawain gets the trophy of the hunt in exchange for the two kisses,
2. 'You will be rich if you carry on such trade', 3. walls, 4. 'And on many
occasions At both supper and afterwards many fine songs ...', 5. she,
6. Gawain, on account of his breeding, would not fail to 'respond' to the
lady's amorous glances even though their purpose bewildered him.

Ande ther thay dronken, and dalten[1], · and demed eft new
To norne on the same note · on Newe Yeres even;
1670 Bot the knight craved leve · to kayre[2] on the morn,
For hit was negh at the terme · that he to schulde.
The lorde him letted of that, · to lenge him resteyed,
And sayde, 'As I am true segge, · I siker my trawthe
Thou schal cheve to the grene chapel · thy charres[3] to make,
1675 Leude, on New Yeres light, · longe bifore pryme.
Forthy thou lye in thy loft · and lach thyn ese,
And I shal hunt in this holt, · and halde the touches,
Chaunge with the chevisaunce, · bi that I charre hider;
For I haf fraysted thee twys, · and faithful I fynde thee.
1680 Now "thrid time throwe best" · thenk on the morne,
Make we mery whyl we may · and minne upon joye,
For the lur may mon lach · when-so mon likes.'
This was grathely graunted, · and Gawayne is lenged,
Blithe broght was him drink, · and thay to bedde yeden
1685   with light.
              Sir Gawayne lis and slepes
              Ful stille and softe al night;
              The lorde that his craftes kepes,
              Ful erly he was dight.

1690 After messe a morsel · he and his men token;
Miry was the mornyng, · his mounture he askes.
Alle the hatheles that on horse · shulde helden him after
Were boun busked on hor blonkkes · bifore the halle gates.
Ferly fayre was the folde, · for the forst clenged;
1695 [4]In rede, rudede upon rak, · rises the sunne,
And ful clere costes · the cloudes of the welkin.
Hunteres unhardeled[5] · bi a holt syde,
[6]Rocheres roungen bi rys · for rurde of her hornes;
Summe fel in the fute · wer the fox bade,
1700 Trailes ofte a traveres · bi traunt of her wiles;
A kenet[7] kries therof, · the hunt on him calles;

1. contended, 2. travel, 3. affairs, 4. 'In red, reddened upon cloud-rack, rises the sun', 5. unleashed (the hounds), 6. 'Rocks rang aloud in the woods from noise of their horns', 7. small dog.

His felawes fallen him to, · that fnasted ful thike,
Runnen forth in a rabel · in his right fare,
And he fiskes hem bifore. · Thay founden him sone,
1705 And when thay seghe him with sight · thay sued him fast,
Wreyande him ful weterly · with a wroth noise;
And he trantes[1] and tornayees · thurgh mony tene greve,
Havilounes[2], and herkenes · bi hegges ful ofte.
At the last bi a littel dich · he lepes over a spenne[3],
1710 Steles out ful stilly · bi a strothe rande[4],
Went haf wilt of the wode, · with wiles fro the houndes;
[5]Thenne was he went, er he wist, · to a wale trister,
Ther thre thro at a thrich · thrat him at ones,
      al graye.
1715   He blenched agayn bilive
            And stifly start on-stray,
            With alle the wo on live
            To the wod he went away.

Thenne was hit lif upon list · to lithen[6] the houndes
1720 When alle the mute[7] hade him met, · menged togeder:
Suche a sorwe at that sight · thay sette on his hede
As alle the clamberande cliffes · hade clatered on hepes;
Here he was halawed, · when hatheles him metten,
Loude he was gayned · with garande speche;
1725 Ther he was threted · and ofte thef called,
And ay the titleres at his tayl, · that tary he ne might;
Ofte he was runnen at, · when he out rayked,
And ofte reled in agayn, · so Reniarde was wily,
And ye he lad hem bi lagmon, · the lorde and his meyny,
1730 [8]On this maner bi the mountes · while mid-over-under,
Whyle the hende knight at home · holsumly slepes
Withinne the comly cortines, · on the colde morne.
Bot the lady for luf · let not to slepe,
Ne the purpose to payre[9] · that pight in hir hert,

---

1. dodges and doubles. 2. redoubles on his tracks. 3. spinny. 4. edge of
a wood. 5. 'Then had he come upon, before he knew it, a hunting station
Where three fierce dogs at a rush attacked him together ...' (However, the fox
evades thém and is off again into the wood). 6. hear. 7. the pack of hounds.
8. While the fox hunt was in progress Gawain was dozing cosily in bed. 9. fail.

1735 Bot ros hir up radly, · rayked hir theder
In a mery mantyle, · mete to the erthe,
That was furred ful fyne · with felles wel pured,
No hues goud on hir hede · bot the hager stones
Trased aboute hir tressour · be twenty in clusteres;
1740 Hir thryven face and hir throte · throwen al naked,
Hir brest bare bifore, · and bihinde eke.
Ho comes withinne the chambre dore, · and closes hit hir
after,
Wayves up a wyndow, · and on the wighe calles,
And radly thus rehayted him · with hir richewordes,
1745 with chere:
‘A! mon, how may thou slepe,
This morning is so clere?’
He was in drowping depe,
Bot thenne he con hir here.

1750 In drey drouping of dreme · draveled[1] that noble,
As mon that was in morning · of mony thro thoghtes,
How that destine shulde that day · dele him his wyrde[2]
At the Grene Chapel, · when he the gome metes,
And bihoves his buffet abide · withoute debate more;
1755 Bot when that comly[3] com · he kevered his wittes,
Swenges out of the swevenes[4], · and swares with hast.
The lady luflich com · laghande swete,
Felle over his faire face, · and fetly him kyssed;
He welcumes hir worthily · with a wale[5] chere.
1760 He see hir so glorious · and gayly atired,
So fautles of hir fetures · and of so fine hewes,
Wight[6] wallande joye · warmed his hert.
With smothe smyling and smolt[7] · thay smeten into merthe,
That al was blis and bonchef · that breke hem bitwene,
1765 and wynne[8].
Thay lanced wordes gode,
Much wele then was therinne;

1. muttered, 2. fate, 3. that comely lady, 4. dreams, 5. gracious, 6. ardent,
7. gentle, 8. joy.

[1]Gret perile bitwene hem stod,
  Nif Mare of hir knight mynne.

1770 [2]For that princece of pris · depresed him so thikke,
  Nurned him so neghe the thred, · that nede him bihoved
  Other lach ther hir luf, · other lodly refuse.
  He cared for his cortaysye, · lest crathayn[3] he were,
  And more for his meschef, · if he schulde make sinne,
1775   And be traytor to that tolke[4] · that that telde aght[5].
  'God shylde,' quoth the shalk, · 'that shal not befalle!'
  With luf-laghing a lit · he layd him bisyde
  Alle the speches of specialte · that sprange of her mouthe.
  Quoth that burde to that burne, · 'Blame ye disserve,
1780   Yif ye luf not that lyf · that ye lie nexte
  Bifore alle the wighes in the world · wounded in hert,
  Bot if ye haf a lemman, a lever, · that you likes better,
  And folden fayth to that fre, · festned so harde
  That you lausen[6] ne list – · and that I leve nouthe;
1785   And that ye telle me that now truly, · I pray you,
  For alle the lufcs upon live, · layne not the sothe
        for gile.'
      [7]The knight sayde, 'Be sayn Jon,'
      And smethely con he smyle,
1790   'In fayth I welde right non,
      Ne non wil welde the while'.

  'That is a worde' quoth that wight, · 'that worst is of alle,
  Bot I am swared[8] for sothe, · that sore me thinkkes.
  Kisse me now comly, · and I shal cach hethen,
1795   I may bot mourne upon molde, · as may that much loves.'
  Sikande[9] ho swewe doun · and semly him kissed,
  And sithen he severes him fro, · and says as ho stondes,
  'Now, dere, at this departyng, · do me this ese,
  Gif me sumwhat of thy gifte, · thi glove if hit were,

1. 'Great peril between them stood Had not Mary minded her knight',
2. 'For that dear lady importuned him so intensely, Urged him so near the
limit, that it became necessary for him Either to accept her love or roughly
repel it', 3. churl, 4. man, 5. (that that) house owned, 6. release, 7. Gawain
declares that there is *no* 'other woman', 8. answered, 9. sighing.

1800 [1]That I may minne on the, mon, · my mournyng to lassen'.
'Now I-wisse,' quoth that wighe, · 'I wolde I hade here
The levest thing for thy luf · that I in londe welde,
For ye haf deserved, for sothe, · sellyly ofte
More rewarde bi resoun · then I reche might;
1805 Bot to dele yow for drurye, · that dawed bot neked,
Hit is not your honour · to haf at this tyme
A glove for a garysoun · of Gawayne's giftes,
And I am here an erande · in erdes uncouthe,
And have no men with no males · with menskful thinges;
1810 That mislykes me, lady, · for luf at this tyme,
Iche tolke mon do as he is tan, · tas to non ille
                    ne pine.'
              'Nay, hende of highe honours,'
              Quoth that lufsum under lyne,
1815   'Thagh I hade noght of youres,
              Yet shulde ye have of myne.'

Ho raght him a riche rink[2] · of red golde werkes,
With a starande ston · stondande alofte
That bere blusschande bemes · as the bright sunne;
1820 Wit ye wel, hit was worth · wele ful hoge.
Bot the renk hit renayed[3], · and redily he sayde,
'I wil no giftes for gode, · my gay, at this tyme;
I haf none you to norne[4], · ne noght wil I take.'
Ho bede hit him ful bisily, · and he hir bode wernes,
1825 And swere swifte by his sothe · that he hit sese nolde.
And ho sore that he forsoke, · and sayde therafter,
'If ye renay my rink, · to riche for hit semes,
Ye wolde not so highly · halden be to me,
I shal gif you my girdel, · that gaines you lasse.'
1830 Ho laght a lace lightly · that leke umbe hir sydes,

1. 'That (with your glove as a keepsake) I may think on thee, man, my
grieving to lessen'. But Gawain has nothing to give that is worthy her receiving; he has with him no train of retainers bearing bags of treasures; no, he has
nothing good enough to give her. Nevertheless, *she* has something to give him,
2. ring, 3. refused, 4. offer. He refuses the ring but later – under pressure – accepts her gift of the green silk girdle.

Knit upon hir kirtel · under the clere mantile,
Gered hit was with grene silke · and with golde shaped,
Noght bot arounde brayden, · beten with fingres;
And that ho bede to the burne, · and blithely bisoght,
1835 Thagh hit unworthi were, · that he hit take wolde.
And he nay that he nolde · neghe in no wyse
Nauther golde ne garysoun, · er God him grace sende
To acheve to the chaunce · that he hade chosen there.
'And therfore, I pray yow, · displese yow noght,
1840 And lettes be your bisinesse, · for I baythe hit you never
      to graunte;
            I am derely to you biholde
            Bicause of your sembelaunt,
            And ever in hot and colde
1845   To be your true servaunt.'

[1]'Now forsake ye this silke,' · sayde the burde thenne,
'For hit is simple in hitself, · and so hit wel semes?
Lo! so hit is littel, · and lasse hit is worthy;
[2]Bot who-so knew the costes · that knit ar therinne,
1850 He wolde hit prayse at more prys, · paraventure;
[3]For what gome so is gorde · with this grene lace,
While he hit hade hemely · halched aboute,
Ther is no hathel under heven · tohewe him that might,
For he might not be slayn · for slight upon erthe.'
1855 Then kest the knight, · and hit come to his hert,
Hit were a juel for the joparde · that him jugged were,
When he acheved to the chapel · his chek for to fech;
Might he haf slipped to be unslayn, · the sleght were noble.
[4]Thenne he thulged with hir threpe · and tholed hir to speke,
1860 And ho bere on hym the belt · and bede hit hym swithe –

1. 'Do you refuse this silk (girdle),' said the lady then, 'Because it is simple in itself?...', 2. 'But whoever knew the virtues that are woven into it, He would esteem it more highly', 3. 'For whatever man is so girded with this green lace, While he has it firmly girdled on, There is no fellow under heaven that can slay him ...'. The girdle seems to Gawain such a sovereign remedy against the dangers of his coming engagement with the Green Knight that he accepts it. She enjoins him not to tell of the gift, 4. 'Then he complied with her insistence and suffered her to speak'.

And he granted – and him gafe · with a goud wille,
And bisoght hym, for hir sake, · discever hit never,
Bot to lelly layne fro hir lorde; · the leude him acordes
That never wighe shulde hit wit, · I-wysse, bot thay twayne

1865   for noghte;
       He thonkked hir oft ful swithe,
       Ful thro with hert and thoght.
       [1]Bi that on thrynne sïthe
       Ho has kist the knight so toght.

1870 Thenne lachches[2] ho hir leve, · and leves him there,
For more mirthe of that mon · moght ho not gete.
When ho was gon, Sir Gawayne · geres him sone,
Rises and riches him · in araye noble,
Lays up the luf-lace[3] · the lady him raght,
1875 [4]Hid hit ful holdely, · wher he hit eft fonde.
[5]Sithen chevely to the chapel · choses he the waye,
Prevely aproched to a prest, · and prayed him there
That he wolde lifte his lif · and lern him better
How his sawle shulde be saved · when he shuld seye hethen.
1880 There he shrof him shyrly · and shewed his misdedes,
Of the more and the minne, · and merci beseches,
And of absolucioun · he on the segge[6] calles;
And he asoiled him surely, · and sette him so clene
As domesday shulde haf ben · dight on the morn.
1885 And sithen he mace him as mery · among the fre ladies,
With comlich caroles · and alle kinnes joye,
As never he did bot that daye, · to the derk night,
           with blis.
       Eche mon hade daynte thare
1890   Of him, and sayde, 'I-wisse,
       Thus myry he was never are,
       Sin he com hider, er this'.

Now him lenge in that lee, · ther luf him bityde!

1. 'By that she has kissed thrice the knight so tough', 2. takes, 3. i.e. the girdle, 4. 'Concealed it very carefully', 5. Gawain then confesses, and receives absolution, and afterwards entertains the ladies, 6. man, i.e. the priest.

[1]Yet is the lorde on the launde · ledande his gomnes.

1895   He has forfaren this fox · that he folwed longe;
      As he sprent over a spenne · to spye the shrewe,
      Ther as he herd the houndes · that hasted him swithe,
      Renaud com richchande · thurgh a roghe greve,
      And alle the rabel in a res · right at his heles.

1900   The wighe was war of the wylde, · and warly abides,
      [2]And braydes out the bright bronde, · and at the best castes.
      And he shunt[3] for the sharp, · and shulde haf arered;
      A rach rapes him to, · right er he might,
      And right bifore the hors fete · thay fel on him alle,

1905   And woried me this wily · with a wroth noise.
      The lorde lightes bilive, · and caches him sone,
      Rased him ful radly · out of the rach mouthes,
      Haldes heghe over his hede, · halowes faste,
      And ther bayen him mony · brath houndes.

1910   Huntes highed hem theder · with hornes ful mony,
      Ay rechatande aright · til thay the renk seen.
      Bi that was comen · his compeyny noble,
      Alle that ever ber bugle · blowed at ones,
      And alle thise other halowed · that hade no hornes.

1915   Hit was the myriest mute · that ever men herde,
      The rich rurd that ther was · raysed for Renaude saule
              with lote.
          Hor houndes thay ther rewarde,
          Her hedes thay fawne and frote,
1920   And sithen thay tan Reynarde,
          And tyrven of his cote.

      And thenne thay helden to home, · for hit was niegh night,
      [4]Strakande ful stoutly · in hor store hornes.
      The lorde is light at the laste · at his lef home,
1925   Findes fire upon flet, · the freke ther-biside,
      Sir Gawayne the gode, · that glad was withalle,
      Among the ladies for luf · he ladde much joye.

1. 'Meanwhile (while Gawain is at ease in the castle) the lord in the country is pursuing his sport', 2. 'And draws out the bright sword', 3. flinched, 4. The hunting party return 'calling full boldly on their great horns'.

He were a bleaunt of blue · that bradde to the erthe,
His surkot semed him wel · that softe was forred,
1930 And his hode of that ilke · henged on his shulder,
Blande al of blaunner · were bothe al aboute.
He metes me this god mon · inmiddes the flore,
And al with gomen he him gret, · and goudly he sayde,
[1]'I shal fille upon first · oure forwardes nouthe,
1935 That we spedly han spoken, · ther spared was no drink'.
[2]Then acoles he the knight · and kisses him thries,
As saverly and sadly · as he hem sette couthe.
'Bi Kryst,' quoth that other knight, · [3]'Ye cach much sele
In chevisaunce of this chaffer, · if ye hade goud chepes.'
1940 'Ye, of the chepe no charg,' · quoth chefly that other,
'As is pertly payed · the chepes that I aghte.'
'Mary,' quoth that other mon, · 'myn is bihynde,
For I haf hunted al this day, · and noght haf I geten
Bot this foule fox felle · (the fende haf the godes!)
1945 And that is ful pore for to pay · for such prys thinges
As ye haf thright me here thro · suche thre cosses
                              so gode.'
                'Inogh,' quoth Sir Gawayn,
                'I thonk you, bi the rode,'
1950   And how the fox was slayn
                He tolde him as they stode.

With merthe and minstralsye, · with metes at hor wille,
Thay maden as mery · as any men moghten –
With laghing of ladies, · with lotes of bordes
1955 Gawayne and the gode mon · so glad were thay bothe –
Bot if the douthe had doted, · other dronken ben other.
Bothe the mon and the meyny · maden mony japes,
Til the sesoun was seen · that thay sever moste;
Burnes to hor bedde · behoved at the laste.
1960 Thenne lowly his leve · at the lorde first
Fochches this fre mon, · and fayre he him thonkkes:

1. 'I shall fulfil first our pact ...', 2. 'Then (Gawain) embraces the knight
and kisses him thrice, As vigorously (*sadly*) and with relish as he could', 3. 'You
meet good luck in earnings from this trade, if you got such goods as that!'.

'Of such a selly sojourne · as I haf hade here,
Your honour at this highe fest, · the highe Kyng you yelde!
I yef you me for on of youres, · if youreself lykes,
1965 For I mot nedes, as ye wot, · meve to-morne,
¹And ye me take sum tokle · to teche, as ye hight,
The gate to the Grene Chapel, · as God wil me suffer
To dele, on New Yeres day · the dome of my wyrdes.'
'In god faythe,' quoth the god mon, · 'with a goud wille;
1970 Al that ever I you hight · halde shal I rede.'
Ther asingnes he a servaunt · to sett him in the waye,
²And coundue him by the downes, · that he no drechch had,
For to ferk thurgh the frith · and fare at the gaynest
        bi greve.
1975   The lorde Gawayne con thonk,
        Such worchip he wolde him weve.
        Then at tho ladies wlonk
        The knight has tan his leve.

With care and with kissing · he carppes hem tille,
1980 And fele thryvande thonkkes · he thrat hom to have,
And thay yelden him agayn · yeply that ilk;
Thay bikende him to Kryst · with ful colde sikinges.
Sithen fro the meyny · he menskly departes;
Eche mon that he mette, · he made hem a thonke
1985 For his servise and his solace · and his sere pyne,
That thay with busynes had ben · aboute him to serve;
And eche segge as sore · to sever with him there
As thay hade wonde worthyly · with that wlonk ever.
Then with ledes and light · he was ladde to his chambre
1990 And blythely broght to his bedde · to be at his rest.
Yif he ne slepe soundyly, · say ne dar I,
For he hade muche on the morn · to mynne, yif he wolde,
        in thoght.
        Let him lyye there stille,
1995   He has nere that he soght;

1. 'And appoint some man to show me, as you said you would, The way
to the Green Chapel', 2. 'And conduct him through the mountains so that
he had no trouble'.

And ye wil a while be stille
I shal telle you how thay wroght.

IV

Now neghes the New Yere, · and the night passes,
The day drives to the derk, · as Drighten[1] biddes;
2000 Bot wilde wederes of the worlde · wakned theroute,
Cloudes kesten kenly · the colde to the erthe,
With nighe innoghe of the northe, · the naked to tene;
The snawe snitered ful snart, · that snayped the wilde;
The werbelande winde · wapped fro the highe,
2005 And drof eche dale ful · of driftes ful grete.
The leude[2] listened ful wel · that ley in his bedde,
[3]Thagh he lowkes his liddes, · ful littel he slepes;
Bi ech kok that crue · he knew wel the steven[4].
Deliverly he dressed up, · er the day sprenged,
2010 For there was light of a laumpe · that lemed in his chambre;
He called to his chamberlayn, · [5]that cofly him swared,
[6]And bede him bring him his bruny · and his blonk sadel;
That other ferkes him up · and feches him his wedes,
And graythes me Sir Gawayne · upon a grett wise.
2015 First he clad him in his clothes · the colde for to were,
And sithen his other harnays, · that holdely was keped,
Bothe his paunce and his plates, · piked ful clene,
The ringes rokked of the roust · of his riche bruny;
And al was fresh as upon first, · and he was fayn thenne
2020   to thonk;
            He hadde upon eche pece,
            Wypped ful wel and wlonk;
            The gayest into Grece,
            The burne bede bring his blonk.

2025 While the wlonkest wedes · he warp on himselven –
His cote with the conysaunce · of the clere werkes

1. God, 2. i.e. Gawain, 3. 'Though he closes his eyelids, full little he sleeps', 4. hour, 5. who promptly answered him, 6. 'And ordered him to bring his suit of mail and his horse's saddle'.

Ennurned upon velvet, · vertuus stones,
Aboute beten and bounden, · enbrauded semes,
And fayre furred withinne · with fayre pelures –
2030 Yet laft he not the lace[1], · the ladies gifte,
That forgat not Gawayne · for gode of himselven!
Bi he hade belted the bronde · upon his balge[2] haunches,
Thenn dressed he his drurye · double him aboute,
Swithe swethled umbe his swange[3] · swetely that knight
2035 The gordel of the grene silke, · that gay wel bisemed,
Upon that ryol red clothe · that ryche was to schewe.
[4]Bot wered not this ilk wighe · for wele this gordel,
For pryde of the pendauntes, · thagh polyst thay were,
And thagh the glyterande golde · glent upon endes,
2040 Bot for to saven hymself, · when suffer hym bihoved,
To bide bale withoute dabate · of bronde him to were
  other knyffe.
   Bi that the bolde mon boun
   Winnes theroute bilive,
2045   [5]Alle the meyny of renoun
   He thonkkes ofte ful rive.

Thenne was Gryngolet graythe, · that gret was and huge,
And hade ben sojourned saverly · and in a siker wyse,
Him list prik for point, · that proude hors thenne.
2050 The wighe winnes hym to · and wites on his lyre,
And sayde soberly hymself · and by his soth sweres:
[6]'Here is a meyny in this mote · that on menske thenkkes,
The mon hem mainteines, · joy mot thay have;
The leve lady on live, · luf hir bityde;
2055 Yif thay for charyte · cherisen a gest,
And halden honour in her honde, · the Hathel hem yelde
That haldes the heven upon highe, · and also you alle!
And yif I might lyf upon londe · lede any while,

1. i.e. the green girdle, 2. swelling, 3. waist, 4. Gawain did not wear
the girdle out of pride, but as a protection against the coming encounter,
5. He thanks the entire company of renown, 6. After the harnessing of
Gringolet he thanks the lord for his entertainment and invokes God's
blessing on his household.

I shuld rech you sum rewarde · redyly, if I might.'
2060 Thenn steppes he into stirop · and strydes alofte;
His shalk shewed hym his shelde, · on shulder he hit laght,
Gordes to Gryngolet · with his gilt heles,
And he startes on the ston, · stod he no lenger
to praunce.
2065   His hathel on hors was thenne,
That bere his spere and launce.
'This kastel to Kryst I kenne,
He gef hit ay god chaunce.'

The brigge[1] was brayde doun, · and the brode gates
2070 Unbarred and born open · upon bothe halve.
The burne blessed him bilive, · and the bredes passed –
Prayses the porter · bifore the prynce kneled[2],
Gef him God and goud day, · that Gawayne he save –
And went on his way · with his wighe one[3],
2075 That shulde teche him to tourne · to that tene place
Wer the ruful race · he shulde resaive[4].
Thay boghen bi bonkkes · ther boghes ar bare,
Thay clomben bi clyffes · ther clenges the colde.
[5]The heven was up halt, · bot ugly ther-under;
2080 Mist muged on the mor, · malt on the mountes,
Ech hille hade a hatte, · a mist-hakel huge.
Brokes byled and breke · bi bonkkes aboute,
Shyre shaterande on shores, · ther thay doun shoved.
Wela while was the way · wer thay bi wod shulden,
2085 Til hit was sone sesoun · that the sunne ryses
that tyde.
Thay were on a hille ful highe,
The white snaw lay bisyde;
[6]The burne that rod him by
2090 Bede his mayster abide.

1. i.e. the drawbridge, 2. Who had 'before the prince knelt', 3. 'with his one man', i.e. the guide, 4. receive, 5. 'The sky was updrawn, but ugly thereunder; Mist drizzled on the moor, dissolved in rain on the mountains, Each hill had a hat (and) a huge mist-cloak. Brooks boiled and broke', 6. 'The man who rode with him'.

'For I haf wonnen you hider, · wighe, at this tyme,
And now nar ye not fer · fro that note place
That ye han spied and spuryed · so specially after.
Bot I shal say you for sothe, · sithen I you knowe,
2095 And ye ar a lede upon live · that I wel lovy,
[1]Wolde ye worche bi my witte, · ye worthed the better.
The place that ye prece to[2] · ful perelous is halden.
Ther wones a wighe in that waste, · the worst upon erthe,
For he is stiffe and sturne, · and to strike loves,
2100 And more[3] is he then any mon · upon middelerde,
And his body bigger · then the best foure
That are in Arthure's hous, · Hestor[4], other other.
[5]He cheves that chaunce · at the Chapel Grene.
Ther passes non bi that place · so proude in his armes
2105 That he ne dinges him to dethe · with dint of his honde;
For he is a mon methles[6], · and mercy non uses,
For be hit chorle other chaplain · that bi the Chapel rides,
Monk other masseprest, · other any mon elles,
Him think as queme him to quelle · as quick go himselven.
2110 [7]Forthy I say the, as sothe · as ye in sadel sitte,
Com ye there, ye be killed, · may the knight rede,
Trawe ye me that treuely, · thagh ye had twenty lives
to spende.
He has wonyd here ful yore,
2115   [8]On bent much baret bende,
    Agayn his dintes sore
    Ye may not you defende.

[9]'Forthy, goude Sir Gawayne, · let the gome one,
And gets away sum other gate, · upon Goddes halve!
2120 [10]Cayres bi sum other kith, · wer Kryst mot you spede,
And I shal high me hom agayn, · [11]and hete you fyrre

1. 'If you follow my advice you will fare all the better', 2. press forward
towards, 3. bigger, 4. Hector, 5. 'He conducts the affair at the Green Chapel',
6. violent, 7. 'Therefore, I tell you, as sure as you sit in saddle, If you go
there you'll be killed', 8. 'On the field bent on much quarrel', 9. The guide
tries to dissuade Gawain from keeping such a fatal appointment, 10. 'Travel
by some other way', 11. 'and promise you firmly'.

That I shal swere bi God · and alle his gode halwes,
As help me God and the halydam, · and othes innoghe,
That I shal lelly you layne, · and lance never tale
2125 That ever ye fondet to fle · for freke that I wist.'
'Grant merci,' quoth Gawayne, · and gruching he sayde:
'Wel worth the, wighe, · that woldes my gode,
And that lelly me layne · I leve wel thou woldes.
Bot helde thou hit never so holde, · and I here passed,
2130 Founded for ferde for to fle, · in fourme that thou telles,
I were a knight kowarde, · I might not be excused.
Bot I wil to the Chapel, · for chaunce that may falle,
And talk with that ilk tulk · the tale that me liste,
Worthe hit wele other wo, · [1]as the wyrde likes
2135   hit hafe.
                    [2]Thaghe he be a sturn knape
                    To stightel, and stad with stave,
                    Ful wel con Drightin[3] shape
                    His servauntes for to save.'

2140 'Mary!' quoth that other mon, · 'now thou so much spelles,
That thou wilt thyn awen nye · nime to thyselven,
And the list lese thy lyf, · the lette I ne kepe.
Haf here thi helme on thy hede, · thi spere in thi honde,
And ride me doun this ilk rake · bi yon rokke side,
2145 Til thou be broght to the bothem · of the brem valay;
Thenne loke a littel on the launde, · on thi lyfte honde,
And thou shal se in that slade · the self Chapel,
[4]And the borelich burne · on bent that hit kepes.
Now fares wel, on Godes half, · Gawayne the noble!
2150 For alle the golde upon grounde · I nolde go with thee,
Ne bere the delawship thurgh this frith · on fote fyrre.'
Bi that the wighe in the wod · wendes his brydel,
Hit the hors with the heles · as harde as he might,
Lepes him over the launde, · and leves the knight there
2155   al one.

    1. 'As destiny decides', 2. 'Though he be a stern fellow To deal with ...',
3. God, 4. 'And the turbulent stream that guards it on the ground nearby'.

'Bi Goddes self,' quoth Gawayne,
'I wyl nauther grete ne grone;
To Goddes wile I am ful bayn,
And to Him I haf me tone.'

2160 Thenne girdes he to Gryngolet, · and gederes the rake,
Shoves in bi a shore · at a shawe[1] side,
Rides thurgh the roghe bonk · right to the dale;
And thenne he waited him aboute, · and wylde hit him thoght,
And seghe no signe of resette[2] · bisydes nowhere,

2165 Bot highe bonkkes and brent, · upon bothe halve,
And rughe knokled knarres[3] · with knorned stones;
[4]The skues of the scowtes · skayned him thoght.
Thenne he hoved, and withhilde · his hors at that tyde,
And ofte chaunged his cher · the Chapel to seche.

2170 He seye non suche in no syde, · and selly him thoght
Sone, a littel on a launde, · a lawe[5] as hit were;
[6]A balg berg bi a bonke · the brymme bisyde,
Bi a fors of a flode · that ferked thare;
The borne[7] blubred therinne · as hit boiled hade.

2175 The knight kaches his caple[8], · and com to the lawe,
Lightes doun luflyly, · and at a linde[9] taches
The rayne and his riche · with a roghe braunche.
Thenne he bowes to the berge, · aboute hit he walkes,
Debatande with himself · what hit be might.

2180 Hit hade a hole on the ende · and on ayther syde,
And overgrowen with gresse · in glodes aywhere,
[10]And al was holwe inwith, · nobot on olde cave,
Or a crevisse of an olde cragge, · he couthe hit noght deme
with spelle.

2185   'Wel! Lorde,' quoth the gentyle knight,
'Whether this be the Grene Chapelle?
Here might aboute midnight
The Dele[11] his matinnes telle!

1. small wood, 2. shelter, 3. gnarled rocks, 4. 'It seemed to him that the clouds were grazed by the crags', 5. mound, 6. 'A protuberant mound by a bank, alongside the stream, By the force (or fall) of a fall of water …', 7. stream, 8. horse, 9. branch, 10. 'And all was hollow inside, nothing but an old cave', 11. Devil.

'Now I-wisse,' quoth Wowayn, · 'wisty[1] is here;
2190   This oritore is ugly, · with erbes overgrowen;
Wel bisemes the wighe · wruxled in grene
Dele here his devocioun · on the Develes wyse.
Now I fele hit is the Fende, · in my five wittes,
That has stoken me this steven · to strie me here.
2195   This is a Chapel of Meschaunce, · that chekke hit bityde!
Hit is the corsedest kirk · that ever I com inne!'
With heghe helme on his hede, · his launce in his honde,
He romes up to the rokke · of tho rogh wones.
Thene herde he of that highe hil, · in a harde roche
2200   Biyonde the broke, in a bonk, · a wonder breme noyse.
What! hit clatered in the cliff, · as hit cleve shulde,
As one upon a grindelston · hade grounden a sithe.
What! hit wharred and whette, · as water at a mulne[2].
What! hit rusched and ronge, · rawthe to here.
2205   Thenne 'Bi Godde' quoth Gawayne · [3]'that gere, as I trowe,
Is riched at the reverence me, · renk to mete –
               bi rote.
            Let God worche! We loo[4],
            Hit helppes me not a mote.
2210   My lif thagh I forgoo,
            Drede dots me no lote.'

Thenne the knight con · calle ful highe:
'Who stightles in this sted · me steven to holde?
For now is gode Gawayne · goande right here.
2215   If any wighe oght wil, · winne hider fast,
Other now, other never, · his nedes to spede.'
  [5]'Abide!' quoth one on the bonke · aboven over his hede,
'And thou shal haf al in hast · [6]that I the hight ones.'
[7]Yet he rushed on that rurde · rapely a throwe,
2220   And with whettyng awharf, · er he wolde light;

---

1. desolate, 2. mill, 3. 'The gear, I believe, Is prepared for my saluta-
tion – battle with man – on the way', 4. Ah well!, 5. ' "Wait!" said someone
on the bank above his head', 6. 'that I promised you once', 7. 'Yet he went
on with that noise for a while, And turned to the whetting of his axe, before
he would descend'.

[1]And sithen he keveres bi a cragge, · and comes of a hole,
Whyrlande out of a wro · with a felle weppen,
A denes ax new dight, · the dynt with to yelde,
With a borelych bitte · bende by the halme,
2225 Fyled in a fylor, · foure fote large –
[2]Hit was no lasse bi that lace · that lemed ful bright –
[3]And the Gome in the Grene · gered as fyrst,
Bothe the lyre and the legges, · lokkes and berde,
Save that fayre on his fote · he foundes on the erthe,
2230 Sette the stele to the stone, · and stalked bisyde.
When he wan to the watter, · wer he wade nolde,
He hipped[4] over on his ax, · and orpedly[5] strydes,
Bremly brothe on a bent · that brode was aboute,
              on snawe.
2235   Sir Gawayne the knight con mete,
              He ne lutte him nothyng lowe;
              That other sayde, 'Now, sir swete,
              Of steven[6] mon may the trowe.'

'Gawayne,' quoth that Grene Gome, · 'God the mot loke!
2240 I-wisse thou art welcom, · wighe, to my place,
And thou has tymed thi travayl · as truee mon shulde,
And thou knowes the covenauntes · kest us bytwene:
At this tyme twelmonith · thou toke that thee falled,
And I shulde at this New Yere · yeply thee quite.
2245 And we ar in this valay · verayly oure one.
Here ar no renkes us to ridde, · rele as us likes.
Haf thy helme of thy hede, · and haf here thy pay.
[7]Busk no more debate · then I the bede thenne
When thou whipped of my hede · at a wap one.'
2250 'Nay, bi God,' quoth Gawayne, · [8]'that me gost lante,
I shal gruch the no grue · for grem that falles.
Bot stightel[9] thee upon on strok, · and I shal stonde stille

1. The Green Man approaches with the great axe he has been sharpening,
2. 'It was no less (in length) by that thong that gleamed full bright', 3. 'The
Man in the Green geared as at first', 4. hopped, 5. actively, 6. appointment,
7. 'Proffer no more arguing than I did to you When you whipped off my
head at a single blow', 8. '... who gave me spirit, I shall hold no grudge
against you on account of any harm that befalls me', 9. limit yourself.

And warp the no werning · to worch as thee likes,
nowhare.'

2255   He lened with the nek, and lutte,
          And shewed that shyre[1] al bare,
          And lette as he noght dutte;
          For drede he wolde not dare.

Then the Gome in the Grene · graythed[2] him swithe,
2260   Gederes up his grymme tole · Gawayne to smyte;
          With alle the bur[3] in his body · he ber hit on lofte,
          Munt as maghtily · as marre him he wolde;
          Hade hit driven adoun · as dregh as he atled[4],
          Ther hade ben ded of his dint · that doghty[5] was ever.
2265   Bot Gawayne on that giserne[6] · glyfte[7] him bisyde,
          As hit com glidande adoun · [8]on glode him to shende,
          And shranke a litel with the shulderes · for the sharp irne.
          [9]That other shalk with a shunt · the shene withhaldes,
          And thenne repreved he the prince · with mony proude
          wordes:
2270   'Thou art not Gawayne,' quoth the gome, · 'that is so goud
          halden,
          [10]That never arghed for no here · by hille ne be vale,
          And now thou fles for ferde · er thou fele harmes!
          Such cowardise of that knight · couthe I never here.
          Nawther fyked I ne flawe, freke, · when thou mintest,
2275   Ne kest no kavelacion[11] · in kynges hous Arthor.
          My hede flaw to my fote, · and yet flaw I never.
          And thou, er any harme hent, · arghes[12] in hert;
          Wherefore the better burne · me burde be called
          therfore.'
2280   Quoth Gawayne, 'I shunt ones,
          And so wyl I no more;
          Bot thagh *my* hede falle on the stones,
          I con not hit restore!

1. fair flesh, 2. prepared himself, 3. might, 4. 'as forcefully as he intended',
5. i.e. Gawain, 6. long-handled axe, 7. glanced at, 8. 'to destroy him there
on the ground', 9. 'That other fellow with a jerk the bright axe blade with-
holds', 10. 'That never quailed on account of any hostile force anywhere',
11. objection, 12. cringes.

Bot busk,[1] burne, bi thi fayth, · and bryng me to the poynt.
2285 Dele to me my destine, · and do hit out of honde,
For I shal stonde the a strok, · and start no more
Til thyn ax have me hitte: · haf here my trawthe.'
'Haf at the thenne!' quoth that other, · and heves hit alofte,
And waytes as wrothely · as he wode were.
2290 [2]He mintes at him maghtyly, · bot not the mon rives,
Withhelde heterly his honde, · er hit hurt might.
Gawayne graythely hit bides, · and glent with no membre,
Bot stode stille as the ston, · other a stubbe[3] auther
That ratheled[4] is in roche grounde · with rotes a hundreth.
2295 Then muryly efte con he mele[5], · the Mon in the Grene:
'So, now thou has thi hert holle, · hitte me bihoves[6].
[7]Halde thee now the highe hode · that Arthur the raght,
And kepe thy kanel at this kest, · yif hit kever may!'
Gawayne ful grindelly · with greme[8] thenne sayde:
2300 'Wy! thresh on, thou thro[9] mon, · thou thretes too longe.
I hope[10] that thi hert arghe · wyth thyn awen selven'.
'For sothe,' quoth that other freke, · 'so felly thou spekes,
I wil no lenger on lyte · lette thin ernde
right nowe.'
2305 Thenne tas he him strithe to stryke,
And frounses bothe lippe and browe.
No mervayle thagh him mislyke
That hoped of no rescowe.

[11]He liftes lightly his lome[12], · and lette hit doun fayre
2310 With the barbe of the bitte · bi the bare nek;
Thagh he homered heterly, · hurt him no more,
Bot snirt hym on that on syde, · that severed the hide.
The sharp shrank to the fleshe · thurgh the shyre grece,
That the shene blod over his shulderes · shot to the erthe.

1. prepare, 2. The Green Man heaves up his axe but suspends the blow,
3. tree-stump, 4. embedded, 5. hold forth, 6. 'It behoves me to hit',
7. 'Hold now your high hood that Arthur gave you, And keep your wind-
pipe after this blow, if you can!', 8. anger, 9. bullying, 10. suppose, expect,
11. The Green Man lets fall a blow that just nicks Gawain enough to draw
blood. Immediately after this – the agreement fulfilled – Gawain leaps away
and prepares for defence, 12. weapon.

2315 And when the burne segh the blode · blenk on the snawe,
     He sprit forth spenne-fote · more then a spere lenghe,
     Hent heterly his helme, · and on his hed cast,
     Shot with his shulderes · his fayre shelde under,
     Braydes out a bright sworde, · and bremely he spekes –
2320 Never sin that he was burne · borne of his moder
     Was he never in this worlde · wyghe half so blythe –
     'Blynne, burne, of thy bur, · bede me no mo!
     I haf a stroke in this sted · withoute stryf hent,
     And if thou reches me any mo, · I redyly shal quite,
2325 And yelde yederly agayn, · and therto ye tryst,
                    and foo[1].
               Bot on stroke here me falles
               (The covenaunt shap right so,
               Fermed in Arthure's halles)
2330   And therfore, hende, now hoo!'

     The hathel heldet him fro, · and on his ax rested,
     [2]Sette the shaft upon shore, · and to the sharp lened,
     And loked to the leude · that on the launde yede,
     How that doghty, dredles, · dervely ther stondes
2335 Armed, ful awles. · In hert hit him lykes.
     Thenn he meles muryly · with a much steven,
     And with a rinkande rurde[3] · he to the renk sayde:
     [4]'Bolde burne, on this bent · be not so grindel.
     No mon here unmanerly · the misboden habbes,
2340 Ne kid, bot as covenaunde, · at kinge's kort shaped.
     I hight thee a strok and thou hit has, · halde thee wel payed:
     I relece thee of the remnaunt · of rightes alle other.
     If I deliver had bene, · a boffet paraunter
     I couthe wrotheloker haf waret, · to thee haf wroght anger.
2345 Fyrst I mansed[5] thee muryly · with a mint[6] one,
     And rove thee with no rof sore, · with right I thee profered
     For the forwarde that we fest · in the fyrst night,

1. strenuously, 2. The Green Man 'set the shaft of the axe on the ground and rested on its blade', 3. ringing noise, 4. 'Bold man, on this ground don't be so angry. No one here has treated you unmannerly', 5. threatened, 6. *mint* (and later *munt*), blow.

And thou tristyly the trawthe · and truly me haldes,
Al the gayne thou me gef, · as god mon shulde.
2350 That other munt for the moren, · mon, I thee profered,
[1]Thou kissedes my clere wyf! – · the cosses me raghtes
For bothe two here I thee bede · bot two bare mintes
boute scathe.
True mon true restore,
2355 Thenne thar mon drede no wathe.
[2]At the thrid thou fayled thore,
And therfor that tappe ta thee.

For hit is my wede that thou weres, · that ilke woven girdel,
Myn owen wyf hit thee weved, · I wot wel for sothe.
2360 Now know I wel thy cosses, · and thy costes als!
And the wowing of my wyf! · I wroght hit myselven.
I sende hir to asay[3] thee, · and sothly me thinkkes
On the fautlest freke · that ever on fote yede.
As perle bi the white pese[4] · is of prys more,
2365 So is Gawayne, in god fayth, · bi other gay knightes.
Bot here you lakked a lyttel, sir, · and lewte you wonted;
Bot that was for no wilide[5] werke, · ne wowing[6] nauther,
Bot fro ye lufed your lyf: · the lasse I you blame.'
That other stif mon in study · stod a gret while,
2370 So agreved for greme · he gryed withinne.
Alle the blode of his brest · blende in his face,
That al he shrank for shome · that the shalk talked.
The forme worde upon folde · that the freke meled:
[7]'Corsed worth cowarddyse · and covetyse bothe!
2375 In you is vilany and vise · that vertue disstries.'
Thenne he kaght to the knot, · and the kest lawses,

---

1. 'You kissed my fine wife! – in return for which I gave you the two
feints with my axe.' The Green Man proves to be Gawain's host at the castle,
2. third: Gawain 'failed' at his third encounter with his hostess inasmuch as
he did not disclose – and give – to the lord of the castle the Green Girdle
which the lady had given him, in return for the fox taken on the third day's
hunt, 3. tempt, 'I sent her to tempt thee, and truly I think you One of the
most faultless men that ever went on foot', 4. pea, 5. cunning, underhand,
6. love-making, 7. Gawain, ashamed of the cowardice and covetousness that
the acceptance of the belt involved, hands it over to the Green Man.

Brayde brothely the belt · to the burne selven:
'Lo! ther the falssing, · foule mot hit falle!
For care of thy knokke · cowardyse me taght
2380 To acorde me with covetyse, · my kinde to forsake,
That is largess and lewte · that longes to knightes.
Now I am fawty and falce, · and ferde haf ben ever
Of trecherie and untrawthe: · bothe bityde sorwe
and care!
2385   I biknowe you, knight, here stille,
       Al fawty is my fare;
       Letes me overtake your wille
       And efte I shal be ware.'

[1]Thenn loghe that other leude · and luflyly sayde:
2390 'I halde hit hardily hole, · the harme that I hade.
Thou art confessed so clene, · beknowen of thy misses,
And has the penaunce apert · of the poynt of myn egge,
I halde the polysed of that plight, · and pured as clene
As thou hades never forfeted · sithen thou was first borne:
And I gif thee, sir, the gurdel · that is golde-hemmed,
2395 For hit is grene as my goune. · Sir Gawayne, ye maye
Thenk upon this ilke threpe[2], · wer thou forth thringes
Among prynces of prys, · and this a pure token
Of the chaunce of the Grene Chapel · at chevalrous knightes.
2400 And ye shal in this Newe Yer · agayn to my wones[3],
And we shin revel the remnaunt · of this ryche fest
ful bene.'
       Ther lathed him fast the lorde
       And sayde: 'With my wyf, I wene,
2405   We shal you wel acorde,
       That was your enmy kene!'

'Nay, for sothe,' quoth the segge, · and sesed his helme,
And has hit of hendely, · and the hathel thonkkes,
'I haf sojorned sadly: · sele yow bityde,

1. He laughed at Gawain's chagrin at being found out, 2. encounter,
3. residence.

2410 And He yelde hit you yare · [1]that yarkkes al menskes!
And comaundes me to that cortays, · your comlich fere,
Bothe that on and that other, · myn honoured ladies,
That thus hor[2] knight with hor kest · han koyntly biguiled.
Bot hit is no ferly[3] · thagh a fole madde,
2415 And thurgh wyles of wymmen · be wonen to sorwe,
For so was Adam in erde · with one bigyled,
And Salamon with fele sere, · and Samson eftsones –
Dalyda dalt him his wyrde – · and Davith therafter
Was blended with Barsabe, · that much bale tholed[4].
2420 Now these were wrathed with her wyles, · hit were a winne
huge
To luf hom wel, and leve[5] hem not, · a leude that couthe.
For thes wer forne the freest, · that folwed alle the sele
Excellently of alle thyse other, · under hevenriche
that mused:
2425 And alle thay were biwyled
With wymmen that thay used.
Thagh I be now bigyled,
Me think me burde be excused.

[6]'Bot your gordel' quoth Gawayne · 'God you foryelde!
2430 That wil I welde with good wille, · not for the winne golde,
Ne the saynt, ne the silk, · ne the syde pendaundes,
For wele ne for worchyp, · ne for the wlonk[7] werkkes,
Bot in synge of my surfet · I shal se hit ofte,
When I ride in renoun, · remorde in myselven
2435 The faut and the faintyse · of the fleshe crabbed,
How tender hit is to entyse · teches of filthe;
And thus, when pryde shal me prik · for prowes of armes,
The loke to this luf-lace · shal lethe my hert.
Bot on I wolde you pray, · displeses you never:
2440 Syn ye be lorde of the yonde londe · wer I half lent inne
With you with worshyp – · the Wighe hit you yelde
That uphaldes the heven · and on high sittes –
How norne ye youre right nome, · and thenne no more?'

1. 'Who ordains all honours', 2. their, 3. marvel, 4. suffered, 5. trust
them not, 6. 'But for your girdle ... that will I take', 7. splendid, proud.

'That shal I telle thee truly,' · quoth that other thenne,

2445 'Bercilak de Hautdesert · I hat in this londe.

Thurgh might of Morgne la Faye, · that in my hous lenges,

And koyntyse of clergye, · bi craftes wel lerned –

The maystres[1] of Merlyn · mony ho[2] has taken.

For ho has dalt drury · ful dere sumtyme

2450 With that conable klerk[3], that knowes · alle your knightes
at hame:

Morgne the goddes

Therfore hit is hir name.

Weldes non so high hawtesse

2455 That ho ne con make ful tame.

Ho wayned me upon this wyse · to your winne halle

For to assay the surquidre[4], · yif hit soth were

That rennes of the grete renoun · of the Rounde Table;

[5]He wayned me this wonder · your wittes to reve,

2460 For to haf greved Gaynour · and gart hir to dighe

With goping of that ilke gome · that gostlych speked

With his hede in his honde · bifore the highe table.

That is ho that is at home, · the auncian lady;

Ho is even thyn aunt, · Arthure's half-suster,

2465 The duches doghter of Tintagelle, · that dere Uter after

Hade Arthur upon, · that athel is nouthe.

Therfore I ethe thee, hathel, · to com to thy naunt[6],

Make myry in my hous. · My meny thee lovies,

And I wol thee as wel, · wighe, bi my faythe,

2470 As any gome under God · for thy grete traughe.'

And he nikked him naye, · he nolde bi no wayes.

Thay acolen[7] and kissen · and kennen ayther other

To the Prynce of Paradise, · and parten right there
on coolde.

2475 Gawayne on blonk ful bene

To the kinges burgh buskes bolde,

1. mysteries, arts, 2. she, 3. namely Merlin, 4. pride, 5. Morgan the
Fay contrived the spectacle of the Green Man at Arthur's Christmastide feast
'In order to have grieved Guinevere and caused her to die At beholding that
same Green Man', 6. aunt, 7. embrace and commit each other ... To the
Prince of Paradise.

And the knight in the enker grene
Whiderwardeso-ever he wolde.

Wylde wayes in the worlde · Wowen now rides
2480 On Gryngolet that the grace · hade geten of his live.
Ofte he herbered in house · and ofte al theroute,
And mony aventure in vale, · and venquyst ofte,
That I ne tight at this tyme · in tale to remene.
The hurt was hole · that he hade hent in his neck,
2485 And the blykkande belt · he bere theraboute
Abelef as a bauderik · bounden bi his syde,
Loken under his lyfte arme, · the lace, with a knot,
In tokening he was tane · in tech of a faute.
And thus he commes to the court, · knight al in sounde.
2490 Ther wakned wele in that wone · when wist the grete
That gode Gawayne was commen; · gayn hit him thoght.
The kyng kisses the knight, · and the quene alce,
And sithen mony siker knight · that soght him to haylce,
Of his fare that him frayned; · and ferlyly he telles,
2495 Biknowes alle the costes · of care that he hade,
The chaunce of the Chapel, · the chere of the knight,
The luf of the ladi, · the lace at the last.
The nirt in the nek · he naked hem shewed
That he laght for his unleute · at the leude's hondes
2500   for blame.
          [1]He tened when he shulde telle,
          He groned for gref and grame;
          The blod in his face con melle,
          When he hit sulde shewe, for schame.

2505 'Lo! lorde,' quoth the leude, · and the lace hondeled,
'This is the bende of this blame · I bere in my neck,
This is the lathe and the losse · that I laght have,
Of cowardise and covetyse · that I haf caght thare;
This is the token of untrawthe · that I am tan inne,
2510 And I mot nedes hit were[2] · wyle I may last.

1. 'He suffered when he had to tell, He groaned for grief and chagrin ...',
2. wear.

For non may hyden his harme, · bot unhap ne may hit,
For wer hit ones is tachched · twynne wil hit never.'
The kyng comfortes the knight, · and alle the court als
Laghen[1] loude therat, · and luflyly acorden
2515 That lordes and ladis · that longed to the Table,
Eche burne of the brotherhede, · a bauderyk shulde have,
A bende abclef him aboute · of a bright grene,
And that, for sake of that segge, · in suite to were.
For that was acorded the renoun · of the Rounde Table,
2520 And he honoured that hit hade · evermore after,
As hit is breved in the best · boke of romaunce.
Thus in Arthurus day · this aunter[2] bitidde,
The Brutus bokes therof · beres wittenesse;
Sithen Brutus, the bolde burne, · boghed hider fyrst,
2525 [3]After the segge and the asaute · was sesed at Troye,
                I-wisse,
            Mony aunteres here-biforne
            Haf fallen suche er this.
        [4]Now that bere the croun of thorne,
2530   He bryng us to his blysse! AMEN.

HONY SOYT QUI MAL PENCE

1. laugh, 2. adventure, 3. See line 1, 4. 'Now (He) that ...'.

NOTE

Sir Gawayne and the Grene Knight, together with three other poems – Holy
Patience, Holy Purity, and Pearl – is preserved in a single MS., dated about
1400. These four poems, which have no titles in the MS., are in the same handwriting which is probably that of a scribe, working either from the original or
from one or more intermediary copies, for the evidence points to the poems
having been composed within the period 1360–1400.

All four poems are in the North-west Midland (Cheshire or South Lanca-
shire) dialect. Sir Gawayne and the Grene Knight contains many words of Norse
origin, which may (some of them, at least) have been in the spoken dialect of
that region. This and other evidence suggests that the poem may have had
Norse, as well as French, ancestors.

JOHN GOWER

*

Medea as Queen of Air and Darkness

    Jason to Grece with his preie[1]
    Goth thurgh the See the rihte weie;
    Whan he ther com and men it tolde,
    Thei maden joie yonge and olde.
5   Eson[2], whan that he wiste of this,
    How that his Sone comen is,
    And hath achieved that he soughte,
    And hom with him Medea broughte,
    In al the wyde world was non
10 So glad a man as he was on.
    Togedre ben these lovers[3] tho
    Til that thei hadden sones two,
    Wherof thei weren bothe glade,
    And olde Eson gret joie made
15 To sen th'encress of his lignage;
    For he was of so gret an Age

        Jason to Greece with his prey
        Goes through the sea the direct way;
        When he came there and told it to men,
        Young and old made joy.
5   *Eson, when he knew of this,*
        How that his son is come,
        And has achieved what he sought,
        And brought Medea home with him,
        In all the wide world was no-one
10   *So glad a man as he was.*
        These lovers are together then
        Until they had two sons,
        Whereof they were both glad,
        And old Eson made great joy
15   *To see the increase of his lineage;*
        For he was of so great an age

1. i.e. the Golden Fleece, 2. The aged father of Jason whom Medea is to rejuvenate, 3. Jason and Medea.

That men awaiten every day
Whan that he sholde gon away.
Jason, which sih his fader old,
20   Upon Medea made him bold,
Of art magique, which she couthe,
And preith hire that his fader youthe
She wolde make ayeinward[1] newe.
And she, that was toward him trewe,
25   Behihte[2] him that she wolde it do
Whan that she time sawh therto.
Bot what she dede in that matiere
It is a wonder thing to hiere,
Bot yit for the novellerie
30   I thenke tellen a partie[3].

   Thus it befell upon a nyht:
Whan ther was noght bot sterreliht
She was vanyssht riht as hir liste,
That no whyt bot hirself it wiste
35   And that was ate mydnyht tyde.
The world was stille on every side.
With open hed and fot al bare,
[4]Hir her tosprad she gan to fare,
(Upon hir clothes gert she was)
40   Al specheles and on the gras
She glod[5] forth as an Addre doth.
Non otherwise she ne goth
Til she can to the freisshe flod,
And there a while she withstod.
45   Thries she torned hire aboute,
And thries ek she gan doun loute[6]
And in the flod she wette hir her[7],
And thries on the water ther
She gaspeth with a drecchinge onde[8]:
50   And tho[9] she tok hir speche on honde.
Ferst she began to clepe and calle
Upward unto the sterres alle,

1. again, 2. assured, promised, 3. part, 4. 'Her hair spread out …',
5. glided, 6. bowed, 7. hair, 8. tormenting breath, 9. then.

To Wynd, to Air, to See, to lond
She preide, and ek heild up hir hond
55   To Echates[1], and gan to crie,
Which is goddesse of Sorcerie.
She seide, 'Helpeth at this nede,
And as ye maden me to spede,
Whan Jason cam the Flees to seche,
60   So help me now, I you beseche'.
With that she loketh and was war,
Doun fro the Sky ther cam a char[2]
The which Dragouns aboute drowe.
And tho she gan hir hed doun bowe,
65   And up she styh[3], and faire and wel
She drof forth bothe char and whel
Above in th'air among the Skyes.
The lond of Crete and tho parties
She soughte, and faste gan hire hye,
70   And there upon the hulles[4] hyhe
Of Othrin and Olimpe also,
And ek of othre hulles mo,
She fond and gadreth herbes suote[5]:
She pulleth up some be the rote,
75   And manye with a knyf she sherth,
And alle into hir char she berth.
Thus whan she hath the hulles sought
The flodes ther foryat she nought –
Eridian and Amphrisos,
80   Pencic and ek Spercheidos,
To hem she wente and ther she nom
Bothe of the water and the fom,
The sond and ek the smale stones,
Whiche as she ches out for the nones,
85   And of the rede See a part,
That was behovelich to hire art,
She tok, and after that aboute
She soughte sondri sedes oute
In feldes, and in many greves,

1. Hecate, 2. car, 3. ascended, 4. hills, 5. sweet.

90 And ek a part she tok of leves.
 Bot thing which mihte hire most availe
 She fond in Crete and in Thessaile.
  In daies and in nyhtes Nyne,
 With gret travaile and with gret pyne,
95 She was pourveid of every piece,
 And torneth homward into Grece.
 Before the gates of Eson
 Hir char she let awai to gon,
 And tok out ferst that was therinne;
100 For tho she thoghte to beginne
 Such thing as semeth impossible,
 And made hirselven invisible,
 As she that was with Air enclosed
 And mihte of no-man be disclosed.
105 She tok up turves of the lond,
 Withoute helpe of mannes hond,
 Al heled with the grene gras,
 Of which an Alter made ther was
 Unto Echates the goddesse
110 Of art magique and the maistresse,
 And eft an other to Juvente,
 As she which dede hir hole entente.
 Tho tok she fieldwode and verveyne[1] –
 Of herbes ben noght betre tweine –
115 Of which anon withoute let
 These alters ben aboute set.
 Two sondri puttes[2] faste by
 She made, and with that hastely
 A wether which was blak she slouh,
120 And out therof the blod she drouh,
 And dede into the pettes[2] two
 Warm melk she putte also therto
 With hony meynd[3]: and in such wise
 She gan to make hir sacrifice,
125 And cride and preid forth withal
 To Pluto – the god infernal,

1. any plant of the genus *verbena*, 2. pits, 3. mixed.

And to the queene Proserpine.
And so she soghte out al the line
Of hem that longen to that craft –
130   Behinde was no name laft –
And preide hem all, as she wel couthe,
To grante Eson his ferste youth.
    This olde Eson broght forth was tho.
Awei she bad alle othre go
135   Upon peril that mihte falle;
And with that word thei wenten alle,
And leften there hem two alone.
And tho she gan to gaspe and gone[1],
And made signes manyon,
140   And seide hir wordes therupon:
So that with spellinge of hir charmes
She tok Eson in both hire armes,
And made him forto slepe faste,
And him upon hire herbes caste.
145   The blake wether tho she tok,
And hiewh the fleissh, as doth a cok.
On either alter part she leide,
And with the charmes that she seide
A fyr doun fro the Sky alyhte
150   And made it for to brenne lyhte.
Bot whan Medea sawh it brenne,
Anon she gan to sterte and renne
The fyri aulters al aboute.
Ther was no beste which goth oute
155   More wylde than she semeth ther.
Aboute hir shuldres hyng hir her
As thogh she were oute of hir mynde
And torned in an other kynde.
Tho lay ther certein wode cleft,
160   Of which the pieces now and eft
She made hem in the pettes wete,
And put hem in the fyri hete,
And tok the brond with al the blase

1. groan.

And thries she began to rase
165   Aboute Eson, ther as he slepte.
And eft with water, which she kepte,
She made a cercle aboute him thries,
And eft with fyr of sulphre twyes;
Ful many an other thing she dede,
170   Which is noght writen in this stede.
Bot tho she ran so up and down
She made many a wonder soun:
Somtime lich unto the cock,
Somtime unto the Laverock,
175   Somtime kacleth as a Hen,
Somtime spekth as don the men.
And riht so as hir jargoun strangeth
In sondri wise hir forme changeth.
She semeth faie and no womman.
180   For with the craftes that she can
She was, as who seith, a goddesse,
And what hir liste, more or lesse,
She dede, in bokes as we finde,
That passeth over mannes kinde.
185   Bot who that wole of wondres hiere
What thing she wroghte in this matier,
To make an ende of that she gan,
Such merveile herde nevere man.

Apointed in the newe Mone,
190   Whan it was time for to done,
She sette a caldron on the fyr
In which was al the hole atir[1],
Wheron the medecine stod,
Of jus, of water and of blod,
195   And let it buile in such a plit[2]
Til that she sawh the spume whyt.
And tho she caste in rynde and rote,
And sed and flour that was for bote,
With many an herbe and many a ston,
200   Whereof she hath ther many on.

1. apparatus, 2. manner.

And ek Cimpheius the Serpent
To hire hath alle his scales lent,
Cheldire hire yaf his addre's skin,
And she to builen caste hem in;
205   A part ek of the horned Owle,
The which men hiere on nyhtes howle;
And of a Raven, which was told
Of nyne hundred wynter old,
She tok the hed with al the bile;
210   And as the medicine it wile,
She tok therafter the bowele
Of the Seewolf, and for the hele[1]
Of Eson, with a thousand mo
Of thinges that she hadde tho,
215   In that Caldroun togedre as blyve[2]
She putte, and tok thanne of Olyve
A drie branche hem with to stere –
The which anon gan flowre and bere
And waxe al freissh and grene ayein.
220   Whan she this vertu hadde sein
She let the leste drope of alle
Upon the bare flor doun falle.
Anon ther sprong up flour and gras
Where as the drope falle was
225   And wox anon al medwe grene
So that it mihte wel be sene.
Medea thanne knew and wiste
Hir medecine is forto triste[3],
And goth to Eson ther he lay,
230   And tok a swerd was of assay,
With which a wounde upon his side
She made, that therout mai slyde
The blod withinne, which was old
And sek and trouble and fieble and cold.
235   And tho she tok unto his use
Of herbes al the beste jus,
And poured it unto his wounde

1. health, 2. quickly, readily, 3. reliable, trustworthy.

That made his veynes fulle and sounde:
And tho she made his woundes clos,
240 And tok his hand, and up he ros.
And tho she yaf him drinke a drauhte
Of which his youthe ayein he cauhte,
His hed, his herte and his visage,
Lich unto twenty wynter Age.
245 Hise hore heres were away,
And lich unto the freisshe Maii
Whan passed ben the colde schoures,
Riht so recovereth he his floures.

From *Confessio Amantis*,
Book V, II, 3927–4174.

NOTE

The *Confessio Amantis*, completed about 1390, is the formidably long English work of John Gower. Gower is often named alongside Chaucer in literary histories. Though he is lucid, his imaginative pressure is low, and his impulse to explore the possibilities of the language (when contrasted with Chaucer) was rarely stirred. But his powers were clearly stimulated by his handling of Ovid's story illustrating Medea's expertise in drugs.

ANONYMOUS

*

The Towneley First Shepherds' Play
Incipit Pagina Pastorum
[*Enter* FIRST SHEPHERD (*Gyb*)]

FIRST SHEPHERD. Lord, what they are weylle · that hens ar
     past,
     For thay noght feylle · theym to downe cast.
     Here is mekylle unceylle · and long has it last,
     Now in hart, now in heylle, · now in weytt, now in blast,
5   Now in care,
     Now in comfurthe agane,
     Now in fayre, now in rane,
     Now in hart fulle fane,
          And after fulle sare.

10   Thus this warld, as I say, · farys on ylk syde,
     For after oure play · com sorows unryde,
     For he that most may, · when he syttes in pryde,

The Towneley First Shepherds' Play
Here begins the Pageant of the Shepherds
[*Enter* FIRST SHEPHERD (*Gyb*)]

FIRST SHEPHERD. *Lord, they are well off who are dead and gone,*
     For they do not suffer vicissitudes.
     Here is much unhappiness, and it lasts long,
     Now in sickness, now in health, now in wet, now in blast,
5   *Now in care,*
     Now in comfort again,
     Now in fair weather, now in rain,
     Now in heart full of gladness,
          And after of sorrow.

10   *Thus goes this world, I say, on every side,*
     For after our play follow bitter sorrows,
     And he that is able to do most things, when he sits in pride,

437

When it comys on assay · is kesten downe wyde,
    This is seyn;
15   When ryches is he,
    Then comys poverte,
    [1]Hors man Jak Cope
        Walkys then, I weyn:

I thank it God · (hark ye what I mene),
20   For even or for od · I have mekylle[2] tene,
As hevy as a sod · I grete with my eene,
[3]When I nap on my cod · for care that has bene,
    And sorow.
    Alle my shepe ar gone,
25   I am not left oone,
    The rot has theym slone,
        Now beg I and borow.

My handes may I wryng · and mournyng make,
Bot if good wille spryng, · the countre forsake,
30   Fermes[4] thyk ar comyng, · my purs is bot wake[5],
I have nerehand nothyng · to pay nor to take.
      I may syng
    Withe purs penneles,
    That makes this hevynes!
35   Wo is me this distres,
        And has no helpyng.

Thus sett I my mynde · [6]truly to neven,
By my wytt to fynde · to cast the warld in seven.
My shepe have I tynde[7] · by the moren fulle even;
40   Now if hap wille grynde · God from his heven
        Send grace.
To the Fair wille I me,
To buy shepe, perde,

---

1. 'Horseman Jack Cope Walks then, I guess', 2. much, 3. 'When I rest on my pillow …', 4. rents, i.e. *demands* for rent, 5. light. His purse is too empty to meet demands, 6. 'truly to say', 7. lost.

And yit may I multyple,
45   For alle this hard case.

[*He is about to leave for the Fair when the* SECOND SHEPHERD (*John Horne*) *enters*]

SECOND SHEPHERD (*to the audience*). [1]Benste, benste, · be us emang,
And save alle that I se · here in this thrang!
He save you and me · [2]overtwhart and endlang,
That hang on a tre, · I say you no wrang.
50   Cryst save us
From alle myschefys,
From robers and thefys,
From those mens grefys,
          That oft ar agans us.

55   Both bosters and bragers · God kepe us fro,
That with thare long dagers · dos mekylle wo,
[3]From alle bylle-hagers · with colknyfes that go,
Siche wryers and wragers · gose to and fro
          For to crak.
60   Who so says hym agane,
Were better be slane:
Bothe ploghe and wain
          Amendys wille not make.

He wille make it as prowde · a lord as he were
65   With a hede lyke a clowde · felterd[4] his here,
He speakys on lowde · with a grim bere,
I wold not have trowde · so galy in gere
          As he glydys.
I wrote not the better,
70   Nor whedder is gretter,
The lad or the master,
          So stowtly he strydys.

1. Benedicite. 2. 'crosswise and lengthwise', i.e. whether 'upside-down or t'otherwise'. 3. 'From all bill-packers who go with cabbage-knives, Such twisters and wranglers ...'. 4. entangled.

[1]If he hask me oght · that he wold to his pay,
Fulle dere bese it boght · if I say nay;
75 Bot God that alle wroght, · to Thee now I say,
Help that thay were broght · to a better way
For thare sawlys,
And send theym good mendyng
With a short endyng,
80 And with Thee to be lendyng
When that Thou callys.
[*To the* FIRST SHEPHERD]
How, Gyb, good morne! · wheder goys thou?
Thou goys over the corne! · Gyb, I say, how!
FIRST SHEPHERD. Who is that? Johne Horne? · I make God
a vowe!
85 I say not in scorne · Thom, how fares thou?
SECOND SHEPHERD. Hay, ha!
Ar ye in this towne?
FIRST SHEPHERD. Yey, by my crowne.
SECOND SHEPHERD. I thoght by your gowne
90 This was youre aray.

FIRST SHEPHERD. I am ever elyke[2], · wote I never what it
gars[3],
Is none in this ryke[4] · a shepherd fares wars.
SECOND SHEPHERD. Poore men are in the dyke, · and oft
tyme mars,
The warld is slyke[5], · also helpars
95 Is none here.
FIRST SHEPHERD. It is sayde fulle ryfe
'A man may not wyfe
And also thryfe,
And alle in a yere.'

100 SECOND SHEPHERD. Fyrst must we crepe · and sythen go.
FIRST SHEPHERD. I go to buy shepe.

1. If he (such a tyrant as described) demands anything of me then I pray for
it dearly if I refuse, 2. alike, 3. causes, 4. realm, 5. thus (such like).

SECOND SHEPHERD. Nay, not so;
     What, dreme ye or slepe? · where shuld they go?
     Here shalle thou none kepe.
FIRST SHEPHERD. A, good sir, ho!
     Who am I?
105   I *wylle* pasture my fe![1]
     Where so ever lykes me,
     Here shalle thou theym se.
SECOND SHEPHERD. Not so hardy,

     Not oone shepe taylle · shalle thou bryng hedyr.
110 FIRST SHEPHERD. I shalle bryng, no faylle, · a hundrethe
     togedyr.
SECOND SHEPHERD. What, art thou in ale? · longes thou
     oght whedir?
FIRST SHEPHERD. Thay shalle go, saunce[2] faylle; · [3] go now,
     Belle Weder!
SECOND SHEPHERD. I say, Tyr!
FIRST SHEPHERD. I say, Tyr, now agane!
115   I say skyp over the plane.
SECOND SHEPHERD. Wold thou never so fane,
     Tup, I say, whyr!

FIRST SHEPHERD. What, wylle thou not yit, · I say, let the
     shepe go?
     Whap!
SECOND SHEPHERD. Abyde yit.
FIRST SHEPHERD. Wilt thou, bot so ?
120   Knafe, hens I byd flytt, · as good that thou do,
     Or I shalle thee hytt · on thi pate, lo,
     Shalle thou reylle.
     I say, gyf the shepe space!
SECOND SHEPHERD. Syr, a letter of youre grace,

---

1. flock. 2. without. 3. What happens from this point to the entry of
Slow-pace is that Gyb, destitute of sheep but intending to buy some, and
John Horne either pretend to see hundreds of sheep where none are, or they are
deluded into thinking that they see them.

125   Here comys Slaw-pase
                    Fro the mylne whele[1].
            [*Enter the* THIRD SHEPHERD (*Slow-pace*)]
    THIRD SHEPHERD. What a do, what a do · is this you be-
            tweyn?
        A, good day, thou, and thou.
    FIRST SHEPHERD. Hark what I meyn
            You to say: –
130   I was bowne[2] to buy store,
        Drofe my shepe me before,
        He says not oone hore[3]
                Shalle pas by this way;

        Bot, and he were wood,[4] · this way shalle thay go.
135 THIRD SHEPHERD. Yey, bot telle me, good, · where ar
            youre shepe, lo?
    SECOND SHEPHERD. Now, sir, by my hode, · yet se I no mo,
        Not syn I here stode.
    THIRD SHEPHERD. God, gyf you wo
            And sorow!
        Ye fyshe before the nett,
140   And stryfe on this bett,
        Siche folys never I mett
                Evyn or at morow.

        It is wonder to wyt · where wytt shuld be fownde,
        Here ar old knafys[5] yit · standys on this frownde
145   These wold by thare wytt · make a ship be drownde,
        He were welle quitt · had sold for a pownde
                Siche two.
        Thay fyght and thay flyte
        For that at comys not tyte[6];
150   It is far to byd 'hyte'
                To an eg or it go.

1. mill-wheel, 2. bound, 3. hair of them, i.e. the sheep, 4. mad, 5. Gyb
and John Horne are – to Slow-pace – two old quarrelsome knaves, and they
resemble Moll who is always counting her sheep though in fact she has but
one, 6. quickly.

[1]Tytter want ye sowlle · then sorow I pray!
Ye brayde of Mowlle · that went by the way.
Many shepe can she polle[2] · bot oone had she ay,
155   Bot she happynyd fulle fowlle, · hyr pycher, I say,
        Was broken.
    'Ho, God,' she sayde,
    Bot oone shepe yit she hade,
    The mylk pycher was layde,
160   The skarthis[3] was the tokyn.

Bot syn ye ar bare · of wysdom to knawe,
Take hede how I fare, · and lere at my lawe
(Ye nede not to care · if ye folow my sawe –
Hold ye my mare – · this sek[4] thou thrawe
165   On my bak)
Whylst I, with my hand,
Lawse[5] the sek[4] band,
Com nar and by stand
    Both Gyg and Jak;

[Slow-pace demonstrates that the sack – which he has brought in – is empty]

170   Is not all shakyn owte · and no meylle[6] is therein?
  FIRST SHEPHERD. Yey, that is no dowte.
  THIRD SHEPHERD. So is youre wyttes thyn.
    And ye look welle abowte, · nawther more nor myn,
    So gase your wyttes owte · evyn as it come in.
        Geder up
175   And seke it agane.
  SECOND SHEPHERD. May we not be fane!
    He has told us fulle plane
        Wysdom to sup.

  JAK THE BOY. Now God gif you care, · folys all sam!
180   Saghe I never none so fare · but the foles of Gotham.
    Wo is hir that you bare, · youre syre and youre dam,

1. 'Sooner want food than sorrow I pray! You resemble Moll...', 2. count,
3. (broken) fragments, 4. sack, 5. loose, 6. meal.

Had she broght furthe an hare, · a shepe, or a lam,
　　　Had bene welle.
　　Of alle the foles I can telle,
185　　From heven unto helle,
　　Ye thre bere the belle;
　　　　God gyf unceylle!¹
　　　　　[*Enter* THE BOY, (*Jack*)]

FIRST SHEPHERD. How pastures oure fee?² · say me, good
　　Pen.
THE BOY. Thay ar gryssed³ · to the kne⁴.
SECOND SHEPHERD. Fare falle thee!
THE BOY.　Amen!
190　　If ye wille ye may se, · youre bestes ye ken.
FIRST SHEPHERD. Sytt we downe alle thre, · and drynk
　　shalle we then.
THIRD SHEPHERD. Yet, torde, I am lever ete;
　　What is drynk with oute mete?
　　Gett mete, gett,
195　　　　And sett us a borde,

The may we go dyne · our bellys to fylle.
SECOND SHEPHERD. Abyde unto syne.
THIRD SHEPHERD. Be God, sir, I nylle!
SECOND SHEPHERD. I am worthy the wyne, · me thynk it
　　good skylle,
　　My servyse I tyne⁵, · I fare fulle ille,
200　　　　At youre mangere.
FIRST SHEPHERD. Thus go we to mete,
　　It is best that we trete,
　　⁶I lyst not to plete
　　　　To stand in thi dangere!

205　　Thou hast ever been curst · syn we met togeder.
THIRD SHEPHERD. Now in saythe, if I durst, · ye are even my
　　broder.

1. unhappiness, 2. flock, 3. grassed, 4. The boy reports that Gyb's
sheep are not lost but are (on the contrary) well-pastured, 5. waste, 6. I care
not to put myself under your obligation by receiving food from you.

SECOND SHEPHERD. Syrs, let us cryb[1] furst · for oone thyng
or oder,
That thise wordes be purst[2], · and let us go foder
Our mompyns[3].
210   Lay furthe of oure store![4]
Lo here browne of a bore!
FIRST SHEPHERD. Set mustard afore,
Oure mete now begyns;

Here a foote of a cowe · welle sawsed, I wene,
215   The pestelle of a sowe · that powderd has bene, ·
Two blodynges[5], I trow, · a leveryng[6] betwene;
Do gladly, syrs, now, · my breder bedene[7],
With more.
Both befe, and moton
220   Of an ewe that was roton;
Good mete for a gloton,

Ete of this store.

SECOND SHEPHERD. I have here in my maylle[8] · sothen[9] an
rost
Even of an ox taylle, · that wold not be lost;
225   Ha, ha, goderhaylle! · I let for no cost,
A good py or we faylle, · this good for the frost
In a mornyng.
And two swyne gronys[10],
Alle a hare bot the lonys,
230   We myster no sponys
Here, at oure mangyng.

THIRD SHEPHERD. Here is to recorde · the leg of a goys,
With chekyn endorde[11], · pork, partryk, to roys;
A tart for a lorde, · how thynk ye this doys?

1. crib. The meaning is: 'Let us join together at the crib or bowl, and end
our bickering by feeding our bellies', 2. dismissed, 3. teeth, 4. As the lost
sheep were found, so now good things to eat are drawn forth out of the once
empty bag, 5. blood-puddings?, 6. liver-pudding?, 7. 'my brothers twain',
8. bag or scrip, 9. seethed, 10. snouts, 11. 'gilded' with egg-yoke.

235   A calf lyver skorde · with the veryose¹,
     Good sawse,
   This is a restorete²
   To make a good appete.
  FIRST SHEPHERD. ³Yee speke alle by clerge,
240   I here by your clause.

   ⁴Cowthe ye by youre gramery · reche us a drynk
   I shuld be more mery. · Ye wote what I thynk.
  SECOND SHEPHERD. Have good aylle of Hely⁵, · bewar
    now, I wynk,
   For and thou drynk drely · in thy polle wylle it synk.
245 FIRST SHEPHERD. A, so!
   ⁶This is boyte of our baylle.
   Good halsom aylle.
  THIRD SHEPHERD. Ye hold long the skaylle⁷,
    Now lett me go to.

250 SECOND SHEPHERD. I shrew those lyppys · bot thou leyff
    me som parte.
  FIRST SHEPHERD. Be God, he bot syppys, · begylde thou
    art;
   Behold how he kyppys⁸.
  SECOND SHEPHERD. I shrew you so smart,
   And me on my hyppys, · bot if I gart
255   Abate.
   Be thou wyne, be thou aylle,
   Bot if my brethe faylle,
   I shalle sett thee on saylle;
    God send thee good gate.

260 THIRD SHEPHERD. ⁹Be my dam saulle, Alyce, · it was sadly
    dronken.

---

1. verjuice, 2. restorative, 3. Paraphrase: You speak learnedly, 4. 'Could ye by your learning pass us a drink', 5. i.e. Ely, 6. The ale is 'remedy of our woe' – a formulary used also of Christ, 7. bowl, 8. belches, 9. 'By my mother's soul …'.

FIRST SHEPHERD. Now, as ever have I blys, · to the botham
    is it sonken.

SECOND SHEPHERD. Yit a botelle here is.

THIRD SHEPHERD. That is welle spoken!
    By my thryft we must kys.

SECOND SHEPHERD. That had I forgoten.
        Bot hark!

265   Who so can best syng
        Shall have the begynnyng.

FIRST SHEPHERD. Now prays at the partyng
    I shalle set you on warke.

      [The Shepherds sing]

    We have done oure parte · and songyn righte weylle,
    I drynk for my parte.

270 SECOND SHEPHERD. Abyde, lett cop reylle[1].

FIRST SHEPHERD. Godes forbot, thou spart[2], · and thou
    drynk every deylle.

THIRD SHEPHERD. Thou has dronken a quart, · therfor
    choke thee the deylle.

FIRST SHEPHERD. Thou rafys![3]
    And it were for a soghe[4]

275   Ther is drynk enoghe.

THIRD SHEPHERD. I shrew the handes it droghe.
      Ye be bothe knafys.

FIRST SHEPHERD. Nay we knaves alle, · thus thynk me best,
    So sir, shuld you calle.

SECOND SHEPHERD. Furth let it rest;
    We wille not bralle.

280 FIRST SHEPHERD. Then wold I we fest
    This mete who shalle into panyere kest.

THIRD SHEPHERD. Syrs, herys,
    For oure saules let us do
    Poore men gyf it to.

1. 'let the cup go round', 2. 'spare it, lest thou drink the whole lot',
3. ravest, 4. sow.

285   FIRST SHEPHERD. Geder up, lo, lo,
              Ye hungre begers frerys.

    [*They collect the remnants of the feast to give to the poor*]

    SECOND SHEPHERD. It draes nere nyght, · trus, go we to rest;
    I am even redy fyght, · I thynk it the best.
    THIRD SHEPHERD. For ferde we be fryght · a crosse let us
        kest,
290   [1]Cryst crosse, benedyght, · eest and west,
           For dreede.
    Jesus o'Nazorus,
    Crucyefixus,
    Marcus, Andreas,
295   God be our spedē!

        [*The* ANGEL *sings*]
    ANGEL. Herkyn, hyrdes[2], awake, · gyf lovyng ye shalle,
    He is borne for youre sake, · lorde perpetualle,
    He is comen to take · and rawnson you alle,
    Youre sorowe to slake, · kyng emperialle,
300   He behestys;
    That chyld is borne
    At Bethelem this morne,
    Ye shalle fynde hymn beforne
        Betwix two bestys.

305   FIRST SHEPHERD. A, Godys dere dominus, · what was that
        sang?
    It was wonder curiose · with smalle notes emang.
    I pray to God save us · now in this thrang,
    I am ferd by Jesus · somewhat be wrang!
        Me thoght,
310   Oone scremyd on lowde,
    I suppose it was a clowde,

---

   1. In this crossing of themselves (and in the terms of their prayer) *immediately before* the Angel's news of the Incarnation we have a conspicuous as well as a dramatic example of the medieval view of Time as something other than mere sequence. 2. shepherds.

In myn ears it sowde,
  By hym that me boght!

SECOND SHEPHERD. Nay, that may not be, · I say you
  certan,
315 For he spake to us thre · as he had been a man.
When he leinyd[1] on this lee · my hart shakyd than,
An angelle was he · telle you I can,
  No dowte.
He spake of a barne,
320 We must seke hym, I you warne,
That betokyns yond starne,
  That stands yonder owte.

THIRD SHEPHERD. It was marvelle to se, · so bright as it
  shone,
I wold have trowyd, veraly, · it had bene thoner-flone[2].
325 Bot I saghe with myn ee, · as I lenyd to this stone,
It was a mery gle, · siche hard I never none,
  I recolde.
As he sayde in a skreme,
Or els that I dreme,
330 We shuld go to Bedleme,
  To worship that lorde.

FIRST SHEPHERD. That same childe is he · that prophetes of
  told,
Shuld make them fre · that Adam had sold.
SECOND SHEPHERD. Take tent[3] unto me, · this is inrold,
335 By the wordes of Isae, · a prynce most bold
  Shalle he be,
And kyng with crowne,
Set on David trone,
Sich was never none,
340 Seyn with oure ee.

1. tarried, poised, 2. thunder-bolt, 3. pay heed.

THIRD SHEPHERD. Also Isay says, · oure faders us told,
That a vyrgyn shuld pas · of Jesse, that wold
Bryng furthe, by grace, · a floure so bold.
That vyrgyn now has · these wordes uphold
345   As ye se.
Trust is now we may
He is borne this day
Exiet virga
      De radice Jesse.

350 FIRST SHEPHERD. Of hym spake more · Sybylle as I weyn
And Nabugodhonsor, · from oure faythe alyene,
In the fornace where thay wore · thre childre sene,
The fourt stode before, · Godes son lyke to bene.
SECOND SHEPHERD. That fygure
355 Was gyffen by revelacyon
That God wold have a son:
This is a good lesson,
      Us to consydure.

THIRD SHEPHERD. Of hym spake Jeromy, · and Moyses also,
360 Where he saghe hym by · a bushe burnand, lo,
When he cam to espy · if it were so,
Unburnyd was it truly · at commyng therto,
      A wonder.
FIRST SHEPHERD. That was for to se
365 Hir holy vyrgynte,
That she unfylyd[1] shuld be,
      Thus can I ponder,

And shuld have a chyld · sich was never sene.
SECOND SHEPHERD. Pese, man, thou art begyld; · thou
    shalle se hyr with eene,
370 Of a madyn so myld · greatt mervelle I mene;
Yee, and she unfyld, · a vyrgyn clene,
      So soyne[2].

1. undefiled, 2. soon.

THE TOWNELEY 'FIRST SHEPHERDS' PLAY'

FIRST SHEPHERD. Nothyng is impossybylle
    Sothly that God wylle;
375   It shalbe stabylle
        That God wylle have done.

SECOND SHEPHERD. Abacue and Ely · prophesyde,
    Elezabeth and Zachare, · and many other mo,
    And David as veraly · is witnes therto,
380   Johne Baptyste sewrly, · and Daniel also.
THIRD SHEPHERD. So sayng,
    He is Godes son alon,
    Without hym shalbe none,
    His sete and his trone,
385   Shalle ever be lastyng.

    Virgille in his poetre · sayde in his verse,
    Even thus by gramere · as I shalle reherse:
    [1]'Jam nova progenies coelo demittitur alto,
    Jam rediet virgo, redeunt Saturnia regna'.
SECOND SHEPHERD. Weme, tord, what speke ye · here in
390   myn eeres?
    Telle us no clerge, · I hold you of the freres!
      Ye preche!
    It semys by youre Laton
    Ye have lerd youre Caton!
395 FIRST SHEPHERD. Herk, syrs, ye fon,
      I shalle you tech: –

    He sayde from heven · a new kynde is send,
    Whom a vyrgyn to neven[2], · oure mys[3] to amend,
    Shalle conceyve fulle even, · thus make I an end;
400   And yit more to neven, · that samyne shalle bend
      Unto us,
    With peasse and plente,
    With ryches and menee,

1. See Vergil *Eclogue IV* – 'the Messianic eclogue', but the order of the two lines quoted should be transferred and for 'rediet' read 'redit et', 2. to declare, 3. fault.

Good luf and charyte
405   Blendyd amanges us.

THIRD SHEPHERD. And I hold it trew, · for ther shuld be,
    When that kyng commys new, · peasse by land and se.
SECOND SHEPHERD. Now brethere, adew, · tak tent unto me,
    I wold that we knew · of this song so fre
410   Of the angelle.
    I hard by hys steven[1],
    He was send downe fro heven.
FIRST SHEPHERD. It is truthe that ye neven,
    I hard hym welle spelle.

415 SECOND SHEPHERD. Now, by God that me boght, · it was
        a merry song;
    I dar say that he broght · foure and twenty to a long.
THIRD SHEPHERD. I wold it were soght · that same us emong.
FIRST SHEPHERD. In fayth I trow noght · so many[2] he
        throng
            On a heppe;
420   Thay were gentylle and smalle,
    And welle tonyd with alle.
THIRD SHEPHERD. Yei, bot I can theym alle,
        Now lyst, I lepe.

FIRST SHEPHERD. Brek outt youre voce, · let se as ye yelp.
425 THIRD SHEPHERD. I may not for the pose · bot I have help.
SECOND SHEPHERD. A, thy hert is in thy hose.
FIRST SHEPHERD. Now in payn of a skelp[3],
    This sang thou not lose.
THIRD SHEPHERD. Thou art an ylle quelp[4]
        For angre!
SECOND SHEPHERD. Go to now, begyn.
430 FIRST SHEPHERD. He lyst not welle ryn,
THIRD SHEPHERD. God lett us never blyn[5],
        [6]Take at my sangre.
            [He sings]

    1. voice, 2. notes of music, 3. blow, 4. whelp, 5. cease, 6. 'take up my
song'.

FIRST SHEPHERD. Now an ende have we doyn · of oure song
    this tyde,

SECOND SHEPHERD. Fayr falle thi growne · welle has thou
    hyde.

435 THIRD SHEPHERD. Then furthe lette us ron, · I wylle not
    abyde.

FIRST SHEPHERD. No sych makethe mone · that have I
    aspyde;
              Never the les
      Let hold oure beheste.

SECOND SHEPHERD. That hold I best.

440 THIRD SHEPHERD. Then must we go eest,
              After my ges[1].

FIRST SHEPHERD. Wold God that we myght · this yong
    babe see?

SECOND SHEPHERD. Many prophetes that syght · desyryd
    veralee
    To have seen that bright.

THIRD SHEPHERD. And God so hee

445   Wold shew us that wyght, · we myght say, perde,
              We had sene
      [2]That many sant desyryd,
      With prophetys inspyryd,
      If thay hym requyryd,

450   Yit closyd ar thare eene.

SECOND SHEPHERD. God graunt us that grace –

THIRD SHEPHERD. God so do.

FIRST SHEPHERD. Abyde, syrs, a space; · lo, yonder, lo!
    [3]It commys on a pase · yond sterne us to.

SECOND SHEPHERD. [4]It is a grete blase, · oure gate let us go

455   [5]Here he is.

THIRD SHEPHERD. Who shalle go in before?

1. guess. 2. 'That which many a sant desired'. 3. 'It comes on apace –
you star towards us'. 4. 'It (the star) is a great blaze, our way we take'.
5. either 'Here the Infant is', or 'Here (is the place where) the Infant is'. The
shepherds, in a turn or two about the stage, have left their fields – following
the star.

FIRST SHEPHERD. I ne rek, by my hore.
SECOND SHEPHERD. Ye ar of the old store,
   It semys you, iwis.

  [They approach the Holy Infant]

460 FIRST SHEPHERD. Haylle, kyng I thee calle! · haylle, most
   of myght!
   Haylle, thee worthyst of alle! · haylle, duke! haylle,
   knyght!
   Of greatt and smalle · thou art Lord by right,
   Haylle, perpetualle! · haylle, faryst wyght!
    Here I offer;
465   (I pray the to take
   If thou wold, for my sake)
   [1]With this may thou lake –
    This lytylle spruse cofer.

SECOND SHEPHERD. Haylle, lytylle tyne mop! · rewarder of
   mede!
470 Haylle, bot oone drop · of grace at my nede!
   Haylle, lytylle mylk sop! · Haylle, David sede!
   Of oure crede thou art crop, · haylle, in God hede!
    This balle
   That thou wold resave,
475   Lytylle is that I have,
   This wylle I vowche save,
    To play thee with alle.

THIRD SHEPHERD. Haylle, maker of man! · haylle, swetyng!
   Haylle, so as I can, · haylle, praty mytyng!
480 I couche to thee than · for fayn nere gretyng,
   Haylle, Lord! here I ordan · now at oure metyng,
    This botelle.
   It is an old by-worde,
   It is a good bowrde,
485   For to drynk of a gowrde,
    It holdes a mett potelle[2].

1. 'With this may thou play – this little spruce coffer' (handing the present),
2. a measured quantity.

MARIA. He that alle myghtes may, · the makere of heven,
That is for to say · my son that I neven,
Rewarde you this day, · as he sett alle on seven,
490　　　　He graunt you for ay · his blys fulle even
　　　　　　　　Contynuyng;
　　　　He gyf you good grace,
　　　　Telle furth of this case,
　　　　He spede youre pase,
495　　　　　　　And graunt you good endyng.

FIRST SHEPHERD. Fare well, fare Lorde! · with thy moder
　　　　also.
SECOND SHEPHERD. We shalle this recorde · where as we go.
THIRD SHEPHERD. We mon alle be restorde, · God graunt
　　　　it be so!
FIRST SHEPHERD. Amen, to that worde, · syng we therto
500　　　　　　　On hight,
　　　　To joy alle sam,
　　　　With myrthe and gam,
　　　　To the laude of this lamb

　　　　　　Syng we in syght.
EXPLICIT UNA PAGINA PASTORUM

NOTE

The 'Towneley' Cycle is so called from the family name of the former
possessors of the MS., and is believed – the evidence is inconclusive – to have
been the text for the plays performed at Wakefield. What is more certain is
that an anonymous writer of great and original power – he is commonly referred to as 'The Wakefield Master' – revised, and in revising intensified, if
not transformed, a large proportion of the Cycle, including both the *Shepherds' Plays*.

ANONYMOUS

*

The York Play of the Crucifixion

(The thirty-fifth play in the Cycle)

FIRST SOLDIER. Sir knyghtis, take heede hydir in hye,
This dede on-dergh we may noght drawe,
Yee wootte youre selffe als wele as I,
How lordis and leders of owre lawe
5   Has geven dome that this doote shalle dye.
SECOND SOLDIER. Sir, alle thare counsaile wele we knawe,
Sen we are comen to Calvarie,
Latte ilke man helpe nowe as hym awe.
THIRD SOLDIER. We are all redy, loo,
10   That forward to fulfille.
FOURTH SOLDIER. Late here howe we shall doo,
And go we tyte ther tille.

FIRST SOLDIER. It may noght helpe here for to hone,
If we shall any worshippe wynne.

The York Play of the Crucifixion

FIRST SOLDIER. *Sir knights, take heed those gathered here together,*
This deed without trouble we cannot carry out,
You know yourselves as well as I,
How the lords and captains of our law
5   *Have given judgement that this fool shall die.*
SECOND SOLDIER. *Sir, all their plans we have known well*
Since we have come to Calvary.
Let each man help now as he ought.
THIRD SOLDIER. *We are all ready, lo,*
10   *That arrangement to carry out.*
FOURTH SOLDIER. *Let's hear what we are to do,*
And let us go to it quickly.

FIRST SOLDIER. *It does not help us to delay here,*
If we are to win any honour.

456

15   SECOND SOLDIER. He muste be dede [1]nedelyngis by none.
    THIRD SOLDIER. Than is good tyme what we begynne.
    FOURTH SOLDIER. Late dynge[2] hym doune! Than is he done.
      He shall nought dere us with his dynne.
    FIRST SOLDIER. He shall be sette and lerned sone,
20   With care to hym and all his kynne.
    SECOND SOLDIER. The foulest dede of all
      Shalle he dye for his dedis.
    THIRD SOLDIER. That menes: Crosse hym we shall.
    FOURTH SOLDIER. Behalde so right he redis[3].

25   FIRST SOLDIER. Thanne to this werke us muste take heede,
      So that oure wirkyng be noght wronge.
    SECOND SOLDIER. None othir noote to neven[4] is nede,
      But latte us haste hym for to hange.
    THIRD SOLDIER. And I have gone for gere, goode speede,
30   Bothe hammeres and nayles large and lange.
    FOURTH SOLDIER. Thanne may we boldely do this dede.
      Commes on, late kille this traitoure strange.
    FIRST SOLDIER. Faire myght ye falle in feere,
      That has wrought on this wise.
35   SECOND SOLDIER. Us nedis nought for to lere,
      Suche faitoures[5] to chastise.

    THIRD SOLDIER. Sen ilke a thyng es right arrayed,
      The wiselier nowe wirke may we.
    FOURTH SOLDIER. The crosse on grounde is goodely graied[6],
40   And boorede even as it awith to be.
    FIRST SOLDIER. Lokis that the ladde on lengthe be layde,
      And made me thene unto this tree.
    SECOND SOLDIER. For alle his fare he shalle be flaied,
      That one assaie sone shalle ye see.
45   THIRD SOLDIER. Come forthe, thou cursed knave,
      Thy comforte sone shall kele[7].
    FOURTH SOLDIER. Thyne hyre here shall thou have.
    FIRST SOLDIER. [8]Walkes oon, now wirke we wele.

1. 'necessarily by the ninth hour' (Mark xv. 33), 2. knock, 3. advises, 4. say (or add), 5. impostors, 6. prepared (with holes already bored to receive the nails), 7. cool, 8. Walk on (the cross which is laid flat on the ground).

JESUS: Almyghty god, my Fadir free,
50   Late this materes be made in mynde:
Thou badde that I shulde buxsome[1] be,
For Adam plyght for to be pyned[2].
Here to dede I obblisshe me
Fro that synne for to save mankynde,
55   And soveraynely be-seke I thee,
That thai for me may favoure fynde;
[3]And fro the Fende thame fende,
So that ther saulcs be saffe,
In welthe withouten ende.
60   I kepe nought ellis to crave.

FIRST SOLDIER. We! herke, sir knyghtis, for manoundis bloode![4]
Of Adam-kynde is all his thought.
SECOND SOLDIER. [5]The warlowe waxis werre than woode,
This doulfull dede ne dredith he noght.
65 THIRD SOLDIER. Thou shulde have mynde, with mayne and moode,
Of wikkid werkis that thou haste wrought.
FOURTH SOLDIER. [6]I hope that he had bene as goode
Have cesed of sawes that he uppe sought.
FIRST SOLDIER. Thoo sawes shall rewe hym sore
70   For all his saunteryng sone.
SECOND SOLDIER. Ille spede thame that hym spare
Tille he to dede be done!

THIRD SOLDIER. [7]Have done belyve, boy, and make the boune,
And bende thi bakke un-to this tree.
[Jesus lies down]
75 FOURTH SOLDIER. Byhalde, hym-selffe has laide hym doune,
In lenghe and breede[8] as he shulde bee.

1. obedient, 2. tortured, 3. 'And keep them from the Devil', 4. 'By Mahomet's blood.' No historical sense! 5. 'The sorcerer waxes worse than mad', 6. 'I think he might have been decent enough to have stopped such sayings', 7. 'Have down quickly, boy, and get moving', 8. length and breadth.

FIRST SOLDIER. This traitoure here teynted of treasoune,
Gose faste and fette hym than, ye thre.
And sen he claymeth kyngdome with croune,
80   Even as a kyng here have shall hee.
SECOND SOLDIER. Nowe, certis, I shall noght feyne[1]
Ere his right hande be feste.
THIRD SOLDIER. The lefte hande thanne is myne,
Late see who beres hym beste.

85   FOURTH SOLDIER. Hys lymmys[2] on lenghe than shalle I lede,
And even unto the bore[3] thame bringe,
FIRST SOLDIER. Unto his heede I shall take hede,
And with myne hande helpe hym to hyng.
SECOND SOLDIER. Nowe sen we foure shall do this dede,
90   And medill with this unthrifty[4] thyng,
Late no man spare for speciall speede,
Tille that we have made endyng.
THIRD SOLDIER. This forward may not faile,
Nowe are we right arraiede.
95   FOURTH SOLDIER. This boy here in oure baile
Shall bide full bittir brayde[5].

FIRST SOLDIER. Sir knyghtis, saie, howe wirke we nowe?
SECOND SOLDIER. Yis, certis, I hope I holde this hande.
THIRD SOLDIER. And to the boore I have it brought,
100   Full boxumly with-outen bande.
FOURTH SOLDIER. Strike on than harde, [6]for hym thee boght.
FIRST SOLDIER. Yis, here is a stubbe[7] will stiffely stande,
Thurgh bones and senous it shall be soght.
This werke is well, I will warande.
105   SECOND SOLDIER. Saie, sir, howe do we thore,
This bargayne may not blynne[8].
THIRD SOLDIER. [9]It failis a foote and more,
The senous are so gone ynne.

1. hang back, 2. legs, 3. the hole drilled to take the nail, 4. unsuccessful. The execution is taking time and trouble, 5. blow, 6. 'For the sake of him who bought (redeemed) thee.' The soldier uses a Christian believer's oath, and the inconsistency is arresting, 7. here 'nail', 8. halt now, 9. The 'sinews have shrunk' so that hand and boring no longer correspond.

FOURTH SOLDIER. I hope[1] that marke a-misse be bored.

110 SECOND SOLDIER. Than muste he bide in bittir bale.

THIRD SOLDIER. [2]In faith, it was overe skantely scored;
That makis it fouly for to faile.

FIRST SOLDIER. Why carpe ye so? faste on a corde,
And tugge hym to, by toppe and taile.

115 THIRD SOLDIER. Ya, thou comaundis lightly as a lorde,
Come helpe to haale[3], with ille haile.

FIRST SOLDIER. Nowe certis that shall I doo,
Full suerly as a snayle.

THIRD SOLDIER. And I shall taeche hym too,

120 Full nemely with a nayle.

This werke will holde, that dar I heete,
For nowe are feste faste both his handis.

FOURTH SOLDIER. Go we all foure thanne to his feete,
So shall oure space be spedely spende.

125 SECOND SOLDIER. [4]Latte see, what bourde his bale myght
beete?
Tharto my bakke nowe wolde I bende.

FOURTH SOLDIER. Owe! this werke is all unmeete,
This boring muste all be amende.

FIRST SOLDIER. A! Pees man, for mahounde!

130 Latte noman wotte that wondir,
A rope shall rugge hym doune,
Yf all his synnous go a-soundre.

SECOND SOLDIER. That corde full kyndely can I knytte[5],
[6]The comforte of this karle to kele.

135 FIRST SOLDIER. Feste on thanne faste that all be fytte,
It is no force howe felle he feele.

SECOND SOLDIER. Lugge on ye both a litill yitt.

THIRD SOLDIER. I shalle nought sese, as I have seele[7].

FOURTH SOLDIER. And I shalle fonde hym for to hitte.

140 SECOND SOLDIER. Owe, haylle![8]

1. think, 2. the hole 'was somewhat too carelessly drilled', 3. haul (on
the rope which is to stretch the arm), 4. 'Let see, what jest his miserable
anguish might brighten?', 5. tie, 6. 'To cool the comfort of this churl',
7. joy, 8. haul (on the rope attached to the legs).

FOURTH SOLDIER. Hoo nowe, I halde it wele.

FIRST SOLDIER. Have done[1], dryve in that nayle,
 So that no faute be foune.

FOURTH SOLDIER. This wirkyng wolde noght faile,
 Yf foure bullis here were bound.

145 FIRST SOLDIER. Ther cordis have evill encressed his paynes,
 Ere he wer tille the booryngis[2] brought.

SECOND SOLDIER. Yaa, assoundir are both synnous and vey-
 nis,
 On ilke a side, so have we soughte.

THIRD SOLDIER. Nowe all his gaudis[3] no thyng hym gaynes,
150 His sauntering shall with bale be bought.

FOURTH SOLDIER. I wille goo saie to oure soveraynes
 Of all this werkis howe we have wrought.

FIRST SOLDIER. Nay sirs, a nothir thyng
 Fallis firste to you and me,
155 I badde we shulde hym hyng,
 On heghte that men myght see.

SECOND SOLDIER. [4]We woote wele so ther wordes wore,
 But sir, that ded will do us dere.

FIRST SOLDIER. It may not mende, for to moote[5] more,
160 This harlotte muste be hanged here.

SECOND SOLDIER. The mortaise[6] is made fitte therfore.

THIRD SOLDIER. Feste on youre fyngeres than, in feere[7].

FOURTH SOLDIER. I wene it wolle nevere com thore.
 We foure rayse it noght right, to yere.

165 FIRST SOLDIER. Say man, whi carpis you soo?
 [8]Thy liftyng was but light.

SECOND SOLDIER. He menes ther muste be moo
 To heve hym uppe on hight.

1. now that the feet are aligned with the boring, 2. augur holes. Christ was stretched till his extremities corresponded with the holes prepared in the cross, 3. tricks, 4. 'We know very well that their orders were (to elevate), But sir, that deed will be hard work', 5. argue, 6. the mortice or socket dug to receive the butt of the cross, 7. all together, 8. 'You were not pulling your weight'.

THIRD SOLDIER. Now certis, I hope it shall noght nede
170 To calle to us more companye.
  Me-thynke we foure shulde do this dede,
  And bere hym to yone hille on high.
FIRST SOLDIER. It muste be done, with-outen drede,
  Nomore, but loke ye be redy;
175 And this parte shalle I lifte and leede,
  On lenghe[1] he shalle no lenger lie.
  Therfore nowe makis you boune[2],
  Late bere hym to yone hill.
FOURTH SOLDIER. Thanne will I bere here doune,
180 [3]And tente his tase untill.

SECOND SOLDIER. We twoo shall see tille aythir side,
  For ellis this werke will wrie all wrang.
THIRD SOLDIER. We are redy, in Gode, sirs, abide,
  And late me first his fete up fang.
185 SECOND SOLDIER. Why tente ye so to tales this tyde?
FIRST SOLDIER. Lifte uppe!
    [*All lift the cross together*]
FOURTH SOLDIER. Latte see!
SECOND SOLDIER. Owe! lifte a-lang.
THIRD SOLDIER. [4]Fro all this harme he shulde hym hyde
  And he war God.
FOURTH SOLDIER. The devill hym hang!
FIRST SOLDIER. For grete harme have I hent,
190 My shuldir is in soundre.
SECOND SOLDIER. And certis I am nere schente[5],
  So lange have I borne undir.

THIRD SOLDIER. This crosse and I in twoo muste twynne,
  Ellis brekis my bakke in sondre sone.
195 FOURTH SOLDIER. Laye doune agayne and leve youre dynne,
  This dcdc for us will nevre be donc.
    [*They lay it down*]

1. i.e. pronc, 2. rcady, 3. 'And attend to his toes'. The Fourth Soldier
is going to attend to the base of the cross in this operation, 4. 'He would
avoid all this trouble and pain to himself if he were God', 5. done in.

FIRST SOLDIER. Assaie, sirs, latte se if any gynne[1],
May helpe hym uppe, with-outen hone;
For here shulde wight[2] men worshippe wynne,
200   And noght with gaudis al day to gone.
SECOND SOLDIER. More wighter men than we
Full fewe I hope ye fynde.
THIRD SOLDIER. This bargayne will noght bee,
For certis we wantis wynde[3].

205   FOURTH SOLDIER. So wille of werke nevere we wore,
[4]I hope this carle some cautellis caste.
SECOND SOLDIER. My bourdeyne satte me wondir soore,
Unto the hill I myght noght laste.
FIRST SOLDIER. Lifte uppe, and sone he shall be thore,
210   Therfore feste on youre fyngeres faste.
THIRD SOLDIER. Owe! lifte!

[*They start to erect the cross again*]

FIRST SOLDIER. We, loo!
FOURTH SOLDIER. A litill more.
SECOND SOLDIER. Holde thanne!
FIRST SOLDIER. Howe nowe!
SECOND SOLDIER. The werste is paste.
THIRD SOLDIER. He weyes a wikkid weght.
SECOND SOLDIER. So may we all foure saie,
215   Ere he was heved on heght,
And raysed in this array.

FOURTH SOLDIER. He made us stande as any stones,
So boustous[5] was he for to bere.
FIRST SOLDIER. Nowe raise hym nemely for the nonys,
220   And sette hym be this mortas[6] heere.
And latte hym falle in all at ones,
For certis that payne shall have no pere.

1. contrivance, 2. strong, 3. 'For in fact we are out of breath', 4. 'I think this fellow cast some spells', 5. huge, 6. mortice (see above). The idea is to let the butt of the cross jar into position as violently as possible.

THIRD SOLDIER. Heve uppe!

FOURTH SOLDIER. Latte doune, so all his bones
Are a-soundre nowe on sides seere.

[*The cross is erected*]

225 FIRST SOLDIER. This fallyng was more felle,
Than all the harmes he hadde,
Nowe may a man wele telle,
The leste lith of this ladde.

THIRD SOLDIER. Me thynkith this crosse wil noght abide,
230 Ne stande stille in this morteyse yitt.

FOURTH SOLDIER. Att the firste tyme was it made overe
wyde,
That makis it wave, thou may wele witte.

FIRST SOLDIER. It shall be sette on ilke a side,
So that it shall no forther flitte,
235 Goode wegges[1] shall we take this tyde,
And feste the foote, thanne is all fitte.

SECOND SOLDIER. Here are wegges arraied
For that, both grete and smale.

THIRD SOLDIER. Where are oure hameres laide,
240 That we shulde wirke with all?

FOURTH SOLDIER. We have them here ever atte oure hande.

SECOND SOLDIER. Gyffe me this wegge, I shall it in dryve.

FOURTH SOLDIER. Here is anodir yitt ordande.

THIRD SOLDIER. Do take it me hidir belyve[2].

245 FIRST SOLDIER. Laye on thanne faste.

THIRD SOLDIER. Yis, I warrande.
I thryng thame same, so motte I thryve,
Nowe will this crosse full stabely stande,
All if he rave thei will noght ryve.

FIRST SOLDIER. Say, sir, howe likis thou nowe,
250 This werke that we have wrought?

FOURTH SOLDIER. We praye youe sais us howe,
Ye fele, or faynt ye ought?

1. wedges, 2. quickly.

JESUS. Al men that walkis by waye or strete,
Takes tente ye shalle o travayle tyne.
255   By-holdes myn heede, myn handis, and my feete,
    ¹And fully feele nowe ere ye fyne,
If any mournyng may be meete
Or myscheve mesured unto myne.
My Fadir,² that alle bales may bete,
260   For-giffis thes men that dois me pyne.
What thai wirke wotte thai noght,
Therfore my Fadir I crave
Latte nevere ther synnys be sought,
But see ther saules to save.

265 FIRST SOLDIER. We! harke! he jangelis like a jay.
    SECOND SOLDIER. ³Me thynke he patris like a py.
THIRD SOLDIER. He has ben doand all this day,
And made grete meyvng of mercy.
FOURTH SOLDIER. Es this the same that gune us say,
270   That he was Goddis sone almyghty?
FIRST SOLDIER. Therfore he felis full felle affraye,
And demyd this day for to dye.
SECOND SOLDIER. Vah! qui destruis templum ...⁴
THIRD SOLDIER. His sawes wer so, certayne.
275 FOURTH SOLDIER. And sirs, he saide to some
He myght rayse it agayne.

FIRST SOLDIER. To mustir that he hadde no myght,
For alle the kautelles⁵ that he couthe kaste,
All if he wer in worde so wight⁶,
280   For all his force nowe he is feste.
Als Pilate demed is done and dight.
Therfore I rede that we go reste.
SECOND SOLDIER. This race mon be rehersed right,
Thurgh the worlde thoth este and weste.
285 THIRD SOLDIER. Yaa, late hym hynge here stille,
And make mowes⁷ on the mone.

1. 'And fully sympathize before you pass on', 2. 'Who all ills can remedy', 3. 'Methinks he patters like a magpie', 4. See Mark xiv. 58, and Iohn ii. 19, 5. tricks, 6. mighty, 7. 'faces'.

FOURTH SOLDIER. Thanne may we wende at wille.
FIRST SOLDIER. Nay goode sirs, noght so sone.

For certis us nedis anodir note,
290   This kirtill¹ wode I of you crave.
SECOND SOLDIER. Nay, nay, sir, we will loke be lotte²,
Whilke of us foure to to have.
THIRD SOLDIER. I rede we drawe cutte for this coote,
Loo, se howe sone alle sidis to save.
295 FOURTH SOLDIER. The shorte cutte shall wynne, that wele
ye woote,
Whedir itt falle to knyght or knave.
FIRST SOLDIER. Felowes, ye thar noght flyte,
For this mantell is myne.
SECOND SOLDIER. Goo we thanne hense tyte,
300   This travayle here we tyne.

1. kirtle, 2. decide by lot.

NOTE

The Cycle of plays, performed on the Feast of *Corpus Christi* at York by the craft-gilds of the city, is preserved in a MS. of which the handwriting is principally fifteenth century. The Cycle was performed throughout the fourteenth and fifteenth centuries. The Reformation eventually enforced a discontinuance about 1580.

The Cycle consists of forty-eight plays starting with the Creation and ending with the Last Judgement. Each of the trade-gilds had the perquisite of a particular play (the subject often being in some way appropriate to the craft or trade of those performing in it). *The Crucifixion*, for instance, was acted by the Gild of Painters and Pinners.

APPENDIX

Compiled by Margaret Tubb
Revised by Charles Page

LIST OF ABBREVIATIONS

E.E.T.S.	Publications of the Early English Text Society		Philology	S.T.S.	Publication of the Scottish Text Society
		M.Ae	Medium Aevum		
		M.L.R.	Modern Languages Review	ed.	edited, edition
E.E.T.S.E.S.	E.E.T.S., Extra Series			abr.	abridged
				mod.	modernized
E.L.	Everyman's Library	M.P.	Modern Philology	repr.	reprinted
				rev.	revised
E.L.H.	English Literary History	P.M.L.A.	Publications of the Modern Language Association	trans.	translation
				b.	born
E. & S.	Essays and Studies			fl.	flourishing
				d.	died
J.E.G.P.	Journal of English and German	R.E.S.	Review of English Studies	c.	circa
				cent.	century

Under each author or work, the aim has been to list first a standard biography (if any), second a standard edition, and third a selection of books and articles for further study (listed in alphabetical order of authors).

FOR FURTHER READING AND REFERENCE

GENERAL BACKGROUND

General History

Bennett, H. S. *The Pastons and their England* (Cambridge, 1922; 1968)

Bindoff, S. T. *Tudor England* (Penguin Books, 1950)

Brewer, D. S. *Chaucer in His Time* (London, 1964)

Coulton, G. C. *Mediaeval Panorama: the English Scene from Conquest to Reformation* (Cambridge, 1938; 1961)

Crump, G. G., and Jacob, E. F. *The Legacy of the Middle Ages* (London, 1926; 1952)

Huizinga, J. *The Waning of the Middle Ages* (London, 1924; Penguin Books, 1965)

Jacob, E. F. *The Fifteenth Century 1399–1485* (Oxford, 1961)

Kendall, P. M. *The Yorkist Age* (London, 1962)

Kingsford, C. L. *Prejudice and Promise in Fifteenth-Century England* (London, 1925; 1962)

Myers, A. R. *England in the Late Middle Ages* (Penguin Books, 1953)

Power, E. *Medieval People* (London, 1951; 1963)

Powicke, F. M. *Medieval England: 1066–1485* (London, 1931)

Rickert, E. *Chaucer's World* (New York, 1948; 1962)

Salzmann, L. F. *English Social Life in the Middle Ages* (London, 1936)

Southern, R. W. *The Making of the Middle Ages* (London, 1953)

Stenton, D. M. *English Society in the Early Middle Ages* (Penguin Books, 1951)

Tawney, R. H. *Religion and the Rise of Capitalism* (London, 1926; Penguin Books, 1938)

Social and Economic History

Bennett, H. S. *Life on the English Manor, 1100–1400* (Cambridge, 1937)

Brewer, D. S. *Chaucer in his Time* (London, 1964)

Homans, G. C. *English Villagers of the Thirteenth Century* (New York, 1960)

Jusserand, J. J. *Wayfaring Life in the Middle Ages* (London, 1889; 1950)

Maitland, F. W. *Township and Borough* (Cambridge, 1898)

Mead, W. E. *The English Mediaeval Feast* (London, 1931; 1967)

Salzman, L. F. *English Trade in the Middle Ages* (Oxford, 1931; 1964)

Thrupp, S. L. *The Merchant Class of Mediaeval London* (Chicago, 1948)

PART FIVE

Education

Leach, A. F. *The Schools of Medieval England* (London, 1915)

Potter, G. R. 'Education' (Cambridge Medieval History, VII, 1935)

Rashdall, H. *Rashdall's Mediaeval Universities* (Oxford, 1895; ed. and rev. by F. M. Powicke and A. B. Emden, 1936)

Waddell, H. *The Wandering Scholars* (London, 1927)

The Church

Blench, J. W. *Preaching in England in the late Fifteenth and Sixteenth Centuries* (Oxford, 1964)

Dawson, C. *Medieval Essays* (London, 1954)

Gasquet, F. A. *Parish Life in Medieval England* (London, 1936)

Gilson, E. *The Spirit of Medieval Philosophy* (London, 1936)

Jacob, E. F. *Studies in the Conciliar Epoch* (Manchester, 1950; 1962)

Knowles, M. D. *The Evolution of Medieval Thought* (Cambridge, 1962)

Knowles, M. D. *The Religious Orders in England* (3 vols, Cambridge, 1948–59)

Leff, G. *Medieval Thought* (London, 1958)

Moorman, J. R. H. *Church Life in England in the Thirteenth Century* (Cambridge, 1946)

Owst, G. R. *Preaching in Medieval England* (Cambridge, 1926; New York, 1965)

Pantin, W. A. *The English Church in the Fourteenth Century* (London, 1955; Notre Dame, 1963)

Poole, R. L. *Illustrations of the History of Mediaeval Thought and Learning* (London, 1880; rev. ed. 1920; repr. New York, 1963)

Power, E. *Medieval English Nunneries* (Cambridge, 1922)

Powicke, F. M. *The Christian Life in the Middle Ages* (London, 1935)

Powicke, F. M. *The Reformation in England* (London, 1941; 1961)

Smalley, B. *The Study of the Bible in the Middle Ages* (Oxford, 1952)

Trevelyan, G. M. *England in the Age of Wycliffe* (London, 1929)

The Arts

Anderson, M. D. *Misericords. Medieval Life in English Woodcarving* (London, 1956)

Borenius, T., and Tristram, E. W. *English Medieval Painting* (Paris, 1927)

Cave, J. P. *Roof Bosses in Medieval Churches* (Cambridge, 1948)

Coulton, G. G. *Art and the Reformation* (Cambridge, 1953)

Evans, J. *English Art, 1307–1461* (Oxford, 1949)

Harman, R. A. *Medieval and Early Renaissance Music* (London, 1958)

Harrison, F. L. *Music in Medieval Britain* (London, 1958)

Harvey, J. H. *Gothic England* (London, 1948)

Hughes, A. and Abraham, G. *Ars Nova and the Renaissance 1300–1540* (New Oxford History of Music, 1960)

Mellers, W. *Music and Society* (London, 1946; 1950)

Oakeshott, W. *The Sequence of English Medieval Art* (London, 1950)

Pevsner, N. *Outline of European Architecture* (Penguin Books, 1943)

Reese, G. *Music in the Middle Ages* (New York, 1940)

Rickert, M. *Painting in Britain: The Middle Ages* (Penguin Books, 1954)

Saunders, O. E. *English Illumination* (Paris, 1930)

Saunders, O. E. *A History of Art in the Middle Ages* (Oxford, 1932)

Stone, L. *Sculpture in Britain: The Middle Ages* (Penguin Books, 1955)

Varty, K. *Reynard the Fox* (Leicester, 1967)

Webb, G. *Architecture in Britain: The Middle Ages* (Penguin Books, 1956)

Wood, M. *The English Mediaeval House* (London, 1965)

See also the bibliography in Evans, op. cit.

LITERATURE

Bibliography

Cambridge Bibliography of English Literature (5 vols., 1940–57; 1967)

Renwick, W. L., and Orton, H. *The Beginnings of English Literature to Skelton* (London, 1952)

Wells, J. E. *A Manual of the Writings in Middle English, 1050–1400* (New Haven, 1916–26)

Literary History

Auerbach, E. *Literary Language and Its Public* (1958; trans. London, 1965)

Auerbach, E. *Mimesis* (Princeton, 1953; New York, 1957)

Bennett, H. S. *Chaucer and the Fifteenth Century* (Oxford History of English Literature, II, 1, 1947)

Bennett, H. S. *English Books and Readers 1475–1557* (Cambridge, 1952)

Cambridge History of English Literature (Vols. I, II, Cambridge, 1907–16)

Chambers, E. K. *English Literature at the Close of the Middle Ages* (Oxford History of English Literature, II, 2, 1945)

Chaytor, H. J. *From Script to Print: An Introduction to Medieval Literature* (Cambridge, 1945; 1967)

Curtius, E. R. *European Literature and the Latin Middle Ages* (London, 1953)

Ker, W. P. *English Literature, Medieval* (London, 1912)

Legge, M. D. *Anglo-Norman Literature and its Background* (Oxford, 1963)

Lewis, C. S. *English Literature in the Sixteenth Century (excluding Drama)* (Oxford History of English Literature, III, 1954)

Mason, H. A. *Humanism and Poetry in the Early Tudor Period* (London, 1959)

Middle English Survey: Critical Essays ed. E. Vasta (Notre Dame, Indiana, 1965)

Owst, G. R. *Literature and Pulpit in Medieval England* (Cambridge, 1933; Oxford, 1962)

Schlauch, M. *English Medieval Literature and its Social Foundations* (Warsaw, 1956)

Wilson, R. M. *Early Middle English Literature* (London, 1939; 1968)

Wilson, R. M. *The Lost Literature of Medieval England* (London, 1952)

Poetry

Berdan, J. M. *Early Tudor Poetry* (London, 1920)

Everett, D. *Essays on Middle English Literature* (Oxford, 1955)

Hibbard, L. *Medieval Romance in England* (Oxford, 1924)

Kane, G. *Middle English Literature* (London, 1951)

Ker, W. P. *Epic and Romance* (London, 1908; New York, 1957)

Lewis, C. B. *Classical Myth and Arthurian Romance* Oxford, 1932)

Lewis, C. S. *The Allegory of Love* (London, 1936)

Loomis, F. M. *Celtic Myth and Arthurian Legend* (New York, 1927)

Loomis, R. S. *The Development of Arthurian Romance* (London, 1963)

Loomis, R. S. (ed.) *Arthurian Literature in the Middle Ages* (Oxford, 1959)

Oakden, J. P. *The Poetry of the Alliterative Revival* (Manchester, 1930–35; repr. 1968)

Spearing, A. C. *Criticism and Mediaeval Poetry* (London, 1964)

Speirs, J. *Medieval English Poetry: The Non-Chaucerian Tradition* (London, 1957; rev. 1962)

Speirs, J. *The Scots Literary Tradition* (London, 1940; 1962)

Weston, J. L. *From Ritual to Romance* (Cambridge, 1920; New York, 1957)

Wittig, K. *The Scottish Tradition in Literature* (London, 1958)

Prose

Bennett, H. S. 'Fifteenth-Century Secular Prose', *R.E.S.*, XXI (1945)

Chambers, R. W. *On the Continuity of English Prose*, *E.E.T.S.* (1932)

Coleman, T. W. *English Mystics of the Fourteenth Century* (London, 1938)

Colledge, E. *The Medieval Mystics of England* (London, 1962)

Knowles, D. *The English Mystical Tradition* (London, 1961)

Owst, G. R. *Literature and Pulpit in Medieval England* (Cambridge, 1933; Oxford, 1962)

Prins, A. *French Influence in English Phrasing* (Leiden, 1952)

Underhill, E. 'Medieval Mysticism' (Cambridge Medieval History, VII. 1935)

Workman, S. K. *Fifteenth-Century Translation* (Princeton, 1940)

Drama

Anderson, M. D. *Drama and Imagery in Medieval English Churches* (Cambridge, 1963)

Berry, Francis. 'A Towneley Pageant's Syntactic Tense' in *The Poet's Grammar* (London, 1958)

Bevington, D. M. *From Mankind to Marlowe* (Cambridge Mass., 1962)

Chambers, E. K. *The Medieval Stage* (Oxford, 1903)

Craig, H. *English Religious Drama of the Middle Ages* (Oxford, 1955)

Gardiner, H. C. *Mysteries End; an investigation of the last days of the medieval religious stage* (London, 1946, 1967)

Kolve, V. A. *The Play Called Corpus Christi* (London, 1967)

Prosser, E. *Drama and Religion in the English Mystery Plays* (Stanford, 1961; London, 1962)

Rossiter, A. P. *English Drama from Early Times to the Elizabethans* (London, 1950)

Speirs, John. *Medieval English Poetry: The Non-Chaucerian Tradition* (London, 1957)

Tiddy, R. J. E. *The Mummers' Play* (Oxford, 1923)

Wakefield Pageants in the Towneley Cycle, The, ed. A. C. Cawley (Manchester, 1958)

Welsford, E. *The Court Masque*, Chs. I, II (Cambridge, 1927; New York, 1962)

Wickham, G. W. G. *Early English Stages 1300–1600* (2 vols., London, 1959–63)

Young, K. *The Drama of the Medieval Church* (Oxford, 1933)

AUTHORS AND ANONYMOUS WORKS

ANTHOLOGIES

Fourteenth Century Verse and Prose ed. K. Sisam (Oxford, 1921; rev. 1955)

Fifteenth Century Prose and Verse mod. ed. A. W. Pollard (Arber's English Garner, 1903; New York, 1964)

Early Middle English Texts ed. B. Dickins and R. M. Wilson (Cambridge, 1951)

Middle English Literature ed. A. Brandl and O. Zippel (New York, 1955)

A Handbook of Middle English ed. F. Mosse, trans. J. A. Walker (Baltimore, 1952)

Literary Middle English Reader ed. A. S. Cook (Boston, 1915)

Middle English Metrical Romances ed. W. H. French and C. B. Hale (New York, 1930; 1964)

Middle English Verse Romances ed. D. B. Sands (New York, 1966)

English Verse between Chaucer and Surrey ed. E. P. Hammond (Durham N. C., 1927; New York, 1965)

Later Mediaeval English Prose ed. W. Mathews (New York, 1963)

The Thought and Culture of the English Renaissance: An Anthology of Tudor Prose ed. E. M. Nugent (Cambridge, 1955)

Scottish Poetry from Barbour to James VI ed. M. M. Gray (London, 1935)

AUTHORS

ASCHAM, ROGER (1516–68): Humanist: b. Yorkshire (?); St John's College, Cambridge; prominent Greek scholar; *Toxophilus*, on archery and education, published 1545; tutor to Princess Elizabeth, 1548; secretary to English ambassador to Charles V, 1550–3; Latin secretary to Queen Mary, 1553; private tutor and secretary to Queen Elizabeth, 1558; said to have lived and died in poverty owing to addiction to dicing and cock-fighting; chief work on education, *The Schoolmaster*, published 1570.

Life by Dr Johnson
English Works ed. W. A. Wright (Cambridge, 1904)
See L. V. Ryan, *Roger Ascham* (Stanford, 1963)

CAXTON, WILLIAM (c. 1422–91): Printer and translator: b. Kent; received good education; apprenticed to cloth merchant; successful commercial career; learned art of printing in Cologne, 1471; set up own printing press Westminster, 1476; printed works of Chaucer, Malory, Gower, and Lydgate.

Prologues and Epilogues ed. W. J. B. Crotch (*E.E.T.S.*, 1928; 1956)
See N. S. Aurner, *Caxton: a Study of the Literature of the First English Press* (London, 1926)
A. T. P. Biles, 'William Caxton as a Man of Letters', *The Library*, 4th Series, 15 (1935)
C. F. Buhler, *William Caxton and his Critics* (Syracuse, 1960)

CHARLES OF ORLEANS (1391–1455): Nephew of Charles VI of France: captured at Agincourt; remained prisoner in England till 1440; wrote poems in both English and French; shows influence of Froissart; friend of Duke of Suffolk.

> *The English Poems of Charles of Orleans* ed. R. Steele (*E.E.T.S.*, ccxv, ccxx, 1941–6)

CHAUCER, GEOFFREY (c. 1340–1400): Poet, diplomat, and civil servant: b. London; son of John Chaucer, vintner; page to Countess of Ulster 1357; fought in French wars 1359; esquire to Edward III who gave him annuity 1367; lifelong association with court circles partly responsible for French influence in work; visits to France on diplomatic missions 1370–8 increased his interest in French literature; visits to Italy 1372 and 1378 educated him in Italian literature; (*Hous of Fame*, first work showing Italian influence, written c. 1379); active public life from 1374 increased his wide knowledge of society and command of colloquial English; position as Controller of Customs for Wool 1374–86 gave him contact with London citizens; (*Canterbury Tales* probably begun c. 1387); Clerk of King's Works 1389; additional pension from Richard II 1394; sued for debts 1398; sent *Complaint to his Empty Purse* to Henry IV 1399 and received additional pension; leased house in Westminster but died few months later.

> D. S. Brewer, *Chaucer* (London, 1953)
> E. Legouis, *Geoffrey Chaucer* (Paris, 1910; trans. 1913; New York 1961)
> *Works* ed. F. N. Robinson (London, 1957)
> *Works* ed. W. W. Skeat (Oxford, 1897, etc.)
> *Chaucer's Poetry: an Anthology for the Modern Reader*, ed. E. T. Donaldson (New York, 1958)
> See J. A. W. Bennett, *The Parlement of Foules* (Oxford, 1957)
>> M. S. Bowden, *A Commentary on the General Prologue to the Canterbury Tales* (London, 1949)
>> M. S. Bowden, *A Reader's Guide to Chaucer* (New York, 1964; London, 1965)
>> H. F. Brooks, *Chaucer's Pilgrims* (London, 1962)
>> *Chaucer Criticism; I: The Canterbury Tales; II: Troilus and Criseyde* Ed. R. J. Schoek and J. Taylor (Bloomington, 1959–61)
>> W. H. Clemen, *Chaucer's Early Poetry* (Cologne, 1938; trans. London, 1963)
>> T. W. Craik, *The Comic Tales of Chaucer* (London, 1964)
>> W. C. Curry, *Chaucer and the Mediaeval Sciences* (London, 1926; rev. ed., 1960)
>> D. Everett, *Essays on Middle English Literature* (Oxford, 1955)
>> G. L. Kittredge, *Chaucer and his Poetry* (Cambridge, Mass., 1915; 1946)
>> J. L. Lowes, *Geoffrey Chaucer* (London, 1934; 1944)

J. Manly, *Chaucer and the Rhetoricians* (London, 1926)

C. Muscatine, *Chaucer and the French Tradition* (Berkeley, 1957; 1964)

R. O. Payne, *The Key of Remembrance* (New Haven, 1963)

K. Schaar, *The Golden Mirror* (Lund, 1956; 1967)

Sources and Analogues of Chaucer's Canterbury Tales, ed. W. F. Bryan and G. Dempster (Chicago, 1941; repr. New York, 1958)

J. Speirs, *Chaucer the Maker* (London, 1951; rev. ed. 1962)

C. Spurgeon, *Five Hundred Years of Chaucer Criticism and Allusion* (London, 1914–25; New York, 1960)

DOUGLAS, GAVIN (1475–1522): Poet and bishop: aristocratic background; M.A. St Andrews University; Bishop of Dunkeld; longest poem *The Palace of Honour* published 1501 is in tradition of *Romance of the Rose*; maturest poem *King Heart* is allegory of man's life and death; greatest work is translation of the *Aeneid*.

Works ed. J. Small (4 vols., Edinburgh, 1874)

Aenid ed. D. F. C. Coldwell (4 vols., S.T.S., 1960–64)

Selections ed. D. F. C. Coldwell (Oxford, 1964)

See C. S. Lewis, *The Allegory of Love* (London, 1936)

C. S. Lewis, *English Literature in the Sixteenth Century (Excluding Drama)* (Oxford History of English Literature, III, 1954)

G. G. Smith, *Scottish Literature: Character and Influence* (London, 1919)

J. Speirs, *The Scots Literary Tradition* (London, 1940; rev. ed. 1962)

DUNBAR, WILLIAM (c. 1460 – c. 1520): Poet: aristocratic background; B.A. St Andrews 1477; employed at Scottish court and received pension from James IV c. 1500; literary life probably began then; accompanied mission to London to negotiate marriage between James IV and Margaret Tudor 1501; exercised some of functions of poet laureate for both English and Scottish courts.

J. W. Baxter, *William Dunbar* (Edinburgh, 1952)

Works ed. W. Mackay Mackenzie (Edinburgh, 1932)

Poems ed. J. Kinsley (Oxford, 1958)

See I. Hyde, 'Primary Sources and Associations of Dunbar's Aureate Imagery', *M.L.R.,* LI (1956)

E. Morgan, 'Dunbar and the Language of Poetry', *Essays in Criticism,* 2 (1952)

See also Lewis, Smith and Speirs (cited under Douglas)

GOWER, JOHN (1330?–1408): Poet: b. Kent; amassed considerable wealth probably through trade; liberal benefactor of churches; friend of Chaucer; in service of Henry, Earl of Derby 1393; in later years had apartment in priory of St Mary Overy, Southwark.

Works ed. G. C. Macaulay (4 vols., Oxford, 1899–1902)

English Works ed. G. C. Macaulay (2 vols. *E.E.T.S.*, 1900–1901; repr. 1957)

Selections ed. J. A. W Bennett (Oxford, 1968)

See G. Coffman, 'John Gower, Mentor for Royalty', *P.M.L.A.*, LXIX (1954)

W. G. Dodd, *Courtly Love in Gower and Chaucer* (Boston, 1913; New York, 1958)

J. H. Fisher, *John Gower, Moral Philosopher and Friend of Chaucer* (New York, 1964; London, 1965)

Lewis (cited under Douglas)

HENRYSON, ROBERT (c. 1425–c. 1500): Poet and schoolmaster; possibly received university education abroad and at Glasgow University; probably master at Benedictine Abbey grammar school, Dunfermline.

M. W. Sterns, *Robert Henryson* (New York, 1949)

Works ed. H. Harvey Wood (Edinburgh, 1933; rev. 1958)

Poems ed. C. Elliott (Oxford, 1963)

Testament of Cresseid ed. D. Fox (London, 1968)

J. MacQueen, *Robert Henryson: A Study of the Major Narrative Poems* (Oxford, 1967)

See Lewis, Smith and Speirs (cited under Douglas)

HEYWOOD, JOHN (c. 1497–c. 1580): Playwright, musician, and professional entertainer: entered royal service at early age; friend of Sir Thomas More; played interlude with his children before Princess Mary c. 1537; enjoyed great favour in reign of Mary but, because of his Catholicism, lost favour on accession of Elizabeth and fled to Belgium.

The Foure P's, Johan Johan . . . and Sir Johan the Preeste, The Play of the Wether in *The Chief Pre-Shakespearean Dramas* ed. J. Q. Adams (Boston, 1924)

HILTON, WALTER (d. 1396): Augustinian canon of Thurgarton, Notts: wrote ostensibly for a nun who had become recluse, but actually for larger audience; great influence on spiritual life of late 14th cent. and later; shows influence of Rolle and *Cloud of Unknowing*; gives many directions for piety and for overcoming Deadly Sins.

The Scale of Perfection mod. ed. E. Underhill (London, 1923); mod. trans. G. Sitwell (London, 1955)

The Ladder of Perfection, mod. trans. L. Sherley-Price (Penguin Books, 1957)

The Goad of Love, mod. ed. C. Kirchberger (London, 1952)

Minor Works ed. D. Jones (London, 1929)

See R. W. Chambers, *On the Continuity of English Prose* (*E.E.T.S.*, 1932)

M. Deanesly, 'Vernacular Books in England in the Fourteenth and Fifteenth Centuries', *M.L.R.* xv (1920)

H. L. Gardner, 'Walter Hilton and the Mystical Tradition in England'. *E. & S.*, XXII (1937)

M. D. Knowles, *The English Mystics* (London, 1927)

E. Underhill, '*Medieval Mysticism*' (*Cambridge Medieval History*, VII, 1935)

JULIAN OF NORWICH (b. c. 1343, d. after 1413): Mystic: recluse in cell attached to church of St Julian, Norwich; during illness experienced revelations; twenty years later experienced further revelations which illuminated previous ones; record of experiences in two forms; shorter version probably records original visions more accurately; work shows acquaintance with Hilton.

Comfortable Words (shorter version) trans. D. Harford (London, 1911)

Revelations of Divine Love (fuller version) ed. R. Hudleston (London, 1952); ed. Sister A. M. Reynolds (London, 1957)

A Shewing of Divine Love ed. Sister A. M. Reynolds (London, 1958)

Selections ed. P. F. Chambers (London, 1955)

See Knowles (cited under Hilton)

P. Molinari, *Julian of Norwich: the teaching of a Fourteenth Century English Mystic* (London, 1958)

R. H. Thouless, *The Lady Julian* (London, 1924)

Underhill (cited under Hilton)

R. M. Wilson, 'Three Middle English Mystics,' (*E. & S.*, New Series IX, 1956)

KEMPE, MARGERY (b. c. 1373): Mystic: daughter of former mayor of Lynn; married John Kempe, *worshipful burgess*; underwent spiritual change after Christ appeared to her and restored her reason during fit of insanity after birth of first child; saw visions and made pilgrimage to Jerusalem; visited Julian of Norwich; travelled widely; tendency to hysteria; autobiography has great value as human document and picture of medieval life.

The Book of Margery Kempe ed. H. E. Allen and S. B. Meech (*E.E.T.S.*, 1940; 1961)

The Book of Margery Kempe mod. abr. ed. E. Butler-Bowdon (London, 1954)

See Wilson (cited under Julian of Norwich)

LANGLAND, WILLIAM (b. c. 1331): Poet; biography based only on notes in manuscript and allusions in poem; illegitimate son of Eustace de la Rokayle (?); Benedictine school, Malvern (?); took minor orders (?); earned living in London by singing psalms.

Piers Plowman ed. W.W. Skeat (Oxford, 1957)

Piers Plowman A-Version, ed. G. Kane (London, 1960)

Piers Plowman B-text, passus I–VII, ed. W. W. Skeat (Oxford, 1900)
Piers Plowman mod. ed. H. W. Wells (London, 1938); D. and R. Attwater
(*E.L.*, 1957); J. F. Goodridge (London, 1959).

See M. W. Bloomfield, *Piers Plowman as a Fourteenth-Century Apocalypse*
(New Brunswick, 1962)

    R. W. Chambers, *Man's Unconquerable Mind* (London, 1939)

    E. T. Donaldson, *Piers Plowman; The C-text and its Poet* (New Haven, 1949)

    R. W. Frank, *Piers Plowman and the Scheme of Salvation* (Oxford, 1957)

    G. Hort, *Piers Plowman and Contemporary Religious Thought* (London, 1937)

    J. Lawlor, *Piers Plowman: An Essay in Criticism* (London, 1962)

    J. P. Oakden, *The Poetry of the Alliterative Revival* (Manchester, 1930–35; repr. 1968)

    E. Salter, *Piers Plowman: An Introduction* (Oxford, 1962)

    E. Vasta, *The Spiritual Basis of Piers Plowman* (The Hague, 1965)

    H. W. Wells, 'The Construction of *Piers Plowman*' (*P.M.L.A.*, XLIV, 1929); 'The Philosophy of *Piers Plowman*' (*P.M.L.A.*, LIII, 1938)

    E. Zeeman, '*Piers Plowman* and the Pilgrimage to Truth' (*E. & S.*, New Series, II, 1958)

LAWMAN: A priest living on the banks of the Severn, at Lower Arley
or Arley Regis; wrote long history of the Britons from the time of
Brutus (its legendary founder) to the year 689, in vigorous, semi-
alliterative verse – perhaps between 1170 and 1210; based on Anglo-
Norman verse chronicle and many other as yet unidentified sources, is
first treatment of the Arthurian stories in English, and one of the few
which maintain a high, heroic note throughout.

    The Brut ed. and trans. Sir F. Madden (3 vols., London, 1847)

    Brut Ed. G. L. Brook and R. F. Leslie (*E.E.T.S.*, 1963–)

    Selections ed. G. L. Brook (Oxford, 1963)

    See H. C. Wyld, 'Lawman as an English Poet', RES, 6 (1930)

    J. S. Tatlock, *The Legendary History of Britain* (Berkeley, 1950)

LINDSAY, SIR DAVID (c. 1485–c. 1550): Poet; courtier of James IV; in
charge of early education of James V (born 1512), whom he served
later as herald and ambassador; work closely associated with life of the
court (*Ane Satyre of the Thrie Estatis* grew from a royal entertainment),
but draws strength from popular tradition of humour and satire.

    W. Murison, *Sir David Lyndsay, Poet and Satirist of the Old Church in Scotland* (Cambridge, 1938)

    Works ed. D. Hamer (4 vols. *S.T.S.*, 1931–6)

    Ane Satyre of the Thrie Estatis ed. J. Kinsley (London, 1954)

    Squyer Meldrum ed. J. Kinsley (London, 1959)

    See Lewis and Spiers (cited under Douglas)

LYDGATE, JOHN (c. 1370–c. 1450): Poet; entered monastery of Bury St Edmunds, 1385; enjoyed patronage of Henry V, and later Humphrey, Duke of Gloucester; Prior of Hatfield Broadoak, 1421; after eleven years in political life, retired to Bury St Edmunds; vast output of verse documents the whole range of cultivated, aristocratic interests in his time; the *Troy Book*, the *Pilgrimage of the Life Man*, the *Fall of Princes*, the *Life of Our Lady* are among many tasks of translation or adaptation to which he applied his eloquence.

W. F. Schirmer, *John Lydgate: A Study in the Culture of the XVth Century* (1952; trans. London, 1961)

Minor Poems ed. H. N. MacCracken (*E.E.T.S.*, 1910–1933; repr. 1961)

Poems ed. J. Norton Smith (Oxford, 1966)

See E. P. Hammond, *English Verse between Chaucer and Surrey* (Durham, N.C., 1927; repr. New York, 1965)

A. Renoir, *The Poetry of John Lydgate* (London, 1967)

MALORY, SIR THOMAS: Author of *Morte D'Arthur*: son of Warwickshire gentleman; in service Earl of Warwick; at Calais c. 1415; knighted before 1442; M.P. 1445; led lawless and turbulent life; imprisoned several times; possibly obtained books from library in house of the Grey Friars, near Newgate; probably died in prison.

W. Mathews, *The Ill-Framed Knight: A Skeptical Inquiry into the Identity of Sir Thomas Malory* (Berkeley, 1966)

Works ed. E. Vinaver (London, 1954)

Morte D'Arthur ed. E. Vinaver (3 vols., Oxford, 1947)

The Tale of the Death of King Arthur ed. E. Vinaver (Oxford, 1955)

Morte D'Arthur mod. ed. (2 vols., *E.L.*, 1906)

J. A. W. Bennet (ed.), *Essays on Malory* (Oxford, 1963)

R. M. Lumiansky (ed.), *Malory's Originality* (Baltimore, 1964)

MANNYNG OF BRUNNE, ROBERT (fl. 1288–1338): Poet: native of Bourne, Lincs.; probably spent some time at Cambridge where met Robert Bruce; belonged to Gilbertine priory, Sempringham, and later to Gilbertine priory, Sixhill, Lincs.; *Handlyng Synne* designed for common people as counter-attraction to inns; finished *Rhyming Chronicle of England* 1338.

Handlyng Synne ed. F. J. Furnivall (*E.E.T.S.*, 1901–3)

See Ruth Crosby, 'Robert Mannyng of Brunne: A new Biography', *P.M.L.A.*, LVII (1942)

Francis Berry, 'Mannyng's Dancers of Colbeck', *Life and Letters To-day* x (London, 1949)

MORE, SIR THOMAS (1478–1535): Author, scholar, and statesman: son of famous London lawyer; brought up in household Archbishop Morton; Oxford; became lawyer; friend of Erasmus; M.P. 1503–4; from 1516 prominent at court; present at Field of Cloth of Gold 1520; undertook many diplomatic missions; Lord Chancellor 1529; refused to take oath denying Pope's supremacy; confined in Tower and executed.

Lives of St Thomas More by William Roper and Nicholas Harpsfield, ed. E. E. Reynolds (*E.L.*, 1963)

R. Ames, *Citizen Thomas More and his Utopia* (Princeton, 1949)

Works ed. W. E. Campbell and A. W. Reed (2 vols., London, 1931)

Works: Vol. 2, *The History of King Richard III* ed. R. S. Sylvester (New Haven, 1963); Vol. 4 *Utopia* ed. E. Surtz and J. Hexter (New Haven, 1965)

Utopia, and *Dialogue of Comfort*, trans. R. Robinson (*E.L.*, 1926)

See R. W. Chambers, *Thomas More* (London, 1935)

J. H. Hexter, *More's Utopia: The Biography of an Idea* (Princeton, 1950)

C. S. Lewis, *English Literature in the Sixteenth Century (Excluding Drama)* (Oxford History of English Literature, III, 1954)

H. A. Mason, *Humanism and Poetry in the Early Tudor Period* (London 1959)

E. Surtz, *The Praise of Pleasure: Philosophy – Education – Communism in More's Utopia* (Harvard, 1957)

E. Surtz, *The Praise of Wisdom: A Commentary on the Religious and Moral Backgrounds of St Thomas More's Utopia* (Chicago, 1957)

PASTONS (1422–1509): famous letter-writers: wealthy Norfolk family; their letters give detailed picture of lives of three generations; description of middle-class society, preoccupied with money matters, leases, the management of property and lawsuits; description of domestic life, the use of leisure and upbringing of children; show that middle classes now writing in English rather than Latin.

Paston Letters ed. J. Gairdner (6 vols , London, 1904; New York, 1967)

Paston Letters, mod. selection (2 vols., *E.L.*, 1924)

Paston Letters ed. N. Davis, Selection (Oxford, 1958)

See H. S. Bennett, *The Pastons and their England* (Cambridge, 1922)

ROLLE, RICHARD, OF HAMPOLE (d. 1349): Mystic and hermit: b. Thornton Dale, near York (?); left Oxford aged nineteen for religious reasons; settled as hermit on estate of Dalton family where composed some of early works; lived for time in Richmondshire; finally settled at Hampole; probably died of plague; regarded as saint though not formally canonized; works frequently copied and imitated.

Writings Ascribed to Richard Rolle, Hermit of Hampole, and Materials for his Biography, H. E. Allen (New York, 1927)

English Writings of Richard Rolle, Hermit of Hampole ed. H. E. Allen (Oxford, 1931)

The Fire of Love, mod. ed. F. M. M. Comper (London, 1914)

The Mending of Life mod. ed. D. Harford (London, 1913)

The Form of Perfect Living mod. ed. G. E. Hodgson (London, 1910)

See T. W. Coleman, *English Mystics of the Fourteenth Century* (London, 1938)

F. M. M. Comper, *The Life and Lyrics of Richard Rolle* (London, 1927)

Wilson (cited under Julian of Norwich)

SACKVILLE, THOMAS (1536–1618): Poet: aristocratic background; Inner Temple; collaborated with Thomas Norton in *Gorboduc* (1561) and contributed to the *Mirror for Magistrates* (1563); then devoted himself to public career – Earl of Dorset, Lord Treasurer of the Privy Council, Chancellor of Oxford University.

P. Bacquet, *Un Contemporaine d'Elisabeth I: Thomas Sackville* (Geneva, 1966)

Gorboduc in *Five Elizabethan Tragedies* ed. A. K. McIlwraith (World's Classics, 1938)

Mirror for Magistrates ed. L. B. Campbell (Cambridge, 1938; New York, 1960)

See Lewis (cited under More)

SKELTON, JOHN (c. 1460–1529): Poet, scholar, and priest: Cambridge; became poet laureate 1489; took holy orders; tutor to young Prince Henry, later Henry VII; structure of verse characteristic of fifteenth century but satiric quality anticipates period of Reformation; described by Caxton as humanist scholar.

H. L. R. Edwards, *Skelton; the Life and Times of an early Tudor Poet* (London, 1949)

Works ed. A. Dyce (London, 1843, repr. 1968)

Complete Poems mod. ed. P. Henderson (London, 1931)

See S. E. Fish, *John Skelton's Poetry* (New Haven, 1965)

K. Garvin (ed.), *The Great Tudors* (London, 1935)

W. O. Harris, *Skelton's Magnyfycence and the Cardinal Virtue Tradition* (Chapel Hill, 1966)

A. R. Heiserman, *Skelton and Satire* (Chicago, 1961)

Lewis (cited under More)

W. Nelson, *John Skelton, Laureate* (London, 1939; New York, 1964)

SPENSER, EDMUND (1552–99): Poet; b. London: Merchant Taylor's school; took M.A. Cambridge 1576, where met Gabriel Harvey and absorbed Calvinist tendencies expressed in *Shepheard's Calendar*; employed by Leicester 1579; secretary to Governor of Ireland 1580; visited London 1590–1 and 1596 to publish *Faerie Queene* and make frustrated appeals for court promotion; satirized court in *Colin Clout's*

Come Home Again (1595) and *Mother Hubbard's Tale* (1591); married
1594 – courtship recorded in *Amoretti*; advocated repressive measures
in prose work *A View of the Present State of Ireland*; became Sheriff of
Cork; visited London with dispatches about revolt of Tyrone 1597;
died at Westminster.

A. C. Judson, *The Life of Edmund Spencer* (London, 1946)

Works, Variorum Edition, ed. E. Greenlaw, C. G. Osgood, R. Gottfried
et al. (10 vols., Baltimore, 1932–58; 1966)

Poetical Works ed. J. C. Smith (Oxford Standard Authors)

Faerie Queene ed. W. J. Hales (2 vols., *E.L.*, 1910)

Mutabilitie Cantos ed. S. P. Zitzner (London, 1968)

See Lewis (cited under Douglas)

W. Nelson, *The Poetry of Edmund Spenser* (New York, 1963)

M. P. Parker, *The Allegory of the Faerie Queene* (Oxford, 1960)

W. L. Renwick, *Edmund Spenser* (London, 1925; 1965)

T. P. Roche, *The Kindly Flame: A study of the 3rd and 4th Books of
Spenser's Faerie Queene* (Princeton, 1964)

Janet Spens, *Spenser's Faerie Queene: An Interpretation* (London, 1934;
New York, 1967)

R. Tuve, *Allegorical Imagery* (Princeton, New Jersey, 1966)

E. Welsford, *Spenser's Fowre Hymns* (Oxford, 1967)

SURREY, HENRY HOWARD, EARL OF (c. 1517–47): Poet, scholar,
soldier, courtier; spent much of childhood at Windsor with Richmond,
son of Henry VII; brilliant but tumultuous career; wrote some of best
verses during imprisonment for striking political enemy; wrote most
amusing poem, a mock apology, when imprisoned for breaking windows in city; won literary reputation with use of the sonnet, blank
verse, and poulter's measure; beheaded on ridiculous charge of treason.

E. Casady, *Henry Howard, Earl of Surrey* (New York, 1938)

Poems ed. F. M. Padelford (rev. ed., Seattle, 1928)

Poems ed. E. Jones (Oxford, 1964)

Aeneid ed. F. H. Ridley (Berkeley, 1963)

See Lewis (cited under Douglas)

THOMAS OF HALES (fl. 1250): Poet: native of Hales, Gloucester;
Franciscan; distinguished scholar; *Luve Ron* probably written early in
reign Henry III.

A Luve Ron (*Early Middle English Texts*, 103–9)

TREVISA, JOHN (d. 1402): Translator, scholar, and priest; b. Cornwall;
contemporary of Wycliff at Oxford; Fellow of Exeter Coll. 1362;
Fellow of Queen's Coll. 1372; expelled 1379 probably because of

Wycliffite leanings; spent most of subsequent life as vicar of Berkely in Gloucestershire; most important translations made at command of Thomas, Lord Berkely; one of most important prose writers of time.

Life in A. J. Perry's introduction to three of Trevisa's shorter works (*E.E.T.S.*, 1924)

Mod. selections from trans. of *De Proprietatibus Rerum* in Robert Steele, *Medieval Lore* (London, 1893)

Polychronicon (trans. from R. Higden), ed. C. Babington and J. R. Lumby (9 vols., Rolls Series, London, 1865–86)

See E. H. Wilkins, *Was John Wycliffe a Negligent Pluralist; also John de Trevisa his Life and Work* (New York, 1916)

WYATT, SIR THOMAS (1503–42): Poet and statesman: son of Sir Henry Wyatt; Cambridge; distinguished but precarious career at court; on diplomatic missions to Italy and France 1525–7; introduced Petrarchan sonnet into England 1527; High Marshal Calais 1529–30; imprisoned 1526 at time Anne Boleyn's downfall; wrote verse epistles condemning life at court c. 1536; ambassador to Emperor 1537; imprisoned on fall of Cromwell, his supporter at court; on release retired to castle at Allington where wrote satires; Knight of Shire for Kent 1542; d. at Sherborne.

K. Muir, *The Life and Letters of Sir Thomas Wyatt* (Liverpool, 1963)

Poems ed. K. Muir (London, 1949)

The Poems of Sir Thomas Wyat ed. A. K. Foxwell (2 vols, London, 1913; repr. New York, 1964)

See D. W. Harding, 'The Rhythmical Intention in Wyatt's Poetry' in *Scrutiny* XIV, 2 (1946)

Lewis (cited under Douglas); Mason (cited under More)

R. Southall, *The Courtly Maker* (Oxford, 1964)

P. Thomson, *Sir Thomas Wyatt and His Background* (London, 1964)

WYCLIF, JOHN (c. 1328–84): Priest, ecclesiastical reformer and writer: b. Yorkshire; Oxford c. 1345; Master of Balliol, 1360; rector of Fillingham, 1361; rector of Ludgershall, 1368; Doctor of Theology, 1372; rector of Lutterworth, Leicestershire, from 1374; inspired initiation of English version of Bible; attacked church endowments and denied right of Church to interfere with secular matters; attacked doctrine of transubstantiation c. 1379 and was publicly condemned in Oxford, 1380; spent rest of life in Lutterworth and spread doctrines among people through 'poor preachers'.

H. B. Workman, *John Wyclif: A Study of the English Medieval Church* (2 vols., Oxford, 1926)

English Works ed. F. D. Matthew (*E.E.T.S.*, 1880)

Select English Works ed. T. Arnold (3 vols., Oxford, 1869–71)

Select English Works ed. H. E. Winn (London, 1929)
The Wycliffite Bible ed. J. Forshall and F. Madden (4 vols., Oxford, 1850)
The New Testament and *The Psalms, Job*, etc., ed. W. W. Skeat (London, 1879 and 1881)
See M. Deanesley, *The Lollard Bible* (Cambridge, 1920)
    S. L. Fristedt, *The Wycliffe Bible* (Stockholm, 1953)
    K. B. MacFarlane, *J. Wyclif and the Beginnings of English Nonconformity* (London, 1952)
    B. L. Manning, Cambridge Medieval History, VII, xvi (1935)

ANONYMOUS WORKS

POETRY

ATHELSTON (14th cent.): Swiftly-moving romance of violent events in pre-Conquest England; one of the finest of the large group of tail-rhyme romances produced in the east-midland area from 1350 onwards.

    Ed. A. McI. Trounce (*E.E.T.S.*, 1951; 1957)
    See A. McI. Trounce, 'The Middle English Tail Rhyme Romances', *M.Ae.*, I, II, III, (1932, 1933, 1934)

AWNTYRS OF ARTHUR (14th cent.): In three MSS.; one of several Northern romances illustrating virtues and describing adventures of Gawain; describes meeting of Gawain and Guinevere with ghost near Wadling Tarn; Gawain accepts and wins challenge; in fifty-five 13-line stanzas, verses linked by rhetorical repetition as in *Pearl*.

    Ed. F. J. Amours, *Scottish Alliterative Poems* (Scottish Text Society, 1897; repr. New York, 1968)
    See J. Speirs, *Medieval English Poetry, the Non-Chaucerian Tradition* (London, 1957; rev. ed. 1962)

BALLADS: No marks of personal authorship; great controversy about origins and dates; different theories discussed by Louise Pound in *Poetic Origins and the Ballad* (New York, 1921; 1961).

    The English and Scottish Popular Ballads ed. F. J. Child (London, 1882–98; repr. New York, 1965), abr. ed. G. L. Kittredge (Cambridge, Mass., 1904)
    The Ballad Book ed. M. Leach (New York, 1955)
    See W. J. Entwistle, *European Balladry* (London, 1939; 1951)
        G. H. Gerould, *The Ballad of Tradition* (Oxford, 1932; 1960)
        M. J. C. Hodgart, *The Ballad* (London, 1950; 1962)
        C. J. Sharp, *English Folk Song; Some Conclusions* (London, 1907; 1965)
        L. C. Wimberley, *Folklore in the English and Scottish Ballads* (Cambridge, 1928; repr. New York, 1965)
        Speirs (cited under Douglas)

BRETON LAYS: Bretons had reputation for story-telling, probably because of *lais* of Marie de France; their shorter tales possibly had musical form and setting in Brittany; when such tales were written in English in fourteenth century, *lais* are described as belonging to distant past (e.g. opening passage of *Le Freine*); whether English romance is classed as Breton lay depends on whether (a) it describes itself as one (*Sir Orfeo*, *Le Freine*), (b) has Brittany setting (*Sir Degare*), or (c) tells story based on one of *lais* of Marie de France (*Sir Launfal*).

> Ed. T. C. Rumble, *The Breton Lays in Middle English* (Detroit, 1965)
> See R. Bromwich, 'A Note on the Breton Lays', *M.Ae.*, XXVI (1957)
>> L. Hibbard Loomis *Medieval Romance in England* (Oxford, 1924; rev. ed. New York, 1963)
>> Spiers (cited under *Awntyrs of Arthur*)

Le Freine (early 14th cent.): Based on Marie de France's *Lai de Fresne*; has prologue which was characteristic of *lais*; same prologue in *Sir Orfeo* which suggests same author; ending missing.

> Ed. Rumble (cited under *Le Freine*)

Sir Degare (c. 1300–25): Probably composed in S. Midlands; written in short couplets; Brittany setting; combines romance and folklore.

> Ed. W. H. French and C. B. Hale, *Middle English Metrical Romances* (New York, 1930)
> Ed. Rumble (cited under *Le Freine*)
> See C. P. Faust, *A Study of the Texts and Narrative Structure* (London, 1936)

Sir Launfal (14th cent.): Arthurian romance; based on Marie de France's *Lai de Lanval*.

> Ed. French and Hale (cited under *Sir Degare*)
> Ed. A. J. Bliss (London, 1960)
> Trans. J. L. Weston, *The Chief Middle English Poets* (Boston, 1914)

Sir Orfeo (c. 1300): Composed in South; same prologue as *Le Freine*: a medieval version of story of Orpheus and Eurydice.

> Ed. French and Hale (cited under *Sir Degare*)
> Ed. A. J. Bliss (Oxford, 1954)
> Trans. Weston (cited under *Sir Launfal*)

HAVELOCK (c. 1285): Probably originally composed in North Midland dialect of Lincolnshire; illustrates exile and return theme; well-constructed plot; author probably minstrel little acquainted with courtly life; vigorous, realistic portrayal of humble life.

> Ed. W. W. Skeat, revised by K. Sisam (Oxford, 1915)
> Trans. L. Hibbard, *Three Middle English Romances* (London, 1911)
> See Speirs (cited under *Awntyrs of Arthur*)

KING HORN (C. 1225): Like *Havelok* is based on earlier French narrative but reflects spirit of English common people; intended for recitation to popular audience; probably composed in South; exile and return theme; shows influence of French short couplets on traditional metre.

Ed. J. Hall (Oxford, 1901)

Ed. French and Hale (cited under *Sir Degare*)

Trans. Weston (cited under *Sir Launfal*), and Hibbard (cited under Havelok)

See W. H. French, *Essays on 'King Horn'* (Ithaca, N.Y., 1940)

Hibbard (cited under *Breton Lays*)

Speirs (cited under *Awntyrs of Arthur*)

KINGIS QUAIR (C. 1423): Still controversy concerning authorship and date; generally attributed to James I who was prisoner in England for eighteen years and had abundant opportunity to acquire knowledge of Chaucer shown in poem; on release married Joan Beaufort; was known in own century as poet; description in poem of imprisonment and courtship possibly autobiographical.

W. Balfour-Melville, *James I, King of Scots, 1406-37* (London, 1936)

Ed. W. M. Mackenzie (London, 1939)

LYRICS:

General: Ed. E. K. Chambers and F. Sidgwick, *Early English Lyrics* (London, 1907; 1967)

Early Middle English Texts, ed. B. Dickins and R. M. Wilson (Cambridge, 1951)

Ed. Carleton Brown, *English Lyrics of the XIII Century* (Oxford, 1932)

Ed. R. T. Davies, *Medieval English Lyrics, a critical anthology* (London, 1963)

Religious: Ed. Carleton Brown, *Religious Lyrics of the XIV Century* (Oxford, 1924; rev. ed. G. V. Smithers, 1952)

Ed. Carleton Brown, *Religious Lyrics of the XV Century* (Oxford, 1939)

Secular: Ed. G. L. Brook, *The Harley Lyrics* (Manchestert 1948; 1964)

Ed. H. A. Person, *Cambridge Middle English Lyrics* (Seattle, 1962)

R. H. Robbins, *Secular Lyrics of the Fourteenth and Fifteenth Centuries* (London, 1952; 1955)

Carols: Ed. R. L. Greene, *The Early English Carol* (London, 1935)

Ed. R. L. Greene, *Carols. A Selection* (Oxford, 1962)

Francis Berry, 'The Grammar of Two Poems' in *Poet's Grammar* (London, 1958)

E. K. Chambers, *English Literature at the Close of the Middle Ages* (Oxford History of English Literature, II, 2, 1945)

H. J. Chaytor, *The Troubadours and England* (Cambridge, 1923)

P. Dronke, *Mediaeval Latin and the Rise of the European Love Lyric* (Oxford, 1965–66)

G. Kane, *Middle English Literature* (London, 1951)

S. Manning, *Wisdom and Number: Toward a Critical Appraisal of the Middle English Religious Lyric* (Lincoln, Nebraska, 1962)

A. K. Moore, *The Secular Lyric in Middle English* (University of Kentucky Press, 1951)

Speirs (cited under *Awntyrs of Arthur*)

Helen Waddell, *Medieval Latin Lyrics* (London, 1929)

MORTE ARTHURE (14th cent.): Moving poem in alliterative verse, describing last two battles and death of King Arthur; composed in North of England (c. 1350–1400) and based on Geoffrey of Monmouth's Latin Chronicle, *Historia Regum Britanniae*, and other sources.

Ed. Brock (*E.E.T.S.*, 1871; 1961)

Ed. E. Björkman (Heidelberg, 1915)

Abr. ed. J. Finlayson (London, 1967)

See Everett (cited under Chaucer)

W. Mathews, *The Tragedy of Arthur* (Berkeley, 1961)
Oakden (cited under Langland)

OWL AND THE NIGHTINGALE (c. 1200): Much controversy concerning authorship and exact date of composition; earlier MS including poem contains also an Anglo-Norman chronicle which stops 1216; extant texts go back to earlier copy which was not author's original; therefore deduced that poem written several years before 1216; reference to Henry II implies death of King Henry II died 1189; therefore poem written after 1189; references in poem to Master Nicholas of Guildford suggest that he was author.

Ed. and trans. both texts by J. W. H. Atkins (Cambridge, 1932)

Ed. J. H. Grattan and G. F. Sykes (*E.E.T.S.*, 1935)

Ed. E. G. Stanley (London, 1960)

See J. W. H. Atkins, *English Literary Criticism: The Medieval Phase* (Cambridge, 1943; repr. New York, 1967)

D. L. Peterson, *The Owl and the Nightingale* and Christian Dialectic, *J.E.G.P.*, LV (1956)

R. M. Wilson, *Early Middle English Literature* (London, 1939)

PARLEMENT OF THE THRE AGES (14th cent.): Has moral and critical quality of *Piers Plowman*; similar to *Pearl* and *Patience* in general plan – i.e. author puts forward proposition which offers opportunity for long narrative illustration; has been attributed on inadequate evidence to author of *Wynnere and Wastoure*.

Ed. I. Gollancz (London, 1915, *E.E.T.S.*, 1897; rev. M. Y. Offord, 1959)

See Speirs (cited under *Awntyrs of Arthur*)

PEARL (c. 1400): Found in same MS. and in same dialect as *Sir Gawayne*, *Patience*, and *Purity*; assumed that *Pearl*, *Patience*, and *Purity* by same author; *Sir Gawayne* shows difference of tone and subject-matter but may be work of same author at maturer stage of development; usual interpretation that *pearl of price* was poet's own child challenged by W. H. Schofield who claimed that pearl is merely symbol of purity; most authorities agree that poet mourns loss of real child, if not necessarily own child.

> *Pearl, Sir Gawayne* ed. A. C. Cawley (E.L., 1962)
> *Pearl*, ed. E. V. Gordon (Oxford, 1953)
> *Pearl, Cleanness, Patience, Sir Gawain* ed. I. Gollancz (*E.E.T.S.*, 1922, 1931)
> *Patience* ed. H. Bateson (Manchester, 1918)
> *Cleanness (Purity)* ed. M. Day (London, 1933)
> *The Complete Works of the Gawain Poet* Trans. by J. Gardner (Chicago, 1965)
> See O. Gargill and M. Schlauch, 'The Pearl and its Jeweller' *P.M.L.A.*, XLIII (1928)
>> Everett (cited under Chaucer)
>> E. V. Gordon and C. T. Onions, 'Notes on the Text and Interpretation of *Pearl*', *M.Ae.*, I, II (1932–3)
>> M. P. Hamilton, 'The Meaning of the Middle English *Pearl*' *P.M.L.A.*, LXX (1955)
>> W. S. Johnson, 'The Imagery and Diction of *The Pearl*' *E.L.H.*, XX (1953)
>> M. Madeleva, *Pearl. A Study in Spiritual Dryness* (London, 1925)
>> *Sir Gawain and Pearl; Critical Essays* ed. R. J. Blanch (Bloomington, 1966)
>> A. C. Spearing, 'Symbolic and Dramatic Development in *Pearl*' *M.P.*, LX (1962)

ROBERD OF CISYLE: Preserved in three fourteenth-century and five fifteenth-century MSS.; composed before 1370 in S.E. Midlands; written in didactic vein – relates how angel brought about complete change of heart in King Roberd.

> Ed. French and Hale (cited under *Sir Degare*)

SIR GAWAYNE AND THE GRENE KNIGHT (c. 1375): Dialect and allusions in poem suggest that author belonged to North-West Midlands; shows preoccupation with theological questions and familiarity with court life; French element in vocabulary suggests either high social status or wide acquaintance with French literature; possibly by author of *Pearl* (see above).

> Ed. R. T. Jones (Natal, 1961)
> Ed. J. R. R. Tolkien and E. V. Gordon (Oxford, 1936; rev. ed. 1968)

See L. D. Benson, *Art and Tradition in Sir Gawain and the Green Knight* (New Brunswick, 1965)

J. A. Burrow, *A Reading of Sir Gawain and the Green Knight* (London, 1965)

D. Pearsall, 'Rhetorical "Descriptio" in *Sir Gawain and the Green Knight*' *M.L.R.*, L (1955)

Sir Gawain and Pearl: Critical Essays, Ed. R. J. Blanch (Bloomington, 1966)

Everett (cited under Chaucer), Oakden (cited under Langland), Speirs (cited under *Awntyrs of Arthur*)

SIR GOWTHER (c. 1400): One of romances showing ecclesiastical influence; version of legend of Robert the Devil; story of sinful man who repents and atones; composed in North; has 757 lines in 12-line stanzas.

Ed. K. Breul (Oppeln, 1886)

See Hibbard (cited under Breton Lays)

SIR PERCEVAL OF GALLES (14th cent.): Tells part of story found in Chretien's *Perceval*; in Northern dialect; written in 16-line stanzas; shows little of Chretien's influence; does not mention Holy Grail.

Ed. Campion and Holthausen (Heidelberg, 1913)

Ed. French and Hale (cited under *Sir Degare*)

See Speirs (cited under *Awntyrs of Arthur*)

WYNNERE AND WASTOURE (c. 1352): Probably earliest of alliterative poems of moral and social protest; allusions in prologue suggest that author was Western man, probably a professional minstrel.

Ed. Gollancz (London, 1920, and *E.E.T.S.*, 1897)

See Speirs (cited under *Awntyrs of Arthur*)

PROSE

ANCRENE RIWLE (c. 1200?): Most important prose work of period; devotional manual, originally composed for guidance of three young women who had withdrawn from world to live as anchoresses.

English Text of the Ancrene Riwle, B.M. Cotton MS. Nero A. XIV ed. M. Day (*E.E.T.S.*, 1952; 1957)

Ancrene Wisse, Corpus Christi College Cambridge, MS.402, ed. J. R. R. Tolkien (*E.E.T.S.*, 1962)

Trans. repr. as *The Nun's Rule* by F. A. Gasquet (London, 1926)

Mod. ed. M. B. Salu (London, 1955)

Ancrene Wisse, pts 6 and 7, ed. G. Shepherd (London, 1959)

See Chambers and Knowles (cited under Hilton)

A. Prins, *French Influence in English Phrasing* (Leiden, 1952)

Wilson (cited under *Owl and the Nightingale*)

CLOUD OF UNKNOWING (c. 1400): One of most advanced of mystical treatises; intended for those suited for contemplative life; distinguishes between false and true mysticism; author possibly also wrote six shorter treatises, including an *Epistle of Privy Counsel*.

> *Cloud of Unknowing, Epistle of Privy Counsel*, ed. P. Hodgson (*E.E.T.S.*, 1943; 1958)
> Mod. eds. J. McCann (London, 1952); I. Progoff (London, 1959); C. Wolters (London, 1961)
> *Denis Hid Divinite* ed. P. Hodgson (*E.E.T.S.*, 1958)
> *The Cell of Self-Knowledge*, mod. ed. E. G. Gardner (London, 1910)
> Four short treatises in E. G. Gardner, *The Cell of Self-Knowledge* (London, 1910)
> See T. W. Coleman, *English Mystics of the Fourteenth Century* (London, 1938)
> > Gardner, Knowles, Underhill (cited under Hilton)

HALI MEIDENHAD (c. 1175–1200?): Semi-alliterative prose homily exalting virginity; proverbial expressions and satiric touches reminiscent of *Ancrene Riwle*; three other works *Juliana, Margaret,* and *Katherine* on same theme appear in same MS.; all written in West Midlands; dialect suggests Herefordshire.

> Ed. A. F. Colborn (Copenhagen, 1940)
> Ed. and tr. F. J. Furnivall (*E.E.T.S.*, 1922)

MANDEVILLE'S TRAVELS (14th cent): Guide-book for pilgrims travelling to the Holy Land, and description of the marvels of the Orient; unique mixture of information and entertainment; said to be written by Sir John Mandeville of St Albans, is in fact a compilation made first in French (c. 1356–7) and translated into English in the later fourteenth century; 300 MS witness to its popularity.

> Ed. P. Hamelius (*E.E.T.S.*, 1919, 1923, 1960–61); M. Letts, Hakluyt Society, 2 vols (1953)
> Ed. M. C. Seymour (World's Classics; Oxford, 1967)
> See J. Bennett, *The Rediscovery of Sir John Mandeville* (New York, 1954)
> > M. Letts, *Sir John Mandeville* (London, 1949)

DRAMA

MIRACLE OR MYSTERY PLAYS (in 15th cent. MSS.): Cycles existed in about twelve towns; performance usually on Corpus Christi day; two plays have survived from Coventry cycle, one from Norwich and one from Newcastle; two plays of *Abraham and Isaac* have not been localized; York, Chester, *N-towne* and Wakefield (*Towneley*) cycles almost completely preserved.

Everyman and Mediaeval Plays ed. A. C. Cawley (*E.L.*)
Mediaeval Mysteries, Moralities and Interludes Ed. V. F. Hopper and G. B.
  Lahey (New York, 1962)
Ten Miracle Plays ed. R. G. Thomas (London, 1966)
See Speirs (cited under *Awntyrs of Arthur*)

Chester Cycle: 24 plays preserved; possibly derived from French
originals; Whitsuntide not Corpus Christi plays; performed occasionally as late as 1575; more homogeneous than other cycles – possibly
work of single author who may have been Ranulf Higden, the chroni-
cler; inferior in dramatic quality to York and *Towneley* plays.

Ed. H. Deimling and Dr Matthews (2 vols., *E.E.T.S.E.S.*, 1893–1916;
  1959)
Mod. ed. (for acting) I. and O. Bolton King (London, 1930)
Selection, mod. ed. M. Hussey (London, 1957)
See P. M. Salter, *Mediaeval Drama in Chester* (London, 1956)

N-towne (probably East Anglian) *Cycle:* Often called *Ludus Coventriae*
because of mistaken identification in 17th cent. with Coventry plays;
plays given in instalments; cycle has 42 sections, beginning with
Creation and ending with Doomsday; performances took place on
Sundays.

Ed. K. S. Block (*E.E.T.S.E.S.*, 1922; 1960)

Towneley Cycle: 32 plays preserved; has some plays in common with
York cycle; contains also five plays of much higher quality, including
Noah and the two Shepherds' plays.

Ed. G. England and A. Pollard (*E.E.T.S.E.S.*, 1897; 1952)
The Wakefield Pageants in the Townley Cycle ed. A. C. Cawley (Manchester,
  1958)

York Cycle: 48 plays preserved; performed as early as 1378 and as late
as 1580; themes cover whole of Biblical history; probable that plays frequently altered according to different occasions – hence variations in
tone.

Ed. L. T. Smith (Oxford, 1885, repr. New York, 1960); J. S. Purvis
  (London, 1957)
Abr. ed. J. S. Purvis (London, 1951)

MORALITIES (15th and 16th cent.): Plays in which characters represent
abstract qualities (i.e. Gluttony, Wisdom etc) or generalized types (i.e.
Everyman etc); allegorical treatment of themes which expound religious
or ethical lessons; abstract figures are given human and contemporary
characteristics.

Castell of Perseverance (early 15th cent.): Earliest and longest of English Moralities; describes man's life from birth to appearance at Seat of Judgement; played out of doors.

> Ed. F. J. Furnivall and A. W. Pollard in *The Macro Plays* (*E.E.T.S.E.S.*, 1904)

Everyman (c. 1500): Greatest of English Moralities (see Essay)

> Ed. A. C. Cawley (*E.L.*, 1943); A. C. Cawley (Manchester, 1961)

Mankynd (late 15th cent.): Example of Morality written for popular stage; Mankynd attacked by three rascals, Nowte, Newgyse, and Nowadays who provide horse-play and low comedy; only morality motive in character of Mercy; performed in inn-yard.

> Ed. in *The Macro Plays* (cited under *Castell of Perseverance*)

Wisdom (c. 1460): Describes how Wisdom, who represents Christ, rescues Mind, Will, and Understanding from enticement of Devil; unsuitable for popular audience; possibly intended to warn monks against evils of deserting their monasteries.

> Ed. in *The Macro Plays* (cited under *Castell of Perseverance*)

INTERLUDES (16th cent.): Term loosely applied to describe plays in first half sixteenth century which were not limited to abstract figures but also employed secular characters for secular diversion; though some interludes were anonymous, many were by known authors.

> *Chief-pre-Shakespearean Dramas* ed. J. Q. Adams (Boston, 1924)
> *English Miracle Plays, Moralities and Interludes; Specimens of the Pre-Eliza-bethan Drama* ed. A. W. Pollard (Oxford, 1927)
> See T. W. Craik, *The Tudor Interlude* (Leicester, 1958)

INDEX